The Question of the Aesthetic

The Question of the Aesthetic

Edited by
GEORGE LEVINE

Great Clarendon Street, Oxford, OX2 6DP,
United Kingdom

Oxford University Press is a department of the University of Oxford.
It furthers the University's objective of excellence in research, scholarship,
and education by publishing worldwide. Oxford is a registered trade mark of
Oxford University Press in the UK and in certain other countries

© the several contributors 2022

The moral rights of the authors have been asserted

First Edition published in 2022

All rights reserved. No part of this publication may be reproduced, stored in
a retrieval system, or transmitted, in any form or by any means, without the
prior permission in writing of Oxford University Press, or as expressly permitted
by law, by licence or under terms agreed with the appropriate reprographics
rights organization. Enquiries concerning reproduction outside the scope of the
above should be sent to the Rights Department, Oxford University Press, at the
address above

You must not circulate this work in any other form
and you must impose this same condition on any acquirer

Published in the United States of America by Oxford University Press
198 Madison Avenue, New York, NY 10016, United States of America

British Library Cataloguing in Publication Data

Data available

Library of Congress Control Number: 2022930037

ISBN 978–0–19–284485–9

DOI: 10.1093/oso/9780192844859.001.0001

Links to third party websites are provided by Oxford in good faith and
for information only. Oxford disclaims any responsibility for the materials
contained in any third party website referenced in this work.

Contents

List of Illustrations   vii
List of Contributors   ix

   Introduction   1
   George Levine

1. TWO THEORIES

1. The Experience of Art   27
   Derek Attridge

2. The Ontology of Artworlds: A Post-Human, Coevolutionary Framework for Aesthetics, Art History, and Art Criticism   42
   Richard O. Prum

2. BEAUTY AND UTILITY

3. Beauty and Her Sisters in the Nineteenth Century and After   71
   Jonah Siegel

4. Gates of Horn in Ivory Towers: On Beauty's Truth   98
   Herbert F. Tucker

3. AESTHETICS AND POLITICS

5. What We Do: The New This and the New That   117
   Isobel Armstrong

6. Can Migrants Be Seen? Some Representations of Migration in Contemporary Art, Film, and Literature   137
   Josephine McDonagh

7. Aesthetic Poison   159
   Edgar Garcia

8. Aesthetic Criticism and the Postcolonial   170
   Ankhi Mukherjee

4. READING CLOSELY: FORM AND MEANING

9. On the Last Paragraph of the 1859 Edition of Darwin's *Origin of Species* 187
   Myra Jehlen

10. Wild Aesthetics: D.H. Lawrence's "Art for *My* Sake" 191
    Philip Davis

11. "Whose Eye Darted Contagious Fire": Aesthetic Form, Performative Action, and *Paradise Lost* 206
    Richard Eldridge

12. Tennyson's Tears, Brooks's Motivations 221
    Susan J. Wolfson

5. OVERVIEW

13. Do Birds Disagree? The Place of Aesthetic Value in Advocacy for the Humanities 243
    Helen Small

Works Cited 263
Index 281

List of Illustrations

2.1a and b	Visualizations of artworlds	49
2.2	Contexts of aesthetic evaluation	55
2.3	The ontology of canons	59
2.4	The hut bower, mossy courtyard, and curated aesthetic collections of a male Vogelkop Bowerbird (*Amblyornis inornata*, Ptilinorhynchidae) in the Arfak Mountains of Irian Jaya, Indonesian New Guinea Photo courtesy of Brett Benz.	65
12.1	Engraving first published in The Illustrated London News, 28 August 1897	239

List of Contributors

Isobel Armstrong is Emeritus Professor of English (Geoffrey Tillotson Chair) at Birkbeck, University of London, Senior Research Fellow of the Institute of English Studies, a Fellow of the British Academy and International Scholar of the American Academy. Over the last few years she has taught at Harvard, the Bread Loaf School of English, and Johns Hopkins University and Princeton. Her *Victorian Glassworlds: Glass Culture and the Imagination 1830–1880* (2008) won the Modern Language Association's James Russell Lowell Prize. Her interests encompass critical and aesthetic theory and feminist writing (see *The Radical Aesthetic*, 2000, and the *Oxford Anthology of Nineteenth-Century Women's Poetry*, 1993) and nineteenth-century literature. The second revised edition of *Victorian Poetry: Poetry, Poetics and Politics* (1993) was published in 2019. Her most recent new work is *Novel Politics: Democratic Imaginations in Nineteenth-Century Fiction* (2017). Poems by her appeared in Shearsman's anthology of poetry by women, edited by Carrie Etter, *Infinite Difference: Other Poetries by U.K.Women Poets* (2010).

Derek Attridge has long had an interest in philosophical approaches to literature, reflected in such books as *Peculiar Language: Literature as Difference from the Renaissance to James Joyce* (Cornell, 1988); *The Singularity of Literature* (Routledge, 2004/17); *Reading and Responsibility: Deconstruction's Traces* (Edinburgh, 2010); and *The Work of Literature* (Oxford, 2015). He edited Jacques Derrida's *Acts of Literature* (Routledge, 1994), and co-authored *The Craft of Poetry: Dialogues on Minimal Interpretation* (Routledge, 2015) with Henry Staten. His other books deal with South African writing, the history and forms of poetry, and the work of James Joyce, and he is completing a book on modernist form in fiction since Joyce. He is Emeritus Professor at the University of York, UK, and a Fellow of the British Academy.

Philip Davis is Emeritus Professor of Literature and Psychology, University of Liverpool, where he was Director of the Centre for Research into Reading, Literature and Society (CRILS). His books include *The Victorians 1830–1880*, *Reading and the Reader*, *The Transferred Life of George Eliot*, and *Reading for Life*, all published by Oxford University Press. *My William James* is forthcoming in 2022 as part of a new series with Oxford University Press, *My Reading*, which he edits along with the series *The Literary Agenda*. He is also editor of 'Studies in Bibiotherapy' with Anthem Press.

Richard Eldridge is a Lecturer in Philosophy at the University of Tennessee, Knoxville and Charles and Harriett Cox McDowell Professor Emeritus of Philosophy at Swarthmore College. He is the author of *The Persistence of Romanticism* (2001); *An Introduction to the Philosophy of Art* (2003, 2104); *Literature, Life, and Modernity* (2008); *Werner Herzog: Filmmaker and Philosopher* (2019); and several other books. He is the General Series Editor of *Oxford Studies in Philosophy and Literature* and the Editor of *The Oxford Handbook of Philosophy and Literature*.

Edgar Garcia is a poet and scholar of the hemispheric cultures of the Americas. He is the author of *Skins of Columbus: A Dream Ethnography* (Fence Books, 2019); *Signs of the Americas: A Poetics of Pictography, Hieroglyphs, and Khipu* (University of Chicago Press, 2020); *Infinite Regress* (Bom Dia Books, 2021); and *Emergency: Reading the Popol Vuh in a Time of Crisis* (University of Chicago Press, 2022). He is Associate Professor in the Department of English Language and Literature at the University of Chicago, where he also teaches in the department of Creative Writing.

Myra Jehlen is Professor Emeritus of English at Rutgers University. Her essays and books comprise readings whose common thread is a view that the meaning of a literary work is in the writing.

George Levine is Professor Emeritus, English, Rutgers University. Among his edited volumes are *Realism and Representation: Essays on the Problem of Realism in Relation to Science, Literature, and Culture* (1993); *Aesthetics and Ideology* (1994); *The Cambridge Companion to George Eliot* (2001, 2019); and *The Joy of Secularism* (2011). Among his publications dealing with themes related to this volume are *The Realistic Imagination: English Fiction from Frankenstein to Lady Chatterly* (1981); *Dying to Know: Narrative and Scientific Epistemology in Victorian England* (2002); *Darwin Loves You: Natural Selection and the Re-Enchantment of the World* (2006); *Realism, Ethics and Secularism: Essays on Victorian Literature and Science* (2008); and *Darwin, the Writer* (2011).

Josephine McDonagh is George M. Pullman Professor in the Department of English Language and Literature at the University of Chicago. Before coming to Chicago she taught in a number of universities in Britain and Ireland, most recently King's College London. She is the author of *Literature in a Time of Migration: British Fiction and the Movement of People 1815–1876* (2021); *Child Murder and British Culture, 1720–1900* (2003); *George Eliot* (1997); and *De Quincey's Disciplines* (1994), and has co-edited several volumes on topics including gender politics, literature's encounters with nineteenth-century science, Dickens and the French Revolution, colonial commodity culture, and migration studies. She is currently Director of the Nicholson Center for British Studies at the University of Chicago, and an editor of *Modern Philology*.

Ankhi Mukherjee is Professor of English and World Literatures at the University of Oxford and a Fellow of Wadham College. She is the author of *Aesthetic Hysteria: The Great Neurosis in Victorian Melodrama and Contemporary Fiction* (Routledge, 2007); *What Is a Classic? Postcolonial Rewriting and Invention of the Canon* (Stanford University Press, 2014); and *Unseen City: The Psychic Lives of the Urban Poor* (Cambridge University Press, 2021). *What Is a Classic?* won the British Academy prize for English literature in 2015. Mukherjee has published articles on a wide range of topics—Victorian literature and culture, postcolonial studies, and intellectual history—in peer-reviewed journals such as *PMLA*, *MLQ*, *Contemporary Literature*, *Criticism*, *Parallax*, and others. She has edited *A Concise Companion to Psychoanalysis, Literature, and Culture* (2014, with Laura Marcus); *After Lacan* (2018); and *Decolonising the English Literary Curriculum* (2022, with Ato Quayson). Mukherjee was visiting fellow at the Humanities Research Centre, Australian National University, in 2014, and the John Hinkley Visiting Professor at Johns Hopkins University in 2019.

Richard O. Prum is the William Robertson Coe Professor of Ornithology in the Department of Ecology and Evolutionary Biology at Yale University, and Curator of Ornithology at the Yale Peabody Museum of Natural History. Prum has done research on avian phylogeny, anatomy, behavior, song, feather development and evolution, plumage coloration, sexual selection, and aesthetic evolution. Prum's book *The Evolution of Beauty—How Darwin's Forgotten Theory of Mate Choice Shapes the Animal World—and Us* (Doubleday), was a 2018 Pulitzer Prize Finalist in general non-fiction.

Jonah Siegel is Distinguished Professor of English and co-director of the British Studies Center at Rutgers University. He is the author of *Desire and Excess: The Nineteenth-Century Culture of Art* (Princeton University Press, 2000), *Haunted Museum: Longing*, Travel, and the *Art-Romance Tradition* (Princeton University Press, 2005), and *Material Inspirations: The Interests of the Art Object in the Nineteenth Century and After* (Oxford University Press, 2020), as well as the editor of *The Emergence of the Modern Museum: An Anthology of Nineteenth-Century Sources* (Oxford University Press, 2008). His most recent monograph, *Overlooking Damage* (Stanford University Press, 2022), is a study of the cultural politics of antiquities at risk.

Helen Small is Merton Professor of English Language and Literature Merton College, at the University of Oxford. Her books include *The Long Life* (Oxford University Press, 2007) (awarded the Truman Capote Award for Literary Criticism, and the British Academy's Rose Mary Crawshay Prize for 2008) and *The Function of Cynicism at the Present Time* (Oxford University Press, 2021). Her 2013 book *The Value of the Humanities* is a critical account of the principal arguments most often used to defend the value of the Humanities. It is widely credited with clarifying and sharpening the terms of contemporary public debate.

Herbert F. Tucker holds the John C. Coleman Chair in English at the University of Virginia, where he serves as an editor for the Victorian series and for *New Literary History*. He has written books on Browning, Tennyson, and the British epic poem during the long nineteenth century, and some hundred essays and reviews chiefly to do with Romantic and Victorian poetry and poetics. Edited volumes include *Under Criticism, Victorian Literature 1830–1900*, and *A New Companion to Victorian Literature and Culture*. His online scansion tutorial *For Better for Verse* remains a work in progress open to all comers. His next book seeks to correlate the ineffability of charm with the irreference of spell-casting language.

Susan J. Wolfson, Professor of English at Princeton University, has had a long care for the subtle dynamics of poetic formings, first explored in her award-winning *Formal Charges: The Shaping of Poetry in British Romanticism* (1997). Subsequent books include *Borderlines: The Shiftings of Gender in British Romanticism* (2006); *Romantic Interactions: The Social Turns of Literary Action* (2010); *Reading John Keats* (2016); and *Romantic Shades and Shadows* (2018); *On he flared* (a contextualized close reading of four letters by Keats, 2021). Forthcoming is *A Greeting of the Spirit* (also on Keats), and *The First of a New Genus: Mary Wollstonecraft's Vindication of the Rights of Woman* (2023).

Introduction

George Levine

1. The Urgency of the Beautiful

I write in the shadow of Covid-19, and its scarily evolving variants. I sit at this computer now, hoping not to die before there is sufficient vaccine to protect me. In such conditions, it seems odd, to say the least, that I am writing not about failures in the distribution of the vaccine, not about the political malfeasance that has allowed and in effect caused so many deaths, but about "the question of the aesthetic." And I write with a sense of urgency as I orchestrate a set of deeply engaged, creative, fresh and very various explorations of why and how the aesthetic matters to human psychological, social, and economic flourishing. Don't I have better things to do? More important things to worry about? Did I need to enlist a dozen or so critics and scholars to engage this issue while Rome and the rest of the world are burning? Obviously, getting the aesthetic right will do nothing to protect me or the millions of others from the deadliness of the pandemic, or from the political violence and intrinsic injustices that are further emerging with the extension of globalization. The aesthetic has nothing to do with survival, reproduction, or money (well, let's keep that in reserve and settle for adding the word "directly" to follow "nothing").

That "nothing" is part of the point, but the "directly" is equally important, a kind of hedge, implying of course, that in the long run, though only indirectly, the aesthetic does have something to do with the very basic conditions of our lives. It is an old point and, by now, a much embattled one. Anyone at all interested in the subject has been through the routine that runs from Baumgartner to Kant, with a little Schiller thrown in; has shrugged with leftist defiance or scientistic contempt at the idea that any human product, anything at all extant in the world, can somehow be cut loose either from constraining context or the survivalist and reproductive energies of all life. If it survives and thrives (this is the basic argument of ultra- Darwinism and most evolutionary psychology) it is functional, embedded in the normal algorithmic processes of natural selection. It seems that all sides cannot be right: we can't accede to the overwhelming evidence that all life is constrained by the rules of survival and reproduction and by the cultural forces impinging on everything we do, and at the same time argue for the existence of elements that are miraculously free of those constraints.

That, however, is where the "aesthetic" this book sets out to defend and affirm finds itself. Or almost. It is that seemingly impossible position that makes for its singular power, and for its singular difficulty in cultures in which utility is all. I am not arguing, nor would any of the contributors to this volume, that there is anything entirely free from the constraints of the material and cultural conditions in which we have our being—not even our understanding, our deeply personal feelings, our reason. And yet the art and literature with which the essays in this book are concerned, and whose contextual importance, at the moment of their production, is obviously the primary motive for their particular existences, enter the world in forms that, however paradoxical it may seem, resist the universal and irresistible constraints. That's one of the reasons the Kantian ideal of purposeless purpose, worked out in his voluminous and complex consideration of perception and judgment, keeps emerging, even as it is so regularly dismissed in modern criticism as merely idealistic. The essays in this volume are themselves all over the place in relation to this idea, but I think it fair to say that all of them, in their variety, accept the idea that the aesthetic occupies a peculiar and indispensable place in the epistemological and ethical and biological economy that constitutes ordinary human life. All else, outside of the world of play (which evolutionary psychology would also include as utilitarian), is immediately and fully subservient to the exigencies of necessity and utility. The aesthetic defers that subservience sufficiently to represent, at least imaginatively, possibilities and satisfactions beyond the limits of immediate usefulness, and in so doing becomes variously and powerfully useful.

With this volume, I am not proposing even to try to resolve the problem upon which, through centuries, we have never been able to reach agreement. The primary object is, perhaps ironically, more practical: to bring the aesthetic unembarrassedly to the center of critical attention, to affirm its importance and explore its singularity and its potentialities, and along the way to be unapologetic and occasionally even sentimental about it. In the face of diminished support for degree programs in literature and the arts, and of culture-wide assumptions, with significant financial consequences, about the inutility of aesthetic studies, it is important to make a case for what is distinct, what is singular about the subject, and about what, in its singularity, it brings to the table. The aesthetic—with all its aura of inutility—needs defending. Within the literary professions themselves there is considerable doubt that a case for literary education can be sustained without demonstration of immediate practical, moral efficacy. With all the important developing interest in the aesthetic, "Literary studies," claims Michael Clune, "is paralyzed not because it has no compelling rationale, but because it is divided by two incompatible visions of its work: as artistic education and as moral education" (Clune 2019). Confronting the question of the aesthetic, this book is unapologetically committed to making a case for "artistic education," to demonstrating the critically important role it plays in our culture. Exploring it afresh is one goal of this book; demonstration of its compatibility with a wide range of critical approaches—some of them often regarded as incompatible with an aesthetic emphasis—is an essential component of the exploration. Such demonstration is aimed at disarming the critique, from outside and inside, of the uselessness of the aesthetic. The outside resists support of the arts and humanities disciplines (despite sometimes significant investment in the arts), the inside swerves to the work of the more ostensibly useful social sciences.

My argument here, however complicating the variations on it in the essays, begins with this: the aesthetic is a fundamental element in all forms of sentient life. While it opens a space of excess, in the sense that it entails something other than mere utility, it is no excrescence. It is the space of excess and of creativity and change that is regularly underestimated just because it can seem so detached from usefulness and necessity. It is the very basis of art and literature, not simply belletristic but essential to its shaping, its forms, its capacity to engage and break free in imagination of alternatives from the constraining necessities of survival and reproduction. Each instance of art comes laden with meaning and possibilities that can stretch out far into politics and large social and cultural problems of the day and deep into the personal and the intimate, and almost always into the particular. That literature can engage such problems may well be a truism among a generation of remarkable literary scholars who have trained themselves so impressively as historians and social scientists. But unlike the knowledge that other disciplines produce, it produces knowledge with affect, knowledge tinged with moral energy. The usefulness of the aesthetic is not directly "practical"; its value lies in its peculiarly humanizing force, in its capacity to expand boundaries of thought and feeling beyond the practical norms of every day and the linear thinking of non-fiction. If we are to "sell" English and language departments to universities and the societies that support them, it must be because we value artistic education and talk about how, whether it gets it right or wrong, art does things that other modes of expression can't do; it opens up, explores, reveals, and creates new angles of perception. The knowledge it generates is not discursive and generalizing but persistently singular. It poses critical questions that disciplines and discourses, not engaged with problems like form or "beauty," cannot.

As the writers in this volume affirm the centrality of the aesthetic in their understandings of literature and art, they engage, almost inescapably, with the kinds of problems that have become increasingly important to criticism as it leans toward ethical education and is directed with moral passion and determination to address injustices, inequality, prejudices, imperialism, sexism, racism, economic disparities. Herbert Tucker gets at one of the points that led to the development of this book. He claims that attention to the demands that the aesthetic imposes on creativity and criticism "can put a salutary check on the rush to relevance in contemporary humanities study, which will labor to better effect, even in service to the causes that summon it most urgently, as it redoubles attention to the resources of artistic form, and the unsuspected truth that beauty harbors" (this volume, Chapter 4). Both sides of this bold assertion are crucial to my point: the importance of attention to the aesthetic; the value of the aesthetic when put to the uses of "the causes that summon it most urgently."

Undertaking this sort of book, I would be, to say the least, disingenuous, if I didn't recognize how embroiled the subject is in conflicts about politics and cultural relevance. My own earlier efforts to reconcile a concern for the aesthetic with the various political agenda that were coming to prominence in critical discourse were often broadly contested, both as analysis of what was going on and as retrograde retreat from politics. Michael Bérubé's strong critique of my *Aesthetics and Ideology* (1994), beautifully formulates a question which I thought I was asking then, and which is a significant part of the rationale for this book: "Is it necessary to overlook the specific properties of literature in order to read literary works in terms of their relations to larger cultural formations?" (Bérubé, 1998, p. 13). His answer and mine are the same: "no." If we differ it is primarily about the degree to which the distinctive work of the aesthetic is in fact often obscured by what Tucker has called in Chapter 4 the "rush to relevance," and on what is lost with that obscuring. More recently, another attack on my earlier work takes a rather different line. Joseph North claims that the effort to give priority to the aesthetic in criticism, "in the absence of any positive commitment to the political per se, in fact quickly turns it into the enemy" (North, 2017, p. 135). My differences here are of course far greater than they are with Bérubé's. But on one factual point, I agree. Politics are not the point of my argument. Artistic education is. Attentive and politically insightful criticism can indeed operate together. But while I am eager to insist on the compatibility of an emphasis on the aesthetic and a commitment to a political reading, politics are not my point, though they do not consequently become the enemy. I want to argue, and demonstrate through the essays gathered here, that not making politics the point does not preclude recognizing political implications, the politics both of the art and of the criticism of the art. Art and the aesthetic do not emerge from a vacuum. The aesthetic might be thought of as "a means to," that is, the condition that allows a particular mode of attention to virtually any subject, any object. Attention to the aesthetic strategies by which the artist creates the work can open the way to an effective kind of political concern that is specific to what art can do and other discursive forms cannot. That attention to the aesthetic is not incompatible with attention to politics is, then, a crucial part of the point of this enterprise. I must leave it to the essays included here to demonstrate. Isobel Armstrong (Chapter 5), for example, argues forcefully and with stunning examples that not only are they not incompatible, but that the disappearance of the aesthetic from central focus is intimately connected to a parallel disappearance of the political. Similarly, Frederic Garcia (Chapter 7) inspects with poetic intensity the materials of art to get at what might be thought of as political, cultural meanings, otherwise invisible.

In Chapter 8, Ankhi Mukherjee provides strong evidence that recognition of "larger cultural formations" is not only totally compatible with emphasis on the aesthetic; thinking about it heightens and intensifies recognition of the force of those formations. Chapter 6, Josephine McDonagh's essay on immigrants and immigrant literature, demonstrates the way in which attention to art, to the aesthetic elements integral to the work, allows for distinct and extremely valuable insights about a particularly crucial and inadequately treated human crisis.

I don't want to be disingenuous here: obviously, as Tucker has implied, the bias of the arguments I am trying to make is that it is a mistake to take the work of literary criticism as primarily that of addressing, and actively addressing, political problems. But it is crucial to the book's own more or less political objective to be clear that while my major object is to focus attention on the aesthetic, another is to break down the binary between aesthetics and politics, to demonstrate how attention to the aesthetic can intensify and heighten political energies. The aesthetic operates wherever there is story, music, art. It is, as it explores all ranges of human experience, a source of pleasure, or, put perhaps less decadently, of intensified feelings. What I want to emphasize here is that attention to the aesthetic allows for endless variations, is not an impediment to concern with those large cultural matters that Bérubé invokes.

Art is the nearest thing to life, George Eliot argued, and art, not politics, is the direct object and subject of this book. If for some readers that means that the book is either conservative or radical, so I have to leave it. The criticism I am urging here would attend to the aesthetic, and go wherever that might take us, but it is not, as North (2017) would have it, designed to make what it attends to better. The aesthetic and aesthetic criticism is work of "judgment"; that judgment may have political implications, and may not. But this book's insistence on the singularity of the aesthetic does, after all, have a political object (in part by claiming that the aesthetic in itself is politically neutral): to help establish a firmer standing ground for literature and the criticism that studies it in a university culture and among institutions that regularly devalue or ignore them.

In one of the strongest among many recent efforts to re-establish in criticism the importance of "form," Caroline Levine has claimed that her book "like many others in the humanities, is an attempt to think about how we might make our world more just" (2015, p. xii). I suppose, given that I think of myself as a fairly nice guy, I would say that this book too is such an attempt. But the thinking about form, language, beauty, art, to which this volume is committed is not "an attempt to think about how we might make the world just." It is, rather, to make a case for the valuing of and the study of the aesthetic. We can, and often do, put the aesthetic to moral use, but obviously there is no inevitable link between aesthetics, aesthetic criticism, art, and moral improvement. Although I almost inevitably assumed, as I progressed through the lit./crit. profession, that there was something inherently good-making about art and literature, I had to deal with the reality that a lot of many unattractive projects written by many unattractive people were part of my developing canon of beautiful and moving works. I might find myself, and have found myself, in company with much finer criticism than mine, judging approvingly work that I found, let us say, uncongenial. The power of the aesthetic to attract can certainly be read in a moral mode, but the first step is to watch and understand its movement. The element beyond analysis in literary works, an element evoked variously here by the essays of Philip Davis and Susan Wolfson (Chapters 10 and 12, respectively), requires attention. Art is a medium through which all of us experience emotion, uncover emotion, share emotion. Yes, of course, I am morally engaged, but the interest of this book is to account for the experience of the aesthetic and its multiple possibilities, to explore more fully and self-consciously the singularity of the aesthetic.

I believe it necessary to back away from the idea that professional consideration of the aesthetic requires, morally speaking, some larger end: moral or political transformation. North is no enemy of many of the tools that this book will employ and endorse: close reading, for example, which will necessarily entail implicit or explicit attention to the formal qualities of the texts. But this close reading, he insists, taking as his model I. A. Richards, is aimed at moving beyond mere scholarship that analyses culture and moving on from the analysis for the sake of improving it (North 2017). The break here between the work of getting things right, explaining things, accounting for their power, attending to the strategies of meaning and the work of transformative injunction is striking. In this formulation, the direct object of art and the criticism that illuminates it is to make the world better. My argument, which is precisely the one that North rejects, is that while literature can be used as an instrument, it is not an instrument. The objective of some ultimate good is an object once-removed. Certainly, I—and I take it all the writers gathered here—believe deep in their professional and personal souls, that the world is better for art, and better for the criticism that lives on and off it. But the aesthetic, as Philip Davis here emphasizes and as is central to the work of Elizabeth Grosz, is a site of *not* knowing—a site of openness and exploration. Where we get in the course of our explorations is an open question, and the consequences of the search and the "arrival," if we ever arrive, are unpredictable. They are the "once-removed."

The idea of the "once-removed" has—as I will suggest when I turn to considering, of all things, Darwin's theory of sexual selection—critical importance in sustaining the distinction I am wanting to preserve, between North's (2017) and Caroline Levine's (2015) commitment to the immediate good, and my commitment to the aesthetic. To get there, I will have to move again, though in a very unKantian way, to the notion of purposeless purpose.

The association of the aesthetic with the useless and the excessive is part of the reason it is so frequently associated with the morally retrograde, the merely self-indulgent, the politically quietist, and thus rejected. In North's argument, the turn, as he sees it, from the immediate intention to improve is a symptom of the dominance of neo-liberal ideology. But I take the idea of uselessness, which makes for excess, to open a way to understand the creativity of art, the crucial importance of form, the distinctness of art among the multiple possibilities of discourse. The quality, the word, "beauty," has similar importance and similar affects. I am here committed to arguing unabashedly for the centrality of the "beautiful," which is, as Jonah Siegel (Chapter 3) plays out in an allegory of the aesthetic, the third and least morally respectable of the three sisters who compose it—ethics, knowledge, and beauty. The sister "in the attic" as it were, but without whom the others lose their efficacy. (It is worth noting that outside of this introduction and Siegel's essay, the word "beauty" does not emerge as a significant overt topic of any of the essays, and in Derek Attridge's (Chapter 1) meticulous theorizing positively drops from consideration in discussions of art). Yet when I was attracted to art and criticism it was certainly in part because art was "beautiful." Art begins by attracting, even if in highly developed forms, it manifests itself as importantly repulsive, or unattractive, a deliberate violation of our instinct for the beautiful. If particular works engaged me intellectually and, say, politically, it was not because I shared their politics (though that certainly helped), but because it was—let's say it—"beautiful."

Beauty, is of course, a loaded word, with a long history of definitions and understandings but, on the whole, with a reputation—at least at this historical moment—for leading critics and scholars down the primrose path to quietism and conservatism, that is, to precisely the self-image against which there is such a strong reaction in literary study. Here, however, I am going to be loading on to "beauty" elements of its other aesthetic sisters. And beyond that, I am going to follow some of the directions laid out by Elizabeth Grosz and Richard Prum (Chapter 2), among others, to make claims for the creative, even activist implications of "beauty." Beauty, far from being the last resort of the self-indulgent, the plaything of the haute bourgeoisie, is a generative, creative force. It is the excess that creates new forms, that, in creating those forms, adds value and gives meaning. It makes for the distinctive work the aesthetic does and can do, which its sisters, knowledge and ethics, cannot do without her. I contend that the aesthetic, however widely it opens up, gets its power from beauty, and that its morally dubious position is unjustified.

It's best to make clear here that I am not thinking of "beauty" as a thing that inheres "in" aesthetic objects. Obviously, the old cliché holds: beauty is in the eye of the beholder, and beauty is, for example, part of our experience of "nature"—beautiful cliffs, forests, flowers. Although Attridge excludes it as an identifying quality of art and would almost certainly disagree with this part of my argument, I see "beauty" as a concept entirely compatible with his view of art, not as an object but as an event. In the elaboration of the possible significances of "beauty," elaborately considered in Jonah Siegel's essay, the idea of the beautiful is compatible with developments in art that are distinctly not "beautiful" in any conventional sense. Richard Prum, like Attridge, does not see the beautiful as a thing inherent in an object but as an experience, an exchange between perceiver and perceived. The beautiful, in that sense, is what attracts one viewer to the other, and that thing may not be what we conventionally think of as pretty. This curious insubstantial but totally material condition helps account for the almost endless variety of definitions to which the aesthetic has been subject. But whatever its nature, beauty, though not perhaps a criterion of art, remains stubbornly in its vicinity—and without it an account of the aesthetic is impoverished. Aesthetics has, historically, been seen as "a branch of philosophy dealing with the nature of beauty." Fair enough, I say, though to say so is only a beginning.

This volume is not a work of philosophy (though philosophical it will become from time to time), but what I would like to think of as a common-sense effort to re-affirm the value of the "aesthetic" in its most current senses, which are helpfully vague and multiple, but which point us to efforts to understand, critique, absorb, learn from, enjoy art in any of its forms, in any of its contexts. My starting point is that, however fuzzy the edges of its definition, the aesthetic is distinguished from the instrumental purposes of virtually every other product of human labor and human expression. It is, by its nature, excessive—more than is necessary (where "necessary" points to utility). To do its job on your omelet or your pork chop, did that fork have to be designed just as it is? To house those people efficiently, did that house have to be designed like that? To assert the horrors of war, and particularly the war in Spain, did we really need "Guernica"? The turn to the beautiful, even in objects that are understood as "functional," is a form of excess. What's going on here?

The "morally dubious" element of the "aesthetic" has to do with the undeniable fact that it, and the beauty with which it is concerned, lug around a vague perfume of the aesthete—the dandyish preoccupation with orchids and lilies, and peacock feathers, and decadence, and a rather snotty hierarchy of taste. But delight in "attractive" things is not the exclusive property of the rich and self-indulgent. Benjamin's attack on the attempt to establish firm boundaries for the aesthetic has taken firm root in modern criticism, though he himself was seduced by the "aura" he saw surrounding art, and his argument was situated in a critical moment of new fascist domination. Politicizing art, partly as a consequence of his powerful arguments, has become for many an essential condition of criticism. But it seems to me that in our moment, the rejection of focus on the aesthetic comes from a culture bound to a dangerous economic rationalism, from that very neo-liberal energy that banishes all but the practical, all but the power of wealth. Oddly then, "Beauty," which in the Benjaminian context has largely become the embarrassing sister, surrendering to an ethical polemic, can in our present context be regarded as a critical element in resisting the fascism with which Benjamin associated it. Without trying to seal the aesthetic off from the living contexts in which it emerges, I want to emphasize in this book what I might call in relation to Benjamin's critique, the "non-fascist" aspects of the aesthetic. I would add yet another complication to these arguments by way of Jonathan Kramnick's remarkable treatment of the subject in *Paper Minds*. Critically for my purposes here, he identifies two modes of the aesthetic and of the beautiful. The one, which he develops in considering the word "handsome," is intimately engaged with representing the world close to hand and of use, an ecologically engaged mode of representation. The other is "aesthetics as contemplation": a quiet viewing of the beautiful as not close to hand, but out there, to be admired passively (Kramnick, 2018, p. 84). I take it that it is the latter form of aesthetics that Benjamin (and North) was resisting.[1]

The attractiveness of beauty digs down to roots in sexuality, and the aesthetic obviously transcends even those extraordinary peacock feathers whose extravagance so upset Darwin on his quest for a unified theory of evolution. Mathematicians think of their theorems and solutions as "beautiful." Remarkable athletic performance is often described, even by the most macho of us, as "beautiful." "Design" is a critical element in almost any product that is circulated in human society. Beauty, though natural objects may be beautiful, implies art of virtually any kind, and certainly more than mere prettiness, including matters of form and style, but also matters of knowledge, and, among the three allegorical sisters, ethics (and therefore, politics). Although, despite Keats, truth is not equivalent to beauty, and beauty not equivalent to truth, the argument here is that the aesthetic should be recognized to imply that beauty gives access to a kind of knowledge that might not emerge without it. The idea of "justice" is not baked into nature; it is a human imagination of equality, of equitableness, of balance, of form. It is a conception in excess of natural processes that evolve not on grounds of justice or desire, but in response to the pressures of necessity. The world (if not humans) would get on quite well without justice, but it wouldn't be nearly as much fun.

It is important to note that the *Oxford English Dictionary* definition of the aesthetic that emphasizes "beauty" is the second. The first is "of or pertaining to sensuous perception." And I want to swerve from the idealistic elements of the Kantian tradition by emphasizing that root in the sensuous, the material—a materialized Kantianism. In any case, the tortuous history of the word until it emerges here as another entrant in a two-century-long debate cannot disguise its root in the senses. We may have left behind the Greek root, probably derived from an ur word *aw., to perceive, but the aesthetic is all about sense perception. Even the dandified form of it, with its emphasis on taste, invokes a word rooted in the

---

[1] A detailed reading of Kramnick's remarkable analyses would almost certainly qualify my persistent argument for "inutility," and "indirection." But I think that on the whole, his reading is compatible with the arguments I make here, particularly in recognition of the materiality of the aesthetic, and also in relation to the development of the aesthetic through sexual selection, in which the recognition of the beautiful is also immediately social and transformative.

material: "taste." However idealistic aesthetic theory can become, it never completely loses its fundamental connection with the senses. The aesthetic, the beautiful—these are not, as they have been taken often by both friends and enemies of the humanities, mindful luxuries to be considered only after attention to the serious business of life, economics, politics. They are sources not only of pleasure—something that as "serious" critics we are likely to underestimate—but of different ways of thinking and feeling. Although I want to include here in the idea of the aesthetic an unabashed commitment both to the beautiful and the simple pleasures that follow from it, the responsibility of this book is to make a case for the distinctive things that aesthetic work *can* do even as its province is so often worlds elsewhere, worlds imagined. Several of the essays here examine works that unfold their meanings primarily through strategies of representation, techniques, forms.

It takes no deep insight to notice how, as the pressures of the pandemic intensified and spread, as we became isolated in our own bubbles via lockdowns and quarantines, people emerged on balconies singing; zoom concerts for full orchestras and choirs circulated around the world; novels, music, museum collections online for viewing, movies, became fundamental to the daily lives of millions of people all over the world. A whole genre of the extended serial and the booming habit of binge-watching blossomed. Given that human contact is absolutely essential to the well-being of us social animals, we have struggled to find ways to make our lives supportable again, and the world of art, in all its various forms, has been central to that struggle. During this time of constraint, suicides have increased and mental health problems and domestic violence have surged. Marriages have disintegrated. And almost universally, in resistance to the inescapable constraints that have exacerbated all these problems, we have turned to art in all its varieties, great and improvised, ingenious and crude, clichéd and clumsy, and often very beautiful. These things, in excess of the various vaccines and antibodies essential to our survival, are demonstrably fundamental to human life. The aesthetic, that province of aesthetes, of snobs, matters. As I write, the very future of the city of New York depends significantly (and economically) on whether the theaters and museums and concert halls will be able to reopen before it is too late. People, says Mr. Sleary, "mutht be amuthed. They can't be alwayth a-learning, nor yet they can't be alwayth a-working, they an't made for it" (Dickens, 1966, bk 3, ch. 8, p. 222).

Perhaps the emphasis in the aesthetic on sense perception points to a more solipsistic condition, one in which the individual absorbed in his feelings, in private sense perceptions, is cut off from that community and is all the more vulnerable to Covid-bred isolation. But as Isobel Armstrong points out in her essay here, the aesthetic is powerfully social—Septimus Smith and Clarissa Dalloway, from worlds apart, unite without meeting over "Fear no more the heat of the sun." The experience of the beautiful is rarely solo—the need to share it is part of our most common discourse. That "tastes differ" is clear, and it's rare that everyone agrees about what is beautiful or not, but the beautiful thrives on exchange. Lives now in solitude have, by sharing the experiences of art, sought consolation in the beautiful, and through it have made human connection, manifested sympathy, encouraged, consoled, shared. If anything, then, the nightmare of Covid-19 has only re-enforced the view that the aesthetic matters enormously. Manifesting itself in its form as conscious art, as intentional beautification, it is, and has been from the known beginnings, fundamental to human life. It is vital without being able to protect us from bacteria and viruses, from death, from all those threats to survival, economic as well as physical, that we construct our lives to resist as long as possible. Its powers of useful uselessness are integral to human development and to human history. Here is the ultimate indirection: the beautiful is fundamental to human life just because it isn't much use.

Yes, distinctions will have to be made—was Mr. Sleary actually worrying about things "aesthetic," or did he simply want to take people's minds off the problems to do with their own survival and quality of life? Is the "beautiful," or aspiration thereto, something intrinsic to all forms of art and entertainment? Are poetry and pushpin just about equivalent? I have learned to take Mr. Sleary more seriously than I had been taught to do from critiques of *Hard Times* that I most admired when I was in graduate school, critiques that insisted on the inadequacy of Dickens' response to the terrible conditions of industrial England that he had so powerfully dramatized. Mr. Sleary was not a political man. The circus he ran did not address the social and political problems Dickens had engaged. And this kind of critique of the aesthetic is distinctly a work of the aesthetic: if we judge Mr. Sleary inadequate it is because he does not weigh sufficiently against the pressures of the rest of the book. It is, that is to say, a matter of failure of form that allows and justifies a political and ethical judgment.[2] Mr. Sleary was, let us say, the "aesthete" of the working class, standing out against the utilitarian emphasis of early Victorian industrial culture. While it is certainly possible to blame him and Dickens, who invented him, for shifting attention so as to keep the exploited working classes quiet as industry ground them down, I credit them both with good faith, because they both were right. "People mutht be amused." (The criticism that addresses these issues in *Hard Times* depends in part for its readings and judgment on the symmetry or asymmetry of the character, "Sleary," with Gradgrind

---

[2] Anne Humpherys, in a reading of the novel that exemplifies finely the relation between attention to the aesthetic and concern with political issues, the constraints of form and the possibilities of meaning, notes in concluding: "while we must be amused, we must also be reminded again and again of the universal human needs for art and play, for moral virtues and compassion not only in personal relations, but also in the workplace and in government, and, above all, for the imaginative power to understand and sympathize with the lives of others, a power that literature like *Hard Times* always gives us."

and Bounderby and the life of the factory—the form of the book is intrinsic to its politics.) Written not as a tract but as a "novel," its attractiveness—let me say, its beauty—becomes a means, through particular narratives and particular conditions, to engage the very serious questions of industrial life in ways outside the calculations of political economy and outside our modern versions of that field.

I am not equating the aesthetic with pushpin, but I am insisting that a critical element in the aesthetics' relation to the beautiful is just the presence of pleasure in the experience, a pleasure that is infinitely various but essential. Elizabeth Grosz, drawing on Darwinian sources to which I will return shortly, is insistent on the centrality of sensation to art's broader significances:

> Art comes from that excess, in the world, in objects, in living things, which enables them to be more than they are, to give more than themselves, their material properties and possible uses, than is readily given in them. Art is the consequence of that excess, that energy or force, that puts life at risk for the sake of intensification, for the sake of sensation itself – not simply for pleasure or for sexuality, as psychoanalysis might suggest – but for what can be magnified, intensified, for what is more, what is perhaps too much, but through which creation, risk, innovation are undertaken for their own sake. (Grosz, 2011, p. 3)

Grosz even turns here to the otherwise generally despised ideal of art "for its own sake," but with anything but a satisfied self-indulgence and fascist narrowness as its end. The excess that is the essence of art and of the aesthetic, driven by the intensity of feeling that has its deep basis in sexual attraction, is the way to the new, the creative.

Surely, it is in part because we believe it pleasurable that we go once again to watch Desdemona die at Othello's hands, or Cordelia die in that unbearable last act of *King Lear*. Intensification of feeling is the immediate aim. But in intensifying, the aesthetic can also be implicitly political, as, for example, William Morris, the socialist aesthete understood it, because, among other things, in its emphasis on feeling it is resistant to the dominance of the economic (even though it can be exploited, like everything else, so as to become the playground or the tool of the rich). While it is inadequate to think of the aesthetic as somehow a strong counter to the utilitarian (and capitalist) bias of our culture, since it is obvious that any given work or art may, in devious ways pointed out by a generation of critics, be complicit with that bias, it remains in its nature significantly resistant to it. But even given the inescapable evidence of their importance to the very texture of our lives, the arts and the humanities which study them are, particularly in times of crisis, under the pressure of utility, both from those institutions that support them, and from the culture that thrives in part because of them. While aestheticism in its snobbier forms has been condemned for the very reasons that critics condemned the Sleary solution to the economic problems Dickens had dramatized, the aesthetic survives, despite its regular co-option, not only as "amuthement," but as a constant challenge to the values of a utilitarian, money driven, neo-liberal society. And it makes its challenge not so much by direct or implicit resistance to particular ideologies but by requiring attention to values resistant to the dominance of the cash-nexus, even where particular works explicitly or implicitly endorse it. As Auden wrote about Yeats: "Time that with this strange excuse, Pardons Kipling and his views, And will pardon Paul Claudel, Pardons him for writing well."

So, one of the reasons that, in between futile phone calls to find someone to vaccinate me against Covid-19, I push on with investigation of the question of the aesthetic is that all this mess has made me feel even more intensely that the aesthetic matters. Attention must be paid. In the midst of various crises of the humanities, culturally and economically determined, it is critically important that we establish a strong justification for their study—even aesthetes have to seek practical support from institutions and governments—a justification that will entail a clear sense of their intrinsic distinctiveness. In one sense, then, our self-justification is ultimately utilitarian, an attempt to answer the question: what of value do we do, as critics and scholars of the aesthetic, that other disciplines don't and can't? A satisfactory notion of the aesthetic ought to entail a substantiation, a materialization, of the Kantian idealist theory of purposeless purpose. What artists do is "useful" in not being governed by, determined by, socially established ideas and ideals of usefulness. This is the negative formulation, but the more positive would begin with beauty itself, and insist that in not being useful the aesthetic is freed to enhance a life constrained everywhere and always by necessity, to imagine and re-imagine, to explore, to invent, to push beyond the limits that necessity in any of its myriad forms impose upon us. And it is free to speculate dramatically about things as they are, expose through language manipulated without discursive regard for the constraints of logic or the merely "rational," the possibilities of experience itself. We awaken to the millennia of injustices that are built into our culture in all of its forms by way of intensely imagined individual experiences, by way of stories, images, sounds that penetrate through the thick layers of generalization and argument; perhaps our best way toward an understanding is through art itself. Even history, that description of the world's life as in itself it really was, unfolds in narratives whose forms entail new ways of imagining.

The variety of perspectives included by the essays gathered here reflects some resistance to a single, unified theory of the aesthetic, but embodies rather a sense of its multiple possibilities. This introduction, though aiming at something like a synthesis, is as idiosyncratic as any of the other essays, aspiring to an understanding of why the aesthetic matters, how it matters, and suggesting its almost infinite range of possibilities. Although all the contributors to this volume joined because they shared a general sense of the value and urgency of the question of the aesthetic, none has signed off on my particular arguments here, with which, my guess is, there will be no universal agreement. The contributors have not had the opportunity to engage each other and certainly, had we done so, disagreements would have been prominent. The essays are unified neither in recommending a single theory of the aesthetic, nor in affirming a single way to do criticism, but in recognizing the fundamental and distinctive value of the aesthetic, understood as a family of possibilities, and in demonstrating various ways in which it is consequential for the culture at large. Long before Covid, the humanities were becoming the stepsisters of the modern university. The humanities and the arts seemed not to be "essential workers." This book insists that they are. As Isobel Armstrong wrote to me when I proposed this volume, "I am arguing that we are fiddling as a profession while Rome burns—the aesthetic is being eroded everywhere in public life and education."

In her remarkably nuanced and compendious consideration of the value of the humanities at a moment when we need urgently to make their case to a skeptical public, Helen Small considers their importance in matters political and social. That they are important in that way is obvious, but, she says,

> I suggest that we should treat with caution a version [of justification] that lends unduly narrowed and exclusive importance to the humanities on the basis of their serious but not *definitive* role in assisting the informed and properly critical perspectives on social and political life... With those caveats in place, the claim stands that the humanities, centrally concerned as they are with the cultural practices of reflection, argument, criticism, and speculative testing of ideas have a substantial contribution to make to the good working of democracy. (2013, p. 6)

Art is the space where ideas and practices and ways of life and politics and movements can be tested by working through the particularities organized into forms that are distinct and not generalizable. Critics may, of course, judge those forms from the perspective of ethical judgment, but their authority lies in their capacity to detect the moral work a literary form might be implying. It is an aesthetic, not an ethical judgment that justifies literary practice. And the aesthetic is a field of perception and a field of judgment: to enter it is to make a choice, imply a preference: this work is worth the trouble, that one not. If an ethical objective emerges from the work, it is, then, by indirection. But of course, that aesthetic world is the world of possibility, and the power and "usefulness" of its testing in fictions, in images, in sounds, depends on the space that the aesthetic occupies, that the demands of beauty impose. Its aim is not to do good but to be beautiful, in the expanded sense I have been urging.

Criticism has important work to do in justifications of the value of a subject field that is notorious for self-critique and that is not that good at public relations because it is so embedded in a long and contested history and so open to ambivalences, ambiguity, alternative perspectives. Critical practitioners, and those in the culture at large to whom art and literature matter importantly, along with those who regard art and literature as mere frills and diversions from the serious business of life and politics, will in different ways resist the implicit argument of this book that it is crucial that we recognize the "aesthetic" as a condition that makes possible all of the extraordinary work it has, in a vast variety of ways, been shown to do, and for which the words psychological, social, and political are inadequate. The aesthetic is no mere frill. It is a mode of experience. It is also a mode of knowledge—a kind of science of the individual rather than of the general. The forms with which it is concerned are not generalizable, as the discursive language of science, in particular, would require. It entails the entanglement of knowledge and feeling. It is a form of play that stands in for reality and illuminates it; it is a means of discovery, of exploration, which is, unlike most discursive prose, open-ended. It is our passport to the beautiful and its pleasures.

We begin with a trust in the importance of the aesthetic in the same way that, say, a biologist finds out what there is to be found out about nature, not to determine how nature should or might have been, but on how it is, in the conviction that biology itself is valuable. It is part of the consistent nature of the aesthetic that it entails some of those activities Small invokes for the humanities more generally—"reflection, argument, criticism, and speculative testing of ideas." Although I agree with Clune that English departments and other disciplines whose study is the arts can claim the significance of their work by way of their expertise in "artistic education," as opposed to "ethical education," this book is not designed as another piece of artillery in various critical wars in which attention to the aesthetic is pitted against larger, more ethically driven projects in politics, social criticism, and cultural study. With it, I invite beauty back to full sisterhood, and argue that its appreciation is essential to our lives.

2. A Darwinian Theory

I leave it to the essays that follow to provide fruitful examples of ways of thinking about the aesthetic, and ways of working with it. Here I throw in my own two cents, independent of the commitments of any of the contributors, to re-enforce my case for the centrality of the aesthetic to our lives. I do so risking something that, among others, Helen Small warns against in her overview of the work of this book in its last chapter. That is, I invoke "nature" for support of a cultural argument. The history of this sort of invocation is not promising. My own rejection of the current movement of literary Darwinism is partly anchored in that movement's commitment to evolutionary psychology, a practice that, as Prum himself argues in Chapter 2, "explicitly aimed to reduce the humanities, sociology, and psychology to human manifestations of adaptation by natural selection." Literary Darwinism offers natural selection as a kind of key to all mythologies explaining all behavior. The argument there is that the survival of anything in a world governed by natural selection requires adaptive efficacy in that "anything." Such a move ends by turning literature into a kind of handbook of adaptive strategies. I nevertheless continue to believe, with Prum, that it is a mistake to exclude science from our considerations of matters cultural, particularly of the aesthetic. Despite the radical and dangerous misevocation of nature to justify such things as eugenics, nature and nurture are not exclusive of each other. My own dive into "naturalism" has, I would like to think, a more benign point, that is, to support the argument that the aesthetic is not a frill added by culture to human equipment, but something built into the human. And such a perspective opens on some wider implications for the aesthetic.

"We need," says Richard Prum, "to embrace Darwin's *aesthetic* view of life and fully incorporate the possibility of *nonadaptive* arbitrary aesthetic evolution by natural selection" (p. 328). Disqualified as an arbiter in scientific controversy, I nevertheless want to accept Prum's invitation, to adapt what he sees as Darwin's "aesthetic" view of life, the view that across the animal kingdom the work of the aesthetic is fundamental and consequential. And most interestingly to me, it is both "arbitrary" and "non-adaptive." Those words make Prum's argument controversial in the scientific community and beyond, but they are remarkably consonant with some traditional views of the aesthetic, and they have the virtue of strong scientific sanction—that is, at least among some scientists. In the mate choice of Peahens and Manakins and Birds of Paradise, Kant's idealist theory takes material root. Both Prum and Grosz develop this argument, if in very different ways, from their reading of Darwin. Both believe that recognizing the interaction and the connections between science and art becomes a valuable tool in developing an adequate theory of the aesthetic and adequate modes of aesthetic criticism. Darwin's theories might be taken as a palimpsest for the aesthetic, an evolutionary take on the transformations that move from the sexual attraction within animal life to great works of human art.

Among the elements of aesthetic theory intimated (or empirically confirmed) here, is the argument that the aesthetic is not merely an excrescence, an "extra." While it is more than seems to be needed for the fulfillment of the requirements of utility and necessity, it is built into nature, built into animal life itself, a condition inherent in our sexuality, in our very development as humans. Just as humans are born with a capacity for language, so they inherit from their evolutionary ancestors and are born with a capacity for appreciation and judgment of beauty. And just as the capacity for language does not determine which language we will speak—for that is culturally determined—so the aesthetic capacity does not determine the form of the beauty in any given case, for that is culturally determined. In a sense, the particular forms of the aesthetic are "arbitrary," like the variations of cultural mores. As the language faculty does not entail commitment to any particular language, so the aesthetic faculty entails no commitment to any particular aesthetic order. The language one speaks, the "beautiful" one finds attractive, are largely culturally determined. (Obviously, there are correlations with elements of the environment and history in which cultures develop, but the same environments do seem capable of nurturing diverse cultural practices.) The form of the language and the form of the aesthetic vary with cultural difference. Every culture has a language. Every culture has an aesthetic. For Darwin, the presence of this aesthetic faculty, with its consequence of cultural diversity, was part of his argument for the unity of human ancestry—we are, all races, quite literally brothers and sisters.[3] At the same time, the theory releases the aesthetic from any universal characteristics embodied in the aesthetic object, and suggests that in fact the aesthetic depends on an interchange between the perceiver and the perceived. It is the sensuous embodiment of cultural relativism.

Critically for my primary argument about the aesthetic, Darwin's theory of mate choice in sexual selection also provides a model of a force *in* nature that operates against the pressures of utility. "Non-adaptive" is Prum's word for it. At least in appearance, sexual selection often runs counter to the pressures of natural selection, that overriding evolutionary force that, algorithmically (so it is now said), has been thought to account for all evolutionary change. Prum outlines the case against this view and the idea that what seems arbitrary change is actually "honest signaling" is probably still predominant in evolutionary biology (Prum, 2017, pp. 44–8). But sexual selection seems to offer an example of purposeless purpose in nature itself. As Prum describes it, the attraction of one mate to the other, usually, as with birds, of female to male, is "arbitrary." That is, it cannot be tied to the usual evolutionary explanation that it is driven by the adaptive forces that lead to survival and reproductive success. It is driven, on Grosz's and Prum's account, by the whims of desire. Darwin, and scientists who followed him, worked to find a way to reconcile an apparently counter-utilitarian development with a vision of nature that saw utility, in the processes of adaptation and survival, as all-determining. But Darwin remained convinced, against the mainstream of science from his day to ours, and despite his own deep investment in the idea of natural selection as the prime mover of evolution, that sexual selection was another force, not a mere subset of natural selection. He saw the aesthetic sense as something in nature in excess of what was necessary, with real effects that natural selection, in its rigorous narrow procedure of killing all excess as adaptive, or less adaptive, could not have achieved on its own.

This almost paradoxical condition might be understood as an enactment in nature of what I have been calling the action "once removed," or "indirectly" of my very first paragraph. That is, the evolutionary developments that emerge from

---

[3] For extended discussion of this aspect of the theory of sexual selection, see Desmond and Moore, 2009, pp. 362–74.

mate choice are not at all the object of that choice. When the choosing mate, usually the female, is attracted to the male, she is attracted not by his reproductive prowess, but by his sexiness, let us say, his good looks. The analogy to the aesthetic pattern is clear—at least to me. What pulls us toward the aesthetic is—we'll use my controversial shorthand here—its "beauty." At its very deepest root, the aesthetic is based in sexuality itself, in desire. The beautiful is the desirable. When it turns out that the "beautiful" has intellectual, moral, social implications, those effects, in my analogy, are the *indirect* result of the initial attraction: the "purpose," as we so often see it, of the purposelessness of the more fundamental attraction. The birds are not aiming toward greater adaptiveness, not aiming toward the development of a new species: they are aiming at the beautiful; that attracts them, as Prum puts it, arbitrarily. Grosz provides a particularly cogent suggestion about how this purposeless purpose operates:

> Art is of the animal to the extent that art is fundamentally bound up with the two features that characterize all of animal existence: the force of sexual selection, that is, the vibratory power of seduction (attention, attraction, performance, courtship); and the force of territorialization (the loosening of qualities from the milieus in which they originate and function through the construction of a boundary or frame within which these qualities can exist in different form).
>
> (2011, p. 4)

The "boundary or frame," the artfulness, the formal beauty, is a condition for imagination and creation beyond the limits of necessitarian constraint, beyond natural selection's algorithmic ruthlessness. If we push the analogy, we can see how the very possibility of some release from contextual constraints emerges from this view of sexual selection.

Much of this, though based in scientific observation, is speculative. The argument is scientifically challengeable, but it remains a model for what we have normally taken as an idealist mistake. The female here has, according to Darwin's then controversial argument, aesthetic taste, a taste for the beautiful. Even according to Michael Ryan, whose theory is designed in part as a scientific challenge to Prum's insistence on the arbitrary and the non-adaptive pattern I've just described, in such exchanges the female does indeed have *A Taste for the Beautiful* (2018). However the scientific controversy gets resolved, genuine evolutionary change follows from behaviors that seem directed not at that change but at the fullest, the most satisfactory attractions and couplings.

And finally, perhaps yet more controversially, Darwin's theory can suggest that the "aesthetic" might exist not as something "in" an object but, as Derek Attridge puts it in quite another context, as an experience. One of the difficulties aesthetic theory has always faced is that, as the old saying goes, *De gustibus non est disputandum*. As Ryan puts it, using yet another aesthetic cliché as he locates the female's aesthetic sense in the physiology of the female, "Beauty is in the eye of the beholder." While this indisputable fact of aesthetic experience has always caused problems for a unified theory of the aesthetic, it seems an inevitable inference from the Darwinian pattern I've been describing. But it opens aesthetic theory to the widest possible range of variations. For Prum, beauty exists in an interchange between the perceiver and the perceived, an interchange in which both partners are active and creative participants. The female demands the male sing better, look better, and be brighter groomed in his plumage. The male, full of desire, develops over the course of generations lovelier song and prettier plumage. This reciprocity, this "loop," produces what is described in scientific study of sexual selection as a "cascade" that accounts for the growth of non-adaptive traits. The beauty is in the exchange, initiated by attraction. We are back again, not only to cultural difference, but to a theory that implies the sociality of the aesthetic and its multiply creative and constantly transformative condition, as Grosz describes the consequences of Darwin's theory in her *Becoming Undone*. What matters for the purposes of this book is a recognition of the aesthetic as, indeed, multiple, dependent on cultural and even individual variability, but a source of pleasure, of knowledge, of social and cultural exchange and development that is fundamental to human experience.

Sexual selection entails both the intrinsic, inherited, biologically confirmed capacity for the aesthetic, and for cultural relativism about beauty. Objective and subjective; universal and individual. Aesthetics from this perspective, then, is not idealist but materialist. It is based in desire, in pleasure, and for its own sake; it issues in creative achievements (new species), unbound to the constraints of necessity. Of course, in making the analogy to Kant's theory I am cheating grossly, since it is precisely "desire," sexual attraction, that underlies my materialist Kantianism. Purposeless purpose is enacted not in an idealist vacuum, but in the very process of evolution that is influenced by sexual selection. The model I offer, then, with what I hope are Darwinian eyes, is a materialized aesthetic, an aesthetic that is central, physically, intrinsically part of evolving life, and that resists for a long way the oppressive and almost universal demands of utility, escaping, if only in imagination, the limits. And as in sexual selection, the desire for the beautiful, via the cascade of interchanging vision, issues in new species (and often glorious plumage), so the aesthetic in art issues in new imaginations, new forms of knowledge.

It is, of course, a very long way from a Peahen's admiration (if that is what it might be called) of the Peacock's wings and tushy to Bach's "*Wachet auf ruft uns die stimme.*" In Chapter 13, Helen Small makes a strong case in her overview here against taking this kind of assimilation of birds' behavior to human aesthetic choice too seriously. But while, in the end, the foundation of a theory here is extremely speculative, it remains, I believe, a forceful argument for the centrality of beauty to all experience. The full complications and difficulties of the theory require a whole volume to itself, but reading Small's critique as against Prum's elaboration of this "posthuman" aesthetic theory should be helpful. This is, in any case, not the place for an extended rehearsal of the scientific arguments that might support the theory of the aesthetic I have been roughly sketching on Darwinian grounds. The question of greatest importance is how a view of this kind might affect the way we might most forcefully argue the case for the aesthetic.

3. An Overview

This book offers a plethora of possibilities. Singularity implies multiplicity. It is obvious that the essays that follow do not grow organically out of the arguments I have made here. Each is an independent thrust, an exploration. But each depends on the centrality of the aesthetic. They are consistent with the overall objective of this book, that is, to make a credible case for the importance of aesthetic critique and for the study of "the question of the aesthetic," and the arts.

The opening essays offer larger theories of the nature of the aesthetic and of art. Both Derek Attridge (Chapter 1) and Richard Prum (Chapter 2) make strong cases that "beauty," or "art," never exists in isolation. Both point to a non-material understanding of "beauty," or art: in the sense that it depends on an interchange, on perception and conditions of perception. It is distinctly individual and social at the same time. Their paths diverge quite radically on other aspects of the question, but they provide a useful theoretical frame for the diverse essays that follow in Part 2.

Siegel (Chapter 3) and Tucker (Chapter 4) provide demonstrations of how widely the reach of the aesthetic extends, and its compatibility with projects that might, certainly in the current critical context, have been seen as antithetical. These two chapters offer themselves as examples of the ways in which the aesthetic can function as forms of knowledge, and overall, they make a case for the ethical energy that might be taken as already intrinsic to the aesthetic. I hope that the essays will be recognized, in all their variety, as providing strong evidence of the argument that Herbert Tucker makes about how primary attention to aesthetic matters can illuminate even those large cultural, social, political matters that are so central to the concerns of current criticism.

The four essays that constitute Part 3 of this book are all directly concerned with major political issues. In what might be seen as the peroration to her essay, Isobel Armstrong (Chapter 5) captures a great deal of the argument here:

> Delight in words is what links these readers to our profession. Immersion—in language. Professional readers tend to occlude both pleasure and beauty, as if these are frivolous pursuits. But both are a prerequisite of a shared culture, a motivation to discovery, a longing to know. The aesthetic and intellectual

pleasure spur each other on. Perhaps exploration rather than explanation is the founding practice of our work—and the need to communicate it. Beauty is a civic as well as an individual experience. Certainly, people don't experience beauty alone—the instinct is to turn to someone else, to exclaim, to share, to talk, to think, to make words.

Here they are: the centrality of beauty to the work of the aesthetic; the indirection I spoke of at the start of this introduction; the connection of the aesthetic with knowledge; the invocation of Mr. Sleary's objectives—people must be amused, either by the circus or Pink Floyd or Dante; the social nature of the aesthetic; the exploratory work that is entailed in the aesthetic enterprise; the moral engagement that emerges out of that sociality and exploration.

The essays by McDonagh (Chapter 6), Garcia (Chapter 7), and Mukherjee (Chapter 8) all tackle vital political issues by way of attention to the aesthetic means by which they are imagined, evocation of the intensity of the engagements (intensity being, as Grosz has argued, one of the key elements in sexual selection and in art). It might be claimed that these essays would fit as finely into books directly engaged with the social issues they discuss as in this book in focus on the aesthetic. But that is one of the key points: concern with aesthetic means is not incompatible with concern with larger cultural issues; it can, instead, enhance that work through description, clarification, analysis.

When I discussed with Edgar Garcia his own quite beautiful, intense, and painful essay, asking if he might want to pause to get more explicit about the general aesthetic concerns that led to his way of arguing, he explained why he didn't want to do that: "I'm interested in... staying with the trouble and possibility of particulars." His powerful argument here about the "poison" of the aesthetic, is, he wrote me, "just one modality (a key one, as far as I am concerned), but not one that encompasses or defines *the* aesthetic phenomenon." In refusing the generalizing of the aesthetic, Garcia seems to me to confirm one critical element of the aesthetic—that is, its tendency to the particular. Aesthetic discourse resists the generalizing tendency of the discursive through particularity (both of the critic attending to the minute materials of the art work, and of the artists building their art) from which emerge the beautiful, the ethical, particular knowledge. We can see how this works in McDonagh's chapter, which develops a theory of "migrant" art out of the most particular attention to the details and strategic vision of the films she studies. Attention to those strategies produces both a wider understanding of the migrant condition and a deeper feeling—an ethical imperative—in relation to the migrant experience. Which is to say, that the aesthetic blends together and transforms through the attractions of the beautiful both knowledge and ethical engagement.

Part 4 of this book, essays by Myra Jehlen (Chapter 9), Philip Davis (Chapter 10), Richard Eldridge (Chapter 11), and Susan Wolfson (Chapter 12), brings together several distinctly different approaches, via the close reading that aesthetic criticism usually entails, to four distinctly different writers. Jehlen's very short piece is not at all connected with my Darwinian theorizing, but is an exemplary exercise in tracing the intellectual, emotional, and structural work that the aesthetic performs, demonstrating how a reading of the style can turn into a demonstration of contradiction in the writer's meaning, and indeed the impossibility of separating "meaning" out of the very forms of the language. In their differences, these essays variously play out Siegel's allegory of the three aesthetic sisters. Eldridge sees the very shape and language of *Paradise Lost* as an experience that might be understood as another version of Eve's relation to the experiences narrated. His ultimate point makes a powerful claim for the virtues, intellectual and moral, of attending to the beauty of the literary particulars:

> By inviting, sustaining, and shaping active imaginative and reflective engagement in an ongoing process of self-scrutiny, the contagious fire that is the fully absorbing poem (like other works of poetic art, including history, music, and painting, among others, at their highest reaches of achievement) offers our best hope for coming to terms with who we are and what we have made of ourselves.

Philip Davis, turning to D. H. Lawrence, makes manifest in the smallest details of Lawrence's language how important Armstrong's insistence on attention to the materials of literature, to "words," can be. "The most important first act in aesthetics," he concludes, "lies in the ability to point to the nerve-like messages of an art that gets under the skin; to feel the synaptic messages inside the words, through and between or across them, like code." Though their essays seem distant in subject and manner, Davis and Wolfson both point to an element in excess of meaning and form, a vital, emotional element inaccessible to mere professional analysis and judgment. Wolfson's remarkable study of Cleanth Brooks' relation to Tennyson's "Tears, Idle Tears" seems to me to dramatize, in a very different context, the quality to which Davis alludes: that quality that escapes analysis but whose intensity gives to the aesthetic experience its peculiar power. The imperative of the "should," of the necessary, functional, useful, rational, is resisted not by mere sentimentality, but by, as Wolfson puts it, "dramatic sympathy." The aesthetic breaks out into feeling and possibility beyond mere "function." Wolfson plays this out in the tension between emotional response to the poem and the critic's professional responsibility to insist on coherence and explanation. The aesthetic opens a space for a sympathy beyond explanation, for alternatives to the apparently necessary or correct. The aesthetic is, then, as I have been arguing from the start, social; it entails—I unembarrassedly quote myself here with Wolfson's sanction: aesthetic experience is "one medium through which all of us experience emotion, uncover emotion, share emotion." Each essay can stand on its own; together they provide a representative sense of the kinds of claims I hope this book satisfactorily makes for the value, the singularity, the importance of the aesthetic and of critical attention to it.

To conclude the volume with Part 5, I invited Helen Small (Chapter 13) to provide an overview and critique of the entire volume, with an eye to the central question: The Place of Aesthetic Value in Advocacy for the Humanities. This, given the great variety of essays and arguments, was no small task. What she offers, in conclusion, is a synthesis that helps in understanding the relation of the essays to each other and to the nature of the overall case the book makes. She places the crisis (and the ethical/aesthetic ambivalences) historically and practically. Along the way, she offers critiques of the various arguments and the project as a whole, most particularly the dangers of some of my own "naturalistic" arguments. Her summary and critique itself builds to an argument about how the question of the aesthetic might be most effectively addressed. In the end, this overview is also singularly Small's own take on the subject, and at the same time an insightful and constructive guide to the arguments.

PART 1
TWO THEORIES

1
The Experience of Art

Derek Attridge

1. The mode of being of the work of art

What makes a work of art a work of art? What is its ontological status or mode of being? I'm posing this question within the context of "advanced" Western society today, and in the light of centuries of speculation on this topic in Western culture, conscious of the fact that it would need to be approached differently in other contexts. And I'm concentrating on works of art that have been accorded significant value, not to the broader category of imaginative productions.

The most obvious answer to these questions is that a work of art exists as a particular type of material entity (whether a unique object or the particular token of a general type, like the printed instance of a novel), or, in the case of temporal arts such as music, film, or theater, a specific type of material sequence. However, a little consideration makes it clear that the context in which such entities are encountered is also important: a found poem in a poetry collection or a Brillo box in a museum is only an extreme example of a more general condition. Of course, a legitimate response might be that different types of art have such disparate modes of being that these questions remain unanswerable; however, let us for the moment assume that the single phenomenon we term "art" has a single distinctive mode of existence.[1]

Countering the idea that the work of art is fundamentally an object is the suggestion that it should be understood as an *event*—that there is no stable entity enduring from the moment of its production to the moment of its reception, open to different interpretations but unchanged in essence. Rather, the work is understood as coming into being—as a work of art—each time that the sounds, words, visual and perhaps tactile elements that constitute the material object are treated, in a temporal experience, in a particular way.[2] To take this suggestion further, we need to explore what *kind* of experience is involved.

---

[1] In what seems to me a counsel of despair, a number of aestheticians have attempted to follow Wittgenstein in characterizing art as something that can only be defined in terms of "family resemblances," no single feature being attested throughout its varied forms. It has been pointed out, however, that there is an underlying genetic basis for the existence of family resemblances.

[2] I have argued along these lines with reference to literature in *The Singularity of Literature* and *The Work of Literature*. In what follows, I have drawn on the arguments spelled out in these books.

The question of experience has been central to very many accounts of art, explicitly or implicitly.[3] It's implicit in Aristotle's discussion of the emotions evoked by tragedy and in Longinus's emphasis on the emotional effects of the sublime. Burke's account of the beautiful and the sublime considers the different experiences they generate, and Baumgarten's proposed science of "aesthetics" depends on the feelings of pleasure or displeasure aroused by beauty or ugliness. Most influentially for later discussions of the experience of art, Kant deployed the terms of faculty psychology to argue for the distinctiveness of our responses to the beautiful and the sublime (though his central interest was in natural beauty). A host of nineteenth- and twentieth-century philosophers took up the question of the experience of art, some emphasizing the arousal of emotion, some the acquisition of new knowledge, some the "free play of the imagination."[4]

Among the more recent schools of thought to which the notion of experience is central is phenomenology, and the phenomenological tradition includes important forays into aesthetics—most comprehensively by Mikel Dufrenne in *The Phenomenology of Aesthetic Experience* and, with a focus on literature, Roman Ingarden in *The Literary Work of Art* and Wolfgang Iser in *The Act of Reading*. Pragmatism, too, is built on a notion of experience; to take one significant example, John Dewey gave his investigation of this topic the title *Art as Experience*. The project of structuralism was to reduce the multiplicity of experience to specifiable codes; post-structuralist approaches to art rejected this ambition, though in many cases remained interested in the experiences provided by art. The tradition of close reading in literary studies, although most often concerned to treat the text as a "verbal icon," included important proponents of an attention to the reader's experience, among them I. A. Richards, William Empson, and F. R. Leavis.[5] In 1967, Lionel Trilling published an anthology of literary works that he titled *The Experience of Literature*, providing a commentary on each of the fifty-two selections.[6] Still focusing on literature, a number of different approaches

---

[3] German philosophical aesthetics is complicated (or perhaps sharpened) by the existence of two terms for experience, *Erlebnis* (roughly, a singular encounter with outer reality; personal experience) and *Erfahrung* (the accumulated resources gained over a period; objective experience). Dilthey, Heidegger, Gadamer, and Benjamin all exploit the contrast, though in different ways.

[4] Paul Guyer, in *A History of Modern Aesthetics*, provides accounts of all the major philosophers of aesthetics (and several minor ones) from the eighteenth to the early twenty-first centuries, organizing his discussion around these categories. He begins by observing that the "core subject matter of the discipline of aesthetics since its inception in the eighteenth century [has been] the study of the nature and value of aspects of the human *experience* of art and (sometimes) nature" (1) (Guyer's emphasis).

[5] Simon During offers an insightful account of the importance of the category of "experience" to these critics, arguing that it became suspect after the advent of cultural studies and post-structuralism (*Against Democracy*, 60–76).

[6] These commentaries are available separately in Trilling's *Prefaces to "The Experience of Literature."* Despite the title, Trilling doesn't pay particular attention to the reader's experience, offering instead relatively conventional introductions to his chosen texts. For a commentary on literary works—in this case, short stories—that does track the reader's experience through a temporally unfolding reading, see George Saunders, *A Swim in the Pond*.

to the experience of literary works found themselves yoked together in the brief flourishing of "reader-response criticism" in the 1960s, and more recently the role of emotion has become a source of interest to many critics, under the more scientific-sounding label "affect." The turn to the model of science is even more visible in the rise of cognitive approaches, which seek to produce objective accounts of responses to artworks. All these methodologies aim to generalize about the experience of art; none, however, takes as its focus of attention the singularity of individual responses, an issue to which I shall return.

This wide agreement on the importance of experience in determining the nature and importance of art is by no means a universal accord, however. Historical studies tend to proceed as if the historian's own experience of the works being discussed is irrelevant, and often the project of contextualizing those works betrays little interest in how they were experienced at the time. At the other extreme, purely formal approaches tend to treat the artifact as an object to be dissected, not an experienced event. Wittgenstein's insistence on the inaccessibility of inner experience caused many of his followers to look elsewhere for explanations of the distinctiveness of art. Hermeneutic methodologies rely on close inspection of the object in order to arrive at interpretations that can be articulated independently of any account of experience. Political approaches of whatever stripe often proceed as if the artwork could have a direct effect on the world, rather than having to be experienced by individuals before any effects, beneficial or detrimental, can occur. Bourdieu's influential sociological studies focus on the reception of art primarily understood as a process of consumption to be subjected to rational analysis.

The past few decades, in particular, have witnessed the dominance of approaches that, in their pursuit of archival materials, historical contexts, or ideological significance, set aside the experiences of readers, listeners, or viewers. And although in recent years there have been signs of a counter-movement, including methodologies that go under the labels "new formalism" and "post-critique," these alternatives don't always escape from the hypostatization of the artwork as an entity independent of its realizations as singular events; in literary studies, for instance, appeals to such philosophical models as "actor-network theory" or "object oriented ontology" challenge the conventional treatment of objects as passive entities acted upon by human agents and in so doing reduce the role of the latter. "Distant reading" deliberately sets its face against the unique experiences of readers, preferring the tabulation of statistics showing habits across wide populations. And although cognitive approaches are concerned with the individual's response to the artwork, they tend to bypass the variety and complexity of the experiences reported by these individuals in their search for testable generalizations.

By what means, then, can we establish the nature of the experience that brings artworks into being as singular events, while doing justice to the diversity of art?

Introspection is a technique with obvious risks but one that it would be foolish to shun; what's important is that reports on one's own experience are tested against the experiences of others. A second method is the examination of published or otherwise recorded accounts of responses to artworks, of which there are many, going back to the beginnings of what we now call art; there are risks here, too, since what people say on this topic is inevitably colored, and perhaps determined, by the discourses available at the time. It can also be useful to examine the practice of artists themselves, since most artworks are produced as responses to other artworks.

One thing seems clear from such evidence: in examining how listeners, readers, and viewers respond to artworks we're dealing with something extremely complex—more complex than most theories of art have been willing to allow. Listening with full attention to a Mozart symphony in a concert hall may involve any or all of the following (and the list is far from exhaustive): responding to the music's harmonic shifts; feeling its patterns of expectation and satisfaction, tension and release; being stirred by a variety of emotions; following the working out of its structural organization; taking pleasure in the beauty of the melodic line; appreciating the skilled performances of the players; mentally following the conductor's movements; enjoying the varying colors of the instruments; admiring the talent of the composer; learning about the evolution of symphonic form; enhancing one's understanding of Mozart's development; recognizing repeated motifs; mentally comparing this performance with others of the same work; identifying characteristic Mozartian touches; assessing the singularity of the work in relation to others of its time; noticing the influence of earlier composers; finding resonances of the historical and cultural context; evaluating the work in comparison with other symphonies; registering the work's inventiveness; silently humming along; and tapping a foot to the rhythm. Other aspects of the experience may be less focused on the music, such as memories of earlier encounters with the piece, imagined scenes conjured up by the sounds, reflections on the place of Western high culture in a multicultural world, observation of the gender balance of the players, attention to the behavior of other audience members, or fascination with the way the oboist contorts his face.

In the same way, one could enumerate the many ingredients of a full response to a painting hanging on the wall of a gallery, which might include appreciating the artist's skill, tracing the echoes and oppositions within the composition, relishing the vibrancy of the colors, finding satisfaction in the overall balance of the work, gaining insight into the artistic practices of the period, learning about the artist's development, perceiving the imprint of the historical context, sensing the physical application of the paint, and much more. The experience of a work of literature, too, is a combination of numerous elements, some of which might be absorption in the progress of narrative, pleasure in the patterning of sound, empathy with characters, visualization of described scenes, admiration for the writer's accomplishment, physical responsiveness to the rhythm, acquisition of knowledge about other times and places, investment in moral dilemmas, and observation of intertextual echoes.

The question I'm addressing, in the face of this almost overwhelming multiplicity of factors, is which of them is, or are, essential and distinctive in the experience of art. It is obvious that many of our responses to artworks are shared with responses to other entities; the enjoyment of beauty, for instance, is not a category peculiar to the experience of art.[7] To say this is not to imply that these responses are irrelevant to the experience of art; on the contrary, they may constitute a large part of what we enjoy and find important when we look at a sculpture or watch a film. But if that experience *is* distinctive—if, for instance, we feel there is a significant difference between the pleasure we take in a landscape of rolling hills and the pleasure we take in a Picasso drawing—we have to look elsewhere in order to advance our understanding of the peculiar character of art.

2. The power of the work of art

A way forward is to consider more carefully what is meant by saying a work of art is an event rather than a material entity or temporal sequence. An event can be simply an occurrence, or alternatively, as the *Oxford English Dictionary* has it, a "significant or noteworthy" occurrence. But the term also plays a central role in many varieties of continental philosophy, where, in spite of significant differences, a common thread emerges: an event is an unpredictable irruption into the flow of foreseeable occurrences.[8] In its singularity it exceeds the prevailing frameworks of understanding, and these frameworks have to shift in order for it to become part of the existing landscape. The experience which brings the successful artwork into being as art may then be understood as one of being taken into previously unknown and unimagined mental or emotional territory, with the necessary consequence of undergoing some change, temporary or lasting, when this happens. This description accords well with many of the recorded reports on the experience of art: such responses often emphasize surprise, newness, freshness, and tell of being altered, of seeing the world differently, after living through a particularly powerful work. More generally, we can say that to experience an artwork as art is to encounter some kind of otherness—some insight, formal

---

[7] Because I don't see beauty as a distinctive property of artworks, I am hesitant about using the term "aesthetic"; I realize that in doing so I'm turning my back on a central issue for this volume. I trust that what follows will nevertheless be seen as relevant to its concerns.

[8] Among those for whom some version of this concept of the event is important are Heidegger, Deleuze, Badiou, Foucault, Lyotard, and Derrida. My own use of the term in discussing what distinguishes the literary work from other types of discourse derives largely from Derrida, though Lyotard's understanding of the event as unrepresentable and Foucault's account of discursive events have also been important influences on my thinking.

property, imaginative activity, or quality of feeling—that lies outside one's familiar schemata of understanding, appreciation, or emotion. "Art," writes Collingwood, "is the cutting edge of the mind, the perpetual outreaching of thought into the unknown" (*Speculum Mentis*, 107).

Now, to return to our concern with what is distinctive about the experience we're examining, the description I've offered clearly applies just as well to other encounters with elements in the world, including other people. What distinguishes the encounter with the artwork is that the qualities that strike one as new, and that have the power to effect change, are appreciated as the product of the inventive work of one or more creators; the work is felt to possess the attribute of what I have called "authoredness." (When we enjoy a work, this sense of authoredness is often combined with a sense of admiration.) And the experience of the work as made by an inventive creator is an experience of its *form*; or, more precisely, since we are speaking of an event, of its coming into being as material forming and being formed.

I haven't mentioned the satisfaction to be gained from formal unity, harmony, and balance, features often emphasized in accounts of artistic experience, and figuring importantly in most aesthetic theories (often under the heading of "beauty"). Not all artworks provide this satisfaction: sometimes, for instance, the expectation of closure is deliberately thwarted. What this shows is that the anticipation of formal wholeness is a resource available to the artist; it can be satisfied or denied in many ways in the course of the event of the work. Unlike the organic form of an oak tree or a butterfly, an organically unified painting is the product of an inventive act on the part of an artist. In the temporal arts, the creator's skill is manifest as much in the avoidance of closure during the unfolding of the work as it is in the creation of a satisfying ending.[9]

Another frequently noted aspect of the experience of art is a feeling of *recognition*, a feeling that, paradoxical though this may sound, is not opposed to the experience of surprise or newness. The otherness with which the recipient of the artwork engages may at the same time feel entirely appropriate and even familiar, as if fulfilling a lack—albeit a previously unacknowledged one.[10] In making the work, the artist's sense that it is finished, is somehow "right," must stem from the fact that an absence in the cultural field has been made good, and this feeling of an absence being made good may also be experienced by the work's recipient. (It's also part of what makes the experience a pleasurable one.) On the other hand, a

---

[9] Barbara Herrnstein Smith, in *Poetic Closure*, traces in some detail the poetic techniques available to create this experience of satisfaction, and Giorgio Agamben devotes a curious little article to the anomalous status of the poem's last line ("The End of the Poem"). It's an aspect of classical music all composers, and students of music, are well aware of.

[10] I use the word "recipient," *faute de mieux*, as shorthand for "viewer, reader, or listener"; its disadvantage is that it emphasizes only the passive aspect of the simultaneously active and passive process it denotes—what Dewey calls "the complete fusion of what we undergo and what our activity of attentive perception brings into what we receive by means of the senses" (*Art as Experience*, 107).

novelty which is simply that—the kind of novelty that anyone can achieve—provides no experience of rightness or familiarity (except the familiarity of repetition) either for the artist or for the recipient, and effects no change in the individual or the culture. (I should note that the experience of otherness, and the resultant shift in perspective, is seldom on a large scale; it's more often merely a slight but pleasurable venture into new cognitive, emotional, or formal territory with only temporary effects.)

Let me sketch an example. After encountering the British artist Steve McQueen's installation *Year 3* at Tate Britain in 2020, I found I had a changed understanding and appreciation of the value of primary schools—not because I had learned anything factual, but because of the experience I underwent that morning. McQueen arranged for 76,000 of London's Year 3 children (aged 7 to 8) to be photographed in their classes with their teachers and teaching assistants, and mounted the photographs in serried ranks on the walls of the sizable Duveen Galleries. To walk through the galleries, stopping to examine this or that photograph, each one wholly singular, and at the same time to take in the vastness of the entire enterprise (a small model of the vast enterprise of the education of the capital's children), was to experience an extraordinary complex of feelings, including elements of awe, elation, amusement, fascination, wonder, and admiration. As a consequence, I now appreciate more than ever before the commitment and energy of primary school teachers, the liveliness and promise of young children in an educational context, and the huge variety in both groups in a diverse city like London. What I knew to some extent as fact is now ingrained as emotionally grounded awareness; and it's clear that large numbers of viewers shared my experience. McQueen had somehow sensed an absence in contemporary culture, and found a way—which, above all, meant finding a form—to make it good.[11]

It will be evident that my focus is on a relatively small proportion of what are labeled as artworks, and an even smaller number of experiences of those works: something more substantial than the pleasures of a well-known formula being played out, offering the enjoyable reassurance of predictability and repetition. An interest in art's distinctive contribution to culture—and, potentially, in spheres beyond the cultural—must take as its subject the kind of experience that has been most valued by readers, viewers, and listeners, including other artists. This is not to deny the impact of the wider practices of art on cultural, social, and political formations; it's only to say such outcomes are not the product of the distinctive power of art. Good journalism, vivid historical writing, powerful documentary film, articulate argument can all effect significant change without drawing on the

---

[11] The question of how it is possible to find many earlier artworks that were inventive in their time still inventive is not easily answered; as T. S. Eliot puts it, "No good poet wants novelty or eccentricity for its own sake: the element of surprise in good poetry is something which remains for ever, and is not only valid for its own time" (*Poems*, vol. 1, 361–2). I have discussed the issue in *The Singularity of Literature* (63–9) and *The Work of Literature* (194–203).

unique resources of art (though of course they may well do so). We also need to take account of the familiar distinction between art and craft, or between the fine and decorative arts: a beautifully made set of porcelain bowls or a fine cheese may not provide an experience of new perspectives, and are unlikely to have been made by an artist moving into hitherto unknown territory. However, this is not an easily determinable border, and it's always possible that what is received as delightful craft by one cultural group or period will be moving art for another.[12]

How, then, does the experience of art, understood in this manner, contribute to social and political life? My account of the unpredictability of the otherness opened up by the work has a clear implication: the instrumental use of an artwork to further a specific end is distinct from its function as art. This is not to deny that art can be a potent force in effecting political and social change: both artists and commentators can, and frequently do, work toward ethical and political ends. Art has played a significant role in the progress made toward gender and racial justice, environmental awareness, and national liberation—and has also been employed by authoritarian governments to thwart progress. The power of art as political instrument lies partly in the fact that it's experienced as deeply pleasurable, making it a powerful medium for narratives or images that provoke action, whether admirable or reprehensible. In this way its political effectivity is a secondary consequence of its potency as art; as art, however, it cannot be controlled or programmed in advance. Making and receiving art is always risky for this reason; a requirement for both artist and receiver is trust. However, if, as I've argued, inventive art brings into view what has been marginalized by the culture, the chances are that it will have beneficial rather than detrimental effects.

This account of art has obvious consequences for criticism. There's no reason why critical commentaries on artworks shouldn't be concerned with any of the responses I listed earlier; the fuller and more richly detailed the critical work, the greater the range of experiences it will embrace. Even the responses that leave the artwork behind for imagined scenes or private memories can play a part in conveying with the required vividness the experience it has offered the critic. (One might draw the line at the facial contortions of the oboist, however.) Criticism is in part, then, a report on the critic's experience, shared with others in order to discover what is idiosyncratic and what is not, and with the hope of increasing the enjoyment and understanding of those engaging with the work. Since this experience may well be enriched by awareness of historical context and biographical background, or informed by a concern with ethical and political significance, such aspects are as relevant as more direct responses to formal and generic properties and the content they shape.

---

[12] Perhaps the best-known philosophical argument for the distinction between art and craft is R. G. Collingwood's in *The Principles of Art* (15–41). For an eloquent argument against the distinction, see Henry Staten, *Techne Theory*.

What such criticism requires is not only the necessary knowledge to make an informed assessment, a sensitivity to the medium used, and a familiarity with the art form and the particular genre of the work, but also a certain attitude: an openness to the new, a readiness to have one's preconceptions challenged and one's horizons expanded. This hospitality to the other is not only the most fundamental ethical requirement of good criticism; it's also the most fundamental ethical function of art. The artist's achievement is to have been open to what the intellectual, moral, and emotional norms of his or her time had rendered invisible and inaudible and to create visible and audible forms to bring them into existence; and the critic's task is to understand and respect that achievement. When I approach a work of art in this spirit I'm not asking myself, What can I say about this work that is clever and original? Rather, I'm doing my best to shed the consciousness of external goals in order to allow the work to speak to me in its own voice. (Its "own" voice being, of course, the voice of the multiple cultural ingredients fused by the artist in the singular work.) We should also note the possibility that a critical report on experience may be a report on a work's limitations, its *failure* to bring the new into being; such a commentary may be produced in order to counter what the critic sees as mistaken acclaim, or to make a point about the pitfalls that await the artist—though for the most part the wisest course is to let such works languish undiscussed.

The temptation in academic criticism is to devise novel and ingenious interpretations, whether or not these are genuinely part of the critic's experience. The available discourses can be a distorting lens here, affording terms and arguments that generate their own momentum and may leave accuracy and responsibility behind. A commentary that extracts a moral lesson from a work of art, finds evidence for historical phenomena or the author's biography, performs formal analysis, or detects ideological bias can be a valuable contribution to the field, but it's a commentary that treats the work as something other than art. Nor should the goal be to arrive at the "correct" interpretation, as if this were the same for all readers and all time.

I must stress here that the approach I'm outlining doesn't involve an appeal to "subjectivity"; the individual responding to a work of art does so as a product of a culture (or many cultures) and a living embodiment of cultural values, assumptions, modes of thought, expectations, and preferences. If the accusatory label "subjective" really means "idiosyncratic," such responses will not survive conversations and comparisons with others. These conversations are also essential if cultural boundaries are to be breached: I can only respond from my own cultural situation, and the limitations created thereby need to be challenged by others responding from different situations (and vice versa).

The approach might sound like an argument for that old critical chestnut, the autonomy of art, but it's far from being so. The inventive production of a work of art is an event not just in the artist's career but in the culture at large, and it's received not just by an individual but by a culture. The artist has a twin responsibility: to bring into being a work that will enrich the lives of those who will experience it, and to do justice thereby to the otherness being introduced into the culture. The recipient, too, has a twin responsibility: to do justice to the created work and thereby to its maker, and to respond to the work in full awareness of the needs and demands of her own time and place. There is no way a response to an artwork could not reflect to some degree the context within which the recipient is constituted; changing contexts necessarily mean changing works of art, a fact for which there is ample historical evidence. A full response will take account of this fact, though it will often require acknowledgment of the work's original context as well.

3. An example

This account of critical commentary is not intended to suggest that there's a single template, style, or set of requirements to be followed; every response comes from, and occurs in, a different place, and just as each work of art is singular, so each response is singular, reflecting the unique situation of the commentator. (Derrida is among those who have observed that fidelity to the singular work necessarily involves a kind of betrayal.)[13] In what follows, I'll give an example of one way of reflecting the experience that constitutes a temporal artwork: a tracing of the critic's own engagement as the work moves and is moved through time, slowing down for the purposes of commentary what happens very rapidly and partly unconsciously. This critical method highlights the feeling that one is participating in the creation of the work—a feeling often described as gaining access to the maker's intentions, though this may not have any basis in fact (the operation of "intention" in the making of art is, it goes without saying, a far from simple matter).[14] This representation of a temporal process isn't an attempt to describe a single experience; it may be a reflection of many engagements with the work as a whole as well as memorial recollections, research into context, consultation of commentaries, and close attention to particular moments. A musician may try out different ways of playing passages; a reader of poetry may experiment with different ways of performing lines. The experience of non-temporal visual arts is also a temporal sequence, but the work itself doesn't usually suggest the order in which elements are encountered; a critical response intended to reflect the viewer's experience might start with more general impressions before focusing on details,

---

[13] See, for instance, Jacques Derrida, "'This Strange Institution,'" 69.
[14] In *A Swim in the Pond*, Saunders gives a vivid account of the reading experience as a tracing of the artist's (assumed) intentions. Blanchot remarks that the reader "partakes of the work as the unfolding of something in the making" (*The Space of Literature*, 202).

or start with a striking detail and expand to the whole work. In sketching a critical response of this kind I'm not offering a model, simply one way of proceeding to be tested and developed or countered by others.

Since space is limited, I've chosen a short poem, Ben Jonson's "On My First Son." Although I know the poem well and have some prior knowledge of the circumstances under which it was written, I want to reflect on what it might be like to engage with it for the first time and without consciously bringing external information to bear upon it. (Of course, my reading will always be colored by what I know, but this attempt at a virgin reading is a useful strategy to allow the poem to speak in its own voice as strongly as possible.) Where additional information deepens the poem, this can be drawn on to enrich further readings. Like almost all poetry, the work calls out to be read aloud.

I've encountered the poem many times over the years, each time within a different context and as a different reader. Its familiarity doesn't prevent it from springing surprises each time I engage with it. I come to it now as a father with adult daughters, never having gone through the kind of grief the poem records, but in the midst of a pandemic that has robbed many other fathers of their children, among an enormous number of other losses. My experience of the poem cannot but be colored by this background.

I give the poem here as it was first published in 1616 among Jonson's "Epigrammes," and then in a modernized version.

On My First Sonne
Farewell, thou child of my right hand, and joy;
   My sinne was too much hope of thee, lov'd boy,
Seven yeeres tho'wert lent to me, and I thee pay,
   Exacted by thy fate, on the just day.
O, could I loose all father, now. For why
   Will man lament the state he should envie?
To have so soone scap'd worlds, and fleshes rage,
   And, if no other miserie, yet age?
Rest in soft peace, and, ask'd, say here doth lye
   BEN. JONSON his best piece of *poetrie*.
For whose sake, hence-forth, all his vowes be such,
   As what he loves may never like too much.

Farewell, thou child of my right hand, and joy;
My sin was too much hope of thee, lov'd boy.
Seven years thou wert lent to me, and I thee pay,
Exacted by thy fate, on the just day.
O, could I lose all father now! For why
Will man lament the state he should envy?

> To have so soon 'scap'd world's, and flesh's, rage,
> And if no other misery, yet age?
> Rest in soft peace, and, ask'd, say, 'Here doth lie
> Ben Jonson his best piece of poetry.'
> For whose sake henceforth all his vows be such
> As what he loves may never like too much.

The title registers immediately as autobiographical (the pronoun is 'my' not 'his'). It could of course be a dramatic monologue spoken by an imagined character—and a strict New Critic might say that the first-person speaker of a poem is always an imagined character—but there's no need to set aside the obvious import of the words as an utterance by the historical Ben Jonson, whatever complications one might wish to introduce after further consideration. What the title portends we can't tell, though the special place of the first-born son in much of recorded history is clearly significant.

In the same way, the first line carries centuries-old echoes as an utterance of loss and benediction, addressed in imagination to the departed son—now identified as a child—and in fact to the reader. The line establishes the meter of the poem as the familiar iambic pentameter, a more meditative and speech-like form than the main alternative in English verse, the tetrameter or four-beat line.[15] Giving full attention to the striking phrase "child of my right hand"—where the off-kilter stress on "right" produces a deceleration in the rhythm—allows it to work as a moving assertion of closeness and indispensability. Further inquiry reveals a more pointed reference: the words translate the Hebrew name "Benjamin." (Strength of emotion doesn't preclude intellectual agility.) We learn from this, too, that the departed son had the same name as the father, adding further poignancy to the valediction.

The second line presents a surprising paradox: why should having great hopes for a child be counted a sin? Again, there is a moment of emphasis in the rhythm as "lov'd" demands some degree of stress despite being in the offbeat position; and the rhyme of "boy" with "joy" seals the connection between these two ideas. Then the crucial fact is revealed: the boy has died at seven years, the shocking number emphasized by the metrical promotion at the start of the line. The paradox is now explained: a life is not owned but borrowed; longevity is not to be assumed. (Jonson would have encountered this trope in both classical and Christian sources.) The tone is complex, however, the financial metaphor hinting at a degree of irony. Does this father really accept that the loss of his son is the equivalent of

---

[15] Jonson chose iambic tetrameter for his poem on his first daughter's death, which begins, "Here lies, to each her parents' ruth,/Mary, the daughter of their youth," where the more song-like movement is evident. Because of my academic background, I register these metrical niceties consciously; for many readers, they operate without reaching consciousness.

payment demanded on an agreed day? And that not to do so is sinful? (The metrically promoted "just" suggests both exactness and fairness.) At the very least, the participant in a contract is aware beforehand of the terminal date. The analogy can't assuage the pain, and the next line allows some of it to be expressed: "O, could I lose all father now!" It's a remarkably compressed cry; I have to re-read it several times to decide on the sense and the affective force. One paraphrase would be "If only I could rid myself of the emotional bonds that come with being a father!" (The spelling "loose" for modern "lose" is common in the Early Modern period, but it's tempting to read the word as a pun conveying both meanings, "let go of" and "unbind.") Christianity may require that one do so; the reality of grief says otherwise.

In the next three lines the conventional religious consolation that should help in the overcoming of that fatherly feeling is put as a question, one to which there is no simple answer.[16] Does it count as a blessing to have escaped from worldly hatreds, disease, and old age?[17] The line "To have so soone scap'd world, and fleshes, rage" asks to be taken seriously, and its intensity is enhanced by the heavily insistent rhythm, with four successive stresses that include the word "escaped" reduced to a single monosyllable.

The final four lines come as something of a relief; "soft," inserted in the conventional translation of *Requiescat in pace*, is a surprising and comforting touch, slowing the articulation of the line by converting the common opening inversion, /x x/, to /x//. The epitaphic trope of the dead person addressing the living visitor to the grave is given an unexpected twist: here the father tells the dead child how to respond to an enquirer, while providing words to be engraved on the tomb. The obvious answer is the child's name, Ben Jonson (in capitals, as it would appear on the monument), and this is the reading that's first invited; but this is and isn't the child's name—it's also the father's name, the poet who feels that none of his poems matches up to the living being whose existence he was partly responsible for. (Had the newer possessive form "Jonson's" been used instead of the older "Jonson his," this doubleness wouldn't be present.) The italicization of "*poetrie*" is perhaps there to remind us of the word's ultimate derivation from the idea of "making" (much commented on in Renaissance manuals on verse).

One might not have thought that calling one's dead child a piece of poetry could be moving, but on every re-reading I find it powerfully affecting. It's at once intimate and self-aware, the opposite of sentimental; the claim is at once considerable—this art to which I have dedicated my life means less to me than the

---

[16] The meter requires that "envie" be stressed on the second syllable and rhyme with "why," as regularly in Middle English and often in Early Modern English. Compare "lye/*poetrie*" later in the poem.

[17] Colin Burrow glosses "rage" as "passion" (Jonson, *Epigrams*, 45), but the line strikes me as denoting much worse evils.

child I have lost—and under firm intellectual control—I can think together, in a kind of pun, the creation of my poems and the creation of my son.

Then a switch to the third person: again, the tone is complex, a crucial aspect of the poem's singularity. "For whose sake" grammatically refers to the son, but it is the poet's own future he is contemplating. An initial reading of the last line, whose rhythmic simplicity contributes to the feeling of closure, is "beware of liking too much that which you love"—a contradictory sentiment that makes sense as a warning to keep some distance from loved ones, in order to prevent the intensity of grief being felt at this moment by the poet. However, the subject of "may never like" is not the poet but "what he loves." (A common meaning for the verb to "like" in the seventeenth century was to "please"—as in the expression "it likes me not.") Jonson's prayer is that the objects of his future love shouldn't please him in the way his son did: it's a commendation of young Benjamin's perfection and at the same time an articulation of the magnitude of the father's loss.

This reading is confirmed when one learns that that final line is a translation of Martial's Epigram 6.29 on the death of a slave, which ends, "Quidquid ames, cupias non placuisse nimis" ("Whatever you love, pray that it not please too much"). But Jonson could have had another of Martial's epigrams in mind as well: 12.34, to his close friend Julius Martialis, warns against becoming too closely attached to another person—"Gaudebis minus et minus dolebis" ("You will rejoice less and sorrow less"). Perhaps that initial misreading of the final line of Jonson's poem is not a misreading at all, but a secondary meaning that hovers behind the first.

How does the information that Jonson is echoing Martial affect our experience of the poem? We could treat it as a scholarly footnote, demonstrating what we know already, that Jonson was steeped in the classics and that Martial was one of his favorite Roman poets. But if we incorporate it into our reading of the elegy, it expands the work's range: as well as a highly personal lament it becomes an explicit contribution to the centuries-long project of finding in language a resource for the exploration of grief—channeling it, focusing it, understanding it, perhaps overcoming it. A public elegy is, finally, not an address to its subject, or a communing with the poet's self, but an invitation to readers to share, and be altered by, that exploration.

Another piece of information that colors my experience of the poem is that Jonson's son died in 1603 of the plague that was rampant in London that year. Jonson himself was staying at Robert Cotton's house and learned of the boy's death through a letter from his wife, who had remained in London (Jonson, *Informations*, lines 198–205). While not altering my understanding of the poem, this added detail increases its affective power, especially at the time in which I'm writing—early 2021—when the deaths from the Covid-19 virus in the UK have reached 100,000 and look set to increase much further. Whatever fallacies—affective, intentional, genetic, contextual—one may wish to avoid, the experience of poetry is not determined by one's theories but by the full engagement of mind and body, and knowledge of the circumstances of a work's creation—and its possible connection with the environment within which one reads—can't be erased. When ideology, inefficiency, and self-interest have condemned so many to a death that could have been avoided, this reminder of the singularity of every loss carries particular weight.

I can't express in precise terms how the experience of this poem has altered my intellectual and emotional understanding of loss, and of the loss of a loved child in particular; our dealings with powerful artworks elude full articulation. But I'm certain it has, however slightly or temporarily. Living through the process whereby a potentially inchoate outpouring of grief is given a precise form that articulates and contains it through the operation of the intellect and the poetic ear cannot but be transformative. And, remarkably, it's an event, and experience, of less than a minute.

Does this account of my experience of the poem correspond to that of Jonson's first readers? There's no knowing; and this is not the point of the exercise. The death of a child was a vastly more common phenomenon in the early seventeenth century than it is now; but this doesn't mean we should attempt to recalibrate our response to take account of this fact. The poem has survived because it has been re-read again and again in changing contexts, and it continues to live today because it speaks to us where and when we are now.

2
The Ontology of Artworlds
A Post-Human, Coevolutionary Framework for Aesthetics, Art History, and Art Criticism

Richard O. Prum

1. Introduction

Humanism encompasses the intellectual investigation, analysis, and celebration of human agency in culture, art, and society. Over the past half century, numerous external challenges have arisen to an exclusively humanistic perspective. Global warming, climate change, habitat destruction, mass biodiversity extinction, pollution, and deadly pandemics pose expanding, planetary-scale threats to human welfare, thriving, and sustainability. Across all humanistic disciplines, attention has turned to consider these material and environmental challenges and, more broadly, to renegotiate the intellectual relationship to the scientific disciplines to which they are a central focus. These efforts raise the question of whether the humanities are intellectually sustainable in isolation from the sciences.

Given the long history of attempts by various scientific fields or movements to "explain away" the products of human agency as the products of various law-like forces, humanists may be understandably anxious about inviting scientists to become active participants in their disciplines. For example, sociobiology in the 1970s to 1990s, and evolutionary psychology since the turn of the century, have explicitly aimed to reduce the humanities, sociology, and psychology to human manifestations of adaptation by natural selection. These intellectual views have been adopted by various humanists in the form of "literary Darwinism" and "evo-criticism" (e.g., Boyd 2009; Dutton 2009). To me, efforts to understand the arts, art making, and art criticism as the products of adaptation create what I call "flatitudes"—faux-profundities that gain their intellectual appeal by flattening the true complexity of phenomena (Prum 2017: 320). Such efforts, which aspire to explain away human agency scientifically as the product of a natural process, are an intellectual dead end.

In contrast, I am working to interconnect science and the humanities by bringing the humanistic focus on human agency to bear on the many emergent, non-human agencies in the natural world. In this chapter, I present a coevolutionary framework that recognizes the myriad, parallel aesthetic agencies of non-human animals. My goal is to contribute as well to understanding of human aesthetics.

On multiple fronts within my own research as an ornithologist and evolutionary biologist, I have encountered deep intellectual connections between my scientific research and vital topics in the humanities, including aesthetics, sexual autonomy, feminism, and queer theory (Prum 2013, 2015, 2017, 2020). In each of these instances, I have experienced the intellectual productivity of a "post-human" move to focus upon non-human agencies as scientific concepts and hypotheses for investigation and analysis.

Here, I am proposing a distinct use of the term "post-human." Post-humanism is often conceived of as an aspirational, revolutionary *future* development through which we humans "overcome" the current and historical limits of "The Human" through collaboration with technology. Although many people consider this hybrid-cyborg humanism to be a worthy and fascinating goal, this perspective leaves me cold and uninterested. It lacks any of the to-be-hoped-for intellectual benefits to either science or the humanities. (Having never been a fan of science fiction, I freely confess that this might be a lack of imagination on my part.)

However, like Jane Bennett (2010) and other new materialist humanists, I *am* interested in a synchronic post-humanism through which we reimagine, decenter, and recontexualize our understanding of human agency by simultaneously recognizing the qualities, properties, and consequences of non-human biological and material agencies. In organismal and evolutionary biology, the subjects of my own scientific research on behavioral homology, mate choice, and the development and evolution of feathers have been under continual threat of reductive explanations from genetics, cell biology, and adaptationist evolutionary biology. I think that decades of this experience has prepared me well to recognize alternate solutions that connect fields of inquiry without reducing them.

Amidst the multiple urgent challenges posed simultaneously by global climate change, habitat destruction, biodiversity extinction, the current Covid-19 pandemic, and the persistence of racism, sexism, poverty, and hunger, it may seem that focusing our attention—indeed our intellectual lives—on understanding aesthetics is, at best, frivolous elitism, or even morally negligent. Although I speak in my own self-interested defense, I really do believe that working toward a deeper and broader understanding of beauty and aesthetics in the world provides a distinct and excellent opportunity to explore the urgently necessary, more productive, new relationship between science and the humanities more generally.

In *Situated Knowledges*, Donna Haraway (1988) observes that the traditional scientific search for "translation, convertibility, mobility of meanings, and universality" becomes reductive "only when one language (guess whose?) must be enforced as the standard for all translations and conversations" between scientific and cultural knowledges. Accordingly, in much of my work, I have found that the adoption of a traditionally *humanistic* vocabulary and perspective in the understanding of biology and evolution in the non-human world is both scientifically and humanistically productive. Accordingly, aesthetics is an excellent place to explore the broader interface between science and the humanities precisely *because* the topic makes many scientists so uncomfortable—because the concept of the aesthetic agency of animals is destabilizing to a reductive, lawlike conception of the sciences that is so corrosive to many efforts to interconnect the "Two Cultures."

In the five hundred years since Galileo observed the moons of Jupiter orbiting around that planet and proposed the heliocentric universe, the science of cosmology has repeatedly reconceived of, and refined, our conceptions of the organization of the cosmos, placing human beings on Earth at successively more peripheral, inconsequential, indeed boring positions within the universe. To me, these successive decenterings of the human have only enhanced the richness, the exceptional qualities, and the consequent *value* of our experiences as humans. Likewise, moving human beings out of the organizing center of the discipline of aesthetics will *enhance* our understanding of human aesthetic capacity, creativity, and history. This post-human aesthetics decenters human aesthetic production, experience, and history while simultaneously enhancing our appreciation for our unique aesthetic complexity. Post-human aesthetics provides the broader context necessary to understand ourselves better. Inviting into our consideration the fully aesthetic phenomena of plants and animals will not downgrade the human arts and human aesthetics, but create a broader pedestal for understanding them.

I argue that thinking about aesthetics, art, and beauty in today's troubled world is morally responsible, and perhaps even courageous, because it requires insisting upon the survival and centrality of traditional humanistic concerns to the inevitable, post-human intellectual world to come. Making a vital intellectual future in the world for aesthetics, beauty, and the arts contributes to insuring the survival of the humanities—and our own sense of wonder, pleasure, and delight—within the inevitable post-humanities.

2. A Coevolutionary Aesthetics

The complexity, richness, and diversity of human-created aesthetic entities and experiences create a persistent problem for intellectual analysis. The expansion of the scope of aesthetics to encompass the aesthetic agencies, objects, and performances of non-human organisms creates even bigger challenges, but also provides a path toward a new conceptual framework and a set of tools that can aid aesthetic investigation at all levels.

In a previous work (Prum 2013), I have proposed and defended a post-human, coevolutionary aesthetic framework that was inspired by a classic thought experiment in aesthetic philosophy—Arthur Danto's (1964) *The Artworld*—and drew upon my own research on the aesthetic evolution of avian plumages, displays, and songs. In that work, I defined art as *a form of communication that coevolves with its evaluation*. Accordingly, the property of being art is neither manifest in the material object or performance, nor in the subjective experience, but in their history of mutual entrainment, relation, and iterative response.

As Danto perceived, art and aesthetics are necessarily population phenomena, which can only be understood in terms of the communities in which aesthetic phenomena occur, persist, and change. These aesthetic communities are appropriately referred to as artworlds, which include a myriad of non-human species and ecological communities. The goal of this chapter is to explore further the ontology of artworlds, and its impact on our understanding of art, art history, and art criticism as natural, post-human phenomena. First, however, I want to summarize a few of the most fundamental implications of this coevolutionary aesthetic framework.

Coevolutionary aesthetics is an aesthetic theory of art; accordingly, there is no category of art without the phenomenon of aesthetics, and no aesthetic phenomena without art. This view, most frequently associated with John Dewey (1934), has not been a popular since the mid-twentieth century. However, coevolutionary aesthetics has little else in common with Dewey's aesthetic theory which focused upon the special psychological qualities of individual "aesthetic experience."

Aesthetic philosophers and art historians readily recognized that what qualifies as "art" has been, and will continue to be, subject to radical and revolutionary transformation (Danto 1981, 1984, 1997). Erroneously I believe, many philosophers simultaneously regard "the aesthetic" as a static category including sensory, often basic, and perhaps universal affective qualities. Consequently, many conclude that the lessons we learn from historical transformations of what can constitute an artwork—from Eduard Manet's *Olympia*, to Marcel Duchamp's *Fountain*, to Andy Warhol's *Brillo Boxes*, and on—is that the history and future of art has left aesthetics behind.

However, one fundamental consequence of coevolutionary theory of art is that the category of "the aesthetic" is *not* static, but is dynamically coevolving with art itself. The category of aesthetic phenomena appropriately includes *all* phenomena that are relevant to the evaluation of an artwork. Therefore, the aesthetic is not universal, flat, static, or even purely sensory, but coevolves dynamically with art itself. The history of the revolutionary transformations of human art is also the correlated history of the transformation of the category of aesthetic, and revision of the criteria by which artworks are evaluated. The analytical advantage of this perspective is that the apparent discontinuities between the material, sensory, superficial, ornamental features of art, and the conceptual, political, sociological, and moral implications of art disappear. All of these features and responses can be best understood through the historical process of aesthetic coevolution.

Although the applications of coevolutionary aesthetics can span phenomena that have been traditionally considered to be exclusively the realm of the sciences (e.g., bird song) and the humanities (e.g., the fine arts), this is not a reductive theory of human or biotic arts. Rather, this framework is appropriate for the analysis of the many, independent emergent origins of art, through the evolutionary or cultural origins of aesthetic coevolution in different populations, species, and communities. This framework does not propose to replace humanistic, cultural analysis, interpretation, criticism, or history of art, but to provide consciously post-human analytical tools to expand what is possible in these ongoing areas of study. For example, the process of aesthetic coevolution can proceed through either genetic correlation/covariance, or through cultural mechanisms. In both cases it is the coevolutionary feedback—the mutual influences of aesthetic production on aesthetic evaluation, and aesthetic evaluation on aesthetic production—that creates the becoming of art.

Coevolutionary aesthetics provides a naturalistic and empirical theory of aesthetics, by which I mean that aesthetic phenomena arise in the world, and can be investigated like other natural phenomena. This view does not mean, however, that art and aesthetic change can be causally reduced to some singular, non-aesthetic, extrinsic explanatory factor or force such as sensory biology, neurobiology, psychology, or adaptation by natural selection. An intellectual and analytical advance made possible by this framework is that we understand the historical process aesthetic coevolution itself as the causal process in aesthetic change. These explanations may frequently include distinct, emergent, and contingent properties of specific artworlds. This naturalistic view of aesthetic agency and process is inconsistent with Denis Dutton's (2006, 2009) claim that a naturalistic view of art requires adopting a cluster concept of art. Following from Ludwig Wittgenstein (1953) and Morris Weitz (1956), an aesthetic cluster concept asserts that art is an undefinable category that must be based on general, family resemblances, which can be recognized operationally by the possession of a cluster of probable criteria, none of which is individually necessary or sufficient. In contrast, coevolutionary aesthetics provides a naturalistic account of art and aesthetics because it focuses upon a natural process—the coevolution between modes of expression and evaluation.

Coevolutionary aesthetics also provides a naturalistic account of the origin of both aesthetic properties and aesthetic values. Aesthetic properties are coevolved dimensions of evaluator response to aesthetic experience. For example, beauty, balance, unity, cuteness, irony, silliness, innovation, and so on are examples of aesthetic properties—*potential* criteria that may be applied in the evaluation of an artwork. Coevolutionary aesthetics implies that such aesthetic properties are *not* universal, a priori, or materially present in the art. Rather, aesthetics properties arise from the historical details of the coevolutionary relation between aesthetic expression and evaluation within an artworld. Aesthetic properties are not intrinsic or material properties of an artwork, performance, or aesthetic entity. They are evaluator experiences whose qualities emerge from historically contingent aesthetic conventions shaped by the coevolutionary histories of the relevant artworlds. Likewise, aesthetic values—including, for example, esteem, respect, admiration, relative merit, or even price of an artwork or an aesthetic evaluation—arise and are shaped historically by the social within a specific artworld.

In this way, coevolutionary aesthetics is a non-reductive framework that is consistent with many contemporary accounts of the context-dependence of aesthetic properties and values. However, this coevolutionary framework is inconsistent with neo-Hegelian modernist theories of art history that conceived of aesthetic change as headed logically, inexorably toward particular aesthetic goals or ends—such as atonal music, monochrome painting, or stream of consciousness writing. Such theories, and the aesthetic movements or "schools" that invoke them, have contributed to the belief that art will necessarily leave beauty, and other sensible aesthetic properties, behind. However, coevolutionary aesthetics rejects any inherent teleology to aesthetic change. Furthermore, because art is a form of communication, artworks, aesthetic expressions, or production that deny, degrade, or challenge the social relation inherent to aesthetic communication will threaten or endanger the capacity of that art form to coevolve and thus to persist and survive. Abstraction, conceptual complexity, and opacity can all be intriguing and engaging aesthetic properties, but their impact on aesthetic coevolution within an artworld can be precarious. What some modernists have referred to as "anaesthetic art" can become an aesthetic dead-end because the absence and denial of sensory engagement can deaden the social relation with communities of evaluators which necessarily drives aesthetic coevolution.

In a naturalistic account of art, beauty is the experience of coevolved attraction or pleasure, in which the aesthetic stimulus and the attraction to it have shaped one another over time. From a coevolutionary aesthetic perspective, beauty will never be "left behind," dropped, or become irrelevant to the arts. A more sciencey way of stating this is that beauty is the *null aesthetic property*—that is, our first expectation for how artworks engage an audience of evaluators in an artworld, and thus sustain the process of aesthetic coevolution. Beauty is the simplest, most powerful aesthetic value because it functions to maintain positive engagement of its evaluators, and thus drives aesthetic coevolution itself.

In contrast to beauty, other aesthetic values arise through a correlation of aesthetic experience with some other *extrinsic, non-sensory,* or *extra-sensory* factor. Like beauty, aesthetic horror coevolves through the direct engagement with observers but in the opposite valence—coevolved repulsion. The sensory signal coevolves to be repulsive because the perceivable details are associated with risk, noxious experiences, or danger. The prime example of aesthetic horror is aposematism, or warning signals in nature—such as the buzz of a venomous rattlesnake, the brilliant red, yellow, and black colors of a coral snake, or the bold black and white pattern of a skunk. These signals coevolve to be repulsive because of their association with these other, dangerous extrinsic qualities. Likewise, the aesthetic property of opulence engendered by gold leaf, jewels, or highly detailed textiles does not arise in any way from their objective form, sensory properties, or possible functions. Rather, their aesthetic properties arise through the correlation of these sensory experiences with their rarity, their economic value, and the great investment of time to create them. In summary, the aesthetic properties of beauty are intrinsic to the social relation between the producer-evaluator, but other, more complex aesthetic properties gain their meaning through their relations to additional extrinsic factors.

3. Artworld Ontology

A fundamental consequence of a coevolutionary aesthetic framework is to contextualize all aesthetic evaluations, criticisms, and influences within or among various artworlds. Understanding these implications requires establishing an *ontology of artworlds*—that is, a formal concept of the ways in which artworlds exist in the world.

From a naturalistic perspective, I propose that artworlds are a natural kind (i.e., real entities that exist in the world regardless of human regard, concern, observation, or theorizing). However, artworlds are not examples of ontological classes (i.e., they cannot be defined by any essential qualities, aesthetic values, or other criteria). Rather, like individual organisms, biological populations, species, and higher taxa, artworlds are examples of historical individuals—that is, natural kinds that exist by virtue of their origin, or birth, their temporal persistence, their potential to thrive and possible multiply, and their inevitable historical end, death, or extinction. Other examples of ontological individuals include you and me, biological species like *Homo sapiens* or White Oaks *Quercus alba*, planets like Earth and Venus, and astronomical features like the Milky Way galaxy. Thus, artworlds exist as historical entities through the ongoing persistence due to coevolutionary aesthetic processes. Artworlds are ontological individuals.

Of course, by stating that artworlds "have a history," I do not mean a human-made accounting, but an actual, temporal persistence that is independent of human conception, or history making. Thus, animal artworlds—such as the elaborate and unique aesthetic community of Rose-breasted Grosbeaks (*Pheuticus ludovicianus*) which involves bold and brilliant male plumage patterning and tonally and temporally complex male song—exist and persist regardless of human conception, analysis, or historicizing.

This historical ontology of artworlds compliments the processual definition of art itself. Artworlds persist historically through the cultural-social networks of interacting aesthetic producers and evaluators. We can envision these aesthetic networks synchronically, or "horizontally," as the nexuses of aesthetic interactions among producers and evaluators (Figure 2.1a). Of course, in some artworlds, producers and evaluators may be different individuals, but in many other artworlds producers and evaluators are the same individuals exercising both of these aesthetic functions in temporal series, or even simultaneously. We can also visualize the ontology of artworlds allochronically, or "vertically" in time, as a temporally persistent, coevolving network of aesthetic producers and evaluators that give rise to aesthetic change in aesthetic form, content, media, and judgment (Figure 2.1b).

This historical ontology of artworlds raises the current ambiguity in the diagnoses of the category of "artworld" from other simultaneously occurring historical aesthetic entities including genres, styles, "schools," "scenes," and "trends." The complex, multiplicity of human artworlds necessarily creates these ambiguities. In biology, such challenges have given rise to a detailed ontology of historical natural kinds including genes, cells, individual organisms, populations (or demes), subspecies, species, genera, families, orders, classes, ecological communities, biomes, ecosystems, and so on. I will not explore this further here, but a future goal of an historical ontology of artworlds is the establishment of operational distinctions among historical aesthetic categories.

A coevolutionary perspective reveals that aesthetic innovation is not restricted to aesthetic producers; art history is not solely the history of artistic genius. Rather, creative innovations in evaluation and criticism can play an equivalently influential role in the coevolution of aesthetic change. Furthermore, the relative contributions of innovations in aesthetic production and judgment in any particular artworld is an empirical question that can be subject to empirical investigation and analysis.

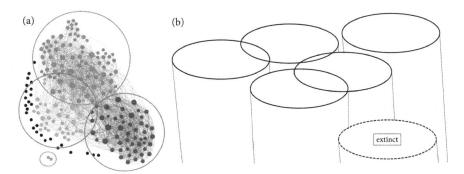

Figure 2.1 Visualizations of artworlds

Notes: (a) Artworlds can be viewed synchronically as a network of aesthetic interactions (lines) among producers and evaluators (nodes). Different artworlds arise from the distinct features of interconnections within and among aesthetic communities. (b) Artworlds can be visualized allochronically as temporally persistent aesthetic communities within which aesthetic coevolutionary processes occur. Artworlds may be isolated, overlapping, or extinct.

The coevolutionary process within an artworld is subject to numerous distinct aesthetic and non-aesthetic (perhaps, more properly extra-aesthetic) effects and influences. Aesthetic influences include innovations in aesthetic production or evaluation innovations that influence sensory perceptions or cognitive responses. "Extra-aesthetic" influences include all those features of the social environment and context of the artworld that can impinge upon aesthetic coevolution, but are not themselves the product of aesthetic coevolution. Some influences are technological innovations—like the printing press, record players, or glasses to correct aberrations in human vision. Others will be a product of material culture such as the scientific discovery of new pigments, or access to new materials through colonialism and capitalism. Indeed, the entire panoply of social factors can serve as aesthetic influences, including economics, gender, class, race, caste, religion, government, nationalism, colonialism and empire, and so on. Extrinsic influences are present in both human and non-human, or biotic, artworlds. For example, a great deal of research indicates that species of birds with learned vocalizations (i.e., culture) have evolved higher frequency songs in urban environments in order to escape acoustic interference created by urban noise (Dowling et al. 2011).

Arthur Danto's (1964) original conception of "The Artworld" was framed explicitly to describe the narrow, elite world of contemporary fine arts produced by fashionable, well-regarded artists, observed, discussed, and emulated by aspiring artists, shown at hip galleries, collected by wealthy patrons and major museums, reviewed in high art and academic publications, curated and exhibited in museums, and studied in studio art graduate programs. This specifically elitist point of view reflected Danto's own aesthetic interests as erstwhile New York abstract expressionist painter. But it also reflected a long tradition of elitism in Anglo-European aesthetic philosophy and art criticism. One can infer from Danto's text that his concept of "The Artworld" in 1964 might not be found in Omaha, and certainly did not exist in Ouagadougou.

An interesting benefit of post-human coevolutionary aesthetic is that the reframing of the discipline to encompass biotic artworlds also exposes and decenters previous Western, Anglo-European, and elitist biases in the conception of aesthetics. As conceived here, there are a myriad of diverse artworlds existing in a nearly uncountable number of non-human species. This tremendous expansion of the breadth and diversity of art may be unsettling to humanists interested in aesthetics. But the expansion comes with the additional benefit of establishing clearly that intellectual interest in aesthetics and aesthetic value are not necessarily tied to elitism, Western chauvinism, patriarchy, capitalism, or hetero-normative conceptions of familial domesticity, as both radical art historians and conservative aesthetic philosopher Roger Scruton (2009) have asserted.

4. Human Artworlds Are Overlapping and Interpenetrating

If artworlds are any historically persisting, coevolving aesthetic networks of producers and evaluators, then virtually every human being is a concurrent participant in multiple simultaneous artworlds: high and low, from the fine arts to pop music, ballet performances to high school dances in a basketball gym, public art museums to shelves of household tchotchkes, cinema to Instagram posts, restaurant cuisine to consumer product packaging, and high fashion to graffiti. I will not invest time here in trying to differentiate which of these phenomena constitute artworlds, genres, styles, and so on. Rather, my goal is to recognize the shared historical ontology of these aesthetic social phenomena.

A ubiquitous feature of human culture is the overlapping, interpenetrating, and dynamic social-material content of human artworlds. Depicted graphically, every person is a simultaneous social participant in multiple partly overlapping artworlds (see Figure 2.1a). However, specific artworlds cannot be defined by their participants—who may come and go individually through birth, migration, recruitment, loss of interest, or death, for example.

Because they are historical entities, artworlds manifest a suite of historical phenomena that will be familiar to historical disciplines, including evolutionary biology, geology, cosmology, history, and art history. For example, the ontological status of artworlds as historical entities means that artworlds can exist, and persist, despite the absence of discreet boundaries or definable limits, or edges. All modern humans are simultaneous participants in multiple, interpenetrating artworlds. Similarly, many bird species are simultaneously participating in the coevolution sexual aesthetics within their species, but also in interspecific artworlds involving the aesthetic coevolution of flowers or fruits with nectivores and frugivores.

The temporal dynamics of artworlds make individual artworlds undefinable by any catalog of participants, description of their aesthetic productions, or their evaluative criteria. Artworlds really exist because their networks of aesthetic production, evaluation, and influence persist over time. Ontological individuality is not threatened or undermined by the instability or fluidity of material or social contents. Although fuzzy borders of, and among, aesthetic communities do not pose a challenge to the ontological reality of artworlds, they can challenge the persistence of specific artworlds at particular points in time. Analogously, the individuality of a human being is not challenged by having a kidney transplant or a blood transfusion, or by eating a meal composed of parts of other organisms. Neither is the individuality of human mothers threatened by the fact that a large percentage of them (perhaps all), retain genetically distinct populations of stem blood cells within their bone marrow that are derived from cells of their offspring that crossed the placenta into their blood streams from each of their offspring (Johnson et al. 2020).

5. Historical Process of Aesthetic Change

Aesthetic change occurs within artworlds through the coevolution of aesthetic production and evaluations. For example, Haydn and Mozart took innovative advantage of the "well-tempered" keyboard (itself a conceptual-technological innovation) to compose music that moved between musical keys within a single piece, creating new modes of emotional expression in music (Rosen 1997). These compositional innovations transformed the audience's capacity to conceive of what music could be and do, which fed back upon future works by these and other composers in the European concert and chamber music artworld, advancing the development of the Classical Style. However, aesthetic change is not simply the history of artistic creative genius. Innovations in evaluation have equivalent potential to further aesthetic change in an artworld. For example, the mid-twentieth-century art critic Clement Greenberg (1986) developed and promoted the idea that twentieth-century avant-garde painting was the realization of a centuries-long progression in Western art toward greater recognition of the unique features of the medium, especially its two-dimensionality and purity of color. Greenberg's work was highly influential in promoting the art of Jackson Pollack and other American abstract expressionists, and his intellectual analysis was an innovation in evaluation that had a tremendous impact on the aesthetic change in mid-twentieth-century Euro-American painting.

Aesthetic change can also proceed through changes—recruitment or diminution—in the composition of the participants in an artworld. For example, the growth of aristocratic female literacy in eleventh- and twelfth-century Europe is thought to have contributed to the development of the secular poetry of courtly love. Change in the composition of the potential evaluators within an artworld transformed the nature of aesthetic productions in the medieval literary artworld (A. J. Sager, Pers. Comm.).

Expanding the concept of art to include coevolving aesthetic productions of non-human organisms also establishes a new dimension of diversity to the mechanisms of aesthetic change—genetic vs. cultural coevolution. In many biotic artworlds, aesthetic coevolution advances by genetic mechanisms. For example, the astoundingly complex ornaments of peacocks, pheasants, and birds of paradise, are the result of the coevolution genes for male display traits and genes for female mate preferences (Prum 2010, 2012, 2017). Genetic coevolution is so materially based that it can be investigated very explicitly. In contrast, however, cultural coevolution in human artworlds proceeds through the influence of aesthetic and cultural ideas, which can result in rapid aesthetic change that obscures its own process. Because the cultural dissemination of aesthetic ideas—in the form of aesthetic productions, evaluations, or extra-aesthetic influences—is less physically constrained and infrequently particulate, it can be more challenging to investigate and analyze. However, as humanists know, people create many material and (now) electronic records of their social interactions, which create resources for the empirical analysis of the process and history of aesthetic change.

6. Origin and Extinction of Artworlds

Analogous to speciation or linguistic dialect and language formation, new artworlds may also form by the diversification, or fission, of an historic or ancestral artworld into descendent artworlds. Descendent artworlds can become distinct through further aesthetic individuation—i.e., continued coevolutionary differentiation of aesthetic production and evaluative criteria between the two descendent aesthetic communities. As in speciation or linguistic diversification, the birth/diversification of artworlds can be fostered by the origin of physical or social compartmentalization, or by the creation of isolation barriers imposed upon the standing aesthetic variation within an artworld.

For example, 1940s and 1950s Rhythm & Blues (R&B) arose from traditionally acoustic blues during the Great Migration of African Americans to northern urban centers. The new social context and isolation-by-distance from the rural communities of origin contributed to individuation of R&B through aesthetic differentiation in instrumentation (acoustic to electric) and a broadening of the R&B audience to include established urban Black communities and some urban Whites. Subsequently, however, this urban, racially diverse R&B aesthetic community may have posed too large a barrier to commercial success within the dominant racist culture, leading specifically to the origin of Rock and Roll, which could market an aesthetically similar musical style to a broader but predominantly White audience. Subsequent individuation in both artworlds led to further establishment of distinct aesthetic histories, trajectories, modes of expression, and audiences.

New human artworlds can also emerge *de novo* by the creation of genuinely new artforms. This process can be instigated by new technologies (e.g., photography, motion pictures, and computers with graphical interfaces). However, aesthetic expression and evaluation in such new aesthetic communities will be greatly influenced by pre-existing aesthetic forms and values from the social environments of the participants in these artworlds.

Artworlds can also go extinct. As in paleontology and conservation, the extinction of artforms and the artworlds in which they were produced can occur in two different ways. First, ongoing aesthetic change within an artworld can render an artform obsolete, non-contemporary "classic," or even canonical (see Section 9). From this perspective, the historical artworld is no longer present because aesthetic change has so transformed it. As in paleontology, taxonomic debates can erupt over when and whether to name a particular, historic chronological section, or era, within an ongoing artworld as distinct.

Another aspect of this process of artworld extinction (and a further confirmation of efficacy of the proposed definition of art as the product of a distinct mechanism of historical change) is that one cannot create a contemporary artwork that is an authentic product of an extinct artworld. If a contemporary writer penned a sonnet in a perfectly Elizabethan style, it could never become an Elizabethan poem, no matter how well it mimicked the composition, vocabulary, orthography, and concerns of those historical antecedents. We recognize such artworks as neo-Classical, neo-cubist, or neo-Dada in recognition of this ontological fact.

Like species, artworlds can also go extinct by complete population attrition (i.e., lack of recruitment of new practitioners and audiences). For example, listening to player piano rolls was replaced as a means of home performance of contemporary music when recorded music and musical radio broadcasts became more available, practical, affordable, and rewarding. Likewise, Mayan calligraphy was greatly diminished by the collapse of Classic Mayan culture in the tenth century, and completely extinct following the Spanish conquest of Mesoamerica in the sixteenth century. The art of scrimshaw—decorative etching on teeth or tusks of sperm whales, narwhals, and walruses—went extinct with the grave endangerment and legal protections of the species used for these artworks. As we can see from these examples, artworld attrition can come about through the intercession of non-aesthetic, cultural or environmental forces—genocide or political suppression, legal protection of source materials, and so on. Artworlds can also be outcompeted by other artworlds in a competition for the finite aesthetic bandwidth in the lives of their participants. Likewise, biotic artworlds go extinct when the species that participate in them do—captured poetically in the title of David Quammen's (1996) book on island biogeography *The Song of the Dodo*.

7. Artworld Contexts of Aesthetic Evaluations

The historical ontology of artworlds means that there is an underlying ontological context to all aesthetic evaluation, influence, criticism, or analysis (Figure 2.2). The nature of aesthetic influence varies with their artworld context because aesthetic evaluations vary in their potential to influence ongoing processes of aesthetic coevolution. Research in aesthetics and art criticism could be enriched by taking into account the diversity of aesthetic contexts. Accordingly, here I identify four distinct contexts for aesthetic evaluation. (A fifth is discussed in Section 9 "Canons".)

7.1 Within an Artworld

The simplest context for aesthetic evaluation is within a single contemporary artworld (Figure 2.2). Aesthetic evaluations can be understood as occurring

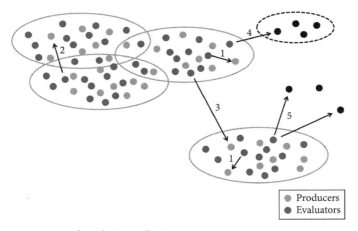

Figure 2.2 Contexts of aesthetic evaluation

Notes: Artworlds create an explicit context for all forms of aesthetic evaluation and art criticism: (1) aesthetic evaluations within an artworld; (2) aesthetic evaluations between overlapping artworlds; (3) aesthetic evaluations between non-overlapping artworlds; (4) aesthetic evaluations of canonical artworks; (5) aesthetic evaluations of non-art. A parallel contextual framework can be applied to aesthetic influences.

"within" an artworld when the artist/producer and the evaluator share a contemporary artworld (i.e., are part of each other's aesthetic community). Within-artworld evaluations have some likelihood of affecting the ongoing process of aesthetic coevolution in that artworld.

For example, if one purchases or reads a new novel or book of poetry by a living artist (in hard or virtual media), then those purchases and readings have the potential to feedback upon aesthetic coevolution by sustaining that artist's aesthetic productions, influencing the artworks subsequently read by the reader, *or* influencing subsequent aesthetic production by that reader-cum-writer. Likewise, if one publishes, or posts on electronic media, a review of a contemporary dance performance or newly released movie, then these aesthetic criticisms have the potential to affect the attendance and attitudes of future viewers of those productions, the sustainability of those dance companies, venues, theaters, or individual artists, and future dances choreographed or movies produced. If one attends an opening of contemporary art in a gallery, and does, *or* does not, purchase a piece of art from the show, then one's decision has the potential to make an impact on the course of aesthetic change in a contemporary artworld. Likewise, mate choices within a bird species based on plumage, song, or display are within-artworld evaluations. Aesthetic change within artworlds necessarily involves within-artworld evaluations such as these.

Of course, not all aesthetic evaluations will succeed in influencing the process of aesthetic coevolution. Just as the existence of the category of art requires the ongoing existence of the examples of failed art (i.e., art that fails to engage its audience or influence the path of future aesthetic change), not all aesthetic evaluations are going to succeed in affecting the ongoing aesthetic coevolution in an artworld. Critiques and opinions may, or may not, influence the trajectory of aesthetic change or stasis in an artworld.

7.2 Between Overlapping Artworlds

The next, more complex context for aesthetic evaluation involves interactions that span partially overlapping artworlds (Figure 2.2). Because the boundaries of artworlds are not fixed, rigid, or even definable, distinct artworlds may overlap, or share some producers and evaluators. Consequently, artworlds may encompass artworks, producers, and evaluators that are shaped or influenced by their shared coevolutionary history with another artworld. Likewise, others may lack the effects of shared aesthetic coevolutionary history. In this context, evaluations have varying potential to affect aesthetic coevolution because of the complexity of the overlapping artworlds.

Ultimately, a full analysis of this context will require committing to criteria for differentiating among the varieties of historical entities within aesthetic communities—artworlds, genres, styles, schools, trends, and so on—which I do not resolve here. However, the larger point about the variation in aesthetic context is still valid regardless of these specific criteria. Here, I present a few potential examples, in which I am assuming artworld status.

The jazz and contemporary dance artworlds have rich histories of both distinct, individuated and shared, overlapping processes of aesthetic change. Evaluations of aesthetic performances of either jazz or dance may vary depending upon the observer's relations to these aesthetic histories. Dancers, jazz musicians, and their audiences may, or may not be, interested in, attentive to, or influenced by productions in these overlapping artworlds. Evaluations of a specific performance of dance or jazz may vary specifically among these possible four categories of observers. Furthermore, the evaluations can differ according to whether the performances themselves do, or do not, share specific aesthetic coevolutionary history with the other artworld (i.e., jazz or dance whose composition, choreography, or performance are, or are not, informed or influenced by shared, overlapping artworld history). Similar comparisons could be made for the overlapping artworlds of opera and literary fiction, sculpture and architecture, painting and poetry, and so on.

Alternatively, a contemporary human feeding on wild blueberries and strawberries would constitute aesthetic judgments between distinct but overlapping artworlds; wild fruits overlap with the broader human artworld of fruits and vegetables which included many domesticated agricultural forms, but the birds and bears that also forage upon wild fruits in biotic artworlds are not participants in human fruit and vegetable artworlds. Clearly, individual human aesthetic preferences for wild fruits will be influenced by their experience of domesticated horticultural fruits and vice versa, whereas the feeding preferences of bears and birds are unlikely to be so influenced. Of course, bears or birds that also feed on fruits grown on human farms or orchards constitute an inverse example of overlapping human–biotic artworlds among animal evaluators.

7.3 Between Non-Overlapping Artworlds

A more remote context for aesthetic evaluation is between aesthetic entities and evaluators from entirely distinct, non-overlapping artworlds (Figure 2.2). Evaluations between non-overlapping artworlds are unable to affect aesthetic coevolution within the other artworld. Consequently, the evaluators' aesthetic judgments lack any shared coevolution history with the aesthetic entities being evaluated. As a consequence, these evaluations are either projections of aesthetic standards, criteria, or values coevolved within a different artworld, or elicitations of entirely novel sensory experiences that have no history of aesthetic coevolution but are cognitively assigned as aesthetic given their novelty.

Examples of aesthetic evaluations between artworlds include listening to recited poetry in an unfamiliar language; watching children from a different culture play an elaborate clapping game or jump a complex double-dutch routine; humans listening to the song of a Rose-breasted Grosbeak or a Humpback Whale (*Megaptera novaeangliae*); or birds listening to the songs of other bird species performed during a dawn chorus.

Although a human cannot become an active participant in a wild animal artworld, there remains the possibility with a human observer of non-overlapping human artworld that a novel aesthetic experience can contribute to the recruitment of that naive observer to become an active participant in that artworld. An opportunity to observe a completely unfamiliar human aesthetic object or performance—such as a person attending a performance of previously unfamiliar Butoh dance, or observing contemporary blown glass sculpture for the first time—might elicit aesthetic responses that remain isolated from these artworlds/genres. However, this human person could also become inspired to become an active participant of that artworld by collecting or learning to make blown glass art, or by attending, studying, or performing additional performances of Butoh.

7.4 Aesthetic Evaluation of Non-Art

The most remote context for aesthetic evaluation is the aesthetic evaluation of non-art– i.e., the aesthetic evaluation of an entity or event whose perceivable form has not, and cannot, coevolve with the aesthetic preferences of any organism

(Figure 2.2). However, this aesthetic context raises a new conundrum. If coevolutionary aesthetics is an aesthetic theory of art, then how can there be aesthetic evaluation of things that are not art? In this context, aesthetic evaluations of non-art are projections of aesthetic standards, criteria, or values that have coevolved within an independent artworld, or they are novel sensory experiences/associations that are categorized by the observer as aesthetic experiences.

Aesthetic experiences of non-art include evaluations of celestial phenomena (i.e., sunsets, sunrises, stars, comets, eclipses, or aurora borealis); the babbling sound of a forest brook; wild scenery and landscapes; alarm calls of birds; and the shapes and colors of wild plant leaves or wild pine cones. The sensible forms of all these objects or experiences are not a product of aesthetic coevolution with any organism. Likewise, any human aesthetic evaluations cannot result in subsequent changes in their form. Sunsets and aurora borealis cannot evolve with our evaluations of them.

8. Artworld Contexts of Aesthetic Influences

Aesthetic influences encompass all the impacts of ideas, concepts, objects, materials, techniques, and methods on the production or evaluation of artworks. In parallel with aesthetic evaluations, the sources of aesthetic influence vary in whether they come from non-art or art, and, in the latter instance, whether they are from the same, an overlapping, or completely distinct artworld.

Both aesthetic evaluations and non-aesthetic influences can impact the process of aesthetic coevolution. Aesthetic influence can be a direct application of an evaluation or an artwork within an artworld. When a novelist is inspired by reading a contemporary novel to incorporate an idea, technique, or structure into a new piece of fiction writing, this direct influence occurs within an artworld. However, when a novelist incorporates a pattern of expression from contemporary rap into their fiction writing, then this would be an influence drawn from overlapping artworlds. If an interior designer selected the color scheme for a fabric or a room based on the plumage colors of a neotropical *Tangara* tanagers (Thraupidae) or a composer incorporated harmonic or temporal structures for a wild bird song, then these would be aesthetic influences drawn between non-overlapping artworlds.

The potential influences of non-art are tremendously broad and diverse. For example, such influences could include: (1) the application or use of materials and devices, like plastics and computers, first developed for non-aesthetic industrial functions, (2) the incorporation of previously non-aesthetic concepts from other areas of culture, such as existential philosophy, the Christian Trinity, or anti-racism, or (3) the inclusion or expression of political concepts such as communist ideology, free-market theory, or fundamental human rights. Likewise, another aspiration of this research is to inspire works or performances of human art that are consciously aware of philosophical implications of coevolutionary aesthetic process and the historical ontology of artworlds.

Aesthetic influences drawn directly from intra-artworld evaluations are intrinsic to the process of aesthetic coevolution itself. Influences from non-overlapping artworlds—such as the painting of a still life of wild fruits and flowers—draw upon aesthetic processes of these other artworlds, but are independent of the artworld of the producer. Aesthetic influences from non-art or from non-aesthetic concepts are entirely extrinsic to the process of aesthetic coevolution. These extrinsic influences can either impinge upon, be brought into, or innovate the process of aesthetic coevolution within an artworld.

Extrinsic social forces can also influence, or impose upon, the process of aesthetic coevolution. Among the most powerful such forces are the impacts of cultural and political institutions, such as governments, political organizations, religious institutions, museums, academics, and the news media. Through investment, inducement, sanction, cooption, hype, and so on, cultural institutions can encourage or constrain the course of cultural coevolution in an artworld.

9. Canons

Looming over this discussion has been the ontological status of historical artworks and the historical and contemporary evaluations of them (Figure 2.3). With the benefit of this framework, I want to turn now to consider the ontology of canons.

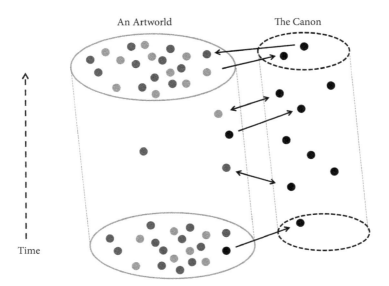

Figure 2.3 The ontology of canons

Notes: A canon (right) is a parallel aesthetic curatorium for historic artworks, evaluations, and criticisms. Contents and qualities of the canon are created through consistent interactions with contemporary aesthetic communities in an effort to shape contemporary criticism, aesthetic discourse, and production.

A canon is a persistent, parallel conceptual conservatory for historical aesthetic entities, evaluations, and aesthetic criticisms. A canon is a conceptual curatorium for "fossil" art and evaluations which functions in relation to dynamic contemporary communities of coevolving aesthetic production, evaluation, and criticism. Canonical artworks gain their status within a canon—often expressed more assertively as "The Canon"—through the evaluations and rhetorical assertions of taste-makers over history.

A canon is different from a "living," ongoing artworld in that the aesthetic entities are static and unchanging (exceptions include degradation with age, and acts of curation, reediting, translation, and restoration). But the specific aesthetic contents of the canon continue to change dynamically, and the evaluations, criticisms, and judgments of canonical works continue to aesthetically coevolve. But how? If contemporary evaluations and criticisms are not coevolving with the stagnant past, what are they co-evolving with? They are coevolving with contemporary trends in elite intellectual goals, specialist aesthetic opinions, and their broader social/cultural purposes (e.g., Kramnick 1997).

Although the traditional defense of canonical artworks is their timeless or immortal status—greatness, creativity, and achievement—the genuine purpose of a canon is to influence contemporary aesthetic evaluations and concepts. The aesthetic functions of canons are more than the encouragement of appreciation for the history of art or sharing the experience of historic artworks. Rather, the contents and evaluations of the canon are deployed—through acts of citation, discussion, and analysis—in the training of artists, art historians, museum curators, gallery operators, collectors, students, and other aspiring taste-makers. Like precedents in the practice of law or achievement records in sports, these historical aesthetic entities are brought to function in the ongoing evaluation of contemporary meanings, uses, and functions of art and aesthetics.

A canon differs from a library, art museum, or repository—all cultural institutions dedicated to the preservation, exhibition, and dissemination of historic aesthetic productions—because a canon is a curated subset of those past productions selected to represent particularly distinguished, exemplary, and historically important aesthetic objects. The artistic contents of canons are in continual revision, reconsideration, and even upheaval. Specific artworks or pieces of criticism are selected for canonical status because of their contemporary functions through aesthetic and intellectual influence. These decisions are the product of networked social interactions and academic trends that are analogous to the discourses and social persuasion that drive many contemporary artworlds.

10. Implications and Applications

In describing this coevolutionary aesthetic framework and an historical ontology of artworlds, I have made numerous proposals that I cannot fully analyze, elaborate, or defend in this chapter. However, I do want to briefly discuss some of the implications and potential applications of this ontology of artworlds.

10.1 Biotic Artworlds

Some of the richest implications of this framework involve the ontological complexities of human aesthetic evaluations of natural, non-human phenomena, including the many forms of biotic art. In this context, it is important to remember that the history of life is a tree, not a *Scala Naturae* of ascending complexity reaching up to humans. Biologically speaking, the myriad of biotic artworlds are not homologous with human art-making. Nor are these biotic artworlds primitive to, antecedent to, or rudimentary versions of any human arts. Rather, these biotic artworlds are entirely independent origins of the aesthetic coevolution that have arisen on multiple distinct branches of the Tree of Life. The phenomena of art have a currently incalculable number of independent origins in the history of life. Since their origins, many of these artworlds have continued to diversify into aesthetic radiations among species and higher taxa. A full regard for the aesthetic agency of non-human life forms requires looking *horizontally* at, not down upon, the achievements and complexities of the aesthetic agencies of other species.

Human aesthetic evaluations of other organisms and their products involve multiple, ontologically distinct kinds of judgments. When we look at and smell a wild rose (*Rosa rugosa*), we are sensing a biotic artwork created in an artworld composed of plant producers and pollinating insect evaluators. These plant productions and insect judgments have coevolved and responded to each other on both evolutionary and behavioral time scales. When we regard a domesticated hybrid rose—such as the white rugosa Blanc Double de Coubert—we are looking at the product of a complex artworld composed of plant producers and human evaluators. Domesticated roses *and* human tastes in roses have both shaped one another over the centuries of agricultural interactions. Aesthetic evaluations of the green leaves of plants are not evaluations of any artform, and constitute a projection of aesthetic standards of *other* origins. However, agricultural cultivars with variegated foliage are agricultural artworks created by humans. These new artforms are made possible by an interaction of innovative input of genetic mutations in plant genomes that create developmental disruptions in the distribution of chloroplasts among the cells of the developing leaves, and the aesthetic values of human horticulturalists selectively breeding plants with those genetic variations. The variegated foliage artforms are a coevolutionary collaboration of plant genetics and human taste.

Not all flowers are biotic artworks. Many trees and grasses, for example, are wind pollinated, and their flowers function entirely through the biophysics of tiny pollen particles and the fluid dynamics of air. Consequently, they have not evolved any attractive, memorable, salient sensory features. Some incredibly showy flowers are actually forgeries of other biotic artworks. Various species of orchids—such as the European bee orchid, *Ophrys apifera*—have evolved to mimic females of specific species of bees in color pattern and scent. When a male bee attempts to copulate with the flower, a pollinium (or conglomeration of pollen grains) is attached to its back. Pollination is only completed, however, when the same male attempts to copulate *again* with another individual of the same species of flower. These orchids are fraudulent interlopers into the coevolved aesthetic value of sexual communication of this bee species. They exploit the aesthetic agencies of the male bees for their own reproductive ends, and they must be quite convincing at it to be effective. Only one visit is not sufficient.

Flowers can also exploit insect pollinators in other ways. For example, the *Amorphophallus* corpse flower (Araceae) and the saprophyte *Rafflesia* flower (Rafflesiaceae) are two gigantic, Southeast Asian flowers that emit overpowering aromas of rotting flesh. Flies are attracted to these flowers, investigate the attractive scent, and become covered in pollen. However, they do not find any rotting flesh on which to lay their eggs, and thus leave the flower deceived. The sensory preferences of flies for rotting flesh is not an aesthetic preference because there is no feature of rotting flesh that has coevolved in order to attract flies. Thus, these floral non-artworks exploit the sensory preferences of the fly for their own reproductive ends. Notably, however, these flowers are *not* beautiful, though they can be attractive to certain morbid human aesthetic tastes—a new kind of aesthetic projection. When a specimen of Sumatran *Amorphophallus* bloomed at the University of Connecticut in 2004—the first example in the northeastern United States in seventy years—over 10,000 people filed through the greenhouse over just a few days to experience it.[1] Notably, *Amorphophallus* and *Rafflesia* are also the *two largest* flowers, or inflourescences, among the more than 300,000 species of flowering plants in the world. Apparently, gigantism is not an aesthetic property in plant-pollinator artworlds.

Other interactions among biotic artworlds can be characterized as aesthetic influence or even as co-optive collage. Most birds that learn their songs learn only from members of their own species (usually not their parents). But dozens of oscine bird species in multiple families, called vocal mimics, have evolved to learn the songs of other bird species. For example, Lawrence's Thrush (*Turdus lawrencii*) from Amazonia has been observed to sing the songs of over 170 other bird species, frogs, and insects (Hardy and Parker 1997). A male Lawrence's Thrush may sing the songs of over fifty different species in a single continuous, uninterrupted bout of singing. The thrushes imitations are very accurate, but they can be distinguished from the songs of the original species by their

---

[1] See https://www.nytimes.com/2004/07/11/nyregion/hold-your-nose-a-corpse-plant-has-bloomed.html?searchResultPosition=2.

excessively sweet, almost saccharine, pure tonal quality. This form of vocal mimicry is not deceptive or aesthetically fraudulent, because avian vocal mimics are not trying to disrupt, or otherwise participate in the artworlds of these other species. Rather, avian vocal mimics have evolved to expand the diversity of acoustic stimuli within their environments that they consider to be salient to their own learning process. Song learning always involves a process of aesthetic evaluation of the songs of available social tutors (usually conspecifics), and a process of vocal emulation that gradually converges on an individual adult vocal repertoire.

The patterns of avian, interspecific vocal mimicry have aesthetically complex consequences. For example, the Marsh Warbler (*Acrocephalus palustris*) is a vocal mimic that nests in northern Europe and winters in sub-Saharan Africa. In an intensive analysis of the vocal repertoire of twenty-nine male Marsh Warblers singing and nesting in one location in Belgium, Françoise Dowsett-Lemaire (1979) identified the songs of 212 different species of birds in the repertoires of male Marsh Warblers, including over 113 species of African birds. By examining the distributions of the most common and the most geographically restricted species of African birds sung by the Belgian Marsh Warblers, Dowsett-Lemaire was able to distinguish among males that wintered in specific regions of East Africa. For example, seven of twenty-nine birds sang imitations of the Grey Sunbird (*Cyanomitra veroxii*), which is narrowly endemic in the lowlands along the Indian Ocean coast from southern Kenya to South Africa.[2] In this example, Marsh Warblers are acquiring a diversity of samples of avian aesthetic cultures of East Africa, incorporating them into their own aesthetic repertoires, and importing them, through the annual intercontinental migrations, to be performed in the marshes of northern Europe. This pattern of trans-Saharan avian aesthetic interchange parallels the trans-Atlantic patterns in English theater performance between London, New York, Charleston, and Kingston during the long eighteenth century that has been documented and analyzed by Elizabeth Maddock Dillon (2014).

Thus, imitative songs are aesthetic samples from the social-sexual artworld of the source species into the social-sexual artworld of the mimic species. The male Superb Lyrebird (*Menura novahollandiae*, Menuridae) is an extraordinary mimic which, upon exposure to human culture, also learns to mimic human-made mechanical sounds. One repeatedly photographed male in a park outside Sydney learned to imitate the sounds of camera shutters and film motor drives.[3] Avian imitations of other bird songs are aesthetic co-options of natural

---

[2] Dowsett-Lemaire was unable to identify another 20 percent of the species imitated by Belgian male Marsh Warblers. These were likely additional species of sub-Saharan African birds whose songs were unknown at that time. No one has repeated this study to identify those additional species.

[3] See https://www.youtube.com/watch?v=VjE0Kdfos4Y.

artworks—like our putting a bouquet of wild daisies in a vase—but avian imitations of a camera shutter, or a car alarm, are not.

Bowerbirds (Ptilinorynchidae) are among the most aesthetically extreme organisms on Earth in terms both of their temporal investment and complex modes of expression (Frith and Frith 2004; Prum 2015, 2017). Male bowerbirds build an ornamental construction of sticks, and adorn it and a surrounding court with an astonishing array of diverse materials found in their environments—which may include flowers, feathers, insects and insect parts, fruits, sticks, shells, lichens, fungus, pebbles, bone, shells, tree sap, masticated fruit pulp, and caterpillar frass. The specifics of bower architecture and ornamental materials used vary among species, and even among some populations. For example, male Satin Bowerbird (*Ptilinorynchus violaceus*) select only royal blue items to ornament the courtyard of their bowers. Although the blue items they now gather include various kinds of blue human trash—blue straws, bottle caps, and other plastic objects—all of the naturally occurring blue materials in their Satin Bowerbird's environment are coevolved artforms in some other artworld—such as blue parrot feathers, fruits, or flowers. Like a human using an egret plume to decorate a hat, Satin Bowerbirds are using a pre-existing artform in their own aesthetically new, composite artwork, or aesthetic collage. Likewise, most of the human trash they gather are examples of branded commercial objects whose form is shaped by commercial artworlds of product advertisements—much like the original supermarket cases of brillo that inspired Warhol's *Brillo Box*. The closely related Great Bowerbird (*Chlamydera nuchalis*) decorates its bower with white items, including bleached sticks, stones, and bones. None of these items are coevolved biotic or human artworks, but they become bowerbird artworks once a male has incorporated them into its courtyard decorations.

The Vogelkop Bowerbird curates the most diverse assemblage of materials in front if its hut bower (Figure 2.4). The male illustrated has gathered (moving from right to left): shiny, black, hydrophobic beetle elytra; enormous waxy red *Pandanus* flowers*; black balls of animal dung; a pile of shredded wood permeated with an aqua-green fungus; fresh blue berries*; large gelatinous red fruits*; and a clump of gooey, amber colored, fresh tree sap(*?). The aesthetic preferences of this population of Vogelkop Bowerbird extend to an unexpectedly creative assemblage of objects and materials—including biotic artworks (marked with an *) and non-artworks—maintained in a very precise and individualized spatial design upon a well-gardened bed of living green moss.

These bowerbirds constitute aesthetic collages that bring together samples of objects and media from diverse sources and presenting them in a new artwork or context. Like human collages, bowerbird decorations bring together an ontologically rich diversity of materials and objects.

Figure 2.4 The hut bower, mossy courtyard, and curated aesthetic collections of a male Vogelkop Bowerbird (*Amblyornis inornata*, Ptilinorhynchidae) in the Arfak Mountains of Irian Jaya, Indonesian New Guinea
Source: Photo courtesy of Brett Benz.

10.2 Artworlds of Oppression

This coevolutionary ontology of artworlds can provide insights into the richness of human artworlds, aesthetic change, and art criticism. For example, contemporary art history and art criticism are extensively interested in the historical and contemporary interactions between aesthetic expressions, evaluation, and aesthetic values with sex, race, class, caste, colonial history, ethnic identity, migration status, and so on. Focus here is often upon analysis of who was historically recognized as an authentic or legitimate participant within a particular artworld, how such recognition was granted or denied, and the aesthetic consequences of such inclusions and exclusions. These intersectional discussions concern the sociological composition, coalescence, and policing of human artworlds. Oppression, prejudice, animus, and social stratification have historical and contemporary impacts on what artworks are recognized as significant, what opinions and evaluations have aesthetic influence, and the consequent path of aesthetic change and innovation.

Although there are examples of idiosyncratic and individualistic artists from oppressed communities who continue as solo, or closet, artists, a common response to social oppression is the creation and persistence of "outsider" artworlds—restricted or completely isolated social sub-networks of aesthetic producers and evaluators from an oppressed minority or identity. This history of outsider status can strongly influence the course of aesthetic change.

Of course, one contemporary response to the recognition of the historical and ongoing social injustices that have contributed to the formation of these "artworlds of oppression" is to promote artworks from these communities to a broader artworld—usually "The Artworld" *sensu* Danto—which is dominated by members of a wealthy, privileged, connected, and empowered aesthetic establishment. An inevitable impact of such efforts will be to transform outsider artworlds through the very act of their recognition. This process can be a mixed blessing. While genuine economic support for artists from oppressed communities can create aesthetic and economic sustainability, the participation of new taste-making individuals and social forces can distort aesthetic values within artworlds of oppression without beginning to address the social forces that contribute to that oppression. Analogous with debates about development vs. gentrification of traditional minority neighborhoods, the ontology of artworlds implies something important about the potential of art, aesthetic philosophy, art history, and art criticism to address histories of oppression.

10.3 Empirical Coevolutionary Aesthetics

A long-term intellectual goal of this effort is to contribute to the development of new, broadly deployable intellectual tools for empirical analysis in aesthetics and art criticism. Such research could take many forms, and advance multiple perspectives within art criticisms.

For example, analyses of the diversity of influences on an individual artwork or individual artist's *ouevre* could take into account the sources of influences within the artists primary artworld, from overlapping, and non-overlapping artworlds, or from entirely outside of current aesthetic communities. *The ontologically distinct sources of influence may have distinct impacts upon the focal artists and their artworld.*

Likewise, one could look at the history of composition, participation, and influences among overlapping, partially individuated artworlds. For example, one could examine historical patterns of aesthetic differentiation, influence, and individuation in seventeenth- and eighteenth-century organ music among the culturally and geopolitically distinct aesthetic communities of Western Europe, including Portuguese, Spanish, French, Flemish and the Low Countries, English, German, Italian, and Austrian traditions. One could analyze the history of diversification among these partially overlapping artworlds, their instruments, technology transfer, musical composition techniques, and performance styles through analyses of correspondence, manuscript exchange, clerical interactions, political alliances, and more. Interestingly, one could expand such work on geographical-cultural aesthetics with analyses of species of oscine bird species—such as Common Whitethroat (*Sylvia communis*, Sylviidae) or Common Nightingale (*Luscinia megaryhnchos*, Muscicapidae)—that have culturally derived aesthetic dialects spread over similarly wide-ranging geographic boundaries.

10.4 Aesthetic Criticism in Coevolutionary Context

Another feature of this coevolutionary aesthetic perspective is that it puts the historical diversity of methods in art criticism into a broadly interconnected intellectual context. For example, Harold Bloom's (1973) classic *The Anxiety of Influence* proposed and analyzed the diversity of creative, aesthetic responses of poets to the psychological impact of reading antecedent poets. Bloom's hypothesized chains of poetic influence are entirely congruent with a coevolutionary account of aesthetic change in which readers (evaluators) become writers (producers), and grapple with the psychological impact of historical achievements within their genre. This ontology of artworlds places the tracing of these chains of influence in an explicit, empirically accessible context of aesthetic coevolution itself.

From the opposite reaches of late twentieth-century literary criticism, Jacques Derrida (1974) and others developed a theory and methods of deconstructing the multiple, context-dependent meanings of texts. Though applicable to all written language, deconstruction was, and is, applied almost universally to aesthetic texts. Deconstruction involves the radical expansion of the role and agency of the reader in interpretation, analysis, and creating meaning from the text.

From a coevolutionary perspective, the works of Bloom and Derrida focus on distinct aspects of aesthetic process.[4]

---

[4] I thank George Levine for his welcoming invitation to participate in this volume. The core ideas presented in this chapter were initially developed for a course taught during my semester as the William Clyde DeVane Professor at Yale University in 2014. The framework was further developed for a conference on "Ökologien des Ausdrucks: Ecologies of Expression" held at the Warburg House, Hamburg in January 2018, at the invitation of Frank Fehrenbach of the University of Hamburg. I thank Alexander John Sager for sharing his thoughts about the aesthetic effects of changes in the composition of medieval literary artworlds. My research was supported by the William Robertson Coe Fund at Yale University.

PART 2
BEAUTY AND UTILITY

3
Beauty and Her Sisters in the Nineteenth Century and After

Jonah Siegel

1. You Will Understand It

Alfred Tennyson's allegorical "Palace of Art" (1832/42) is liable to strike the contemporary reader as all too clear in its meanings. Yet the author evidently feels the need to gloss the theme of the work *and* to elaborately preview its narrative in a brief companion poem that he includes with the piece when he sends it to his friend Richard Trench. "I send you here a sort of allegory (For you will understand it)," Tennyson writes in a peculiar formulation that muddies several issues about the aspirations of the work even while expressing certainty about the poem's clarity.[1] The suggestion is that Trench will have access to a particular insight ("you will understand" being something we say when others may not). Or does Tennyson mean that the allegory is so clear that its tendency is unmissable? That would certainly be a reasonable construal of the claim about a poem with few apparent mysteries.

"The Palace of Art" tells the tale of a self that builds for its soul a perfect location for encountering the culture of the world, a place where the soul remains, indifferent to the sufferings characteristic of the actual lived experience of that same world, until an undermotivated crisis drives it out of the palace in a paroxysm of shame and self-revulsion. A few ambiguities aside, the "Palace" is indeed relatively straightforward, which should make the creation of another poem in order to gloss it redundant.[2] And so there is a quality of excess in the existence as much as in the form of this explanatory poem, which consists of a deeply conventional, if far-reaching, allegory locating humanity between the two extremes of angel and devil, the place of each subject in that spectrum being determined by the object-choices of its passions. This ancillary poem, which the anthologies awkwardly entitle "To ___. With the Following Poem," informs us that "The Palace of Art" is about

---

[1] Tennyson, "To ___. With the Following Poem ["The Palace of Art"]," lines 1–2.
[2] On "The Palace of Art," see Siegel, *Haunted Museum*, 8–12; also Ricks, *Tennyson*, 86–8.

> A glorious Devil, large in heart and brain,
> That did love Beauty only, (Beauty seen
> In all varieties of mould and mind)
> And Knowledge for its beauty; or if Good,
> Good only for its beauty, seeing not
> That Beauty, Good, and Knowledge, are three sisters
> That doat upon each other, friends to man,
> Living together under the same roof,
> And never can be sunder'd without tears.
>
> (lines 5–13)

This improbably equitable, loving relationship among too many subjects is Tennyson's image for the appropriate affective bond between the self and three sisters who are Beauty, Good, and Knowledge, something between a titillatingly chaste harem and a fantasy of perfectly balanced group affection worthy of middle school. Monogamous intimacy with just one sister is out of the question: love all or love none, declares the speaker. But that simple injunction is not so easy to obey. The gloss-poem ends with the Beauty-loving self banished from the bliss of full sisterly affections, a failure that amounts to the betrayal of that particularly human comeliness ("the perfect shape of man") which establishes our condition somewhere between the divine and the demonic. The frank avowal of a single attraction leaves the subject paradoxically excluded from love, bereft of all human connection:

> And he that shuts Love out in turn shall be
> Shut out from Love, and on her threshold lie
> Howling in outer darkness. Not for this
> Was common clay ta'en from the common earth
> Moulded by God and Temper'd with the tears
> Of angels to the perfect shape of man.
>
> (lines 14–19)

It bears noting that, although the claim is that the common clay of the common earth is only perfected by a love distributed equally among Beauty, Good, and Knowledge, the insistence on an even temper of love is not based on an even distribution of charms. On the contrary, the poem is plain evidence that Beauty is the most attractive sister, the one who puts the other affections at risk.

You will understand it. Indeed you will, even though that certainty is addressed to another. But perhaps we should pause in front of an understanding that interpolates us with such force. The conventions of editing have left a blank in the nontitle of this ancillary piece ("To ___"). We could fill in the gap with our own names, or assume that any name could be written into that spot equally well precisely because the theme is so easy to understand. Still, I want to suggest that Tennyson's use of an apparently unsophisticated allegorical construction both confesses to and covers over an extraordinarily difficult topic. While it is hardly unusual to find a structure designed to appear self-evident rising over what is in fact a powerful ambivalence, my argument in this chapter is that both the ambivalence and the strategy of representation are not only characteristic of attempts to address the nature of beauty in the nineteenth century but very much in evidence in later—and very influential—accounts of the topic still common in the twentieth and twenty-first centuries.

The peculiar erotic situation the poem lays out is illustrative of a set of questions of long standing, so it will help to be literal about the relationships on which the allegory is structured. While Beauty, Good, and Knowledge are intimately connected in the way sisters are (that is, having a shared origin and, presumably, some common lineaments), they are also distinct. Their reconciliation will not, in any case, come from tracing their family tree or identifying family resemblances, but from the arrival of a subject, a fourth self who puts the three into a kind of relationship that is an exotic variation on the exogamous adventures of courtship. The relationship of the self to the three, which is bound to be unstable, is always at risk of being further distorted by the outsized attractions of Beauty, which are paradoxically so excessive as to be also present in some measure in the other sisters, but which when experienced solely in *her* are figured as a lust distinct from the form of attraction one experiences in the case of more virtuous attachments. The poem does not address an excessive passion for Good or for Knowledge, though the latter might be said to be the problem at the heart of "The Palace of Art" itself. And so, the claim of a close family relation notwithstanding, Beauty, Good, and Knowledge differ in fundamental ways, as do the feelings each is liable to provoke. Indeed, it is in the very kinds of desires they elicit that the two (Good and Knowledge) are distinct from the one (Beauty), though—just to emphasize the weirdness of the allegory—the categories always risk becoming entangled again when the self loves either one of the two *only* for her Beauty.

Tennyson's allegory may seem heavy-handed to the modern reader, and the judgmental nature of its conclusions may even inspire a bemused condescension, but the poem describes a relationship to the beautiful that is very close to the one we live with every day in modern criticism. For a long time, beauty was out of the running as a topic in advanced discussions of literary studies, and when it has returned it has typically been accompanied by close relations. *We* don't call them sisters, but the widespread unwillingness to name the relationships at issue even figuratively may in itself be symptomatic. How did we go from a situation in which Tennyson might fear our humanity is at risk if we allow ourselves to be dominated by a love of beauty to one in which it is *only* a claim of either knowledge or goodness that justifies the presence of beauty at all? This is an important question, but it should not blind us to the fact that all of Tennyson's sisters are still present in our discussions of beauty; it is only our accounts of the kinds of relationships we should have with them that have changed.

It would evidently surprise the poet to discover that Beauty is the one sister who has been banished from the affections of modern criticism, only allowed to return under strict supervision by the other two, with Knowledge or Good at either side, holding her, not in a sisterly embrace, but in the custodian's firm grip. My aim is not to argue for a need to recover a lost sense of beauty that I am not in fact convinced is gone.[3] Rather, I am interested in reflecting on what happened both to the kind of hard-to-discipline lust about which Tennyson warns and to the complex intersection of knowledge and ethical judgment written into the allegory. My argument opens up in two directions: recognition of the sophistication of Victorian reflections on beauty inevitably brings into view the hard work we do today to keep the force of the topic at bay, the embarrassment provoked by the theme perhaps distorting our work as cultural historians as much as our self-reflections as critics.

The values the three sisters stand for are not liable to be commensurate or harmonious in the normal course of things. To *do* good would lead to a better world. To *know* good may just make one sad, as one recognizes the disjunctions between what one knows and what one can hope for. To *know* the world is to be accurate in one's sense of what is around one, and so it may be to become fit to act effectively because one is unillusioned—or to act well because the positive qualities of the world (sometimes called its beauty or even its goodness) lead as a matter of course to better action. Knowledge itself has lately not been celebrated for its own sake, but insofar as it participates in an ethical project. But this latter sense of the matter needs to assume that the secret at the heart of the world is goodness, that the more we know of it the more oriented toward the good we will become. There have been traditions in which this assumption has not been made, in which the secret of the world is dark, so that to put oneself in harmony with it is neither beautiful nor good. Which is all to say that understanding Knowledge, Goodness, and Beauty as closely related (as akin to sisters) involves a historically specific set of claims and presuppositions about each of the categories and their relations.

Victorian poetry provides many models of the relationship between love, self-love, and beauty. William Morris's "Defence of Guenevere" (1858) is worth citing in this context as a fantastic and contradictory instance of the claim of beauty as evidence—as an alternative form of knowledge or truth: "Will you dare," the adulterous queen demands to know from her accusers, without addressing the factual basis of their allegations, "When you have looked a little on my brow, / To say this thing is vile?" Much of the fascination of the poem resides in its

---

[3] Scarry points out that the sciences have been less fastidious about keeping these topics apart than the humanities. She also describes the vocabulary of beauty as not so much lost as driven underground (*On Beauty and Being Just*, 52, 57).

commitment to the aggressively challenging claims of beauty Morris puts in the mouth of his speaker. A fantastic boldness shapes the formulations of the queen at risk of being burned to death for her affair with Lancelot: "will you care," she pretends to ask, drawing attention to her sinuous body, her lovely face, "For any plausible lies of cunning woof, / When you can see my face with no lie there . . . ?" (lines 236–41). The queen's words keep inviting the caring and daring they interrogate. But they never deny any of the charges against her, which, after all, are true. Instead, she offers an invitation for the experience of Beauty to take the place of Knowledge of her adultery and ultimately of the ethical value we look for in judges (what we might call Goodness). Where better to find terms and structures for the complex relations between attraction, knowledge, and moral judgment characteristic of the aesthetic than in the confusions of the affective life where we so often discover all those elements irresolvably at play? Still, in later periods the relationship of the three elements Tennyson's soul is meant to love equally has come into question. Like the mob gathered around Morris's Guenevere, hesitating to kindle the flame that will burn out of the world the person who fascinates them, modern writers about beautiful things often give the impression of being concerned that either they must pretend to come to judge when in fact they have come to gaze, or that at the moment of gazing on beauty they fear that an imposition is taking place—that perhaps it's all just a trick delaying righteous action until some Lancelot shows up to make that action impossible. If we feel Beauty to be the dangerous sister, likely to lead to the neglect of Good and Knowledge, it may be because we want so much to love only the good and the true.

I am trying to suggest through the pressure I am putting on the terms of Tennyson's allegory that the challenge of beauty was written into nineteenth-century texts in ways our own hesitations on the topic have frequently led us to deflect. Every use of the term "aesthetic" having to do with the appreciation of beauty, and not just perception in general, is ultimately traceable to the nineteenth century (see Siegel, "Victorian Aesthetics"). And yet the kind of discomfort the topic provokes in the era is also clear. For every "He fathers-forth whose beauty is past change / Praise him" of a Gerard Manley Hopkins ("Pied Beauty" (1877), lines 10–11), we have the warning that stands at the threshold of Tennyson's "Palace of Art" (1832): "We cannot live in art."[4] Certainly, women poets in the period were unlikely to leave as they found them the masculine fantasies of desire and agency around which contemporary accounts of beauty often shaped themselves. From Elizabeth Barrett Browning to Christina Rossetti and beyond, one finds a rich tradition of engagement, resistance, and transgressive revision that may be said to reach one of its culminating points in Michael Field's *Sight and*

---

[4] Tennyson cited the statement by Trench as the goad for writing "The Palace of Art" (*Tennyson*, ed. Ricks, 86).

Song (1892), where "A Portrait" addresses "beauty in its cold / And vacant eminence" (line 29). I will return to this poem and a few others below, but before I do, it will be useful to lay out some of the challenges that have shaped treatments of the topic in recent years.

2. Distinctions of the Anti-Aesthetic

Beauty has never been more consistently celebrated as a good than it was in the Victorian period, the same era that taught us a fundamental ambivalence about the sources for that celebration (see Prettejohn, *Beauty and Art*). The biggest challenge to our critical appraisal of the cultural significance of beauty does not lie in the Victorians' overinvestment in the idea, then, nor in their failings given the aesthetic values of later eras, but in what we might read as a fundamental though seldom fully acknowledged inheritance from the period. I hope it's easy to recognize one part of our legacy: the insistence that Beauty always must be placed in relation to Truth and the Good. I believe we have a harder time acknowledging the other: the dangerous attractions of Beauty. But even the more apparently straightforward affiliations merit reappraisal.

The relationship between Knowledge and Beauty can seem all too obvious in our day, at least in the broad sense that we understand the role of knowledge to be to explain to us *why* we find something beautiful. The most influential line of causal analysis is probably that developed by the French sociologist Pierre Bourdieu in *Distinction* (1979) and *The Rules of Art* (1992), studies that place in evidence surveys of French museumgoers in the 1960s and readings of a severely restricted canon of nineteenth-century French literature in order to propose a compelling analysis in which the rise of an ever more abstract formalism is linked to the consolidation of middle-class interest, the existence of which, Bourdieu proposes, blows up Kantian claims for the disinterested nature of beauty.[5] Human experience predisposes us to credit the claim that an ostensibly disinterested judgment is liable to have hypocrisy at its core. In this line of argument, Kant's insistence that the kind of pleasure we feel in response to objects that we need or that we want to consume is distinct from the pleasure we find in objects in which

---

[5] Though the two works are quite distinct, the centrality of autonomy is a constant (see Guillory, "Bourdieu's Refusal"). On the tension between Bourdieu's instances and his claims, see the philosopher John Armstrong, who good-humoredly writes of the "local and period" flavor of Bourdieu's evidence in the course of a quietly devastating discussion, which concludes with this gentle but thoroughgoing condemnation: "The central failing of Bourdieu's analysis is that he insinuates an explanation... where no such explanation is justified" (*Secret Power of Beauty*, 100). Another contemporary aesthetician is less mild: "He appeals to data about the way different social classes have different aesthetic taste. And he thinks that this supports his historicism. But it is difficult to reconstruct steps of reasoning between this empirically supported premise and the general historicist conclusion" (Zangwill, *Metaphysics*, 213). For further discussion of Bourdieu's project, see Siegel, *Material Inspirations*, 13–16, 67–128.

the faculties are moved without those stimulations is identified as at once mystified and deeply impoverished. To hold that our pleasure in seeing a flower or a beautiful landscape is distinct from the one we might take in the sight of a glass of wine we wish to drink or of a person we long to embrace is seen as a refusal of authentic experience, which is perhaps full of the glasses of wine and people we want, but not so well furnished with beautiful sights or sounds. "The whole of legitimate aesthetics has been constructed," as far as Bourdieu is concerned, by "an immense repression" against which his project is to produce the actual "truth of taste" (*Distinction*, 485). The palpable pleasure in reading Bourdieu is the satisfaction of seeing our clear-eyed sagacity confirmed to us by a recondite analysis combining the power of received opinion with the charisma of apparent complexity and some tables that look like data.

In the school of thought of which Bourdieu is among the most important and most straightforward of exponents, Knowledge and Good appear to reach an extraordinary size as Beauty fades almost to insignificance, or to the thinnest veneer covering over a reality that sufficient goodness or knowledge will allow us to pierce. And yet it would be hard to sustain the idea that the argument does away with Beauty, so much as it consigns her to a tighter control by her sisters, or perhaps subjects her to a ritual act of humiliation that fascinates in its own right (like Guenevere before her judges).

If Bourdieu's research and arguments found a sympathetic hearing, it is because they reached an audience interested in the claims he was advancing. *The Anti-Aesthetic*, an influential set of essays published in 1983, four years after *Distinction* was released in France but the year before its English translation was brought out, carries its fundamental challenge in its title. The pieces the art critic and theorist Hal Foster gathered together in that volume are intended to offer an alternative to what the aesthetic is or was. It is striking, then, that in reading Jürgen Habermas's well-known essay on modernity as an incomplete project, which Foster places at the opening of the collection, we find something like a genealogy for Tennyson's sisters. In his discussion of Max Weber's characterization of science, morality, and art as three areas of human endeavor that once had a shared cultural home in the overlapping fields of religion and metaphysics, but which in modernity belong to three distinct autonomous spheres, Habermas identifies an unavoidable set of conceptual distinctions or specializations: "Since the 18th century, the problems inherited from these older world-views could be arranged so as to fall under specific aspects of validity: truth, normative rightness, authenticity and beauty. They could then be handled as questions of knowledge, or of justice and morality, or of taste" (*Anti-Aesthetic*, 9). While the division separating these fields, or "specific aspects of validity," is not accidental but fundamental to the experience of modernity, Habermas emphasizes how the collapse of an earlier system has left a set of inherited problems. With the disintegration of the metaphysical-religious family unit, each kid goes off to pursue her own interests, and the internal logic of specialization inevitably sharpens the distinctions among them even as it leads each specialized field to lose contact with the broader social whole that the family stood for and promoted:

> professionalized treatment of the cultural tradition brings to the fore the intrinsic structures of each of the three dimensions of culture. There appear the structures of cognitive-instrumental, of moral-practical and of aesthetic-expressive rationality, each of these under the control of specialists who seem more adept at being logical in these particular ways than other people are. As a result, the distance grows between the culture of the experts and that of the larger public. (9)

Whatever the start date of the professionalization and institutionalization he describes, Habermas is interested in how the results of that process are experienced *now*: "What accrues to culture through specialized treatment and reflection does not immediately and necessarily become the property of everyday praxis." The echoing abstractions of the phrase instantiate what they declare, that we cannot live in art, of necessity a bloodless realization when it is, as in this case, neither an accusation nor an injunction so much as the declaration of a melancholy inevitability. Like the readout of a powerful diagnostic computer the design of which neglected to include any kind of bedside manner, Habermas's language brings us the bad news in the dispassionate voice of the specialization it is working to describe. In this account of things, it is definitional of art's situation in modernity that we cannot live in it (neither immediately nor of necessity is art part of "everyday praxis").

Habermas tells with characteristically impassive clarity a story that is often relayed in more sentimental or judgmental terms. "With cultural rationalization of this sort," he writes, "the threat increases that the life-world, whose traditional substance has already been devalued, will become more and more impoverished" (9). Habermas describes a double loss: the alienation that accompanies rationalism (the impoverishment of the life-world) entails, on the one hand, a division of elements that had once been imagined as coexisting and, on the other, a separation of the lived world from the newly abstracting concepts and practices that aim to describe and change it—and which had been available in earlier dispensations. Knowledge, morality, and beauty are not only sisters in this model, but they stand for a family relationship lost to every modern subject, an inherently harmonious condition that, when it is gone, will appear to us in fragments, each of which will, of necessity, entail competition for our interest. To make "objective science, universal morality and law, and autonomous art" (9) newly relevant for life is a structural challenge of extraordinary difficulty because it cuts against the grain of those fields and the history of their emergence. Specialized kinds of knowledge, only available through specific practices, conform with difficulty to a world in which the logic governing them will always seem partial—both because it does not fully match up to the richness of the world as it is and because of the residual, but never entirely forgotten, fact that these three things have been, for most of human history, understood to be related.[6]

Hal Foster's introduction to *The Anti-Aesthetic* is as bracing as Habermas's "Modernity" in laying out the challenging project of bringing fields of knowledge, the fundamental shape of which emerge in distinction to the lived world, into a productive conceptual relationship with that world. "'Anti-aesthetic,'" he writes about the awkward term he has chosen to champion in the volume, "signals that the very notion of the aesthetic, its network of ideas, is in question here: the idea that aesthetic experience exists apart, without 'purpose,' all but beyond history, or that art can now effect a world at once (inter)subjective, concrete and universal—a symbolic totality" (xv–xvi). For the aesthetic to be in question is for the relationship of the category to be broken off—from life, from other categories with which it had once been associated. It is that break which is being put into question. The absence of purpose (or "'purpose'") Foster adduces is evidently a reminiscence of Kant's *Zweckmäßigkeit ohne Zweck* (purposiveness without purpose) from the third *Critique*, made over from an important conceptual gambit— an attempt to describe the effect on the faculties of seeing a beautiful form—into a charge of fundamental irrelevance or pointlessness.[7]

Foster's analysis, like Habermas's, entails a number of divisions or separations. But if in Habermas these distinctions are the result of historical processes calling out for reflection, in Foster, as in so many critics of the period, including Bourdieu, they are registered not as historically determined conditions, even definitional ones, of modernity, but as intolerable political disaggregations or abandonments of social solidarity. "Art," Bourdieu charges, "is one of the major sites of denial of the social world" (*Distinction*, 510).[8] If Habermas can sound like he is rewriting an old story, of a fall into knowledge that leads to our banishment from a more harmonious paradise, "denial," in Bourdieu's turn of phrase ("*dénégation*" in the original) feels more like an ongoing betrayal or a psychic weakness, as in those formulations in popular psychology (judgments at once ethical and cognitive)

---

[6] Habermas recognizes the positive aspirations of the emergent specialization he associates with an Enlightenment philosophy that aimed to "utilize this accumulation of specialized culture for the enrichment of everyday life—that is to say, for the rational organization of everyday social life" (10). Compare Eagleton's dialectical account of the Weberian argument, in which the split opens up to a new possibility of freedom as it models a new vision of ethical autonomy (*Ideology of the Aesthetic*, 366–8). In an important variation on the Weberian claim, suggesting why Beauty might be the privileged sister, McKeon proposes the emergence of the aesthetic as "a reaction to and compensation for the early modern division of the arts from the sciences" (*Secret History*, 385).

[7] On purposiveness, see Kant, *Critique of the Power of Judgment*, 47–51 and 106–8. In order to link the topic to Kant's ethical theories, Guyer and Matthews prefer "purposiveness without an end" over the symmetrical rendering of the phrase more typically used. See Guyer, "Editor's Introduction," xlviii.

[8] "*L'art est un des lieux par excellence de la dénégation du monde social*" (Bourdieu, *La distinction*, 596). Bourdieu is well aware of the sociological tradition on which his argument is based. See, for example, his *Practical Reason* (1994), where the topic is cited as something of a truism (83).

whereby people are held to be living in denial when they do not confront (and thereby, presumably, overcome) the ongoing traumas distorting their lives. While Foster is more judicious in his formulations, his own arguments share the tendency to identify a political failing at the heart of modern concepts of beauty. The "anti-aesthetic," Foster writes, "marks a cultural position on the present" from which we ask: "are categories afforded by the aesthetic still valid?" ("Postmodernism: A Preface," xiii). Implicit in the question is a claim about the past and about the concept: at some point what is being called "the aesthetic" was valid and its validity was understood to be recognizable by the presence of a harmonious or at least coherent relationship in which art could "effect a world at once (inter)subjective, concrete and universal—a symbolic totality." Reading Foster with Habermas, we are able to recognize that what Foster is describing is not a new period for which an old solution is inoperable or useless, but one in which a troubling condition of long standing (what Habermas called the unfinished one of modernity) has become intolerable.

3. Resistance

The strength of *The Anti-Aesthetic* at its best resides in its combination of political and ethical commitments with a nuanced understanding of the critical tradition to which the arguments of its contributors are responding. Foster, unlike Bourdieu, does not strand the history of thinking about the aesthetic in the eighteenth century but instead reminds his readers of sophisticated later developments in that field, which comprise an "adventure." The familiar story Foster tells culminates in Theodor Adorno's attempts in *Aesthetic Theory* to rescue the category of the aesthetic as oppositional—as a fundamental mode of critique. But Foster calls this a story in part to be able to mark its end, not to say its failure:

> The adventures of the aesthetic make up one of the great narratives of modernity: from the time of its autonomy through art-for-art's-sake to its status as a necessary negative category, a critique of the world as it is. It is this last moment (figured brilliantly in the writings of Theodor Adorno) that is hard to relinquish: the notion of the aesthetic as subversive, a critical interstice in an otherwise instrumental world. Now, however, we have to consider that this aesthetic space too is eclipsed—or rather, that its criticality is now largely illusory (and so instrumental).   ("Postmodernism: A Preface," xiii)

Foster insists that the urgent demands of the moment require an end to the adventure of the aesthetic: "in the face of a culture of reaction on all sides, a practice of resistance is needed" (xiv). On this view, the only question left to resolve is whether Beauty is the problem or the savior who refuses to help. In either case, if some failing in Beauty is indeed to blame, then reestablishing her sisterhood with Knowledge and Good might do important work in defeating the culture of reaction. The premise seems clear enough. So clear, however, that it opens up another set of questions altogether, starting with a basic one: when will it be permissible to ask, *How is that working out for us?* Has the anti-aesthetic in fact fostered a practice of resistance that is having an effect on the culture of reaction all around us? Have we seen gains in resistance as we see losses in our relationship to beauty?

Is it in poor taste to ask for results? Surely not. When one is busy reconnecting culture to the life-world, surely the only way to measure success or even progress is to look from concept to experience. And we have available to us all the evidence we need to evaluate the claims at either end, that is, as to whether we find in the world an ongoing relationship between power and valorized forms of elite taste, or whether by freeing ourselves from what have been identified as outmoded forms of aesthetic judgment we have achieved a practice of resistance that in fact resists. The alternative to making the connection would be, strangely enough, a disinterested practice of resistance, or one unlinked to the life-world, a specialized practice that would be just one more version (and a particularly mystified one) of the very kind of thing the anti-aesthetic and the de-denegating projects of the 1980s were designed to counter.

The evidence is everywhere around us that there is no necessary relationship between tastes that have been identified as elite and social power. A Diet Coke and some fried chicken at a beauty contest, overpriced whiskey at a staged wrestling match, some shared narcotics at a concert, or a slow ride through a carefully groomed landscape, punctuated by brief episodes of hitting a ball with a stick—these are the cultural situations where power might be encountered these days, or at a yoga retreat, perhaps, with fresh juices squeezed out on demand, or at an impassioned sermon delivered in a vast modern temple. In the meantime, the claims of and for an elite canon of beauty—and for canons in general—are less and less self-evident to anyone. As museums reach out to an indifferent world with fashion shows and popular music, they suggest not overweening confidence but the despair of a superannuated Lothario squeezing himself into jeans and T-shirt in order to confuse those he courts (or himself) about where his charms may lie at this stage in life. Art history departments are perennially close to the chopping block when cuts are discussed at universities. But more telling, perhaps, than the indifference of the wider public is the fact that it would be impossible to mount a credible debate about the curriculum at *any* academic department in which one side was arguing that the beauty of a particular work was a good enough reason for that work to be studied, taught, or even preserved. John Guillory pointed out decades ago how "surprisingly difficult" it had become "to define a progressive political rationale for the teaching of canonical texts" (*Cultural Capital*, 21). The urgency of that observation is underlined by his undeniable point a few years later that academic practice had found its fundamental justification in its identification as "a vehicle of political transformation" ("Bourdieu's Refusal," 370). I mention both of these observations from the 1990s largely to assert that they are so self-evidently true at this point that we may need to be reminded that they were ever novel enough to provoke comment.

In short, the question about results seems particularly worth asking precisely because the strategy of resistance might be said to have been an utter success. But the taste associated with power must surely match up with actual-existing power in some way for claims of political agency to have any purchase, to be more than perverse nostalgic exercises of necrophobia. Evidently, those of us who write on taste will soon find ourselves in a peculiar situation where in order to teach texts that critique the power of elite culture we may well need an extensive critical apparatus to explain what that culture was. Or, should we see ourselves as officiants at a kind of ritual celebration like those at which a villain who was executed centuries before is reconstituted out of rags and hay at regular intervals to be burned all over again? Perhaps our role is to commemorate a victory we don't quite remember. But that would mean the resistance had succeeded, right?

4. Nineteenth-Century Beauty

The challenge mounted by Jacques Rancière in *The Philosopher and His Poor* (1983) against the school of thought represented by the Bourdieu of *Distinction* deserves to be better known for reasons at once methodological and historical, not simply because of the salutary resistance it presents to a number of commonplaces of our own day about class and the politics of taste, but because of the value of the philosopher's nuanced identification of the nineteenth century as the period in which art has "detached itself from its old functions and judges but still has not closed itself up in its autonomy" (*The Philosopher and His Poor*, 199).[9] Rancière's work is motivated by a sympathy rare in recent writers for the affective drives and historical determinants shaping claims about culture. Hence his unironic response to the ambition to unite "freedom and equality with compulsion (rather of respect and submission . . . than of fear) in the aesthetic" (197).[10] These are Kantian concerns, which Rancière develops from a thoughtful reading of Friedrich Schiller,

---

[9] On the importance of Bourdieu for Rancière's project, see Parker's introduction to the volume, "Mimesis and the Division of Labor." See also the chapter "The Sociologist King," 165–202. The fullest engagement with this text in Victorian studies is probably Freedgood, "The Novelist and Her Poor." For a bracing and informed political challenge to Rancière's aesthetic project, see Clune, "Judgment and Equality" (along with Pangia's thoughtful work *Rancière's Sentiments*, which provokes Clune's response).

[10] Rancière is citing Kant's extraordinary appendix, "On the Methodology of Taste," with its densely suggestive play of historical circumstance, struggle, and insistence on the need to harmonize higher culture with natural inclinations (Kant, *Critique of the Power of Judgment*, 229–30).

and so they are philosophical. But they are also recognized as *historical* in his argument, as characteristic of the period following the French Revolution, when art presents the possibility (or even identifies the necessity) of "offer[ing] itself as the aim and privileged support of strategies of reappropriation" (199). In Rancière's provocative argument, the elements of the aesthetic emerge anew as sources for political agency. In a bold set of formulations that unhesitatingly, and with tendentious awkwardness, repurpose terms typically wielded by schools of thought concerned to identify the subjection of disenfranchised groups— "appropriation," "gazing," "dispossession," and "other," not to say Bourdieu's "*dénégation*"—Rancière reorients the vision of self and of other in order to identify a situation in which the aesthetic could become a key element in a politics of recognition rather than being relegated to a practice of negation or unidirectional appropriation. "[T]he 'denegating' aesthetic gaze," he writes about the nineteenth century, "can now take, among the intellectuals of the proletariat, the full force of an other gaze [*d'un regard autre*] upon the property [*propriété*] of the other that becomes an other gaze [*qui devient regard autre*] upon the proletarian's dispossession" (199; translation slightly modified). Rancière's jangling play with possession and gazing is designed to throw into confusion the limiting accounts of possession and recognition so often brought to bear in ostensibly political reflections on the aesthetic. The translators render *propriété* as "propriety," suggesting correct behavior or conformity to accepted standards, but I have modified the citation, as I think the primary meaning of the word is probably more productive. As they gaze on what does not belong to them—and even though they may do so through an internalized version of a gaze itself not originally theirs—members of the proletariat may discover not simply the evident fact of their alienation, but an experience of dispossession that eventuates in a productive development, "an aesthetic and militant passion for reappropriation" (199).

Rancière's target is what he understands to be a deeply destructive set of conventions in progressive thought that amounts to the claim that the love of beauty is always and of necessity an imposition from above shaped around a claim of autonomy, with the consolidation of power as its ultimate tendency. The philosopher refuses the arrogance that appropriates the aesthetic to the privileged elite.[11] And his argument seems ever more clearly vindicated by developments that have taken place in the years since he wrote *The Philosopher and His Poor*. The anti-aesthetic tradition, it is becoming ever more clear, represents less a moment of practical resistance than the hypertrophy of a specialized and theoretically instrumental concept of the aesthetic in which beauty is largely abstracted

---

[11] Cf. Eagleton's attempt to rebut "those on the political left for whom the aesthetic is simply 'bourgeois ideology' to be worsted and ousted by alternative forms of cultural politics" (*Ideology of the Aesthetic*, 8). For a more recuperative challenge to the simpler forms of ideological critique, see Isobel Armstrong, *Radical Aesthetic*. See also the nuanced account of the concept of interest in the earliest period of its formulation in McKeon, *Secret History*, 323–87.

out of the life-world by arguments that see in it only a tool of power, with privilege on one end and disenfranchisement on the other. In order for Knowledge and Good to come to the fore, it would seem that one sister needs to be hidden entirely out of sight. But for Rancière, even Good has a limited role to play in analyses that leave little space for working-class agency or cross-group solidarity—or really any commonality of thought and experience that may tend to support enfranchisement.[12] "In the final analysis," the philosopher writes, "the pedagogy that 'raises consciousness' by unveiling exploitation and its mystifications is a very impoverished virtue" (*The Philosopher and His Poor*, 121).

Rancière's animus is driven by a sense that Bourdieu's project is the latest manifestation of a dynamic whereby fundamental change is held to be impossible due to a mechanism of irreconcilable division that strands us in a familiar situation with, on one side, the intellectual, occupying the position of a knowing and alienated subject, and, on the other, the people, seen as a sullen and possibly dangerous object, blind to itself and its best interests, unable to be more than an obstacle to its own liberation. The alternatives offered by Rancière's Bourdieu are willfully stark and impoverished when they amount to a choice between a perfect and fully self-motivated and autonomous engagement with aesthetic objects—a phenomenon never described because it is indescribable—or an instrumental use of those objects (to achieve or maintain social rank), which is described with great detail and verve. When we discover, as we always will, that the kind of perfection in the first choice is not available in aesthetic experience any more than in any other experience, we are left with an option that has neither the merit of being useful nor of being true.

The philosopher Nick Zangwill has noted the tendency of sociological challenges to the aesthetic to address themselves to a category that is easy to refute in theory in part because of its scarcity in life or philosophy, that is, to "a pure aesthetic approach to art" (209). Zangwill reminds us of what should be obvious: "Beauty does not stand alone. It cannot exist by itself. Things are beautiful because of the way things are in other respects.... Beauty cannot be solitary and we cannot appreciate it as such" (*Metaphysics*, 1; see also Ngai, *Our Aesthetic Categories*,

---

[12] On Bourdieu's indifference to evidence of commonalities of taste among classes, see Zangwill, *Metaphysics*, 212–13. Recent studies that demonstrate the untenable nature to claims of exclusion include Rancière's own *Aisthesis*, Vargo's *Underground History*, with its demonstration of the rich cultural life of Chartism, Hack's *Reaping Something New*, a study of the uptake of what we call Victorian literature in what we call African American literary culture in the nineteenth century, and Lootens's *Political Poetess*, a challenging account of race and what she identifies as the legacy of separate spheres in accounts of nineteenth-century poetry. Hartley has described the aspiration towards "more tolerant and inclusive understanding" of beauty in the period, though that aspiration is, of course, predicated on a number of stark separations (Hartley, "Beauty," 585). Isobel Armstrong drew attention to the aesthetic aspirations of chartists at least as early as *Radical Aesthetic* (see 3, 21n1). See also Sanders, *Poetry of Chartism*. Gikandi's treatment of what he calls the "Counterculture of taste" or "counter poetics" is a particularly bold attempt to address intersections and divergences in taste taking place across the fundamental ruptures of slavery without in any way repairing them (*Slavery*, 233–81).

43–4). What would happen if we heard in Tennyson's unresolved attempt to identify the sisters of Beauty not simply confusion about the ethical limits of a passion for admirable form, but a recognition of the actual complexity of a category that seems to call out to us with a claim of particular distinction yet will not ever fully sustain that claim? Evidently Zangwill is only bothering to deny beauty's solitary existence because the tendency to lose sight of the network of nonbeautiful things required for beauty to exist is a recurrent phenomenon. We know that the lack of a pure experience of justice in the world does not mean we should abandon the concept, any more than the impossibility of experiencing love unaccompanied by elements that we tell ourselves are not integral to that emotion has suggested to anyone beyond adolescence that there is no such thing as love. Beauty tantalizes with the promise of a distinct kind of experience free of so much else. The fact that that promise is never manifested in the pure fullness of the freedom it seems to suggest is recognizable throughout the nineteenth century, which may be an indication not of the naïveté of the period but of its thoughtful engagement with the topic.

The speaker in A. Mary F. Robinson's "Art and Life" (1886) freezes the blossoms of her apple tree by dipping them into the icy well that is art. In this form, their beauty is preserved, but only at the cost of preventing the flowers from ever coming to fruition. The life that art memorializes and on which it depends is protected but chilled, its nutritional value sacrificed for something else: "Therefore, when winter comes, I shall not eat / Of mellow apples such as others prize: / I shall go hungry in a magic spring!" This kind of equilibrium in the dialectic between art and life was often upset in late-century writing, which frequently emphasizes not the artist's hunger for life but the fear of being caught up in natural processes—to freeze one's apple blossoms is, after all, to preserve them. Michael Field render in verse a highly finished portrait of a slender and bejeweled young woman by Bartolomeo Veneto, now in Frankfurt: "A Crystal, flawless beauty on the brows / Where neither love nor time has conquered space" ("A Portrait," 27). But it is the burden of the woman's knowledge of the place of beauty in time (itself a new version of a conventional concern of lyric poetry, of course) that drives the creation she sponsors and shapes. The poem recasts the painting as a staging of her own beauty by the noblewoman who is its subject (she selects the flowers, she decides how much of her body to reveal, and so on). In a perverse revision of Keats's urn (that foster child of slow time), she conquers time in the process of self-memorializing, thereby removing at once the possibility of change and of memory in the permanently perfect present tense at which the poem arrives at its close: "She had no memories save of herself / . . . And gave to art a fair, blank form, unverified by life. / Thus has she conquered death" ("A Portrait," 29).

The distance between Michael Field's "blank form, unverified by life" and the various claims for the vivifying and life-affirming powers of art that run through the period (e.g., Barrett Browning, *Aurora Leigh*: "art / Which still is life"

(5.238–9)) is clear enough. But this kind of contradiction must be recognized as typical of an uncertainty of long standing. The drive to find a space sheltered from what Michael Field called, in their poem on the *Mona Lisa*, "the vicissitudes by which men die" ("La Gioconda," 8), while still in some way reflecting those very vicissitudes, only gathered energy, until, by the end of the century, the often desperate claim of artistic autonomy was left as a major contribution to modernism.[13] It is this tradition Wallace Stevens evokes in 1915 when he has his speaker declare twice that "Death is the mother of beauty" in the course of his deeply stylized celebration of commonplace experience, "Sunday Morning." The golden bird William Butler Yeats placed in a changeless Byzantium of the mind in 1928, a deathless figure, all artifice, singing in a timeless space of what is past or passing or to come, is precipitated out of the despair felt by that paltry thing that is an aged man upon a stick gazing on the passions of the young—themselves too busy loving and dying to care for either the majesty of the bird or the speaker's fragility.

Rancière's historicization of a category that has become detached from old functions and judges, but which we would be wrong to simply see as on its way to a fated autonomy that will easily and as a matter of course separate it from lived experience, may help us to be more generous than has often been the case about main lines of Victorian literature and fine arts that have tended to be characterized by their failure to either achieve autonomy or to deploy the styles that came to be associated with the higher levels of abstraction. We may also read in Rancière's account of the period an invitation to serious new scholarship. The philosopher's most ambitious recent work in this area, *Aisthesis*, includes substantial engagement with Ralph Waldo Emerson, John Ruskin, and Walt Whitman, along with the usual French figures. As this list of names only suggests, the history of modern beauty is a characteristically nineteenth-century one, and like so much that matters from that period, it is characterized by failure, compromise, and uncertainty. Indeed, some of the most interesting critical work on the topic comes from authors such as Bourdieu himself or, more recently, Franco Moretti, when they wrestle with the failure of autonomy to be fully manifested in the nineteenth century, thereby rediscovering with productive chagrin what the evidence amply documents (Bourdieu, *Rules of Art*, 339–48; Moretti, *The Bourgeois*, 137–44).

Ultimately, the relationship between Knowledge and Beauty in much modern criticism is not at its heart a very complicated one: knowledge sets out to identify the real determinants leading to claims that something is beautiful. The nineteenth century offered other ideas. "Beauty is truth, truth beauty" ("Ode on a Grecian Urn," 373), Keats's vase tells the viewer in a phrase the compactness of which is part of its argument. "To look at a thing is very different from seeing a thing,"

---

[13] See Loesberg (*Return to Aesthetics*), Teukolsky (*Literate Eye*), Goldstone (*Fictions of Autonomy*), Belting (*Invisible Masterpiece*), and Krauss (*Originality of the Avant-Garde*).

writes Oscar Wilde, sixty years later: "One does not see anything until one sees its beauty" ("Decay of Lying," 1096). To bracket off Keats's aestheticism as a manifestation of his charming sensuality or Wilde's as derived from a more general antinomian rebellion against a hypocritical middle class philistinism is to ignore the clear evidence of the preoccupations of a period in which beauty is consistently associated with the coming of knowledge, in which not only knowledge is beautiful in itself, but in which recognition of the beautiful is consistently recognized as a form of knowledge.[14] Acknowledging the seriousness of the formulations I have cited and of the tradition to which they belong may allow us to locate between Keats and Wilde an author the first never read but the second certainly did, Georg Wilhelm Friedrich Hegel. So it may be useful to discuss here the main elements of the intersection of knowledge and beauty that is so important in the philosopher's work.

In the *Aesthetics* (1835), Hegel lays out some of the theoretical sources for the vast gap between object and self that is crossed when beauty is experienced. With some important exceptions, the recent tendency has been to imagine that the most compelling relationship between ourselves and the world is one in which we manage to remove ourselves as much as possible from the experience (see Levine, *Dying to Know*). But for Hegel, the notional voidance of the self before the world is merely the necessary first step in a swift dialectic, which is why it only looks like we are playing a zero-sum game in which to perceive the world we first need to abstract it and then give way to its pressures. "As finite intelligences," he writes "we sense ... objects, we observe them, we become aware of them through our senses, we have them brought before our contemplation and ideas, and, indeed, before the abstractions of our thinking understanding which confers on them the abstract form of universality" (*Aesthetics*, 1:112). The commitment to the independence of things seems to require a surrender of the liberty at the moment of perception: "With this one-sided freedom of objects," the argument goes on, "there is immediately posited the unfreedom of subjective comprehension... Truth in that case is to be gained only by the subjugation of subjectivity" (1:112). The next turn in the dialectic is immediate, and it involves a willing— not a passive—relationship to the object world. And so it is that following his account of the loss of freedom of the subject at the moment of encountering the object Hegel turns to the force of the subject submitting objects to its will:

> Thus now it is things which are deprived of their independence, since the subject brings them into his service and treats and handles them as *useful*, i.e. as objects with their essential nature and end not in themselves but in the subject, so that

---

[14] Notable recent treatments of beauty as associated with the coming to knowledge include Scarry, *On Beauty and Being Just*, 46, and Kramnick, especially 57–97. On the complex nature of Victorian concepts of experience see Coombs and Garratt.

what constitutes their proper essence is their relation (i.e. their service) to the
aims of the subject. Subject and object have exchanged their roles. The objects
have become unfree, the subjects free. (1:113; emphasis in the original)

The instrumentalizing of the world makes the things in it unfree objects. It is the task of the beautiful to effectuate the reconciliation of the subject and object at the point of perception. The possibility of a doubled freedom from the constraints built into the subject's inescapable relationship to the world is a role that in Hegel is carried out by beauty. It is not only the object that is freed by being experienced as beautiful; the perceiving being is also granted a new dispensation: "the consideration and the existence of objects as *beautiful* is the unification of both points of view, since it cancels the one-sidedness of both in respect of the subject and its object alike, and therefore their finitude and unfreedom" (1:113).[15] Perhaps Hegel will allow us to recognize the intellectual sources of that Wilde claim I cited above, that "One does not see anything until one sees its beauty." To run the matter in a different direction may even allow us to recognize the aphoristic quality in the philosopher's formulations, such as the proposition that in encountering the beautiful object "the self becomes concrete in itself" (Hegel, 113). The failure to achieve such a concretion of the self might well be figured in Tennyson's fashion: by the evocation of a baffled lover banished to a threshold outside of all affections, unable to realize his human state.

The erotic character of the desire evident in the various figures for beauty I have discussed in my treatment of poetry would take us out of the realm of the beautiful as far as Kant is concerned, which opens up for reflection a more interesting question than it might at first seem: why does erotic attraction emerge as a characteristic figure for the relationship to beauty in the period? To ask this question is to forget that we believe we know the answer: that everything is erotic, for example, or that every significant relationship is an interested one. "I am half sick of shadows," says the Lady of Shalott. We understand that feeling, and we are excited and pleased as she recognizes her true passion when the vision of Lancelot makes her not only see directly, but also participate with a new immediacy in the world she has so far only apprehended in a mirror or as she represents it to herself on her tapestries. Poems such as "The Lady of Shalott" or "Defence of Guenevere" are about beauty, but they are also designed to be beautiful objects in themselves. Victorian literature proposes repeatedly that the erotic life is not simply the source of the fundamental drives being denied in claims about beauty, but a rich model for the complex nature of the experience of beauty itself. The beauty of representation itself has a quality of knowledge folded into it. We feel something in the recognition that part of the world has been brought before us (the inescapability of

---

[15] Hegel's argument is anticipated in Schiller's account of the play drive's reconciliation of formal and material dispositions in *The Aesthetic Education of Man*. See especially letter 14 (Schiller, 95–9).

desire, say, or the power of repression or the vexed nature of the relationship between art and life). To recognize the claim of representation itself is to perhaps open the door to the other sister, Knowledge. But Good still seems some distance away—unless we imagine some good from recognizing pleasure and its vicissitudes.

5. Affordances of Beauty/Significance of Form

At the end of Tennyson's "Palace of Art" the soul, abashed, has been driven out of her stronghold and entered the world. But she leaves the Palace standing, available for a possible return. The subject, whose lust for beauty in "To ___" has made him an outcast, lies howling on the threshold of love at the close of that poem. These culminations suggest that while one may not be able to live in art, one evidently may spend a lot of time having strong feelings around its door.

I proposed at the beginning of this chapter that the stark allegorical forms the poet adapts in these works may be better understood as manifestations of an ongoing ambivalence than as illustrations of a set of clearly resolved ideas. I have also been suggesting that the sophistication of this representation of ambivalence and irresolution becomes all the clearer when viewed from the perspective of the many attempts at clarification of a subsequent era. The poems accurately capture an emotional relationship shaped by inevitable imbalances, which is also a way of saying that to focus on the three extraordinary sisters may be a way to deflect attention from the pathetic subject who is trying to negotiate his relationship among them, and who evidently has more in common with the reader. In this self torn in his relationship to the sisters, rejected, cast out from affection as the punishment for having acted on an unbridled passion, vulnerable, humiliated—human—we may identify much that is avoided in influential recent accounts of the aesthetic. The approach I have associated with Bourdieu has no time for weeping and howling at the threshold; its exponents are inside the house engaged in deep conversation with Knowledge and Good while side-eyeing Beauty. And what is the topic of their conversation? They are talking about that sad deluded stranger lying on the threshold weeping, a social-climber who has confused his greed for advancement for heart-felt emotion.

I have emphasized a period in the 1980s and 1990s during which the critique of an autonomous aesthetic realm was felt to be an urgent project, and I have suggested that while the endeavor has met astonishing success at the institutional level, it has inevitably failed to deliver on its most consequential promises. Analyses of the disappointment attendant on the bold political aspirations of that era have been made repeatedly for the last few decades, to the point that this chapter might itself be felt to belong to a tiresome recent tradition. Still, though the doctrinaire followers of Bourdieu are fewer than they once were, and bold challenges to the aesthetic are seldom advanced with the force we saw in earlier days, it would be a mistake to see the absence of open arguments as a sign of the failure of a set of values. Sometimes people do not talk about things that go without saying.

In more recent decades it can seem we see a version of something like a renewed interest in beauty, insofar as the features of specific aesthetic objects are explored or given some priority in what has been described as a return to form.[16] There are methodological and conceptual reasons for this sense of a return, both in the renewed priority given to specific forms and genres in the course of analysis and in the shift away from causal categories conventionally understood to be distinct from the aesthetic—notably in the schools of thoughts I addressed above in relation to Bourdieu and Foster. While recourse to form from the *fin de siècle* to the first decades of the twentieth century tended to be motivated by an attempt to move the discussion of art beyond questions of morality ("There is no such thing as a moral or an immoral book," Wilde declares in a characteristic aphorism in the Preface to *Dorian Gray*: "Books are well written, or badly written. That is all" (17)), contemporary formalism has typically emerged as an attempt to escape something that may or may not turn out to be quite different, the undue pressures of material, historical, or political circumstances in determining the meaning or value of a work. Insofar as moving beyond abstractions, such as history or power or class is understood to involve a new commitment to specificity, the value of beauty seems to glimmer in the offing. And yet, beauty is hardly at issue in most of the stronger claims that have been made for the category of form. It is rather her sisters who are still coming to the fore. Indeed, Caroline Levine's *Forms*—to cite one influential recent example—is openly a moral project. An attempt to bring to bear the methods of formal analysis of the literary critic in order to identify the political conditions determined by various social forms (forms are "the stuff of politics," Levine declares (3, 7)), its ultimate goal is to promote good being done in the world. And, indeed, while variations on the word politics occur nearly one hundred times in Levine's book, the word "beauty" occurs five times, and never as an object of analysis or reflection. "[T]he south is associated with rural beauty, economic sluggishness, and an accepted gap between peasantry and gentry" (*Forms*, 41), Levine tells us about Elizabeth Gaskell's *North and South*, with the attractions of the region hardly finding themselves in pleasant company in that list of conventions. When beauty occurs as a term of praise, it is typically a synonym for effective conceptualization: Trish Loughran is praised for "a beautiful

---

[16] Out of the many attempts to lay out the stakes of the turn to form we might cite in recent years the thoughtful sweep of Gaskill, "The Close and the Concrete," and the methodological reflections of Kramnick and Nersessian, "Form and Explanation," as well as foundational texts shaping and reflecting on the resurgence of interest in the topic, such as Leighton, *On Form*, Levinson, "What is New Formalism," and Wolfson, *Formal Charges*. The special issue of *Modern Language Quarterly* Wolfson edited with Brown, *Reading for Form*, is important to cite in this context.

example" of the overlapping or collision of various networks in her discussion of the mail in the American colonies prior to the Revolution (120). Beauty in this usage has to entail knowledge and goodness. And indeed, the beauty in Loughran's argument is ultimately traceable to the disruptive nature of the inadequately articulated communication networks in the colonies she identifies, an excellent illustration for Levine's sophisticated and dynamic account of the social life of forms.

There is no reason to blame a critic for failing to do something she is not trying to do, and in Levine's project, which is to transfer what are ostensibly the skills, procedures, and conventions of critics trained in analyzing aesthetic objects to the study of forms not typically understood as falling under our jurisdiction in order to do political work, the benefit of thinking of a particular social form as a network or system does not reside in the opportunity to reflect on its beauty. We *could* imagine our system of highways as beautiful, or even sublime, or our electrical grids, or systems of shifting water or even fuel from place to place. That we don't pause to marvel at them very often is symptomatic of the naturalization of astonishing artificial systems, and of the tendentious and limited nature of what we typically allow ourselves to identify with our aesthetic categories. In any case, the beauty of the forms of the world is not the concern of politically inflected formalism.

It may be helpful to look back to one of the earliest attempts to differentiate the project of form from the question of beauty, a topic that takes us directly to the aftermath of the Victorian period and perhaps even to the emotions moving Tennyson's melancholy lover in "To ___." Though recent debates about form make consistent recourse to Knowledge and the Good and generally leave Beauty unaddressed, we find the topic front and center in one of the great early formalist polemics, Clive Bell's 1913 *Art*. Bell proposes to replace the word "beauty" with "significant form," a quality which he distinguishes from a more common category he associates with the response to butterflies, say, or to attractive individuals, to which he abandons the older term. Wielding a kind of quick and easy Kantianism, Bell works to peel away an idea that in Kant is largely related to nature—the disinterested claim of beauty—and append it almost entirely to works of art. But this is not Kant. In *Art* the aim is to identify the aesthetic experience as an emotion—not a kind of cognition at all, and as such to insist that it is not related to other values one might associate with cognition, namely the acquisition of knowledge or the making of ethical judgments. Bell ultimately comes back to both of these ideas and attempts to recover them, but this first move is a clear indication of the critic's ambivalent relationship with the sisters of Beauty, and possibly with Beauty herself. His account of significant form is based on a relay of emotions: the artist had an aesthetic emotion provoked by perceiving a form in the world, and that is what is relayed to the attentive viewer by the art object. Built into this model is an attempted refusal not just of one sister, but of all three;

Knowledge and Good go by the wayside along with Beauty. Or, at least each sister is greatly reduced in size and power. What is left is a concept of emotion described at a strikingly primitive level, accompanied by a version of mediation that paradoxically needs to be even more basic in order to encompass the heterogeneous sets of objects available to be admired by the cosmopolitan aesthete.

"What quality is shared by all objects that provoke our aesthetic emotions?" asks Bell before listing an assortment: "What quality is common to Sta. Sophia and the windows at Chartres, Mexican sculpture, a Persian bowl, Chinese carpets, Giotto's frescoes at Padua, and the masterpieces of Poussin, Piero della Francesca, and Cezanne?" The response is delivered with a hyperbolic certainty that makes no effort to hide its tendentious nature nor its circularity: "Only one answer seems possible—significant form. In each, lines and colours combined in a particular way, certain forms and relations of forms, stir our aesthetic emotions. These relations and combinations of lines and colours, these aesthetically moving forms, I call 'Significant Form'; and 'Significant Form' is the one quality common to all works of visual art" (8).[17]

One missing element in more recent approaches to form, the loss of which is surprisingly anticipated as early as the work of Bell, is the concept of the art object itself. "Aesthetic object" is sometimes used as a term meaning a thing whose principal affordances arise from its form. Identifying a category of objects whose current first order of use is understood to be aesthetic contemplation, opens the way for dealing with form itself. In that sense the broadening out of the claim of form we find in Levine is a progression from what we see in Bell, and in both cases, the source of the category of analysis lies within the viewer. To ask as Bell does "What quality is shared by all objects that provoke our aesthetic emotions?" is to skip over the more fundamental question about a list the heterogeneity of which is an indication of the triumph of the concept of art (including as it does an entire Byzantine church, now a mosque, in Istanbul, the windows at a medieval French cathedral, unspecified handiwork from unclear locations in Central America, Persia, and China, frescoes in a Chapel in Padua, and easel paintings from the fifteenth, seventeenth, and nineteenth centuries). The definitional challenge presented by the institution of art (what *do* these things have in common?) finds its resolution in the emotions of an individual. In that sense the relay point who matters the most in this process is the critic.

The extravagant and perhaps overconfident celebration of emotion that is so common in English letters of the first half of the twentieth century—typically presented in the Bloomsbury Group as a reasonable and justified reaction to the restraint of middle-class Victorian culture—comes to the fore in this early twentieth-century formulation. "We must therefore give up the attempt to judge

---

[17] On the afterlife of the term, "significant form," in relation to the rise of later formalist approaches, see Gaskill, "The Close and the Concrete."

the work of art by its reaction on life," Bell's great collaborator, Roger Fry, writes in his 1909 "Essay in Æsthetics," as he also repurposes a Kantian tag, "and consider it as an expression of emotions regarded as ends in themselves" (19). And yet, this very celebration of the emotions is a door by which the Good will reenter the argument. "Art is above morals," declares Bell before immediately contradicting himself, "or, rather, all art is moral because, as I hope to show presently, works of art are immediate means to good. Once we have judged a thing a work of art, we have judged it ethically of the first importance and put it beyond the reach of the moralist" (*Art*, 20). With the bracing declarative forcefulness characteristic of his circle when it comes to closing any gap between the emotions and ethical judgments, Bell does not shy away from a remarkably hyperbolic claim. It is not that the Good has been banished after all, but that it is always already there when we have made an aesthetic judgment. In this argument, there is no choice of the sort that tormented the lover in Tennyson's allegory: to see art is to see that rarified phenomenon Bell calls "significant form," which is to see the Good. Moral readings of art works are a nonsense because they are redundant.

In its recent politicized manifestations, form comes near providing a return to the sisterly trio of Goodness, Knowledge, and something like Beauty, which may help to remind us what a short distance we have in fact traveled from a preoccupation with finding a moral claim and a cognitive one inextricably woven into our aesthetic experiences. Still, in the early years of a new millennium, and a century after Bell advanced the gambit of "significant form," it bears reflecting on what we have lost and gained by the move to form as a conceptual category. To see form isn't to see beauty, though it may allow for a kind of return to that very Victorian concern with the process whereby a subject placed in relationship with a highly valorized object is felt to be mobilizing an interplay of cognition and of ethics so closely allied that their correlation can appear to be inevitable. I'd like to suggest that the apparent evolution from beauty to significant form, and ultimately to form *tout court*, may lead us to miss both how much we are still working in response to Victorian preoccupations and also how difficult that response has made it for us to talk about the sister that provoked the most complicated passions in the nineteenth century. It is misleading to use form as a kind of value-neutral stand-in for beauty, because there is no value-neutral stand-in for beauty.

Formalism is often an argument disguised as a perception, when it isn't a work of emotional sharing camouflaged as an account of something more concretely perceivable in the world than the feelings of an individual. Significant form—that modernist transitional object that early twentieth-century British thought tried to put in the place of beauty—cannot be said to get rid of subjects because it depends on emotion. In Bell's argument art relays emotion from individual to individual by means of form. And that process of recognition and relay is precisely what makes it significant. Significant form is a relationship between world and artist in the first instance and then between art object and viewer in the second. The role of the critic is to describe the nature of a relationship we are meant to be feeling, that we will feel if rightly constituted and if the form is effective, and if we clear up some confusions about sentiment and ethics left over from the nineteenth century. And so, art is about artists and viewers, and significant form, which presents itself as beauty stripped of its more contingent human elements, is in fact emotion objectified. Emotion is experience in art understood this way, and all we have of knowledge. It is as though Bell had removed all the constraints on the passionate subject in Tennyson's "To ___," leaving behind only his feelings, now freed from any burden of judgment. And, indeed, the critic is disarmingly clear on this part of his argument: "it may be objected," he acknowledges, "that I am making aesthetics a purely subjective business, since my only data are personal experiences of a particular emotion. It will be said that the objects that provoke this emotion vary with each individual, and that therefore a system of aesthetics can have no objective validity" (*Art*, 8). His answer to the charge of subjectivism is pleasantly stark and forceful, though not for that reason fully satisfactory; indeed, it serves largely as the occasion for him to throw one of Tennyson's sisters under the bus: "It must be replied that any system of aesthetics which pretends to be based on some objective truth is so palpably ridiculous as not to be worth discussing" (8).

In later manifestations of formalism we find ourselves in relation to a form not because someone has felt something and created something, but because systems have been put in place (and the passive form will be the form of this kind of formalism). What this approach opens up is political reflection on systems in which we are always already enmeshed, and toward which we might want to (probably need to) respond. A key word that has emerged along with the renewed interest in form in the last several years is "affordance," a concept drawn from writers on design, but ultimately traceable to the psychologist who coined it, James J. Gibson, and which is sometimes taken to make available a category of experience in which the object world is the most determinant element. But it may turn out that, as is the case with the identification of significant form, so with the discussion of affordances: the claims of the subject are not really left behind in either case. While the chief merit of the category is sometimes understood to be the way it articulates the significance of things while minimizing subjects, this is in fact not the main tendency of the concept in Gibson, in whose work it emerges as part of an intriguingly textured environmental concept of sight—one in which the subject is understood to be fully embedded in the world in a manner that would have been recognizable to Hegel and his nineteenth-century readers: "an affordance is neither an objective property nor a subjective property; or it is both if you like. An affordance cuts across the dichotomy of subjective-objective and helps us to understand its inadequacy (*Ecological Approach to Visual Perception*, 129)."[18]

---

[18] For a subtle and useful account of the concept of affordances, see Kramnick, *Paper Minds*, 5–11.

Beauty, the aesthetic, form: these can seem like various ways of talking about related things, perhaps with different degrees of precision or technical engagement. But the topic changes depending on the term. The category of the aesthetic carries with it a long conceptual history, and its power resides precisely in the things it never fully resolves: the nature of experience, of subjects, of an engagement with the world that may well be charged with force in spite of what we do or do not fully know. Use of the term invites reflection on the social role of individual responses, on the claim to shared experience, and perhaps even on the tendency to judge others through the things that move them, or through their ability to be moved.[19] Form, on the other hand, is always about second-order claims, because no claim about form is recognizable without other similar or related structures against which to declare that this thing belongs to the category in which we are placing it: it is a box, it is a circle, it is a network, a sonnet, a novel. Or the question may be finessed as Bell did: it is "significant," meaning its form matters to me— and so it should to you.

Beauty strikes me as the most productively troubling of these terms because it identifies an experience that engrosses the senses without providing the mind with reasons for that fascination. It is that which reflections on the aesthetic attempt to explain, which formal claims work to organize. Your eye is drawn in a certain direction when something as simple as the line of a cheekbone or the arch of an eyebrow appears at the edge of your vision. The timbre of a voice or the notes of a bird song stop your progress. A piece of poetry keeps coming back to you, troubling or comforting you for reasons not fully related to the evident content of the line. A painting in a gallery suddenly moves you, or (why not?) moves you after long reflection. The shifting clouds in a clear sky call out for attention, or a pair of bridges on a river with the light falling a certain way beneath them. You look, and look again.

While the recognition of form inevitably depends on reflection about a set of experiences, on abstraction from instances, the experience of beauty is always partial, limited, contingent: this beautiful face, that stand of trees with that line of light cutting across it, or even, that tone of voice, that melody. "What is this . . . to me" (*The Renaissance*, ed. Hill, xix–xx) is the fundamental question for the aesthetic critic that Walter Pater describes. The answer to that question, though it is as myriad and unstable as each instance it addresses and as each self who asks it is nevertheless the source of all the facts with which the critic has to do, as far as Pater is concerned. But this is no invitation to easy self-indulgence; it is a project he will ultimately describe as "a desperate effort to see and touch" (*The Renaissance*, ed. Hill, 189). To ask it is to recognize that something has happened,

---

[19] On the complicated nature of the universality written into aesthetic categories, see Ngai, *Our Aesthetic Categories*, 169–73, 284 n93.

that an experience has reached us from the world, but it is not to resolve what that experience amounts to.

Experience itself has consistently been a promise and a challenge in discussions of form, in which the immediate unmediated particularity of the aesthetic object is sometimes presented as its core interest. Indeed, formalism as an approach has been taken to entail the return to a base level of experience, as in Viktor Shklovsky's much-cited formulation about art's mission, "to make the stone *stony*" ("Art as Technique," 12). The immediacy of the relay from sensibility to sensibility involved in the concept of "significant form" is one manifestation of this preoccupation. The fascination with unmediated and therefore immediate aesthetic experience runs through the first decades of the twentieth century; from the ambitious formulations of Imagism to the speculative pedagogy of I.A. Richards and including the attempt to bring aesthetic experience down to the register of physiological responses sometimes associated with the work of Vernon Lee, the period was full of formal approaches designed to return to the most immediate kind of encounter. An "Image," we may recall, is "that which presents an intellectual and emotional complex in *an instant of time*" (Pound, *Literary Essays*, 4, emphasis added; see also Lee and Anstruther-Thomson, *Beauty and Ugliness*; Richards, *Practical Criticism*).

Time usefully enters Caroline Levine's treatment of form in her account of rhythm (*Forms*, 41–81), which is ultimately about contending forms of standardization and repetition, what she describes as the "rhythms of social experience" (51). But it is only from an abstracting distance that any of our experiences can be conceived as regular or even repeated. Pater proposes an arresting image for the failure of perception that insists on patterns; it is only "the roughness of the eye," he notes with an adjective designed to make one pause "that makes any two persons, things, situations, seem alike" (*The Renaissance*, ed. Hill, 189). Immediacy is the fact of experience, and everything that makes it urgently significant. But the experience of that immediate moment is vulnerable to the disposition of the subject and the efficacy of the organs of perception: "Every moment some form grows perfect in hand or face; some tone on the hills or the sea is choicer than the rest; some mood of passion or insight is irresistibly real and attractive to us,—for that moment only" (*The Renaissance*, ed. Hill, 188). *Every moment* is a phrase that might equally suggest comforting copiousness (another opportunity presents itself every moment) or distressing urgency (perfection is coming to fruition at this very moment; blink and you will miss it—again!). It is a matter of the critic's disposition to determine whether pleasure or fear is the proper response to a situation in which "not to discriminate every moment some passionate attitude in those about us, and in the brilliancy of their gifts some tragic dividing of forces on their ways, is, on this short day of frost and sun, to sleep before evening" (*The Renaissance*, ed. Hill, 189; see also Gallagher, "Formalism and Time," 243).

In the allegory that Tennyson's "To ___. With the Following Poem" accompanies, the soul is driven out of her haughty isolation in the Palace of Art by an overwhelming sense of guilt figured in extravagantly Gothic forms, with rotting corpses emerging in unexpected corners of her elaborately designed place of beauty. And yet, though the soul leaves the palace, she refuses to have it torn down, with the thought that she may return again when she has cleansed herself of the guilt she has accrued for taking up residence where one is not supposed to live: "Yet pull not down my palace towers that are / So lightly, beautifully built / Perchance I may return with others there / When I have purged my guilt" (lines 293–6). It is an evocative, ambiguous space, this palace that is treasured and feared, a site the love of which is liable to become a guilty all-engrossing passion revealing monsters needing to be purged from oneself. But it is also a place that requires protection. Burn the beautiful being out of the world, or stare at her lovely figure as she openly beguiles you. Tear down the Palace of Art, or leave it up as a perpetual potential place of return shaped by beauty and distorted by the realization of irresponsibility. The space that opens up after the ending of "The Palace of Art" may represent the most interesting vision of the modern relationship to beauty in the poem: a treasured location charged with the nostalgic force of its near loss as well as with the guilty sense that its absence may be necessary for the full expansion of moral sensibilities, the importance of which does not make the attention they bring to bear any less vulnerable to distraction.[20]

---

[20] This chapter adapts and revises material that first appeared in my essay, "Beauty," *Victorian Literature and Culture* 48 (2020): 745–71. I am grateful to Danny Hack, George Levine, Meredith McGill, and especially Nancy Yousef for generous help in revising the text.

4
Gates of Horn in Ivory Towers
On Beauty's Truth

Herbert F. Tucker

"All art is quite useless" (Wilde (1890), 17). In form, this last and tersest thesis from the preface to *The Picture of Dorian Gray* arrives as a truth claim. In context, however, it is a paratextual component of a work of fictional art, and not just any such work but the most notorious aestheticist novel of the Victorian *fin de siècle*. Shall we then call it true or false? No, which is to say: neither. Or better say, slipping into the wiggle room of Oscar Wilde's gratuitous adverb: not quite. Any aesthetic of utility that, without relegating art to trivial amusement, can withstand the instrumentalization that would reduce art to a propaganda medium, or documentary storage device, needs to make friends with paradox. On the evidence of the poetry and poetics from Wilde's century that this chapter will consider, art's long-range usefulness as an elaborated cultural practice inhered in its immediate uselessness; in its freedom, that is, from the criterion of direct utility that governed the most conspicuous enterprises of industrial society.

In the name of cultural survival within and beyond an era of unpredictable change, it was incumbent on artists to pursue art as if for art's sake alone. The eventual cultural work awaiting the work of art was not laid out for it in advance but remained to be seen. The free imagination of novel forms was primarily obliged to an intrinsically aesthetic mandate whose outcomes and applications were radically unknown to the present, and for that very reason were speculatively precious to the future. Recalling the premises of Romanticism and Aestheticism can put a salutary check on the rush to relevance in contemporary humanities study, which will labor to better effect, even in service to the causes that summon it most urgently, as it redoubles attention to the resources of artistic form, and the unsuspected truth that beauty harbors.[1]

---

[1] In "The Long Lure of Anti-Instrumentality: Politics, Aesthetics, Sustainability" Caroline Levine (2021) takes exception to the indefinite adjournment that some academic humanists on the contemporary left embrace when it comes to practical solutions for even so pressing an issue as climate change. Among other components of "anti-instrumentality," Levine adduces the principle of "artistic autonomy" that my chapter here sets out to illustrate in nineteenth-century contexts and to defend as still valid today. Pointedly recalling how, with a combination of funding at home and propaganda abroad, during the Cold War decades the CIA "figured out how to instrumentalize—we might even say, weaponize—

By way of two or three manifestoes, and a handful of lyric poems traversing Wilde's century, I invite my reader here to inhabit the difference between a set of congruent binaries: the faculties of imagination and reason; experience and empiricism as ways of grasping those faculties' reciprocation; pleasure and profit as their often contrasted outcomes; arts and sciences as their institutional, and especially their academic, correlates. Poetry and truth—*Dichtung und Wahrheit*, as Goethe wittily balanced the two when framing the story of his life—were partners that competing interests within nineteenth-century culture hardened into an opposition whose nearly axiomatic self-evidence across the twentieth retains a force today that it increasingly behooves us to resist. Romantic and Victorian lyric poetry constituted a zone in which the lines dividing major binaries were memorably drawn, then consequentially crossed: not zeroed out, but chiastically linked at a conjunction of paradoxical interdependence.

Conceptually the argument I wish to make was already apparent two centuries ago to Percy Bysshe Shelley, who in "A Defence of Poetry" (1821) wrote with incisive explicitness about both the distinction and the coordination between poetry and truth, aesthetics and epistemology, inspiration and advocacy. Art's incalculable power to affect the world inheres for Shelley in its medium, not its message. That is why a poet "would do ill to embody his own conceptions of right and wrong, which are usually those of his place and time, in his poetical creations" (Shelley 2003: 682). It is also why Shelley's preface to *Prometheus Unbound* (1820) affirms that "Didactic poetry is my abhorrence," not because poetry lacks principles, exactly, but because the enunciation of principles is foreign to its purpose, which is rather to lead the imagination to entertain "beautiful idealisms of moral excellence; aware that, until the mind can love, and admire, and trust, and hope, and endure, reasoned principles of moral conduct are seeds cast upon the highway of life which the unconscious passenger tramples into dust" (232). Precisely because "We want the creative faculty to imagine that which we know" (695), the else-sterile fruits of intellection require sympathetic aesthetic quickening into consciousness: "The great instrument of moral good is the imagination; and poetry administers to the effect by acting upon the cause. Poetry enlarges the circumference of the imagination" (682).

This aesthetic enlargement of experience is a temporal and therefore historical process, which has cognitive dimensions as well. The language of real poetry,

---

the anti-instrumentality of the aesthetic," she enjoins in place of aesthetic and political purism the intermediary compromise of "collective continuance": a stepwise, renewable commitment to sustainability that she calls "a capacitating end, a crucial means of affording a range of other ends." That Levine envisions this worthy program solely in terms of institutional politics (e.g., fossil fuel divestment campaigning) leaves unaddressed whether or how the aesthetic platform of art for art's sake should likewise be pragmatized. My chapter takes the position that it should not: that beauty as its own reason for being is itself already a "capacitating end," whose affordance of "a range of other ends" may finally be the stronger for being currently unforeseeable. On this question see also Robert Archambeau, *Poetry and Uselessness: From Coleridge to Ashbery* (New York: Routledge, 2020).

Shelley says, "is vitally metaphorical; that is, it marks the before unapprehended relations of things and perpetuates their apprehension" (676). Poetic metaphor, that is, constitutes new knowledge about the world, through the integrity of relation it effects among hitherto atomized facts. A like integration typifies the freshly created aesthetic artifact's high degree of coherence, and furthermore consolidates its organization for transmission to the future: the individual reader's memory of a beautiful poem figures, as it partially effects, its perpetuation in the collective mind. And, as is entailed by Shelley's valorization of creativity, the collective mind of futurity will regard the inherited artifact in a new light, according to differences "in place and time" that disclose fresh understandings. This is the sense whereby, in the peroration of the "Defence,"

> Poets are the hierophants of an unapprehended inspiration; the mirrors of the gigantic shadows which futurity casts upon the present; the words which express what they understand not; the trumpets which sing to battle, and feel not what they inspire; the influence which is moved not, but moves. Poets are the unacknowledged legislators of the world. (701)

Shelley's poets are not besotted oracular rhapsodes, although like the rest of us they are ignorant of the future. If they do channel futurity on our behalf, it is thanks to faithful attendance—first theirs, then ours—on those "beautiful idealisms" which they bequeath in intellectual and formal beauty to a changing world, which in receipt of their "legislation" adjudicates and applies it anew.[2]

That's Shelley's general idea, which I confidently adopt two hundred years later as mine too, about how the aesthetic imagination goes to work (within the concretely formed materiality of its medium) and how it travels among minds (with an enlivening difference). The inertia of shaped beauty grounds the diversity of its interpreted truth, both of which hinge not on generality but on the specificities of aesthetic form and receptive milieu, of conveyance and destination. The turn my argument now takes from prose to poetry entails a shift along this same continuum of reception: away from the translucence of paraphrase, which trades one truth for another more or less at parity, and towards the obliquities of literary interpretation, which translates beauty by reading it out as truth. Because art thinks through form, useful access to its truths presupposes unfolding its beauties appreciatively. To phrase the essential binary of aesthetic utility in terms of beauty

---

[2] Two recent books frame this principle of coiled or harbored change in terms, respectively, of poetics and genetics, claiming on the one hand "that a poem's consequence is uncertain – unfixed, in flux, negatively capable – and that such uncertainty makes it possible for a poem to both resist the seeming certainties of current conditions and to potentially remake our common store" (Falci 2020: 17); and on the other hand that, where "there are hidden preferences for sexual traits yet to exist in a species," "the preference landscape is ripe with hidden preferences waiting to be exploited" (Ryan 2018: 59, 157).

and truth, as I have just started doing, is to enlist a powerful ally in John Keats. "Beauty is truth, truth beauty" (Keats 1978: line 49). That sibylline pronouncement at the end of the "Ode on a Grecian Urn" has meant various things to various readers, and indeed the prediction of such variance not only is one of the messages the words harbor but also forms a major clause within the brief that nineteenth-century poetics presented about the utility of aesthetic variability as such.

Before Keats distilled the urn's gnomic utterance in 1819 he had been hazarding things like it for some time. "What the imagination seizes as Beauty must be truth," he wrote in an 1817 letter, with an insistence (not "receives" but "seizes," not "is" but "must be") that shows him persuading himself in the course of tutoring his correspondent. The letter hurries on to another, roughly equivalent formulation; yet this one is more persuasive because more tentative, in a couple of senses: "The Imagination may be compared to *Adam's dream – he awoke and found* it truth" (Keats 2002: 36). "May" replaces "must," and narrative supervenes on manifesto, with literary-historical reinforcement into the bargain. We and Bailey are to recognize the comparison to God's creation of Milton's beautiful Eve from slumbering Adam's rib, and to recognize too the interval between Eve's creation and her reception on Adam's part, seasoning fulfillment with surprise, as essential to Keats's story. That story is a strong allegorical reading, well in excess of anything actually said in *Paradise Lost* (Milton 8.437–90), about how imaginative truth comes to pass. Beauty yields truth over time; before beauty can have its use, it takes a little getting used to.

This temporal dimension carries over powerfully into the odes of 1819. "Beauty is truth, truth beauty" resonates within "Ode on a Grecian Urn" as an epitomizing echo of the poem's imaginative and affective plot, which has led from repeated crests of ecstatic identification with the urn's depictions into repeated valleys of sober desolation. The latter have won the day by the time Keats launches his final stanza with defensively ironical carping at the urn's "fair attitude" (line 41) of mere indifference and "cold pastoral" (line 45) residue of frustration and loss. Its millennial beauty abides, but only to "tease us out of thought" (line 44) and so cheat the poet out of the consoling sort of truth he was expecting to find. What remains is the slender but authentic truth about the truth: on one side the stubborn fugitivity of the real, on the other the ubiquity of distorting interpretation. Keats's over-reading of the "legend" (line 5) incised on the urn's surface has spun its beauties into truths of his own manufacture (most notably, in lines 37–40, an unpeopled and entirely imaginary "little town" that the urn nowhere depicts), which are home truths about the character of a melancholy into which his aspirational hedonic escapism cannot help relapsing.

So also runs the lesson of "Ode to a Nightingale," where at the eleventh hour "The fancy cannot cheat so well / As she is famed to do, deceiving elf" (lines 73–4), and the exposure of a circuitous, gorgeous self-deception puts the poet back in touch with the real. Keats emplots both odes as extended departures from the straight way of truth (intellection as the crow flies?) along the sinuous detour of an instructive error—a correction *of* the aesthetic *by* the aesthetic, which recoups, in the round, imagination's seizure of truth by way of beauty. Likewise, the "Ode on Melancholy" vests the truth of the human condition in immersive aesthesia. Melancholy holds sway "in the very temple of Delight," feasts on "beauty that must die," transient "joy," and "aching pleasure" (lines 21–4). Yet again "Beauty is truth, truth beauty," *and in that order*: the second "beauty" differs from the first, being tempered by the asperities of a belated, hard-won knowledge.

From these severely splendid odes Keats went on to draft, in *The Fall of Hyperion*, a poetic self-inquisition that terminal illness kept him from completing, but whose proem remarkably places the aesthetic recuperation of truth in the hands of posterity, at a date beyond his lifetime. "Fanatics have their dreams, wherewith they weave / A paradise for a sect" (lines 1–2): although they may lack "the fine spell of words" (line 9), nevertheless fanatics are aesthetic utilitarians, convinced in advance as to the truths their woven dreams should rehearse. In contrast, and in an agnostic triumph of negative capability, Keats suspends judgment about the dream-vision on which he is embarking:

> Whether the dream now purpos'd to rehearse
> Be Poet's or Fanatic's will be known
> When this warm scribe my hand is in the grave.
>
> (Lines 16–18)

With heroic open-mindedness, Keats disowns the ability to declare what if any truth—what sectarian or ideological baggage—his work-in-progress may prove to convey. Only time can tell that, when the future history of its reception confers on the manifest beauties of the poem meanings not now foreseeable. While this deference seems extreme, it was already implicit in the odes' vista of multiple "generations," made hungry ("Nightingale," line 62) and laid "waste" ("Urn," line 45) by needs of their own, yet consoled by the powers of song and image to acknowledge those needs in person, meet them in the flesh. When in 1939 W. B. Yeats wrote in the last of his published letters that "Man can embody truth but he cannot know it" (Yeats 1954: 922), he was recapitulating an aesthetic wisdom Keats had found in the urn and taken to the tomb.[3]

A poet Yeats more probably had in mind was Shelley, whose paragraph quoted above from the "Defence of Poetry" performs a chorus of nay-saying that, as it mounts

---

[3] Giorgio Agamben's (2017) recent tour of the aesthetics of taste finds the philosophical tradition foundering perennially on the beauty/truth dilemma, which is "that science knows the truth but cannot enjoy it, and that taste enjoys beauty without being able to explain it" (8). For Plato "Beauty cannot be known and truth cannot be seen" (17); for Kant "The Idea is a concept that cannot be represented or an image that cannot be expounded," but never both (48); and by the later nineteenth century the discourses of "Aesthetics and political economy," respectively blinded and starved by "a knowledge that is not known and a pleasure that is not enjoyed," converge finally, although unsustainably, on the promise of taste as "the experience of a knowledge that enjoys and a pleasure that knows" (67).

from "unapprehended" to "unacknowledged," limns the negative labor of unknowable truth that forms the groundwork for aesthetic recognition. Delayed recognition is the leitmotif of more than one poem that another Shelleyan, Robert Browning, wrote at mid-century about the traffic in art, the investment in futures, and the postponement of returns. One of these, "Popularity" (1855), which directly addresses the situation of avant-garde poetry, goes so far as to end with the name "John Keats." Its bumptious speaker, whom there is no compelling reason not to deem Browning himself, asserts with contagious indignation that the "true poet" he hails must work unrewarded in his own day, being heralded only by the speaker ("I know you") and by God ("he needs you"), who shelters the true poet across "this dark world" and vouchsafes art's "light to spend" in time to come (Browning 1981: lines 1–10).

> His clenched hand shall unclose at last,
>   I know, and let out all the beauty:
> My poet holds the future fast,
>   Accepts the coming ages' duty,
> Their present for this past.
>
> (Lines 11–15)

The Shelleyan poet fastens on the future, ahead of his time in observance of a double "duty": he sustains modern art's obligation to make beauty new, even as he anticipates compensation from the IOU of a "duty" that posterity will bestow as hindsighted back-taxes. This imaginative calculus sharply contrasts with the instant gratification that is both offered and exploited by time-serving artistic contemporaries, the Tom, Dick, and Harry who cultivate ephemeral popularity but are nobodies in the historical big picture. Browning frames the contrast within an extended comparison of the true poet's work to the solitary labor of harvesting a certain sea snail (the dye-murex) and distilling from it a pigment of intense blue. That dye once "refined to proof" and "filtered by degrees" (lines 54–5), it falls to art's retail profiteers to copy and mass-produce it by the bottle:

> And there's the extract, flasked and fine,
>   And priced and saleable at last!
> And Hobbs, Nobbs, Stokes and Nokes combine
>   To paint the future from the past,
> Put blue into their line.
>
> Hobbs hints blue,—Straight he turtle eats:
>   Nobbs prints blue,—claret crowns his cup:
> Nokes outdares Stokes in azure feats,—
>   Both gorge. Who fished the murex up?
> What porridge had John Keats?
>
> (Lines 60–70)

With tart scornful puns on "prints" and "Put blue into their line," Browning exposes an industrial cartel of painter, poet, and entrepreneur, who "combine" to depress art in opportunistic pursuit of the main chance. "To paint the future from the past" is the presentist slogan of derivative imitation, stalled on a fad that feeds the taste of the hour. Such expediency makes manifest contrast with line 15 above: with a view to future ages that exchanges "Their present for this past," the limber imagination of the true poet regards the present moment in historical perspective, as if it were already time past—and well past time for a change. "Their present" invokes by word play an intergenerational gift economy in which the aesthetic, unlike its diluted special-effects knock-off, is not for sale.

All this is good aesthetic Romanticism, albeit tempered by Browning's sense of the philistine enmity to art that another half century of market capitalism has exacerbated, and rendered with a lexical bluntness and prosodic punch no one would mistake for Shelley or Keats. But something else marks this as a Victorian poem, something that approximates it to the sponsoring concerns of the present collection of essays. I mean its long simile portraying the poet as the Tyrian "fisher" (line 23) of shells, which departs from the apostrophized poet in stanza 5 and never really comes back to its tenor, except by winking implication, until the last line raises John Keats from the dead. In a sense Browning's prodigal gamble on the long odds of a single trope enacts the allegiance to imaginative originality that underwrites "Popularity" taken whole. In another sense it lets him perform the new, brusque species of beauty that successors would be prizing him for, half a century later:

> Yet there's the dye, – in that rough mesh,
> The sea has only just o'er-whispered!
> Live whelks, each lip's-beard dripping fresh,
> As if they still the water's lisp heard
> Through foam the rock-weeds thresh.
>
> (Lines 36–40)

That fine last line is one that Ezra Pound would have been proud to claim for the *Cantos*. The entire stanza, through risk-taking rhyme and delicate consonantal impediment, issues true-blue the new sibilant "lisp" of a voice that practices in verse a make-it-new aesthetic that the entire poem preaches.[4] But the two stanzas

---

[4] Browning had practiced this tongue-twisting euphony in *Sordello* (1840)—an experimental epic that Pound especially championed—in a version of much the same image:

> some forgotten vest
> Woven of painted byssus, silkiest
> Tufting the Tyrrhene whelk's pearl-sheeted lip,
> Left welter where a trireme let it slip
> I' the sea, and vexed a satrap.
>
> (3.11–15)

that follow do still more, in an exponential proliferation of nested similes that track beauty all the way down to its erotic root:

> Enough to furnish Solomon
>   Such hangings for his cedar-house,
> That when gold-robed he took the throne
>   In that abyss of blue, the Spouse
> Might swear his presence shone
> Most like the centre-spike of gold
>   Which burns deep in the blue-bell's womb,
> What time, with ardours manifold,
>   The bee goes singing to her groom,
> Drunken and overbold.
>
>   (Lines 40–50)

No birds sing, it's true. But Browning's bees do more than enough to correlate the eye's lust for chromatic intensity—"Astarte's eyes" (line 29) having invoked the aphrodisiac glamour of the ancient Near East's Venus—with lusty desire in overdrive, the buzz of sexual selection up and down the animal kingdom. All this two decades before Darwin's *Descent of Man* (1871) put the preferences of queen bees, or queens of Sheba ("the Spouse"), or divine beauty queens, on the evolutionary agenda. That beauty perseveres, by sovereign virtue of its random, "drunken" arbitrariness, formed part of the legacy Browning adopted from Romantic aesthetics and counterpoised to a Victorian utilitarian rationale.

From a close look at evolutionary theory at mid-century, Alfred Tennyson also drew an appreciation for beauty's capricious effects in nature. But what delighted Browning scared the poet of *In Memoriam* half to death. Subtract providential intelligence from natural-theological design, he inferred, and you only find in

> This round of green, this orb of flame,
>   Fantastic beauty; such as lurks
>   In some wild Poet, when he works
> Without a conscience or an aim.
>
>   (34.5–8)

The Gothic revulsion *In Memoriam* expresses at "Nature, red in tooth and claw" (56.15) is well enough known to obviate further comment. But the stanza just quoted makes a subtler complaint. Its horrified vision of "Fantastic beauty"—mindless, reckless, pointless creation—is a tendentious fantasy in its own right, if one to which a poet may have been conspicuously liable who possessed in equal measure Tennyson's lavish verbal imagination and meticulous craftsmanship.

Still, versions of this fantasy of unpiloted planetary evolution had currency and stamina across Victorian intellectual life. Half a century later it could still generate Thomas Hardy's Immanent Will, which "works unconsciously, as heretofore, / Eternal artistries in Circumstance" (Fore Scene to *The Dynasts*, 1905). Closer to Tennyson's mid-century crisis, Browning had his insouciant mouthpiece Fra Lippo Lippi entertain the theory ("say there's beauty with no soul at all") only to shrug it off: "If you get simple beauty and nought else, / You get about the best thing God invents" (lines 215–18). Such faith, or flippancy, was beyond Tennyson, or beneath him. The "wild Poet" was an inner demon that this control freak needed to find and face down, by facing up to it. In doing so he effected one of his elegy's hard-won reconciliations to what, in spite of himself, he had to concede were the realities inspiring and constraining aesthetic experience.

This was at bottom a Keatsian project, and Tennyson's pivotal confrontation with a wild nature that figured art's essential unruliness occurs, suitably, in his own encounter with the song of a nightingale. The "Wild bird" of lyric 88, here quoted in full, is lyric 34's "wild Poet" apprehended no longer *ab extra* by a spectator but now from the inside by a confessed companion in the art.[5]

> Wild bird, whose warble, liquid sweet,
>   Rings Eden thro' the budded quicks,
>   O tell me where the senses mix,
> O tell me where the passions meet,
>
> Whence radiate: fierce extremes employ
>   Thy spirits in the darkening leaf,
>   And in the midmost heart of grief
> Thy passion clasps a secret joy:
>
> And I—my harp would prelude woe—
>   I cannot all command the strings;
>   The glory of the sum of things
> Will flash along the chords and go.

The poem arises from a multisensory paradise where acoustic, tactile, gustatory, even floral-olfactory inputs combine in a synaesthetic "mix," which line 3 acknowledges en route to a darker inventory of feeling-as-emotion. The complex of "passions" takes ambivalence to "fierce extremes" that coexist in a hidden core, from which given emotions emerge into radiant aesthetic articulation but whose

---

[5] Zon (2017: 72) quotes from Charles A. Witchell's *The Evolution of Bird-Song* (1896) a clause that nearly enough glosses Tennyson's celebrated poem to have been, perhaps, influenced by it: "the language of the wild bird is to it as important as is the language of a wild man to him" (178). See also Curry (2019: 53): "The best birdsong sounds unmistakably improvised within the relevant constraints of the organism, community and ecology – in other words, it is cultural – while the best human improvisers sound unmistakably natural."

central "secret" remains mysterious. This nuclear mystery powers art but resists understanding—and eludes controlling craft. Hence the radical ambiguity of the confessions, and concessions, of Tennyson's third stanza. He wants to sing the blues, but blurts out a glory anthem instead. Or, with equal and opposite syntactic warrant, he sets out to praise "the sum of things" but loses it in a flash and reverts to prelusive lamentation. What is left resembles nothing so much as that "Fantastic beauty" he deploringly reprehended back in lyric 34. The poet now acknowledges his complicity with a summative reality that defies conscientious direction, frustrates purpose and aim, and insists on taking its own way into the future.[6] What flashes "along the chords" of poetry may *go out*, for all the poet knows, and for the time being; but it also *goes forth*, improvident but evolving, into other hands under changing conditions. By the time *In Memoriam* is over, it too has changed, as Tennyson takes this aesthetic correction firmly on board: "I see in part / That all, as in some piece of art, / Is toil coöperant to an end" (128.22–4). The poet can see the creation, and indeed his own artistic creations, only "in part," because in them the reciprocation of beauty with truth is participated and processive. Pieces of art are collaboratively, and therefore provisionally, constructed by those who will have a share in them. The method of self-governance, as it were, for so collective and ongoing an aesthetic evolution is not that of a command economy: its aesthetic "end" is shaped, but not dictated, by an authorial "aim." And so it is also, in the poem's eco-cosmic finale, with that "far-off divine event, / To which the whole creation moves" (Epilogue, lines 143–4).

With mention of evolution and ecology this chapter remembers its Darwinian occasion, and relapses from verse to a few prose writings from the 1860s. Each of the next passages ponders a dialectic of disengagement with instrumentality that rehearses the crucial difference—which sponsors this entire book—between Darwin's 1859 *Origin of Species* and 1871 *Descent of Man, and Selection in Relation to Sex*. As the full title of the latter gently suggests, Darwin there entertained second thoughts about the resolutely utilitarian machinery he had set going when his 1859 theory harnessed the invincible power of natural selection to promote characteristics that let a species prevail in the struggle for existence. What proved useful in that struggle survived, and only what proved useful. Inutilities found no place to speak of in the *Origin*—traits expressed, for example, in color or movement or song that might prove reproductively attractive and therefore get passed along to offspring who shared those traits or a preference for them when mating. But such traits had caught Darwin's eye all the same, and by 1871 he had given them an important role in driving the variegation on which speciation was based. Such ostentatiously useless traits mattered to the evolving theory of evolution

---

[6] Tennyson seems to have been working toward an appreciation like Richard Prum's for the beauty of the "arbitrary" display trait that, "disconnected from any other, extrinsic measure" of species utility, "communicates no other information than its presence" (Prum 2017: 40).

because they decisively, consequentially mattered to members of mate-choosing species who were led by preference to breed with, and so proliferate, those traits' possessors. Generationally reinforced preferences were the result, Darwin reasoned, of what might as well be called an evolved taste for beauty.

That this taste was useless in any practical sense conducing to survival is a major premise of our teammate Richard Prum's remarkable book, *The Evolution of Beauty* (2017), which forfeits none of its striking impact in our day by the care with which Prum shows his case anticipated in a minority party of evolutionary biologists who trace their lineage back to Darwin in 1871. Here let me simply subjoin that Darwin's revised theory was itself anticipated during the preceding decade, not in the life sciences but in Victorian cultural studies that memorably reformulated some of the ideas we have been tracing in poetry and poetics, about the manifest uselessness, but also the deferred if unpredictable utility, of the practice of literary arts.[7]

In 1864 Matthew Arnold published what justly remains one of his best-known essays, "The Function of Criticism at the Present Time." Replace Arnold's "Function" with "Use," or a cognate of your choice, and you have begun framing his essay's argument as the latest installation within a running nineteenth-century aesthetic vindication of the immediate inutility of letters. Arnold constructed on behalf of his chosen vocation criticism—evaluative reflection, that is, on literature and culture old and new—a case that by this point in my chapter should look pretty familiar. Criticism's eventual use, which is the detection of inferior imagination and thought and the advancement of better, is radically a function of its freedom from functions of any other sort that attach it to party or sect. The first duty of criticism, if it is "to produce fruit for the future," is "steadily refusing to lend itself to any of those ulterior, political, practical considerations" (Arnold 1961: 246) which rule the contemporary field of discourse, be it in the 1860s or at any "present time." "Whoever sets himself to see small things as they are" commits to "a very subtle and indirect action" within the proximate current of events, "abandoning the sphere of practical life" (250). And the critic's motive for renouncing direct influence is not ascetic but the reverse. It is indeed robustly aesthetic, "the free play of the mind upon all subjects being a pleasure in itself, being an object of desire" (245).

Shelley and Keats, Browning and Tennyson, are at this point nodding with approval from the gallery. Yet Arnold sets the stakes of criticism still higher, mounting through desirous "pleasure" all the way to beauty's great correlate "love." With the "disinterested love of a free play of the mind on all subjects, for its own sake" (245), we reach the threshold of Victorian Aestheticism, where

---

[7] This is to lend support to Bennett Zon's quarrel with the neo-utilitarian view, held by Steven Pinker among others, "that the sciences influence the arts more than the arts influence the sciences" (Zon 2017: 2).

original craft and critical participation are vitally one: "to have the sense of creative activity is the great happiness and the great proof of being alive" (258; see also Dewey 1934: 52–4). To liberate this creative-critical sense into uncompromised action, in the essay's final words, "will certainly be the best title to esteem with posterity" (258), that ultimate court of aesthetic appeal. To keep criticism a free and liberal art, Arnold took pains to prescribe its action no further than these brief citations have done, much as years later in "The Study of Poetry" (1880) he would crown his "touchstones" defense of poetry with a circumlocutory evasion of anything that savored of analysis. His portable anthology of fail-safe "specimens" wear self-evident marks of "the high, the very highest quality," about which Arnold will say no more than that those marks "are in the matter and substance of the poetry, and they are in its manner and style" (313). They're just beautiful, that's all. Yet the admiration of beauty for its own sake turns out to illustrate, in a valedictory paragraph that appears to have Darwinism in its purview, not "the world's deliberate and conscious choice," but "the instinct of self-preservation in humanity" (327).

"For its own sake."[8] In this Arnoldian phrase, unbeholden beauty's intrinsic self-justification anticipates the classic formulation it received a few years later in A.C. Swinburne's *William Blake: A Critical Essay* (1868): "art for art's sake."[9] "Handmaid of religion, exponent of duty, servant of fact, pioneer of morality, she cannot in any way become" (Swinburne 2004: 380). Like Browning's queens, Keats's Urn and Melancholy, and Prum's (and Darwin's) mating mother-to-be, Swinburne's personified art operates without interference from forces that would encumber her choices by any ulterior motive or message. And Swinburne's *Critical Essay* reaffirms Arnold's paradox about criticism, to the effect that in forswearing any such utility lies art's only hope of proving useful. Once she betroths herself to morality or science, "she is no longer of any human use or value.... The one fact for her which is worth taking account of is simply mere excellence of verse or colour, which involves all manner of truth and loyalty necessary to her well-being" (381). Even the deferred utility of art's "truth," in this sentence, is a byproduct that Swinburne admits only grudgingly. His reluctance on this score jibes with the exaltation of barrenness in his poetry of the 1860s

---

[8] Find this formula appropriated for biology, contra evolutionary utilitarianism, in Prum (2017: 276) ("pleasure for its own sake") and Safina (2020: 184) ("beautiful for beauty's sake").

[9] *L'art pour l'art*, which became a rallying cry in Britain for Pre-Raphaelite and Aesthete vanguards during the later nineteenth century, claimed international adherents as well from France (Théophile Gautier, Charles Baudelaire) and America (Edgar Allan Poe, J.A.M. Whistler). While the slogan has provoked detraction left and right ever since it first arose, halfway between that time and ours it is noteworthy to find aesthetic autotelism defended by theorists as diverse as the Aquinian Catholic Jacques Maritain—"art, as such, is *gratuitous* or disinterested" ("An Essay on Art," 1930, Maritain 1946: 98)—and the Darwinian pragmatist John Dewey, who repudiates the slogan yet roundly defends, among "experiences enjoyable in themselves," and against "that which is merely a utility," art's creative autonomy: "The work of esthetic art satisfies many ends, none of which is laid down in advance" (Dewey 1934: 3, 6, 135).

and after: "Hermaphroditus" (1866), for example, stresses the Louvre statue's sheer beauty by dwelling on "the waste wedlock of a sterile kiss" (line 19) and its "fruitless flowers" (line 38). In this as in much else Swinburne steers to extremity tendencies that were abroad in Victorian culture. John Ruskin moralized art insistently, but preferred by 1879 the beauty of the flower to its manifest destiny of procreation: "The flower exists for its own sake, – not for the fruit's sake. . . . The flower is the end of the seed, – not the seed of the flower" (*Proserpina*, in Ruskin 1903–12, vol. 25: 249–50; see also Levine 2008: 92; Prum 2017: 147; Safina 2020: 203). Likewise, Walter Pater, drafting in 1868 what would become five years later his "Conclusion" to *The Renaissance*, composed a polemic that told against conclusiveness itself: "Not the fruit of experience, but experience itself, is the end" (Pater 1986: 152).

When the "end" is thus resolved back into its means it remains consequential but relinquishes its ostensible purpose. Purpose inheres rather, and inscrutably, in the means: the traits of sexual selection or objects of aesthetic devotion to Keats's "beauty" and "truth," Arnold's "manner" and "matter," Swinburne's "verse or colour... which involves all manner of truth and loyalty." "Beauty happens" (Prum 2017: 72); and staying true to where and when and how it happens is all you know on earth, and all you need to know. By the later nineteenth century it was possible for, and maybe incumbent on, a writer as deeply convinced of the world's abiding providential design as was Gerard Manley Hopkins to attend scrupulously to the happenings of beauty wherever he found them. Hopkins accepted beauty as a trust, and he made the duty of its stewardship a choral burden in "The Leaden Echo and the Golden Echo" (1880), where a chorus of keening maidens having leadenly asked how "to keep / Back beauty, keep it, beauty, beauty, beauty, . . . from vanishing away?" (lines 1–2) find their golden answer in a kind of recantation: "Give beauty back, beauty, beauty, beauty, back to God beauty's self and beauty's giver" (line 19). Beauty's best defense is also its divinely given purpose, which is to be recycled.[10]

Hopkins returned to this question in an 1885 sonnet asking "To What Serves Mortal Beauty?" "See, it does this: keeps warm / Men's wit to the things that are; / to what good means – where a glance / Master more may than gaze" (lines 3–5). Beauty rewards attention to the things of this world, with an eye to beauty's truth (it's what good means) that appreciates the excellence of such truth's mediating features (why, what good means!). Under the mortal shadow of life's transience the experience of beauty must be transient as well, which is why glancing beats gazing—advice to which the poet returns at the close: "What do then? how meet

---

[10] Compare the "sacramental" semiotic that Hopkins's fellow Catholic poet David Jones attributes to "poetry," or beauty, as an addictively "extra-utile" activity of humankind. "These activities are done for a sign. They are significant of something other" (Jones 1978: 178)—to which we may add that the distance between signifier and signified, like that between phenomena and interpretation, entails in transit a temporal deferral.

beauty? / Merely meet it; own, / Home at heart, heaven's sweet gift; / then leave, let that alone" (lines 12–13). Because getting beauty right is not passive spectatorship but a difficult act we perform or "do," it is a deed that like all acts in time has its term. Knowing when to quit is a gift, in Hopkins's variety of aesthetic experience, an essential piece of equipment for the mission of recycling. A timely turning aside from this or that beauty inducts the participant seer into the sonnet's last condition, "God's better beauty, grace" (line 14), which technically theological term finds an apt secular correlate in the Arnoldian free and active play of the observing mind for its own sake.

The aesthete's watchword "sake" is a favorite word with Hopkins too, which pertains to the "Self" that "flashes off face and frame" (line 11) and off the musical signature that marks a "Purcell tune" (line 3) in this sonnet, as it does in an earlier sonnet on the same composer urging "an eye to the sakes of him" as to the identifying plumage spread by "some great stormfowl" for an instant's glimpsing ("Henry Purcell," lines 10–11). The sake of a thing discloses to outward perception the instress or inherence of its mortal beauty, "that in the thing by virtue of which especially it has this being abroad, and that is something distinctive, marked" (Hopkins 2002: 237; see also 259). And its virtue is essential to Hopkins's verbal artistry: "Poetry is speech framed for contemplation of the mind by way of hearing or speech framed to be heard for its own sake and interest even over and above its interest of meaning.... Poetry is in fact speech only employed to carry the inscape of speech for the inscape's sake" (Hopkins 1959: 289).

Beauty is sexy for Keats and Browning, among many others; for Hopkins it is phenomenally sakesy. The peculiar sakes of miscellaneous things in the created world, and of cherished words in the intricate microcosm that is a poem, inform alike the substance and style of Hopkins's best known digest of beauty tips:

> Glory be to God for dappled things –
>   For skies of couple-colour as a brinded cow;
>   For rose-moles all in stipple upon trout that swim;
> Fresh-firecoal chestnut-falls; finches' wings;
>   Landscape plotted and pieced – fold, fallow, and plough;
>   And áll trades, their gear and tackle and trim.
> All things counter, original, spáre, strange;
>   Whatever is fickle, frecklèd (who knows how?)
>   With swíft, slów; sweet, sóur; adázzle, dím;
> He fathers-forth whose beauty is pást change:
>   Práise hím.

An encomium for outliers, a paean to uniqueness, "Pied Beauty" (1877) spares no effort in distancing itself from conventions of poetic form to which it nevertheless idiosyncratically adheres. Structurally it is what Hopkins called a "curtal" sonnet, cropped back from the standard dimension of fourteen lines split into octave and sestet, yet maintaining the standard 8/6 ratio exactly as 6/4.5, sestet plus quatrain plus final hemistich (Preface: 109). Its pentameter prosody features this poet's signature sprung rhythm, in relatively low dosage: some lines (1, 8, 10) effectively iambic, the rest demanding five stresses per line amid a scatter of slack syllables, in a pattern orchestrated by the occasionally meddlesome superscript accents his manuscript imposed; and no two lines quite alike. Each line carries a single image unless, like line 4, it doesn't. The reader is thrown off balance, kept at attention by not knowing just what is coming next.

This do-it-yourself diversity-under-rule matters especially in a poem whose theme is on the one hand the multifarious plenitude of creation but on the other a family resemblance that binds the multifarious into a living whole. The binding work of alliteration in every full line will speak for itself. More nuanced, and telling, is an interior design of double consonants that as it were rhyme on the liquid "l": "dappled," "couple," "stipple," then "tackle," "fickle," "freckled," then "adázzle," are only the mid-word nodes in a line-crossing, poem-long pattern of phonemic reprise that stitches together musically items whose common thread is that each of them is unlike anything else, irreducible to uniformity. At a higher order of magnitude "Pied Beauty" differs from itself in syntax: lines 1–6 present a paratactic shuffle of images loosely dependent on the initial subjunctive exhortation "Glory be to God for . . . ," which lines 7–9 apparently go on to extend until line 10 reveals their inverted grammatical subordination as objects of a declarative subject and verb—"He fathers-forth"—and the declarative Subject of subjects at that, emerged into dominance from the recessive position of the dative in line 1 ("to God"). As nearly always happens with Hopkins, the second part of the sonnet converts to interpretive understanding the array of evidence celebrated during the first, theorizing details into generalization before capping the supervenient order with, in this case, an express order: the imperative spondee "Práise hím." (See Ryan 2018: 46–7 on the animally evolved functions of habituation and generalization.) Beauty precipitates truth that entails consequences. Still, the poet does all he can to keep his quatrain's generalizing empirically honest, holding it to the test of variegation experienced as such, by a series of heterogeneous adjectives in lines 7–8 that are anything but synonyms, and the aesthetic compounding of sensory contrasts in line 9, which is for good measure the most rhythmically sprung of them all.

"Pied Beauty" so meets its constituent mortal beauties, and with such a cherishing glance at their motley sakes, that it may at last wax a little jealous in their defense. The poet's theology, after all, is metaphysical; it postulates a realm of immortal beauty, which at least nominally threatens to translate whatever is "counter" or "fickle" into a permanence that dissolves the very changefulness—internal variegation, temporal transiency—for which it is prized to begin with. The "beauty" named in the title and that of a God "whose beauty is past change" seem incompatible. It might be wisest to read this incompatibility the way students of Hopkins have tended to read it, as a conceptual shimmer imparting to the poet and his poem an enveloping tension that replicates with interest the oxymoronic or paradoxical energy of line 9, which we might rewrite: With aesthétic, órthodox; autotélic, symbólical; extraórdinary, ordáined. But the argument that has been developed in this chapter encourages a sakesier reading, one aligning the doctrine in question with something that this poem otherwise moots, but that the tradition we have sampled tells us to look for: beauty's faith in its own reception by posterity. What if "pást change" were to refer, as Darwin referred a phenotype like "finches' wings," to a history of selections? To dappled differentiation as the outward and visible sign of a venerable process of incessant deferment? What if the truth of the beauty past change were the running subtotal and balance forward of *past changes*, the innumerable accumulation of infinitesimal alterations that have fathered and brought forth whatever today is banked and tangled, who knows how? What if God's creative beauty, whose charged grandeur will flame out in a million times and places, were itself the subtle deposit of "pást change," and by that token were the promise of changes to come in a diversifying future of aesthetic reception, continuous with the present but gloriously indiscernible now?[11]

The unwrapping of a single, laden phrase resumes in little the ramified hermeneutic process that forms part of my larger topic: the inheritance, discovery, and repurposing that impel literary history. Finding fresh application for cultural resources over a century old, I have sought timely truths in what poets have said about beauty, chiefly by attending to the beautiful (and for that reason durable) ways they have said it. To promote aesthetic utility over ideological utility in art has been my object all along. If I haven't proven in general terms that art's uselessness has its uses, that is because mine is a proposition that must be proven, as Keats said, "upon our pulses," and proven in particular cases, or not at all (Keats 2002: 88).

The same holds true for an adjacent thesis in literary history: that even our most candidly ideological interventions will fare better—will disclose more, and do it more cogently—by attending to aesthetic practice than by conscripting art to serve a practical agenda. Let "Pied Beauty" serve once more as illustration. Other readers of Hopkins's curtal sonnet have remarked how its adjectival kaleidoscope all but brings into focus an adjective that it doesn't use, but that his biography conspires with recent developments in literary studies to let us posit as a ground for the poem's entire procedure: *queer* (Saville 2000: 120–5, Hall 2007: 29–30).

---

[11] Morgan 116–17 finds Hopkins's teacher Pater and contemporary Grant Allen attuned to an aesthetic sort of telepathic time-travel. For the latter, "the experience of art makes present the past of the species"; for the former, channeling Winckelmann's veneration of classical statuary a hundred years before, aesthetic experience "offers immediate and semipassive access to a past that can be literally touched."

Pied beauty is the beauty of what's queer, and the poet's sidelong manner of perceiving beauty has much to do with his ambivalent erotic orientation toward, as "To What Serves Mortal Beauty?" declares, "lovely lads," the "World's loveliest – men's selves" (lines 6, 11). The love Hopkins thus trained askance on homosexual desire expands in "Pied Beauty" to embrace heterogeneity as such, within a queered dispensation that deems whatever is "spare, strange" not just curious but beautiful. Better: each exhibit in the poem invites the kind of curiosity that beauty invites, which, prizing categories open, coaxes their contents forth in a lucky catch (Saville 2000: 91). To be dappled, freckled, et cetera, is to be radically irregular, patterned yet nonaligned, irreducible to our default binaries of symmetry and hierarchy. In a later sonnet Hopkins even coined a verb, "Betweenpie," to denote the intermediating way beauty teases out of internal difference something essentially accidental ("My Own Heart Let Me More Have Pity On," line 14). Betweenpied beauty is, as queer studies are teaching us to say nowadays, nonbinary. So indeed is all beauty, when you get close enough to notice. To understand the idiosyncrasy of the beautiful in that granular, nonbinary way is one gift that the contemporary queering of literary studies can bestow on aesthetics: a discipline that, if it knows what it's good for—not to mention what's good for it—will look afresh at beauty in order to renew its truth.

PART 3
AESTHETICS AND POLITICS

5
What We Do
The New This and the New That

Isobel Armstrong

As I was writing this chapter, images of a mob assaulting the Capitol, and Trump's treasonable incitements to sedition, were beamed across the world. The language of Fascism asserted itself. On the same day Covid-19 deaths in the United Kingdom totaled over one thousand in the last twenty-four hours, a record and a cause for mourning. Things fall apart. Not a good time to embark on a discussion of our discipline, one would think. Nevertheless, there is every reason for doing so. Far from being a parochial concern, this is the moment to ask some questions about what we do.

To begin, here are two experiences, both, as it happens, enabled by technology. The first, videos of Roberto Benigni, the Oscar winning star of "Life Is Beautiful," reading Dante to crowded piazzas and squares in Italy, and as far afield as San Francisco. You will find dozens of these on YouTube. The second is a remote encounter. A technician trying to put my email to rights had to send me a test email. At the second attempt what came back were five lines from Pink Floyd's "Echoes" beginning with "Cloudless every day you fall upon my waking eyes." "Pink Floyd," he wrote, "a passion of mine." Here was a man who loved words.

Both the Dante readings and Pink Floyd fan demonstrate an aesthetic need and a passion for words. Do this aesthetic need and the need for words have any relation to our highly professionalized and self-conscious study of texts? Should it? Does it matter if it doesn't? Are there threads of connection between the crowds standing in piazzas, the man typing a pop song, and what we do? Or maybe we should put it the other way round: Tolstoy wrote a famous essay in his reforming phase, "Should we teach the peasant children to write, or should they teach us?" It was a serious question. Maybe the Dante listeners and Pink Floyd fan could teach *us* something about words and aesthetic need, not we them.

To think about this question, I began to look at the claims and theories that have recently circulated in our discipline, the proliferating theses, models, and systems. This is to enter a contested field. What looks at first sight as an avid competition for cultural capital, is more likely an attempt to gain a foothold in the marketized technocracy of today's neoliberal university, an attempt to create a safe, defended intellectual space. Derek Attridge, in his Introduction to *The Work of Reading* (p. 4), has recently characterized the dominant mode of our "insular" research as science-based and "empirico-historical," a response to the decline in numbers enrolling for literary courses and to the privileging of "monetary reward and utilitarian training."

One is spoilt for choice. There is surface reading, there is distant reading, there is postcritical reading, there are two incarnations of formalism—new formalism and what, for want of a term, I will call newer formalism. There is historical poetics, digital humanities, history of the emotions, affect theory, new materialism. There is the costive manifesto of V21. As Georgina Born has noted, we don't talk much about beauty. As I looked, the forms of reading I began by thinking of as disparate seemed strangely uniform. With one exception, politics was eschewed: less noticeably, there was a quiet extirpation of the aesthetic. The exclusion of politics and aesthetics seemed to move in tandem. This chapter explores how an absence of voices in our discipline that might counter the new Fascism (to add another "new") and the lack of interest in aesthetic questions come to be linked.

1. Depthless Reading

I can only take an exemplary critical text from some of these proposals for reading. Each deserves much fuller discussion. My accounts are not definitive, but shaped by the question above—the threads of connection between listeners and readers outside the academy and our practices inside it. Chosen because it was one of the earliest proposals for a new kind of reading, my first text was published a year after the global financial crisis of 2008, Stephen Best and Sharon Marcus's "Surface Reading: An Introduction" (2009).

Best and Marcus want to replace the hermeneutics of suspicion with a new, cool, critical praxis, a hermeneutics of skepticism, perhaps, for the twenty-first century. They see the critic as anatomist or taxonomist, their primary model of the text as "a constellation of multiple surfaces concealing nothing," an entity with "length and breadth but no thickness" (p. 9), a depthless network, a Mobius strip. At other times they offer another paradigm of reading as immersion, to which I will return. But keep the first in mind, for it is invoked to rid criticism of their adversary throughout the essay—the Fredric Jameson of *The Political Unconscious* (1981)—and in addition to junk the old knowledges of the twentieth century, the thinking of Marx and Freud, conveniently elided in Jameson's work. Their hostility is directed to "symptomatic reading," the reading that elicits latent meaning in the text's beyond, "hidden, repressed, deep meaning," "veiled," "latent" meaning read through the gaps and absences that reveal a "deep history" unavailable to the text's surface but which shapes it (p. 2), a mystified presence organized by questions the text itself does not pose (p. 5). They repudiate—one of the most valuable parts of this essay—"an adversarial relation to the object of criticism" (p. 16), what I think of as accusatory criticism, where the hubristic critic's power is wielded over the text, a master–slave relation, displacing it. Jameson is accused of a twofold aberration: his capacity for mystification, in which the epiphenomena of the surface merely serve to block the "real" meaning of the text, and a framing of this unmasking as a heroic act—the critic as hero—abrogating to himself the power that belongs to the text.

As the essay goes on, Jameson becomes a sort of sorcerer or magus, arch-mystifier, calling spirits from the vasty deep. His aberrations cannot be left alone. Twice his thinking is characterized through theological analogies. His affinity with the ancient gnostic tradition, in which truth is "not immediately apprehensible" has connections to "what [Umberto] Eco calls the hermetic theory of interpretation, the idea that words 'hide the untold'" (p. 4). The power of the critic is assimilated to "the God of biblical hermeneutics, who can transcend the blinkered point of view of humankind," and the Augustinian tradition that "viewed God as the best author," where Jameson usurps the position of God (p. 15). Throughout the essay the authors repeatedly draw attention to the fallacy of "the latent meaning behind a manifest one" (p. 3), "the depth model of truth" (p. 10), and to its surface-depth structure: "deep truth too abstract to be visible" (p. 11), "latent voices and hidden transcripts" (p. 12), "relations that are secret, hidden" (p. 13, quoting Foucault), "wresting hidden truths from hidden depths" (p. 13), "wrestling to free the hidden truth" (p. 15), "hidden depths" (p. 18). *What* truths Jameson wrests from the depths do not seem to need to be defined. They belong to the unsaid. It is depth itself that is toxic. The violence of capitalism and its structuring of bourgeois experience understood as a given by Jameson is something the authors seem not to be able to make available to themselves or us as one of Jameson's themes. For them another kind of politics should operate, a politics of freedom, attention to the artwork's freedom (p. 16). Left to itself the artwork, containing its own hermeneutic, will itself enact a politics where freedom is in play with capitalism, and the "left-leaning literary critic" (p. 8) need not add theory to the text because it is already there. (But ideas still have to be elicited: the authors instance Christopher Nealon's exciting essay, "Reading on the Left," as an example of conflict generated in and through the text itself, but Nealon presupposes the work of the critic is active.) Let alone, like a driverless car, the text will do much of the work of criticism. This deference to the text as hero is followed through in a respect, a respect that consorts well with the neoliberal university, for the technological turn of criticism—databases and machine intelligence: "Computers are weak interpreters but potent describers, anatomizers, taxonomists. New media create new forms of knowledge" that can bypass "evaluative energy" and lead to "objectivity, validity, truth" (p. 17). Of course, computers can create new forms of knowledge, but, a truism, they don't have agency: any taxonomy they create is only as good as the organization of its data. Here the authors are on the same trajectory as Jesting Pilate.

The authors do worry that their refusal of depths and the need for "minimal critical agency" (p. 17) may look "politically quietist" (p. 16). Their premise is that "literary criticism *alone* [emphasis added] is not sufficient to effect change" (p. 2). But did anyone ever claim that *alone* it does? Or ever at all? The effect of this refusal of politics is to block any ongoing political enquiry into our subject, such as the recent and profoundly important essay on the systematic occlusion of race in Victorian studies, "Undisciplining Victorian Studies," by Ronjaunee Chatterjee, Alicia Mireles Christoff, and Amy R. Wong. Best and Marcus's serious ethical commitment to the superficial, however, means that they assemble an interesting range of diverse surfaces for critical praxis that appear to resist depth, and co-opt a number of figures. The taxonomy of depthlessness embraces the materialism of cognitive reading supported by neuroscience (Elaine Scarry), the verbal complexity of literary language (I.A. Richards), affective, unmediated experience (Susan Sontag), descriptive accounts of the self-mediating text (Paul de Man), patterns across texts (Clifford Siskin), surface as self-evident, literal meaning (Marcus herself). What we might call these "flat" critiques are finally subsumed in the procedures of new formalism and its "autonomy from ideology" (p. 14), where Marjorie Levinson is invoked through her analysis of the artwork's resistance to the "routinizing instrumentality of capitalist regimes" (p. 14). Is this their alternative reading of capitalism in opposition to Jameson? These regimes are "flattening," a slightly confusing epithet here, because it puts the procedures of surface reading itself in doubt. Notwithstanding this slip, it is here that a genuinely rich and uninhibited understanding of the experience of the artwork as "immersion" emerges as a release from the desensitized experiences of capitalism into a rich commitment to the immediacy of the text, to an unashamed saturation in its sensuous being for its own sake. It is an experience that might have been called "jouissance" in earlier days, and the authors spell out this commitment with a zeal and energy that cannot fail to be resonant.

Yet the figure of "immersion" surely reintroduces the very depth that the metaphor of surface tries so hard to avoid: it is difficult to imagine "immersion" in a fluid element without imagining depth. Liquidity without depth, if you "bathe in the artwork's disinterested purposelessness" (p. 14), is unlikely. (A confused reader, attempting to retain the metaphor of surface, attempting, indeed, to avoid invoking the return of the repressed from a repudiated Freudianism, might try to imagine depthless immersion as the alternative of taking a shower in Kantian idealism.) The provocative metaphor of surface gets into trouble here, but what one takes away from this essay is a wonderful freedom of immersion in the art object that looks hopeful. Nevertheless, though the extirpation of politics is clearly signaled in this essay, it is quieter about its extirpation of the aesthetic: what it looks to is "disinterested purposelessness," a kind of sterilized Kantianism. I wonder what this means in practice. I think of the piazza crowds, the song that invites and incites.

This is in many ways a prophetic essay, and seems increasingly significant now, presaging a turn to depthlessness shared across many types of reading that at first glance look different. It anticipates the much more prolix, *The Limits of Critique* (Rita Felski, 2015), where Bruno Latour's Actor Network Theory (ANT) is another model of depthlessness, and is the single alternative critical procedure in comparison with Best and Marcus's multiplicity of examples. The virtues of ANT are "the act and fact of association, the coming together of phenomena to create assemblages, affinities, and networks...in the sometimes foreseeable, sometimes unpredictable ways in which ideas, texts, images, people, and objects couple and uncouple, attach and break apart" (p. 157). This randomness matches the "messy" realities of reading (p. 153), though it's puzzling what kind of criticism randomness might create. And if we are messy readers does that have to make us messy critics?

Contemporary with this work is another manifesto, that of "V21 Collective, Manifesto of the V21 Collective" (2015), a collective and protest movement whose agenda to some extent matches that of surface reading in its espousal of form and formalism. The frustrations of a group who feel their work is not recognized are palpable in today's contracting academic world. The collective's aggressive stance throws out some demanding ideas (though its cryptic title incorporating the V grapheme seems to retain the ideological historicization of the Victorians from which the collective wishes to escape—try 19thC? And this unfortunate abbreviation evokes that other healthy brand name, V8). Form and formalism and the politics of form (Thesis 7) allied with "*presentism*" (Thesis 8) that maps today's Victorian legacy of "empire, war and ecological destruction," from now backwards, is a way out of a crippling "positivist historicism" (Thesis 1). Though history in digital form appears to be acceptably unfetishized if "in the service of abstraction" (Thesis 6). Ideas, "synthetic thinking" (Thesis 9), are desirable, not "factism." What's not to like about a good deal of this? But what would an abstract, formalist, presentist history look like—surface history, perhaps, when history begins yesterday? Legacy history seems pre-given, as expressed here, mapped onto a passive text, where the possibility that texts themselves make history, and that history itself is conflictual, gets lost. The collective stirs things up, asks questions, makes people uneasy, which is all to the good. But when it speaks of its intention to "break historicism" (Thesis 3) it sounds like a group of vigilantes asking for a purge. This manifesto looks like the exception to the rule in its espousal of politics, but it isn't really. Only the politics it wants will do. V indeed. As with Best and Marcus, there is a significant silence about the category of the aesthetic.

Form is the theme of Jonathan Kramnick and Anahid Nersessian's 2017 "Form and Explanation." This article created significant controversy. Kramnick is a formidably brilliant and well-informed metacritical analyst who can take out flawed ideas with unsparing precision, as his 2011 "Against Literary

Darwinism," for instance, makes clear. It is less form itself, in spite of the "unruliness" of its application, however, that preoccupies Kramnick and Nersessian here, than the importance of establishing "explanation" as the central function of our discipline—"What does form explain?" They take off from the finale of Franco Moretti's *Graphs, Maps, Trees* (2005) where he expresses a preference for "explanation over interpretation" (p. 91) (though they have some reservations about his thinking). Explanation offers a serious account of our discipline as knowledge. They hasten to say that the centrality of explanation does not mean assimilating scientific accounts of form to literature with a spurious empirical gravity. The real project should be to understand what different accounts of form mean for different disciplines and what kind of explanation form can provide for each of them, even when formal explanations, as often in literary criticism, quoting Zenon Pylyshyn, may redefine "its explananda" ("Form and Explanation," p. 651). This reading of explanation and form enables the authors to speak confidently across disciplines, without subordinating critical discourse to them, in a productive and exemplary way. The second section of their essay, "Some Versions of Explanation," arguing for a pluralistic reading of form, is virtuosic. Thus they are in conversation with Elizabeth Anscombe on concepts (to argue that the epistemic understanding of form is embedded in usage), Ned Block on consciousness (the hybrid definitions of a single term), John Dupré on the scientific fallacies of unifying explanation (the need for promiscuous or pluralistic realism), Carl Hempel and Bas van Fraassen, the latter on explanation as "descriptive information" (p. 667).

The authors' "simple premise" is the founding of "literary disciplinarity" on the assumption that "form and explanation work together," a project pursued "without apology or compromise" (p. 652). (But why the need for apology at all?) Form is an explanation but it is also necessary to explain form and accordingly their first section is "Some Versions of Form" (p. 652). As in the earlier context of surface reading, "form" is predicated on a repudiation of "the deep dark below" (quoting Bruno Latour (p. 653), a popular figure) and on a rejection of what is regarded as an unacceptable authoritarian and totalizing politics, where Best and Marcus's surface reading is invoked, reinforced by Rita Felski's *The Limits of Critique*. Once again, Jameson gets a drubbing, assimilated to the "paranoid" structure of critique modeled by Eve Kosovsky Sedgwick in her distinction between paranoid and reparatory criticism. (The respondents in a subsequent issue of *Critical Inquiry* are in agreement, commenting that "theory" is "unfashionable" (Tom Eyers, p. 137), and Marjorie Levinson cites Steven Knapp and Walter Benn Michaels' "Against Theory" in support of Kramnick and Nersessian (p. 154)).[1]

---

[1] The replies to Kramnick and Nersessian deserve much more attention than I can give them. To summarize: Tom Eyers (pp. 136–43) focuses on what for him is a "new descriptivism" of the

It is actually with the second phase of formalism that the authors are concerned, rather than its earlier manifestation, one that Levinson examined so thoroughly in her classic article, "What is New Formalism?" (2007), describing it as a movement rather than a theory. The exhilaration of this early movement, which we might characterize, for instance, in Susan J. Wolfson's *Formal Charges: The Shaping of Poetry in British Romanticism* (1999), is not in their sights. They make a distinction between revisionist and reductive readings of form: the first rests on the ethical fidelity of an art of describing, from which the observer's persona is as far as possible dredged, so that the ontology of a thing emerges in all the lucidity of its objecthood. Heather Love is its practitioner (p. 654). The reductive reader is represented by Sandra Macpherson, and glossed by *The Stanford Encyclopaedia of Philosophy*'s account of reduction as an entity x reduced to y, meaning that y is prior to and constitutes x (p. 655). The authors seem happy with Macpherson's reductionist view that form is "the shape matter[y] (whether a poem or a tree [x]) takes" (p. 655), nothing more or less. Thus marble shapes sculpture, letters, poems (p. 657), free from history. They miss that the "y" of the poem's "x" is not letters but words: words are an order of materia quite different from marble and words always have a history because language is humanly made. A poem is surely more, not less, than its letters.

They are less happy with, indeed, are savage about, the "flat ontology" of another account of form classified as reductionist, Caroline Levine's striking and influential *Forms: Whole, Rhythm, Network* (2015). Yet the project of *Forms* seems to be wholly commensurate with that of surface readers and indeed with that of Kramnick and Nersessian themselves. She is an anti-Jamesonian (p. 135). The repudiation of depth allies her with the "newer" formalist formation: she states at the outset of her book that it is the form of the content, not the "buried content" of the form that concerns her (p. 16). "Deep structures" give way to the multiple, plural play of forms with and against one another. She rejects a metaphysical for a contingent model of non-dialectic collision that organizes social experience, as her bravura account of *The Wire* indicates. All form is political as our lives are

---

"self-evident." Implicitly his phrase "liberal ecumenicism" questions the pluralism of Kramnick and Nersessian. Marjorie Levinson in an eloquent response (pp. 144–55) that restates her earlier understanding that the first phase of new formalism has no theoretical core, is particularly interesting on Carl Hempel and Baas van Fraassen: Hempel asks for a formal theory of explanatoriness as a guide to judgments, whereas van Fraassen believes there can be no explanations in science as the relation between the theory and the thing you are trying to explain is arbitrary. On Moretti she differs from Kramnick and Nersessian in the relationship of interpretation to explanation and the priority of explanation: Moretti arrives at new taxonomies via statistical data, and these taxonomies change the way we work, change how we interpret the field, so there is a dynamic relation between explanation and interpretation. Moretti sees form as force, a social force, and retains a materialist conception of form. Heather Love (pp. 156–63), in addition to questioning "literariness" and the "cheerful pragmatism" of Kramnick and Nersessian, spends time on de Man and the resistance to reading (inflected as negative capability) in order to limit the production of multiple ways of reading. (All articles are listed in the Works Cited, and can be found in *Critical Inquiry* 44 (Autumn 2017).)

organized by structures and conduits of power, whether the educational system, the legal system, or information flows. So form has agency—form is fate. Form, like matter, is constitutive and thus, in a productive tautology, there is no other of form. Kramnick and Nersessian's attack is on "the conceiving of form as anything that exists" (p. 658). But Levine's sin is also to be political. As I understand it (I précis their nearly two and a half pages of forensic analysis) form and politics constitute one another for Levine, and by the sleight of hand that makes form anything that exists, so history comes into being because the existence of things carries with it de facto a historical life. So form and history, form and politics are elided and a circular relation between form, politics, and history is established. Everything becomes elective when there is only a choice between forms. The authors don't look at any of this work as it plays out in practice: and yet Levine's is a revealing form of analysis—see the multiplicity of interacting forms in *The Wire*, or, on a smaller scale, the exemplary and beautifully differentiated reading of "colliding" meters in Elizabeth Barrett Browning's "The Young Queen" (pp. 74–81). They return to the attack in their "A Reply to Our Critics," reiterating their argument and parrying Levine's understandably angry response. (Mindful of the intellectual severity of Kramnick's reputation, other contributors are laboriously courteous in their replies: Love is deemed "convivial" for this (p. 173), with the implication that Levine is not.) I have not space to discuss the minutiae of this further discussion, though was it quite fair to equate Levine's belief in the political force of art with the University of Leicester's crudely instrumental value-for-money reading of arts research (p. 170)? (An oddly British eruption in an otherwise American context.)[2] Levine accuses them of being "bloodless" (p. 130), but there is certainly some blood-letting going on in their reply. What is notable, though, about their response to her response is what they do not mention—the model of "collision." This takes agency away from human actants and confers it on forms, and must worry an interlocutor. Kramnick and Nersessian don't pick up on this political issue: they tend to occlude political questions altogether because they are explicitly uneasy about political readings. "Now is the time to commit to our field's intellectual rationale" (p. 166), form as explanation being one of its concerns. Their pluralism and form's meanings in this rationale "are not waiting to be pre-approved by our politics," and these are not "waiting to be greenlit by our study of aesthetic objects" (p. 166). Of course not. But sometimes the object of criticism asks for *a* politics, sometimes not. And there are moments in the history of our subject when politics needs urgently to be heard, such as today's concern with race. Levine's move to political analysis elicits an excess of ferocity.

---

[2] Having said this, Kramnick and Nersessian are prescient: the University of Leicester has just sacked all the medievalists in its English Department (January 2021).

Kramnick and Nersessian quote Roman Jacobson: "the object of literary science is not literature [or politics] but 'literariness'" (p. 666), and "literariness" is the "special quarry of criticism" (p. 667). In their reply, responding to Love's pressure on the concept of literariness, they reiterate: "Unlike literature, *literariness*, as both substance and quality, declines to repose on canons and traditions and thus keeps the borders of the discipline open." It comprehends the variety of texts and methods that "fall within the everyday practice of literary studies" (p. 173).

Love queries this term tentatively. Less tentatively, but I hope not unconvivially, I ask, what *is* this term? This mysterious higher order category which subsumes everything that falls within the purview, the everyday practice, of literary studies as both substance and quality? An aura? An emanation? We know we are practicing literary studies when we come within, indeed seek, this mystical zone: "... it's a fire, smoke ... no, it's not ... / It's vapour." This seems to be a lapse in an impressive essay that both delimits explanation and form and expands into pluralism, the multiple "explanations bound to questions" with which the first essay ends (p. 669).

What does literariness explain and how do you explain literariness? The different sections of Kramnick and Nersessian's essay—"Some versions of ...," seem to deliberately recall William Empson and his *Some Versions of Pastoral* (1935). But for Empson the "literariness" pastoral implies both reveals and conceals political complexity: if one extends an implied literariness to *Seven Types of Ambiguity* (1930, revised 1947, 1953) and *The Structure of Complex Words* (1951), what one comes up with is a fascination for the way cognitive and aesthetic experience both impede and galvanize one another in the study of language. Nearly a hundred years ago, Empson's literariness was founded on the excitement of words and a recognition of the interaction of aesthetic and cognitive experience.

There *is* a form of history that is acceptable to the regime of surface reading and the "newer" formalism, and that is historical poetics, partly because its history can be assimilated to the paradigms of form. And perhaps it comes nearest to Empson's excitement with words. Yopie Prins's subtle and magisterial "What is Historical Poetics?" (2016), is a classic master-class in historical poetics. Prins opens her essay by differentiating her historical reading of texts through "recognition" rather than through the "cognition" espoused by Simon Jarvis (who wants verse to think through meter), and describes as inseparable what he saw as two distinct ways of reading: "I believe that we cannot separate the practice of reading a poem from the histories and theories of reading that mediate our ideas about poetry. I am committed to a historical poetics that works recursively as a loop, reading simultaneously from inside out and from outside in" (p. 14)—the credo of historical poetics. A poem is the diachronic history of its readings, including misprisions and occlusions, framed by the larger history of prosody. Prins contrasts these "multiple mediations" of voice with I.A. Richard's synchronic, neurone-dominated reading of Browning's "Pan and Luna" (p. 20), concerned as Browning's poem is with transmission, as the myth of Syrinx is mediated through Virgil and through his own wife's poem, "A Musical Instrument" (1860). She demonstrates how, in its turn, "A Musical Instrument" is a mediated text, working with Ovid, Leighton's illustration of the poem, gender politics, theories of meter and of reading, right up to the recent past in Ted Hughes's literal (through sound recording) reading of the poem. Book illustration, early feminism, sound technology, are the multiple cultural contexts for this poem, but the grounding discourse is the history of prosody. Sidney Lanier's *The Science of English Verse* (1880) is the first text to be introduced in her essay.

Even so, Prins's explanatory paradigm here, in Kramnick's terms, would not be metrical form so much as mediation. Though looking at most of the contributions to the issue of *Modern Language Quarterly* (2016) in which Prins's paper appears, the starting point is the empirical ligature of prosody (Andrea Brady, Caroline Levine, Simon Jarvis). And the historical poetics movement has taken off with exuberant archival projects such as the Princeton Prosody Archive initiated by Meredith Martin. So historical poetics is not discontinuous with that transverse rather than vertical orientation—the injunction to read across not deep—of the subject which we have seen effected in other accounts of reading. This is the nearest account of our discipline to what is now usually described as the "old fashioned" ideal of close reading, because it looks meticulously at metrical detail and specifics, mediates language through the schemata of form. My query would be, is historical poetics founded on prosody? If not, what are its parameters? David Nowell Smith's *On Voice in Poetry* (2015) has started a conversation about this: he wants to add to the category of the prosodic the *chronemic*, "higher order contours, phrasing, cadences" (p. 11) and has an interesting argument with Prins on the status of meter as mechanism (pp. 140–1).

Before I move on to the second section of this chapter, I notice a glorious exception to determinedly transverse and depthless readings of form. This is S. Pearl Brilmyer and Filippo Trentin's "Toward an Inessential Theory of Form: Ruskin, Warburg, Foccillon" (2019) which is as much a theory of affect as form. Their form is not "an unchanging shape or pattern to which a thing can be reduced" (p. 484), or that which is essential to an object, and they embark on a reading of their three figures where inessential form can become a "somatic record" (p. 480). Here they return to the long association of the aesthetic with the body, reading Ruskin and Warburg through the somatic record, and Warburg in particular through his pursuit of "pathosformel," a unique welding of decorative form and affect. Forms for them point to nothing other than themselves, "untranslatable and intransitive" (p. 495). Though I wonder if the rhythms of the body discovered in a kind of bio-ornamentation don't belie this claim.

What this discussion does, though, is to bring to the surface the other problem (the first is politics) lurking throughout the discussions I have examined, the unsaid—the aesthetic. Is it part of our remit to be troubled by this question? It should be if we remember the crowds in the piazzas and the passion of the Pink Floyd follower, their demonstrable aesthetic need and love of words. (And we could go beyond this to lovers of rap.) It would be odd if these passions had nothing to do with us.

Part of the problem is that the aesthetic is *not* immediately demonstrable, even though we take it for granted as a category. In a subtle and closely argued essay, "Criticism and Judgment" (2020) (again the brevity of my chapter does not do justice to a superb discussion), Robert S. Lehman takes up the problem of the elusiveness of the aesthetic. His starting point is the gap between "formal analysis and aesthetic judgment," the "inharmoniousness of analysis and judgment" (p. 1106). It is a problem of "the division of presentation from judgment" (p. 1109) deriving from Kant's insight that our cognition does not conform to objects but rather the reverse, a severance that puts "presentation" in question. New criticism is the ostensive definition of this problem: the formal text is not the aesthetic, nor is its analysis, though it may generate aesthetic experience. What this experience may be is difficult to define, as Lehman describes a number of failed and often serio-comic attempts to do so. He concludes that "the essentially private character of aesthetic judgment" (p. 1122) can be made public by a kind of circumstantial location of the experience (for which he invokes philosophical behaviorism) in a range of "publicly-observable behaviours" (p. 1123) that make a "tissue of a particular scene of aesthetic judgment" (p. 1122) publicly available. I wonder, though, if a characteristic of aesthetic judgments, rather than being solipsistic, is a pre-supposition that they are *always already sharable*. Rather than being socially constructed, as Lehman comes very near to saying, they *make sociality possible*. Aesthetic judgments come in words, sharable words. One might say, that it is *discussable* is what makes the judgment aesthetic.

That it is *discussable* is what brings aesthetics and politics together, as I explore in the following section. Dante's listeners, the technician with a passion, do point us to something crucial, the need to share and the beauty and power of words themselves. Rather than speaking of "the" aesthetic one could posit a variety of aesthetic experience (one among many varieties) as the energy that prompts shared discussion, that presupposes the aesthetic experience in the need to discuss it. I am not sure that the technologies of depthless reading would satisfy the energies and desires of people searching for this interactive experience. Can we claim that as specialists we are exempted from being meaningful to anyone but ourselves? Yet ours is one of the disciplines with roots in the everyday and everyday interaction. Unless we put words, shared language, at the center of what we do I do not see how we can describe what we do, or show the peculiar relevance of aesthetics and politics to it. It comes down to language. In my next section, language intertwines aesthetics and politics.

2. Language

A concern with language is assumed to mean "close reading." This is what Franco Moretti says about it:

> But the trouble with close reading (in all of its incarnations, from the new criticism to deconstruction) is that it necessarily depends on an extremely small canon. This may have become an unconscious and invisible premise by now, but it is an iron one nonetheless: you invest so much in individual texts *only* if you think that very few of them really matter. Otherwise, it doesn't make sense. And if you want to look beyond the canon (and of course, world literature will do so: it would be absurd if it didn't!), close reading will not do it. It's not designed to do it. It's designed to do the opposite. At bottom, it's a theological exercise – very solemn treatment of very few texts taken very seriously[3] – whereas what we really need is a little pact with the devil: we know how to read texts, now let's learn how *not* to read them. Distant reading: where distance, let me repeat it, is a *condition of knowledge*: it allows you to focus on units that are much smaller or much larger than the text. (*Distant Reading*, pp. 48–9)

Close reading is for the "theological" wrinklies. This is Moretti at his most provocative, insisting, wrongly, on the total incompatibility of "distant" (a term which began as a joke, see *Distant Reading*, p. 44) and "close" reading. The excitement and passion of his thinking in the brilliantly transformative *Graphs, Maps, Trees* (2005) doesn't actually derive from a repudiation of reading closely (in fact he is a brilliant close reader): rather it comes from a new phenomenology of texts, thinking of texts through morphology, evolution. True, some of Moretti's taxonomies convert texts into data in order that an algorithm can operate, the concept of hegemony, the rise and fall of genres ("Graphs," in *Graphs, Maps, Trees*) or national literatures ("Conjectures on World Literature," in *Distant Reading*). Moretti ignores that the notion of hegemony is itself "theological" and depends on assuming that an old-fashioned "rise and fall" model of competition between genres as between nation states operates as the formative principle of literary production, very much in the mode of bygone continental historical reading (*Distant Reading*, p. 56). (Compare Regenia Gagnier's model of the mutations of liberalism in world literature in *Literatures of Liberalization*, 2018.) The categories he uses, for instance, the silver fork novel, the historical novel (the generalizing definite article gets one a long way) to graph the emergence of forms

---

[3] An issue of *Critical Quarterly*, "Historical Poetics and the Problem of Exemplarity" (2019), addresses the philosophical issue of small sample. A fine article by Natalie M. Houston in *Victorian Studies* (2014) on statistical methods in Victorian poetry echoes Moretti (p. 499). The interesting account of large-scale line length analysis (pp. 506–7), though, has depended on giving the computer a problem and subsequently interpreting data: we don't *not* read. I reiterate this as a truism.

inevitably dependent on prior close readings by others, as he recognizes. The successive redactions of Mitford's *Our Village*, which Moretti charts by means of maps elucidated from the texts, required a considerable feat of close reading (despite their tautological nature). The impressive reading of free indirect style that ends the "Trees" chapter rests wholly on meticulous analysis of syntax. It is difficult to see how this "much smaller unit" could have been arrived at without "close" reading.

It is this—free indirect style—that opens up new possibilities for Moretti, and, as I hope to suggest, for thinking about what we do. And I hope, too, this account of free indirect style carries along with it politics and aesthetics in tandem.

To show this I turn aside from manifestos for critical reading to a literary text, Virginia Woolf's *Mrs Dalloway* (1925), a novel that mediates another text, Shakespeare's *Cymbeline*. Clarissa Dalloway mends a green silk dress in preparation for her party. As she sews, the words of *Cymbeline*'s dirge, "Fear no more the heat o' the sun," enter her mind in a third person voice as a lyrical three-word fragment—"Fear no more." The folds of the green dress and the rhythm of sewing modulate into the rise and fall of waves: Shakespeare's words seem to float on reverie as semiotic particles.

> That is all. Fear no more, says the heart. Fear no more, says the heart, committing its burden to some sea, which sighs collectively for all sorrows, and renews, begins, collects, lets fall. And the body listens alone to the passing bee; the wave breaking; the dog barking, far away barking and barking. (p. 43)

Because the line of verse is shortened even the stress pattern is subtly altered to a series of three regular ictus from what feels like a dactyl in the original. It is not *what* is feared but the psychic depths of fear itself that the words set afloat. Suffering "those sudden thunderclaps of fear" (p. 95), the shell-shocked Septimus (who identifies saving England in the First World War with saving Shakespeare) also recapitulates *Cymbeline*: ". . . while far away on shore he heard dogs barking and barking far away. Fear no more, says the heart in the body; fear no more" (p. 153). The third person voice speaks for his fear.

This recurrence, rather than drawing attention to the circulation of language, is often described as the fusion of two consciousnesses, those of Mrs Dalloway and Septimus. But Woolf is also exploring how words from outside the self, "Fear no more," become part of the self, part of consciousness, the inner speech of the self. Here two characters are actively sharing somebody else's words, Shakespeare's. This sharing of language, even when you are alone, makes poetry a vitally interactive, vitally social experience. Of all the art forms that use words, poetry is the most collaborative. What stops this being a coercive process of invasion? And an ideological invasion at that. Words become part of you, yes, but just as surely the very process of internalization makes them *not* you, other to the self, apart from the self who invokes them. Therefore the self can negotiate language, negotiate the speech community to which it belongs. Negotiated language *is* the speech community. The words here don't merge with consciousness but become a consciously used mantra and charm, a conscious remediation (perhaps contextualized by the sonic violence of the real or imagined barking dogs, the unsolved violence of World War One). Woolf's use of Shakespeare's words is a paradigm of the way the social world is evoked in the act of reading someone else's words. In poetry-reading the self is alert to language and to its otherness, always potentially if not actually in dialogue with it. Affective and critical reading happens simultaneously. Interaction, intersubjective experience, is the essence of the reading of poetry, but it is a type of *all* reading experiences, and by extension a type of *all* verbal exchanges. Dialogism is inherent in the processes of language. Tension, even struggle, is constitutive. For Clarissa Dalloway and Septimus the experience of inner speech is both aesthetic and political.

I am reading dialogism more loosely than Moretti, who invokes Bakhtin's dialogism and Voloshinov's struggle for the sign (and here he is an expert close reader) when he charts a crucial branching of the novel's "tree," "free indirect style" (*Graphs, Maps, Trees*, pp. 81-91). Free indirect style is that syntactic structure that makes a character's thought available and distanced through the third rather than the first person, so that it hovers between an impersonal and a personal statement, a kind of aporia between the two that enables, he thinks, the individual's voice and the voice of the social doxa to be heard simultaneously. One form it takes, he says, in Jane Austen, is the enabling of a reading of the self's freedom along with the constraints of socialization—a "liberal" compromise, he implies (p. 82). There are other more unconstrained and politically adventurous practices of the free indirect style, and these can modulate into the stream of consciousness (which I think spells an individualism with which he is uncomfortable). Free indirect style is never quite dialogic in Bakhtin's terms, but it does set up conflict and become active, as the self finds itself in opposition to the doxa. But to do this consciousness has to negotiate in an impassioned way with what Bakhtin calls "a language filled with other people's words," as Dostoevsky's Raskolnikov finds (p. 83). Here Moretti also invokes Voloshinov's reading of "Quasi-Direct Discourse" as further evidence of the self's negotiation with language. *In* a text dialogism may be problematic, as he says, but for the *reader* of a text dialogism is, I claim, part of the reading process, part of negotiating other people's words. Free indirect speech is the quintessence of social language, but all reading activates social experience. It's what makes both aesthetic and political experience possible.

Moretti uses the term "inner speech" (p. 83), which originated with another Russian, L.S. Vygotsky, who made a more subtle reading than Bakhtin and Voloshinov of the interchange between "inner" speech and the language community (as I describe in *The Radical Aesthetic* (2000), pp. 136-42). My invocation of these three figures is to remind us, first, that in reading poetry and the novel we are always reading something made of other people's words, always engaging in a perpetual interchange between our own language-making and the writer's handling of the social language of the speaking community, a process that ranges from the scarcely noticed to the agonistic. ("There is no language without the putting of language into play and at stake," Steven Connor writes, in his *Beyond Words* (2014).) And second, I invoke these three figures to remind us that they pursued an alertness to language we have all but forgotten in our current thinking about literature. Between them (and they disagreed) they brought into visibility the complexity of a social reading of language-making and its founding principle of interaction, a principle of language-making where the self is subject to the interplay of vital constraints and an equally vital principle of autonomy. They made us self-conscious about the way language and its creativity works. Entering into a literary text is a vital intellectual and imaginative experience. It offers an alertness to language as nothing else does.

Why is it important to think about language now? In what follows, though I am stressing the political valence of our subject, I am assuming that the imaginative charge that is germane to aesthetic experience is a motivating element in alertness to language.

Why is it important to think about language now? Because we are living in the era of the ascendancy of Fascist language—in both the United Kingdom and the USA. Knowing about language and its complexity affords some protection against this moment, the destruction of dialogism. It's the beginning of a counter to it. Fascism knows that when you want to commit an act of violence you must first of all destroy language. This is the prior act of violence. *Take back control: Get Brexit done: Make America great again.* This totalitarian language, using words as missiles, makes it impossible to reply. It produces what looks like univocal certainty while in fact producing empty fiduciary terms. These can be filled with any content the listener prefers—or simply with the surge of affect that appears to ascribe agency—take, get, make—and elective choice to the listener. It is impossible to reply to these injunctions because they eliminate a predicate. To start to ask, control of what? Make great how? Finish what? is to ask for specifics when they have already been eliminated, the ground taken from beneath the respondent's feet. "Show strength," "Fight like hell," Trump said. There is no way this language can be dialogic because its aim is to destroy the possibility of a shared reality in which two agents can participate in dialogue, to cow disagreement and to kill off the interlocutor. It is linguicide.

Christopher Bollas has written about "The Fascist state of mind" in his *Being a Character: Psychoanalysis and Self Experience* (1992), exploring the psychic conditions that enable genocide.[4] His argument that the Fascist state of mind freezes

---

[4] I thank David Russell for this reference (via Adam Phillips) and for discussion and invaluable help with this chapter and its themes.

up the symbolic order by destroying the "polysemousness" that is habitually present (p. 201), foreclosing complex issues, is provocative, but I want to draw attention to the section on intellectual genocide, which he calls "'Committive Genocide" (pp. 207–9) and which is a form of linguistic genocide. There are five categories here, though they merge into one another. *Decontextualization* takes a view held by an opposition out of its proper context to discredit it so that the opponent "will naturally struggle to fill the gaps created by this rhetorical violence." The characterization of Biden's political program as "communism" might be an example, relocating an agenda in bygone Communist Russia. *Denigration* distorts, rendering views ridiculous and destroying "ideation" as the machinery of conflict. Fake news? Virtue signaling? *Caricature*, cartooning the individuals who hold antipathetic views: in England Michael Gove has very successfully described all institutional opposition to his views on education, whether by teachers, unions, or educational specialists as "the Blob." The same goes for the characterization of political activism as "woke," a favorite of the *Daily Mail*. "Loony left" is another favorite. A technique of displacing the specific and by a generality that is assumed to require no definition and as such can't be argued against. *Character assassination* goes further, discrediting the personal character of the holder of a view. Biden's age, Kier Starmer's petty legalism as a trained barrister. *Change of name*, and *Categorization as aggregation*, both ways of making a person lose his identity, are active techniques in England and the USA where Black Lives Matter is concerned (faggots, terrorists, niggers). These are allied with Bollas's second category, "Omittitive Genocide," that erases a group, simply by not referring to it and censoring both its cultural productions and its activities.

That these linguistic techniques are so banal and widespread today might suggest that we don't really need to see them as that threatening—what's a slogan or a caricature more or less? But they are techniques for destroying language, and thus for destroying epistemic possibilities, as Richard J. Evans has shown in his account of Nazi conspiracy theories, *The Hitler Conspiracies* (2020), where lies about the burning of the Reichstag by "Communists" in 1933, for instance, acted as a cover for the Nazi's suspension of civil liberties (pp. 93, 109). And techniques not only for destroying epistemic possibilities but creative linguistic imagining. (We could pair Dasa Drndic's historical novel, *Trieste* (2007), with Evans's work, which explores how silencing itself creates collusively silent bystanders—"There are many bystanders... Blind observers... they play it safe" (p. 84)). There is no shared reality created through language. It is art here that explores the destruction of language.

We have not yet thought seriously about reclaiming our own language, and thus our autonomy, because the liberal arrangements of Western societies still seem intact. Recent events have shown they are not. But the novel and particularly the novel out of Africa has for some time known about the destruction of language and its repercussions. I end by offering some examples of narratives where language counts. African continent writers know about techniques of silencing by a master colonial language. They are an extreme case of language's oppression, to be sure, but for that very reason, instructive. It is a political point made through aesthetic passion.

3. "Shut up!"

From Chinua Achebe's founding novel from Nigeria, the Sophoclean *Things Fall Apart* (1958), to Tsitsi Dangaremba's 2018 novel of Westernized Zimbabwe, *This Mournable Body*, colonial technologies of silencing abound. In Achebe's novel, after the subjugation of elders by the British justice system, "Even when the men were left alone they found no words to speak to one another" (p. 185). Even when released, returning home, "They neither spoke to anyone nor among themselves" (p. 188). Protest is quelled, but worse, communication *between* members of the indigenous community is destroyed. When the District Commissioner intervenes to bring to a halt the communal meeting of the villages, the place of debate and discussion, "There was utter silence" (p. 194). The last English utterance in the novel is "Shut up!" (p. 197), as Obierika attempts to describe the gratuitous atrocity of Okonkwo's suicide in a eulogy over his friend's body. This is how "pacification" proceeds (p. 197). In the sixty years between Achebe and Dangaremba that silencing has been internalized. Educated at an elite school, the protagonist, Tambutzai, possessor of European credentials, narrates throughout via the distancing pronoun, "you," as if the "I" is objectified, deprived of subjectivity. She dreads identification with indigenous Zimbabwian culture and its (to her) squalor. Her response to demands on her ethical, empathic nature is silence. Complicit at a city bus stop to an assault on one of the girls at her hostel, she ignores their reproaches: she cannot reply to her boss when she is responsible for a fiasco in her home village—"You listen and you do not answer" (p. 361). Institutionalized after a mental breakdown and questioned by a psychologist, "the words crawl slowly into your throat" (p. 135). There's a malfunction of the relation between inner and outer speech. Her linguistic maiming is signified by her former occupation, making up slogans in an advertising agency.

African continent novels are dominated by the wars and civil wars whose origins are a complex mix of colonial legacy and internal power relations and which dramatize the position of English as the master language, a language that has the power not only to suppress indigenous culture and language, but also to create misprision and bewilderment. In Dangaremba's Zimbabwe, the war of 1964–79: earlier, Ngũgĩ wa Thiong'o's *Petals of Blood* (1977) has the Mau Mau struggles in Kenya (1952–60) as its context; Buchi Emecheta goes back to the press-ganging of Nigerian men to fight in the Second World War in *The Joys of Motherhood* (1979). More recently, in Chimamanda Ngozi Adiche's *Half of a*

Yellow Sun (2006), the Nigerian/Biafran Civil War of 1967–70 dominates; in Aminatta Forna's *The Memory of Love* (2010), it is the Sierra Leone Civil War of 1991–2002 and its atrocities. In Jennifer Nansubuga Makumbi's Ugandan novel, *The First Woman* (2020) it is the violence of Idi Amin and the Tanzanian–Ugandan war of 1978–9.

In Emecheta's novel the British have employed incomprehensible Hausa militia to force Southern Nigerians into the British army. But these soldiers speak a basic English that reduces the men to herded animals—"Gwo, gwo into the lorry – gwo, gwo!" (p. 161). In later novels the language of power is more indirectly violent. In Adiche's novel, authentic Igbo is constantly compromised. Odenigbo's rapid transitions from Igbo to English and back, from command to informality—"the Igbo of one who spoke English often" (p. 4)—confusing his new houseboy, denotes a perpetually compromised identity. The language of power is in tension with his avowed ethnicity. In Forna's novel, the visiting English psychologist, longing to be inward with Sierra Leona culture, is confounded by the "bluntness" of Krio and the "spaces" its speakers escape into (p. 47). A final irony is a kind of reverse silencing: his own English colonizer's language, a language of power he repudiates, is used against him. An indigenous woman traumatized by the civil war whom he wants to help has his urgent advice translated into her own language and mediated by "a conversation he cannot understand." She terminates dialogue in empty, formal English drained of content: "I am better now. The problems are gone. Thank you Doctor" (p. 204). "No speaking Vernacular" is the notice that meets girls moving up to upper primary school in the 1930's, "No jabbering Lugunda" (p. 269) in Makumbi's novel. The two protagonists live in an almost schizophrenic linguistic, conceptual, and societal world: in one world there is the language of monogamy, in the other the language of polygamy. But the two languages intertwine and cause deep misprision and actual alienation.

It is Ngũgĩ wa Thiong'o's *Petals of Blood* that is most explicit about the destruction of language that overrides and erases identity: "Teach them good idiomatic English" (p. 207). Quoting Shakespeare's speech on degree from *Troilus and Cressida*, the head teacher in an elite school for Kenyan boys "did not therefore want to hear any more nonsense about African teachers, African history, African literature, African this and that . . ." (p. 206). Early in the novel, Karega knowingly warns a skeptical Munira about slogans: "The trouble with slogans or any saying without a real foundation is that it can be used for anything. Phrases like Democracy, the Free World, for instance, are used to mean their opposite. It depends of course on who is saying it where, when and to whom" (p. 70).

And yet Ngũgĩ wa Thiong'o has specifically repudiated the African continent novel in English, the "Afro-European" novel that betrays indigenous African languages. *Petals of Blood* was the last work to be written in English, before he turned to the drama in Gikuyu, *I Will Marry When I Want*, that led to his imprisonment in 1977. In *Decolonising the Mind* (1986), he argues that literature in English, and even campaigning in English, is a betrayal: "While we were busy haranguing the ruling circles in a [English] language which automatically excluded the participation of the peasantry and the working class in the debate, imperialist culture and African reactionary forces had a field day" (p. 26). In an interview of 2017 he describes himself as a "language warrior" for Gikuyu because "[English] Language is a means of spiritual subjugation" by a West that "refuses to take responsibility for their crimes against colonialized peoples." "The right to language is a human right, not a privilege."

The African context, however it might differ from ours in England and the USA, is an extreme case of dispossession that exposes the linguistic oppression that can happen in other contexts—even without the oppressions of imperialist domination. It's an irony that our own imperialist language should have developed a violence turned against itself. Fascist language is circulating in the everyday of our countries right now. One of its objects is to dispossess by silencing speech, that human right. It is peculiarly resistant to argument, which is its objective. But it is not resistant to analysis. Therefore, the larger the number of people in any community who can analyze language, whose business is with words, who understand the manipulation of words, so much the better. As Bakhtin, Voloshinov, Vygotsky, and Virginia Woolf saw, literature is founded on the rhythms of interchange between other people's words and our own. It is profoundly social. It is constantly available as a resource. And literary criticism is a praxis that begins with thinking about words and experiencing words imaginatively. I am not arguing that "close reading" is our salvation or that we should go "back" to "close reading." I am not arguing that literary criticism can change the world either "alone" or otherwise. Simply that language is the core of our discipline. Whatever we do, whatever direction we take, it is founded on language. To have as many trained readers as possible in a democracy, who can resist and understand manipulation—what we do creates that cohort. And I would claim that this cognitive capacity develops *pari passu* with, is driven by the shared energy of aesthetic experience. I.A. Richards's justification for practical criticism, developed in the first era of Fascism, was not as "theological" practice, but as civic education, a means of refusing misprision, an impossible ideal and—actually a rather grim—belief in accurate reading, as safeguard against exploitation (see Armstrong, *The Radical Aesthetic*, p. 88). He forgot the aspect of delight understood by his contemporary, Yeats—"Words alone are certain good."

The listeners hearing Dante in piazzas and the lover of Pink Floyd re-enter at this point. For along with thinking about words, most of us know the energizing pleasure of them. Delight in words is what links these readers to our profession. Immersion—in language. Professional readers tend to occlude both pleasure and beauty, as if these are frivolous pursuits. But both are a prerequisite of a shared culture, a motivation to discovery, a longing to know. The aesthetic and intellectual pleasure spur each other on. Perhaps exploration rather than explanation is the founding practice of our work—and the need to communicate it. Beauty is a civic as well as an individual experience. Certainly people don't experience beauty alone—the instinct is to turn to someone else, to exclaim, to share, to talk, to think, to make words. William Carlos Williams's Flossie exclaims, shares delight, in the roses she has been keeping on ice in wax paper: the roses are not beautiful until they have been recognized by someone else. The last four lines of the poem are dialogic, half way between an exclamation and a question. She shares a "moment beautiful" as the last line has it, even though the shared moment is made fragile by the penultimate line: "for the moment / beautiful." But the poem ends with the word "beautiful," which finally triumphs. And fittingly ends this chapter.

6
Can Migrants Be Seen?
Some Representations of Migration in Contemporary Art, Film, and Literature

Josephine McDonagh

1. Invisible Migrants: Michael Haneke, *Happy End* (2017)

"This is Mohammed, all the way from Nigeria, his wife and two children were burned alive by Boko Haram. It took him a year to get here. Every day for months he's walked from the jungle to the tunnel, in the hope of getting across at last. No luck yet, but where there's life there's hope. This is Youssef from..." (Haneke, p. 54).[1] These are the words of Pierre Laurent (Franz Rogowski), the dissolute and probably deranged son of a rich family, who, toward the end of Michael Haneke's ironically entitled *Happy End* (2017), introduces a group of five African migrants (Jackee Toto and four unnamed actors) to an overwhelmingly white, high bourgeois lunch party. The gathering is to celebrate his mother's engagement to a British businessman, who works for a global financial conglomerate which has just taken over the Laurents' French-based family firm. To the acute embarrassment of the guests, Pierre begins to tell the migrants' harrowing stories, until he is interrupted by his mother, Anne Laurent (Isabelle Huppert), who in a sudden and unexpected burst of extreme physical violence breaks his finger. It gives the scene the air of a Greek tragedy: the dramatic climax in a tense family drama of intergenerational conflict. Yet the presence of the migrants on the margins of the dining room, and at the periphery of our screen, raises the possibility that, despite appearances, the family drama itself might be a distraction from the extreme violence of global displacement that Pierre's commentary only begins to disclose.

I would like to use this troubling scene as a jumping off point for considering the representation of migrants within the contemporary arts and literature. If Haneke's point is that the lives of migrants are concealed within the societies

---

[1] *Happy End*, dir. Michael Haneke (2017). The title of the original French version is in English. Youssef is the name of a 16-year-old Sudanese boy who was killed by a van in a hit and run incident at the mouth of the Eurotunnel on December 3, 2015, and whose death triggered a protest on the part of a group of Sudanese refugees which was suppressed by the police. See Calais Migrant Solidarity (2015); Sanyal (2020, p. 185).

which they inhabit, he is surely persuasive. *Happy End* is set in Calais in the late 2010s, when this region was notorious as the location of the so-called "Jungle," an improvised camp on industrial wasteland, where migrants waited in their quest to cross the Channel to reach the UK, one of the "hotspots" of the European "migrant crisis" (De Genova et al. 2016, pp. 16-22). At the time of the film's release, the "Jungle" was the focus of considerable attention: a site of human dereliction and despair from one perspective; or an enclave of criminality and contagion from another (Sanyal 2020, pp. 161-3). Yet despite this, the migrants in the film remain in the background, barely visible. They provide a backdrop to the film, but one we hardly notice. Toward the beginning, Anne Laurent drives along a stretch of road bordered by a high, wire fence, dotted with security cameras, and topped with coiled razor wire, behind which we can just glimpse in outline the shipping containers that the French government had provided as shelters for migrants (Ticktin 2016, pp. 28-33). At one point in this sequence, we see an ambulance on the hard shoulder, indicating that an accident has happened; probably it involved a migrant, but it isn't clear. Throughout the film, migrants appear in person just four times, mostly fleetingly: a group of Black men hovering outside what looks like a social agency for migrants, located beside a school at which (White) children and their parents are assembling; men wandering aimlessly on a beach fully clothed, among scantily dressed (White) seaside swimmers and sunbathers; walking down the streets of Calais, when they are engaged in conversation by the elderly Georges Laurent (Jean-Louis Trintignant) (Pierre's grandfather)—filmed from a distance, their images indistinct, as though caught by a passerby or perhaps a security camera; and finally, and most substantially, at the lunch party noted above. Each time they are at the edge of the screen, or out of focus, slightly blurred. Muffled background chatter at another bourgeois party reveals that the White residents of the neighborhood consider the migrants a security risk, but the level of anxiety they provoke seems out of proportion with the migrants' relative invisibility in the film. In the film, we generally only notice them because they are Black, and dress differently to the townspeople, with whom they hardly interact. The actors who play them are not even included in the credits to the film. They fade into the background, their human presence no more than a passing detail of everyday life in twenty-first-century Calais.

This positioning of the migrants on the borders of our attention is an important element of the film. Haneke's works famously attend to regimes of seeing and attention, most notably in his earlier film, *Caché* (*Hidden*) (2005), in which technologies of viewing provide the means to explore questions of national amnesia regarding France's colonial past. In *Caché*, the story concerns the host of a highbrow TV show whose childhood maltreatment of an adopted Algerian boy, presumed to have been orphaned in the October 17, 1961 massacre of hundreds of Algerians by the French police in Paris—an event notoriously repressed ("hidden") by the French authorities for many decades—comes back to haunt him. In a film full of scenes many of which take place in a television studio, and in which screens of various kinds come to saturate its *mise en scène*, a central setting to which we return frequently is a room in the protagonist's family house dominated by a large screen, on which he and his wife watch videos that have mysteriously arrived at their house (Ezra and Sillars 2007, pp. 215–21). These videos show the exterior of their own home, secretly filmed over long periods, as though by a detective or spy, or casually on CCTV. The videos are menacing: who made them, or why, is never ascertained; nor is it clear how they should be viewed, or what they reveal. As the couple watch, the outside world invades their private space; they feel vulnerable, exposed. The hidden story evoked by the title of the film, concerning the childhood episode, is not revealed by these videos, but unravels over the course of the film, not through filmic evidence, but through associated events which bring the protagonist and the Algerian man back into contact with each other. In the film their traumatic story becomes something like an allegory for the national disavowal of its history of colonial violence, specifically the 1961 massacre (Gilroy 2007; Fulton 2019); but in its presentation it is stumbled on, to the side of the matters to which our attention is more openly directed, for example by the visual cues embedded in the video.

What is key to Haneke's film is its emphasis on seeing, and the ways in which contemporary media technologies which frame people's view, in a sense, blindside them; but *Caché* holds out the possibility, too, that an habitual point of view can be transformed through the aesthetic work performed by the film. Haneke's achievement in *Caché* is to retrain spectators to reposition their gaze and look elsewhere in order to see things differently; specifically, in this film, this is to read a domestic trauma as a metaphor for, or symptom of, something on a much larger scale. This redistribution of attention through aesthetic representation—its careful juxtaposing of different styles of image in its montage of security video, domestic realism, and hazily presented dream sequences on his own cinematic screen—enables reflection on the difficult questions of postcolonial culpability.[2]

Following in the wake of *Caché*, the aesthetic work carried out in *Happy End* seems both more complex and more troubling. The two films overlap in their sphere of interest and visual idiom: as in *Caché*, *Happy End* draws on everyday screen technologies, now updated to reflect the digital and mobile technologies of the 2010s. Mobile phones, laptop computers, and the Internet mediate all social interactions represented in the film, and dominate its scenes. The devices designate what we can see. As in *Caché*, images on screens are often presented as

---

[2] Not all agree on this point. Haneke's decision to evoke the 1961 massacre in such an oblique way divided opinion as to whether the film enabled its audience to come to a fuller understanding of that event (Fulton 2019, p. 699), or in fact was complicit in the very repressive practices it apparently set out to expose. As Gilroy writes, it is "not so much a clever study of audience complicity, regression or resignation, but rather a conduit for those depressing reactions served up with what looks like bad faith" (Gilroy 2007, p. 233).

puzzles, as though there is a secret concealed in them which we are required to fathom through attentive spectatorship. From the opening shots taken by a young Eve Laurent (Fantine Harduin) on her mobile phone, which record her mother's routine ablutions (brushing her teeth, going to the toilet) before she falls into a coma (induced by poison administered by her daughter), to the closing scenes, also filmed by the girl on the same device, of her grandfather endeavoring to drown himself (aided by the girl), we are asked to consider all the characters in the film in the context of their screen lives. In every case, what they watch and how and when they appear on screen reveal forms of violence that are embedded in every day social interactions: Thomas Laurent's (Mathieu Kassovitz) (the girl's father's) passionate, sadomasochistic extramarital affair conducted online with a classical musician; the death of a construction worker in a building accident on the Laurents' building site, captured digitally by a security camera; the son, Pierre's self-destructive YouTube karaoke performances; and (in a more residual mode) the grandfather's photographs of his deceased wife, whom (he recalls) he had smothered in an act of euthanasia, and so on. Yet unlike in *Caché* where the film turned eyes to a traumatic issue that had been hidden from view, in *Happy End* there is no diversion of attention, no enlargement of sympathy.

Rather than leading us to a larger, we might say, world-historical story, *Happy End* remains fixated on the domestic conflicts of the Laurent family, the more extreme violence of global displacement remains to all intents and purposes unseen, on the margins of representation, figuratively, and usually literally, at the edge of our screen. The migrants remain more or less invisible both within the community—a lurking presence that haunts rather than inhabits the town—and in the film itself, an invisibility signaled by the disturbing fact that the names of the Black actors who played the migrants do not even appear in the film's credits. Unlike the Algerian thread in *Caché*, in *Happy End* the migrants' stories are never drawn into an analysis on a national or international scale, although if we follow through the analysis of global capital that is gestured toward in the film (the takeover of the family firm by globalized capital is part of this story), well might they have done.

Rather, in *Happy End*—more than in *Caché*—we confront the difficult fact of this sidelining head on: what kind of art is it, the film seems to ask, that operates under the conditions in which something or someone is more or less offscreen, only partially seen? *Happy End* makes clear that bourgeois modes of seeing are incapable of noticing migrants, and this is what the film presents to us. It does so both in its presentation of quotidian modes of looking through digital media—phones, cameras, the Internet—as well as in its inclusion of more formal aesthetic works which are spliced into the film—for example, Thomas's lover's impassioned viol performance, privately staged at a family party, and the lavish paintings that adorn the walls of their luxurious family home. In the bourgeois world depicted here, art is decorative, a sign of accumulated wealth, and the images that surround the characters on the screens they see in their daily interactions reflect only interpersonal dramas within a narrow social sphere. Unlike in *Caché*, in *Happy End*, there is no respite from the limitations to these ways of seeing, and the film persists in marginalizing the very subjects of its inquiry.

After Anne's assault on her son, she invites the five Africans to join the party, but at the very moment at which the film might have begun to see properly the migrants for the first time, Georges, who has been trying to end his life throughout the whole film, seizes the distraction it causes as an opportunity to leave the party. Calling on his granddaughter's aid, he goes outside to attempt his own drowning. The camera thus leaves the migrants and follows this odd couple, the old man pushed in a wheel chair by the young girl, down to the ocean until he is immersed to his neck. The camera lingers on an image of the man, head just above the water, explicitly referencing Beckett's *Happy Days* (1961), whose dark comic nihilism is also evoked in the film's title. Now the camera cuts to the girl who has walked away from the shoreline, and calmly takes out her mobile phone to record the drowning. We watch through her screen as she films him in the water, waves lapping around his body, their sound filling the soundtrack; then the sound of running as Anne (her aunt) and Thomas (her father) rush to save him. Here the film ends, the drama suspended, but with the strong sense that the old man's attempt to kill himself will fail, the tortured family dynamics will continue in the same manner as throughout the film, and the migrants' inclusion in the family party will be a one-off event after which they will continue their own inexorable daily (failed) attempts to leave France through the Tunnel.

Despite the film narrative's promise of a denouement, such as is realized in Greek tragedy, in *Happy End* there is no resolution; nothing has changed and nothing will change; everyone is trapped in the same repetitive patterns of behavior. The irony of the film's title is not just that the ending is not happy, but that it sees no end, no change to the situation it presents. Art, the film appears to say about itself, makes no difference, nor can it.

2. Migration Art: A Brief Survey

Is it possible that the particularly bleak view of the aesthetic we witness in Haneke's *Happy End* might be related to the subject matter it appears to exclude: migration? Unlike in the earlier film, in which colonial violence comes to occupy the center of the film's concerns, in *Happy End*, the aesthetic mode that the film adopts instead is caught in a spiral of its own self-negation. It can only lead us to the edge of its scope of vision, and point out to us that the migrants lie beyond this limit. This failure of representation is not a matter of the sublime: no transcendence is offered, only deflection. When Pierre tells the migrants' stories, the shock he elicits is registered rather as embarrassment, and this seems to relate more to the revelation of the catastrophic relationship between Pierre and his mother, than the spectacular violence that had been experienced by Mohammed or Youssef in Africa, or the everyday violence to which they are subject in the human transit camp at Calais. The migrants in this film serve only to remind us of the limits and complicities of bourgeois practices of aesthetic representation. It isn't clear whether one should understand this irony as a biting indictment of bourgeois art practices; or alternatively as the film's unconscious complicity in its own revelation.

The mixed critical responses to the film reflect this ambiguity. Haneke's well-known irony notwithstanding, *Happy End* troubled critics for its failure of empathy, related variously to its perceived formal incoherence, its lack of character development, and its spotlight on an elite social stratum with whom its advantages and behavior make it difficult to sympathize (Elbiri 2017; Marchini Camia 2017; Scharres 2017). But perhaps a more compelling point is that the film itself records—and in doing so repeats—the more egregious failure of recognition on the part of the family and the townspeople in relation to the migrants. In this light, failure of recognition would seem to be the film's point. At the end of the film there is, on the one side, a troubled family looking after itself, its property, and its own continuation, while becoming incorporated into specific forms of international finance capitalism; and on the other side, a wide, empty ocean stretching endlessly into the distance. While *Caché* initiated a retraining of our senses in the interests of addressing collective guilt (even if it failed to convince), in *Happy End*, any work of this kind is incomplete or suspended, and our attention dispersed.

The uncomfortable questions that *Happy End* raises regarding the aesthetic and its possibilities for engaging with contemporary migration resonate because in recent years migration has in reality become a favored theme in the arts and literature. Rather than a failure to represent migrants, there seems to have been an explosion of what we might loosely call migration art, so much so that it sometimes seems *de rigueur* for contemporary works to feature the theme of migration. Literary prizes (there are numerous examples, but one suffices: the T.S. Eliot poetry prize, awarded in 2021 to Bhanu Kapil for *How to Wash A Heart* (2020), an experimental poem exploring "the complex relations that emerge between an immigrant guest and a citizen host" (Kapil, back cover)), themed exhibitions in museums (for example, *Paris–Londres Music Migrations (1962–1989)* at Le Musée national de l'histoire de l'immigration, Paris, March 2019–January 2020),[3] theatrical performances sometimes featuring migrant actors (for example, "The Jungle," a play about the Calais refugee camp, performed by refugee actors, premiered at the Young Vic, London, December 2017, and later transferred to New York) all attest to the prominence of migration art within the contemporary

---

[3] See https://www.histoire-immigration.fr/paris-londres.

art sphere.[4] For many readers and spectators, aesthetic representations of migration are the primary if not sole counterweight to its representation within the news media. The result is an odd division between, on the one hand, mainstream media reports which focus on migrants as either criminals or victims of criminals (people traffickers), often framed by episodes of spectacular violence—dangerous journeys in which migrants risk life and limb, or instances of criminality and violence within facilities for refugees and asylum seekers; and on the other hand, an array of purposefully sympathetic representations of migration within the arts that seek to give voice to, and understand the migrant experience (Sanyal 2020, p. 164). Related to this is a tendency in some aesthetic representations to appropriate migration as a provocation to formal experimentation in a way that can seem detached from the material realities of migration. Even when aesthetic works are in dialogue with these other kinds of media representations, the general effect is of an unusually bifurcated landscape, with little in between two very different types of image. One of the effects of this outpouring of migration art may be in fact to deepen the divisions between representational regimes of art and news media, reinforcing a sense of a separate cultural realm.

In the context of the present volume's theme, therefore, it is worth pausing to survey migration art, to understand something of its methods and its parameters as a body of work that seems, from some angles, to have saturated the contemporary European–American cultural sphere. My survey here selects from recent works of migration art to give a flavor of its formal characteristics, but does not aspire to be either systematic or complete. It is purposefully wide and impressionistic, and includes examples of both avant-garde art and more mainstream, middle-brow works, from across a broad spectrum of media and genres. There is a growing body of interesting critical work on various components of migration art: Erling Björgvinsson et al.'s (2018) edited special issue of the journal *PARSE*, a compilation of creative works and essays focusing on a "crisis of representation" at today's transnational borders, stands out as a rich exploration of this kind of politically engaged art and criticism (Björgvinsson et al. 2020); and, in the field of the visual arts, essays in Saloni Mathur's edited volume, and Emma Chubb's article on migrant orientalism, are important for their discussions of particular works (Mathur 2011; Chubb 2015; see also Demos 2013). My interest here is less in the achievement of specific works, however, than the phenomenon of migration art *in toto*, as it manifests across media. How does the abundance of work dealing with this topic shape contemporary aesthetic practices, both in relation to production and consumption?

Are there any common features that we can identify across this strikingly diverse and uneven body of works—novels, poems, theatrical performances,

---

[4] See https://www.nytimes.com/2018/06/20/theater/the-jungle-a-play-about-refugee-camps-is-coming-.html.

works of visual art in different media, music, and films? It is probably fair to say that there is a shared commitment to social justice for migrants, even though this aim is expressed with different levels of intensity and efficacy. It is hard to identify works of art that take a negative view of migrants, unless one includes anti-immigrant political propaganda, of which the infamous "Breaking Point" poster used by Nigel Farage in the 2016 UK Brexit campaign is a well-known example (Stewart and Mason 2016). For many reasons, not least of all illegality, racist images such as these tend to stand well outside the concerns of cultural institutions, especially those that are publicly funded, and their claims on the aesthetic are much more complicated to assess. The harnessing of aesthetic forms for the positive cause of migrants, on the other hand, is evident in works across genre and media, and in these I identify three recurrent characteristics or tendencies.

The first feature of migration art is that it tends to be informational. There is what we might call an ethnographic and humane impulse to describe and make known the lives of migrants. This is not merely a matter of describing modes of life that are foreign or exotic (as in travel writing), although inevitably this is part of their concern; but the emphasis is always on lives that are exceptional because of the ways in which enforced movement affects them: exceptionally precarious, exceptionally risky, these tend to be lives lived on the brink of death. Especially in narrative fiction and memoir, the unusual and precarious circumstances that cause people's displacement from their home country, the dangers they encounter in transit, and the hazards of settlement, all present ready material for drama and narrative suspense. We can see this in migration novels such as, for instance, Sunjeev Sahota's *The Year of the Runaways* (2015), about illegal South Asian migrant workers in Sheffield in Britain; Mohsin Hamid's *Exit West* (2017), concerning refugees from an unnamed war zone (probably Syria) whose journeys across the world are presented as though they are magical; or in Thi Bui's graphic novel-memoir, *The Best We Could Do* (2017), on her experience becoming a Vietnamese immigrant in America. In each case there is a documentary element in the text, as each records the extraordinary circumstances of modern-day migration. In the course of these narratives, we not only learn about the factors that cause people to move from conflicts and privations; but also, mainly through the delineation of characters, there is an opportunity to identify sympathetically with the lives of others.

The pedagogic component of these narratives, their instruction in cultural diversity, is striking, and it is significant that Hamid and Thi Bui's texts are both explicitly geared toward young adult readerships. Such narratives aim to reveal to readers conditions of life that are presented as being substantially different from, and more dangerous than, what are assumed to be their own. The extreme precarity to which migrants are subject dominates the narratives in ways which draw a clear distinction between migrant and settled lives, between the (endangered) subjects represented and the (secure) assumed readers. Migrants within these texts live in circumstances in which they do not know what will happen next, what dangers they face. In *Exit West* (due to the characters' magical transposition across national borders), they do not know even what country they will occupy next. The knowledge deficit between the protagonists as displaced persons, and the context in which they find themselves, present many opportunities for plot development. Migration provides the conditions for adventure. It creates tension and forms of suspense which can only be resolved by the eventual safety, stability, and settlement of the protagonists.[5]

The narrative pleasure produced by these texts also drives the ethical project that they undertake. Works such as these aim to enlarge our understanding, and engage our sympathies regarding people who are forced to migrate. Perhaps because these texts are sometimes aimed for young adult readers, they are firmer in their direction of readers' attention than we might normally expect. Some works of migration art leverage the sympathy they evoke for specific causes. This instrumental tendency, a direct commitment to a social cause, is the second distinctive characteristic of migration art that I draw attention to. For instance, a connection between the work of art and political and social activism is often celebrated. For example, "Woven: Connections and Meanings," at the National Museum of Mexican Art in Chicago in 2019, an exhibition of works by five Mexican and Mexican American textile artists, foregrounded the ways in which traditional methods of weaving and textile production combined with activism for social justice to represent the crisis at the US–Mexico border (National Museum of Mexican Art 2019); while British textile artist, Alice Kettle's project "Thread Bearing Witness," which used "textiles to learn from, show solidarity with, and raise funds for displaced people," similarly incorporates the craft cultures of migrants in "new monumental stitched artworks" (Thread Bearing Witness 2019).

As in Kettle's project, another feature of migration art is its more or less explicit use in fundraising campaigns. Another example is *In Damascus*, a cantata composed by Jonathan Dove, first performed in 2016, which took a translation of a poem by Syrian writer Ali Safar as its libretto to represent the war-torn city and place of displacement. Although commissioned specifically for a music festival, nevertheless elements of its production appear to have made it a stimulus for fundraising, blurring the line between an audience's appreciation of an aesthetic work and material transactions in the interests of a humanitarian cause (Hall 2016). Its London performance by Mark Padmore, the tenor celebrated for his remarkable renditions of the Evangelist in Bach's Passions, drew this new musical

---

[5] In some cases, when narratives explicitly address questions regarding the immigration systems within nation states, plot resolution tends to revolve around achievement, or not, of settled status within the host country. A good example is Valeria Luiselli's *Tell Me How It Ends* (2017), an account of the author's interactions as a translator for child refugees from Mexico and Central America in New York, where the question of legal settlement lies at the center of a moving exploration of child experience.

work directly into the Christian tradition of sacred musical works and the classical canon, and helped to leverage charitable donations for Syria-related charities. Of course, the idea that aesthetic works might be used directly in the interest of activism or charity is not new. But in migration art the mobilization of this often seems to be a part of the work's structural make up, a precondition for its production.

A third tendency in works of migration art relates to their capacity to provide the means for self-expression for marginalized people; that is to say, to make audible otherwise repressed voices in the interests of both democratic representation and the self-determination of migrants. Sometimes this drive is incorporated in the formal structure of the works. In poetry for instance, the lyric form affords opportunities for some remarkable work by poets who identify as migrants. In these, risk and danger are foregrounded in radically unstable contexts of literary subject formation. Take for example, the young Salvadoran poet, Javier Zamora, whose first collection, *Unaccompanied* (2018), narrates perilous cross-continental journeys to the United States, in one case ironically transforming attempts to evade the bullets of drug cartel snipers as a dance routine; or Eduardo Corral's impressive *Slow Lightning* (2012), which presents elliptical narratives of memory and desire in the context of lives that hover on the borders of life and death, written across the various terrains of his own cross border journeys. Sometimes the extraordinariness of migration is marked explicitly in the experimental form of the poem. In Divya Victor's *Kith* (2017), an arresting account of a migrant domestic worker's return to Colombo is a prelude to a complex and testing exploration of the poet and her family's experience of the South Asian diaspora, in which the very substance of the poem breaks down into fragments that are reorganized and distributed across the work into ultimately meaningless pieces. The poem aestheticizes the experience of dispersal, through recessive and repetitive patterns of words and parts of words, ever smaller, ever more dispersed, evoking states of mental instability connected with physical and emotional deracination.

The form of lyric poetry allows poets to explore their personal history of migration in abstract and allusive ways, but a related phenomenon that is particularly striking in the sphere of migration art is the development of activist and humanitarian projects that develop the therapeutic uses of creative expression as a way of providing psychological and emotional support for migrants. An example is the project, "Stories in Transit," based in London and Palermo, which runs creative writing workshops for migrants, and espouses among its objectives the aspiration to explore large questions, such as whether "culture, and specifically storytelling in any form [can] provide shelter for people who have lost their homes? Can a tale become a home? A *lieu de mémoire*? Can a memory of literature and the process of making it over and over again build "a country of words" (Mahmoud Darwish)? Can narratives build a place of belonging for those without a nation (Stories in Transit 2021)? Performance-based organizations, such as London-based Phosphorous Theatre, which "makes socially engaged performance with, for, and by refugees and asylum seekers," similarly develop out of a belief that aesthetic practice might be a path to self-determination, social integration, and economic stability (Phosphorous Theatre n.d.).

I have tried to capture both the range and recurrent characteristics of this vast body of art and literature. Among these works there are of course huge variations in style, technique, and intention, not to mention quality. From the point of view of the aesthetic, migration art seems to conform to a Kantian conception in establishing a *sensus communis*: it generates sympathy, it allows audiences to expand their knowledge of others, it lessens the distance between strangers, it condemns stigmatization and imagines possibilities for hospitality, as well as for self-expression and empowerment. On the other hand, its lack of disinterestedness, and its open commitment to activism, fundraising, or therapy, undermine expectations of the autonomy of the artistic object. It sometimes seems too motivated, too keen to persuade or pity, too preachy.

From a political perspective, too, these works raise problems. In their representation of people who are migrants, works of migration art sometimes seem condescending, or—worse—accentuate the migrant's otherness from a notional norm. The emphasis on extreme human suffering means that the pathos of migration is one of migration art's keynotes, but this does not always accurately reflect the reality of migrant experience. Not all migrant experience takes people to the brink of death, by any means. Emma Chubb identifies the emphasis in works of migratory art on the "always suffering, illegal, non-white and Europe-bound" migrant as an element in what she calls "migratory orientalism" in contemporary art which paradoxically "re-inscribes the very Euro-American-centrism and the colonial-center periphery model that it purports to disrupt" (Chubb 2015, p. 273). There is moreover a tendency toward the appropriation of migration, to serve as a metaphor for other forms of exile, including psychic displacement and social deracination; or appropriated as a theme or an idea to be explored in formal terms, evacuated of its social meanings in its aestheticization. Migrants sometimes seem to give human face within artworks to a condition of displacement that seems all too easily to be generalizable, and their journeys become metaphors for all kinds of political or psychic estrangement (Chubb 2015, pp. 272–3; see also Björgvinsson et al. 2020). Just as headlines and slogans such as "we are all migrants," or "we are all immigrants," or even, during the pandemic, "we are all refugees,"[6] are repeated so frequently that the sentiment dissipates almost as soon as it has been

---

[6] Entering any of those three phrases into a search engine scores multiple hits of op eds, blogs, and magazine articles, which draw on the sensationalism of the phrase, and proceed to show that it is either (surprisingly) true, or (surprisingly) untrue. A couple of examples suffice: https://www.colorlines.com/articles/millionth-time-we-are-not-all-immigrants; https://www.gq-magazine.co.uk/politics/article/coronavirus-refugees-isolation.

expressed, so too, within works of art and literature, expressions of identification with a migrant condition, at worst, can be bland and empty articulations of little more than a sympathetic disposition.

The problems facing migration art stem from the tension that exists between their all-too-evident ethical intentionality and their actualization as a formal work of art. The philosopher, Rancière identifies this as producing an "indistinct sphere where... the specificity of political and artistic practices [are] dissolved," a place at which the "core of the old term morals: the distinction between fact and law, what is and what ought to be" breaks down, leading to "an unprecedented dramaturgy of infinite evil, justice, and redemption" (Rancière 2006, pp.1–2). Rancière sees this tendency among works of art to take what he names the new "ethical turn" as a defining characteristic of contemporary, neo-liberal art and politics (Rancière 2006; Guénoun 2009). Yet while the genre of migration art is a good example of this new ethics-driven trend, we might ask whether there are some works that manage, even within this frame, to evade the "indistinct sphere"? I propose as an example of a work that I consider to do so successfully, a multimedia, immersive video installation by the Moroccan–French artist, Bouchra Khalili, called *The Mapping Journey Project* (2008–11). Chubb finds Khalili's work to be a prime example of migratory orientalism, and astutely points out its repetition of many orientalist techniques. Yet even so, I find that the work that it performs on its spectators is moving in a way that ultimately challenges the colonizing impulse of orientalism. It is specifically the material form of the work—its oblique presentation of many migrant stories, combined with its large scale—that immerses us in its own complexity, and enables us to maintain a sense of the particularity of each story. Absorbed in the details of this work, we resist being overwhelmed by what Rancière refers to as the "dramaturgy of infinite evil, justice and redemption."

The work consists of a series of eight large screens on which are displayed maps on which an anonymous hand maps the line of a journey (Khalili 2019, *The Mapping Journey Project*). To the side of each map is a set of headphones through which the spectator listens to a recording of a migrant's voice narrating their journey. The narratives tend to parataxis, with an emphasis on description rather than explanation: stages of the journey are presented sequentially, without justification or reason. Each of the migrants' narratives is coordinated with the image on the screen: we watch as a hand appears on the map, and draws a line in a red, blue, or black pen marking the route they have taken. The hand is seen in close-up; the scale of the display magnifies it. Their journeys are extraordinary: usually vast distances undertaken for reasons that sometimes seem contingent and sometimes flimsy; the extreme physical endurance required; and journeys that are elongated and made hazardous by national security.[7] As the maps mark the geopolitical

---

[7] Seven of the maps chart journeys across continents; only no. 3, in Israel/Palestine, is more small-scale, but the journey no less intricate or perilous. On this, see Nawi (2015).

spaces of nation states, they are also occupied by the drawing hand; borders are crossed; oceans traversed; each map is turned into a record of uprooting. Even though each migrant is presented in disembodied form, as a voice and a hand, nevertheless their experience is humanized through the performance staged in the work of art: the hand gives human shape to the map; the recorded voice gives them a three-dimensional acoustic space which they (and we) inhabit; and the colored line that they draw seems to root them—and us—in the shared experience of a journey made, represented, and re-experienced by the viewer. The work produces a sense of what it feels like to be uprooted, deracinated, without home, and, as the migrants in *Happy End*, invisible. The work specifically does not create a feeling of sympathetic identification with migrant others. Rather, as it simulates displacement, it gives its viewers a sense of estrangement from their own environment, of a kind of homelessness, or enforced abandonment of one's place in the world, while at the same time projecting a sense of a social connection with the migrant, however tenuous that might in fact be.

In a separate work, *The Constellations* (2011), a series of eight silk screen prints, Khalili abstracts these journeys still further by plotting them as a series of dots on a vivid Persian blue surface, an unreal shade for the night sky, so that they resemble a constellation of stars etched on mineral surface, or embroidered in a carefully dyed fabric (Khalili, *The Constellations Series*). Inverting the idea that travelers are guided by the stars, Khalili creates constellations from the journeys that her migrants had taken. It makes their journeys epic, connecting them to the deep time of the universe, and to travelers across time who have navigated by the stars. In the flatness of the screen therefore, Khalili creates a kind of temporal and planetary depth, making the migrants, the traces of whose odysseys are memorialized in the work, heroic and timeless.

In common with other works of migration that I have surveyed here, Khalili's *Mapping Journey Project* and *Constellations* provide information about migrant experiences, raise public consciousness regarding migrants, and provide the therapeutic and other benefits of self-expression in migrant people. Yet their special potency lies outside these functions, in the capacity of their images and sounds to absorb us, and immerse us in the spaces that they produce, and displace us from our own. This is a sensual experience: it has the effect of a deracination, which we experience in the context of the works' explicit presentation of migrants' stories. Although the term carries a good deal of baggage, we might identify this as a version of the sublime—the migratory sublime.[8]

---

[8] Rancière's critique of Lyotard's sublime comes to mind here (Rancière 2006, pp. 15–17). But it is important to note that what I identify here as sublime in Khalili's work is not explicitly connected to any idea of the unrepresentable.

3. The Migrant as Shipwreck: Caroline Smith, *The Immigration Handbook* (2016); Caroline Bergvall, *Drift* (2014)

The desire to represent migrants in aesthetic works has a long and complex history that predates the contemporary migration "crisis." In the nineteenth century, migrants in art and literature were frequently depicted as gypsies. These mobile and ethnically distinct mobile people were objects of both repudiation and desire. For many, they were vilified because they existed outside the norms of respectable society; but for others, it was precisely because their style of living transgressed the strictures of rule-bound society that it was admired and desired. Poets and artists even styled themselves as gypsies, as in, for example, Matthew Arnold's "The Scholar Gypsy" (1854) (Nord 2006). When the attractions of gypsy living as a model for the creative life began to fade at the end of the century, the decline coincided with a wave of immigration to Britain from Eastern Europe. It was as though the arrival of these new people made the threat of such immigrant populations more pressing.

Despite the continuing presence of Roma people and other travelers, including the Irish, in contemporary European societies, the figure of the gypsy does not hold the place in the Western cultural imagination that it once did. Nowadays the figure for a migrant that may have replaced the gypsy is that of a shipwreck. This is partly because of the associations between modern day migrants and dangerous and illicit sea travel. Images of shipwrecked migrants have populated the news in recent times: victims of people trafficking, journeying across the Mediterranean in small inflatable boats; the Vietnamese refugees from the war, making perilous journeys across the South China seas from the late 1970s to early 1990s, facing the hazards of pirates and storms; or, relatedly, the desperate migrants who have more recently drowned in attempts to cross the Rio Grande river to gain access to the USA.[9] Specific examples of individual casualties often capture the headlines. These are often children: Alan Kurdi, the 3-year-old Syrian boy whose corpse was found on a Turkish beach in September 2015; or the Sudanese teenager whose corpse was found drowned on the coast close to Calais, having attempted a channel crossing in an inflatable dinghy in August 2020 (Grierson et al. 2020).

Yet the migrant as shipwreck is also a literary image with a history that precedes the contemporary moment. Joseph Conrad's short story, "Amy Foster" (1901), set in place a powerful version of this with his character Yanko, the sole survivor of an emigrant ship that sunk in the North Sea on its way from Poland to the United States. As Yanko is washed up on the shore in Kent, destitute and alone, he is rejected by all the people in the village in which he finds himself, apart from Amy

---

[9] For example, the case of the father and child drowned in the Rio Grande in 2019, whose photograph was widely distributed in the world media, discussed by Edgar Garcia in his "A Migrant's Lotería" (Garcia 2020, p. 252).

Foster, whom he marries. But in the end, even she rejects him, despite their having a child together. Her rejection of him is triggered specifically by his reversion to his native language when he is sick: she finds his language strange and frightening, and this rejection leads to his death. According to Edward Said, Conrad's short story is the "most uncompromising representation of exile ever written," and his assessment has ensured "Amy Foster"'s place as a model for all forms of displaced people in the twentieth- and twenty-first centuries (Said 1984, p. 165; Stonebridge 2018, pp.12–13; Rose 2017, p. 2; McDonagh 2021, pp. 290–6). Compared with the figure of the gypsy who represented freedom from convention, the shipwreck casts the migrant in a different light: on the brink of death, overwhelmed by the ocean, choking, spluttering, enfeebled, alone against the elements, cast adrift by a storm, or a sudden wave, unprotected by the vessel in which they travel, the shipwreck is the person who has risked everything.

The predominance of the image of the shipwreck supports Edgar Garcia's observation that modern day migrancy is defined in terms of risk and danger (Garcia 2020, p. 252). The figure of shipwreck places modern-day migrancy in a longer history of forced migration set in motion by racialized capitalism. In the history of Atlantic world slavery, shipwrecks loom large as the fate of many thousands of enslaved African people. The appalling case of the slave ship, *Zong*, whose entire "cargo" of 130 enslaved people were thrown into the ocean for an insurance claim in 1781, has been analyzed and commemorated in a number of studies and artworks, including most famously, J.M.W. Turner's *The Slave Ship* (1840), as an episode that stands for the atrocities of the Atlantic slave trade (Baucom 2005). In *Zong!* (2008), the poet M. Nbourse Philip takes the case report from the trial regarding the insurance claim—the only surviving documentary evidence of the event—and using only the words, and parts of the words, within that document, creates a lengthy, poetic rumination on the lives and deaths of the 130 deceased. This is a work of "erasure," in which the total dismantling of the language of the report is made to imitate the material experience of death by drowning. The emphasis on the bodies of the enslaved people, whose imagined names (the only words that remain intact) are inscribed in small print as a band that continues across the bottom of each of the pages, is conveyed in part by this violent disaggregation of letters and sounds. It is organized intricately across pages in which the abundance of white space seems like water in which the reader drowns, struggling to make sense of the scattered shards; when reading and vocalization replicate in the body of the reader the visceral feelings of suffocation and expiration. The organization of letters of the page is rhythmic, and has a strobe like effect; reading becomes dizzying—nauseating, even—as we too sink in its sublime emptiness (Klonaris 2011).[10]

---

[10] Helen Klonaris writes, "I begin reading *Zong!* out loud. "w w w   w   a wa" (p. 3). Very quickly, I am whispering, my voice and breath ragged. The letters far from each other sound like voices calling

In *Zong!*, through the formal work of the poem, Philips salvages a memorial to the wreckage of human lives that slavery inflicted from the fragments of the case report, as though the poet herself were a shipwreck cast away on a desert beach, constructing a shelter from the remains of the ship. In other recent works of migration art, we see a similar emphasis placed on salvage as commemoration. A Lampedusa-based artist, Franco Tuccio's simple wooden crosses made from the remnants of vessels that carried migrants to the island, respectfully memorialize the dead and draw them into Christian funerary ritual. Francesca Soliman compares Tuccio's small-scale works favorably with the spectacular exhibit of Swiss artist, Christoph Büchel, at the 2019 Venice Biennale of *Barca Nostra*, a hoisted wreck of a ship that had sunk containing over eight hundred migrant people from Africa who were trapped in its hull, killing almost all of them (Soliman 2019). Büchel's work divided opinion between those who experienced it as a necessary reminder to complacent art audiences of the loss of human life incurred by migration, and others, like Soliman, for whom it "stands out as the worst example of appropriation and exploitation of migrants' deaths" for commercial gain (Soliman 2019).

In Michael Haneke's *Happy End*, the association between the migrant and the shipwreck is registered when the five dark figures wander across the beach, like beachcombers just arrived on the shore. The setting of the film, in Calais, with the port and the resort both present throughout, foregrounds the ocean, which is presented as luminous, calm, but limitless—like a charming blue void which might suffocate you. The final image of the old man almost totally immersed in the water turns him into the shipwreck, rather than the Africans—an image of solipsism in the face of the suffering of others that is a fitting ending to this difficult film.[11]

Not just risk and danger, therefore, the shipwreck embeds a range of associations to do with being carried away, drifting, losing control; of total immersion, engulfing wateriness, endless liquidity; as well as repurposing and recycling, a

---

out from the water, like voices mourning. There is a sense in which words are not the thing here, that words must get out of the way for something else to come through. White space fills these pages, like water. I want to weep, or vomit" (Klonaris 2011).

[11] Hans Blumenberg's intriguing 1997 study, *Shipwreck with Spectator*, explores the recurrence of images of shipwrecks and spectator in the history of philosophy, and provides some context for understanding the profundity of the final image of the film. Blumenberg tracks a long history of instances of scenes in which a spectator watches a shipwreck within philosophical texts stretching back to Epicurus: the spectator, the philosopher, who abstracts significance from the scene; the shipwreck, whose vulnerability to the elements presents humans in their relationship to the Lifeworld. Both figures are metaphors, what he describes as non-concepts, and their importance is the way in which they connect abstract ideas with the material world. They are in a sense connective tissue that allows us to imagine ideas in the world. His study follows these figures through the history of philosophy, finding the two figures wrapped together, dependent on each other. In *Happy End*, Georges's position as both spectator (sitting watching out to sea), and shipwreck (immersed, drowning), suggests the solipsism within the culture which the film critiques. We might see Haneke as marking the ethical limits of the conceptual model that Blumenberg maps.

sense of resourcefulness in the face of exhaustion. The shipwreck indexes the very materiality of life and death, on and in the ocean: the limits of the body as the lungs fill with water; skin that is blotched, swollen, and puckered through soaking; random shards of wood and metal, the remains of the vessel, signs of destruction and possibilities of survival through salvaging; living on the edge, in the waste of the wreck, on the borders of life; living on borrowed time. In migration art, the image of the shipwreck registers simultaneously the resilience and fragility of human lives in transit.

Here are two examples from recent poetry, one formally conservative, the other experimental. The image of the shipwreck persists across stylistic divides. The first is Caroline Smith's *The Immigration Handbook* (2016), a series of well-crafted poems composed when the poet was a case worker for a British Member of Parliament. Having served as an intermediary between migrants and the slow-moving, cruel machinery of the state's immigration system, Smith has produced poems which are particularly affecting because they are based on events that she witnessed. The cases are real cases, and it is this that animates the poems. Smith's focus is on the failures of a bureaucratic system in which claimants wait for years for a resolution of their case, only to be told that their documents have been lost, or that their time has run out. More often than not, it is the inefficiencies of the system that inflict unendurable hardships on fragile people. Dickens's Circumlocution Office (from *Little Dorrit* (1857)) haunts the poems. We meet a series of claimants: Arjun Mehta, in "On Hold," who phones the Home Office repeatedly from a public telephone kiosk, to never get a reply over a period of seventeen years. The phone box is finally sealed, silent like a "sepulchre" or a (Keatsian) "obsidian urn" (Smith 2016, p. 9). Or a boxer (in "The Boxer") whose file has been lost at the Home Office, and his papers, Smith imagines, "brailled" "with mildew" (Smith 2016, p. 10). The metaphors are striking, even when they seem familiar and even clichéd. Sometimes this is because there is something slightly "off" about them that makes us pause: for instance, "braille," one assumes, should make the papers legible rather than illegible, but the misfit here calls us up short, making the environment yet more confusing, putting us in a position like that of a migrant. Sometimes Smith presents bureaucratic documents as poems. "Delay," for instance, is a redacted photocopy of a letter from the Home Office addressed to (one assumes) the lawyers acting for a client whose "No Time Limit application [has] been outstanding since 12 December 2006" (the letter is dated September 2015) (Smith 2016, p. 31). The letter contains instructions on how to proceed: further forms must be completed in order that more official processes might take place. This is grim poetry.

Even when they are not in the language of official documents, the poems adopt a flat mode of diction in blank verse. There is little in the way of formal meter; the sonorous elements of language are muted. Instead, through small linguistic shifts and adjustments—the redactions in the Home Office letter, for instance, or puns, or extended metaphors—they unsettle us, shift our point of view, redistributing our attention and enlarging our sympathy. Some of the poems narrate a moment of self-reflection or even transformation on the part of an official. For example, in "Red Road Flats," which begins

> When the Presenting Officer heard of
> their suicides following the ruling
> it was as if he'd woken up
> and found himself
> a trespasser in his own garden.
>
> (Smith 2016, p. 21, ll. 1–5)

it is not just the simile ("it was as if") but the caesura produced by the breaks between lines 3 and 4, and 4 and 5, that inject into the smooth surface of the complex sentence a kind of gasp of uncertainty, an opening for introspection. The poems that capture such moments are among the most affecting; in an understated way, the transformations they enact seem, at times, almost to be sacred.

The idea of intermediation is central to her project. Just as Smith served in her role as case worker as a mediator between migrants and the state and its functionaries, so too her poems attempt to convey to their readers the affective experience of the exclusions that she had witnessed. The rhetorical techniques which she draws on to achieve this invariably perform a kind of translation, often imaged as a physical transposition between spheres of experience: between the sphere of the state and its processes, and the subjective sphere of feeling and suffering. This is how the image of a shipwreck operates in a poem entitled "I.S. 96." "I.S. 96" is the name given in the UK to the official document that, until recently, conferred the status of "temporary admission" on a person seeking to remain while their immigration case was being considered by the Home Office (it no longer exists). In the poem, the experience of being in possession of an I.S. 96 is presented as being in a state of suspended animation, as though subject to the undulation of the waves (the failure of the system to resolve his case over many years is like "the sinking pull and roll / of pebbles shifting beneath him"). It is like being shipwrecked. From its introduction in line 4, the metaphor is extended through the rest of the poem's twenty-one lines, spatializing the experience. States of abandonment and survival are imagined in relation to the migrant, and projected on to a new landscape that is of his own making. It begins,

> The refusal notice told him he was
> "Appeals rights exhausted." He was.
> After eleven years on Temporary Admission,
> like a shipwrecked survivor
> staggering up the shore,

>   he had collapsed on the tide's edge
>   to the boom of the sea
>   and the cry of the gulls.
>
>   (ll. 1–8)

As his case is not resolved, and he is able to remain, his "his fragile hope" "take[s] root",

>   ...lacing
>   the bleached crowns of matted grass
>   to the quiet leeside of the dunes
>   among the flat, violet stones
>   and brittle bundles of seaweed
>   that drifted across the paths
>   of half-buried sleepers.
>
>   (ll. 16–22)

The beach is an abandoned terrain with its own fragile ecosystem: plant life just about survives on the dunes, alongside the seaweed, and the "half-buried" railway sleepers. The "sleepers" might also be human—half dead, half alive; and the beach a graveyard, of the not-quite-dead.

Smith's poems tread a thin line between sentimentality and being genuinely moving. At their best, their achievement lies in their ability to lead us between spheres of experience and points of view, accomplished through rhetorical devices that enable us to imagine inhabiting alien worlds. In "I.S. 96," the simile signaled by the word "like" ("like a shipwrecked survivor": note, too, the inversion of our expectations—not someone who has survived a shipwreck, but a survivor who has been shipwrecked, the emphasis resting on the condition of extreme survival) acts as a portal between the language of state bureaucracy ("Temporary Admission") and that of the suffering individual. The pun on "exhausted" in line 2—predictable enough—does similar work, shifting us from the domain of official process, to focus on the vulnerability of the migrant's body. The effects of embodiment are incremental. As with all Smith's images, the allusion to the shipwreck stays intact, yet it opens a window to an imaginative inhabiting of a state of abjection that is at once human and hopeful, as well as hopelessly funereal.

In Caroline Bergvall's *Drift* (2014)—a much more complex and demanding amalgam of poetry, performance, commentary, drawing, photography, documentary, and translation (her rendering of the Old English lyric, "The Seafarer")—the figure of the shipwreck operates in more formally complex ways. Through its ten distinct sections, the word "drift" refers to the drift of words, sounds, and grammatical forms between languages and over time; the movement of sounds and images between media, and the sliding between sounds of voice and percussion; psychological and emotional drift experienced by the poet in times of personal stress; and finally, the drift of an overcrowded rubber boat carrying seventy-two African migrants from Tripoli to Lampedusa. Sixty-three of the passengers perished on this ship, so it is presented as a kind of a wreck, even though the ship itself remained intact. In Bergvall's *Drift*, the shipwreck is inserted into, and is central to, a poetics of drifting.

Like Smith, Bergvall refers to a particular case of migration, that of the so-called "Left to die boat," which, when journeying across the Mediterranean in March 2011, ran out of fuel and drifted for twelve days, during which time most of those on board died through starvation and dehydration. At the time, NATO's military intervention in Libya meant that the region was saturated with military aircrafts and ships, and all activities were monitored by multiple agencies. But despite this, and even though the ship was observed and tracked by satellite surveillance systems, no one went to its aid. A report by the humanitarian group, Forensic Archaeology, parts of which Bergvall incorporated verbatim in section 4 ("Report") of *Drift*, combined the testimonies of the few survivors with wind and sea-current data, and satellite imagery, some of which was requisitioned from the military agents who surveyed the region, through which they "reconstructed the liquid traces of this event, producing a report that served as the basis of several legal complaints" (Forensic Architecture 2012). In interviewing the survivors, they explain that, "[r]ather than placing the emphasis on the subjective dimension of his experience, we used various memory aids—such as photographs of naval and aerial assets that were present in the area at the time of the events—to assist him in remembering details that could support the reconstruction of the event, and the identification of the various vessels and aircraft encountered by the vessel while at sea." Once again it is the material traces of the episode that are key, now heavily mediated by digital technologies of satellite surveillance, turning the physical presence of the boat into what they refer to (appropriately) as its "liquid" traces.

In section 8, "Log," Bergvall describes how she came across the case through a newspaper article in April 2012. At this time, she was already immersed in creating *Drift* as a performance piece with a percussionist, based on "The Seafarer."[12] The "Left to die boat" transformed the theme of drift that she had been exploring by reframing drifting as a matter of neglect, the consequence of a failure, or abandonment, in the context of an ethics of care (McMurtry 2018). In collaboration with a photographer, she worked at "macro magnification" of the surveillance photographs taken by the French military aircraft of the migrant ship, adding another layer to her work. These are reproduced in section 3 of *Drift*, "Sightings." The images are indistinct, patterns of lines, like those in a magnified

---

[12] Bergvall's reimagining of the "The Seafarer," and her rethinking of the significance of Old English as source of poetic knowledge and effect which she explores in other works too, constitute the core of *Drift*. See Davies (2018, pp. 200–1) and Daily (2006, pp. 175–204).

textile, or a fingerprint. The enlarged images "encounter the dead as they are still living and sailing". The opacity of the magnified photographs is compared with the fog that she drives through ("My car-lights would hit back at me like a mirror"); or the fog on the ocean in "The Sea Farer"; or the cognitive fog as she learns to read the Old English lines; or our own foggy apprehension of the complex elements of the poem, the fragmented words, the strange letters, the dissonance of the sounds, and the oddness of the images. As the strands of the poem come together we experience a clearing of the fog; a flash, or a sound, of clarity, but only momentarily. In "Log" she refers to the way in which the migrants' tragedy parallels a sense of drift in her own life; she weaves it together with an account of a period of personal breakdown, in which drug experiences cause cognitive drift, and she recalls being saved by a paramedic (Bergvall 2014, p. 151); a cruel contrast between herself and the migrants for whom no one comes to the rescue. Things come together and fall apart. "Being lost is a way of inhabiting space by registering what is not familiar" (Bergvall 2014, p. 139), she tells us. For her, this sense of being lost is connected to her sexuality and intimate relationships; but she also links it to the medieval sagas that are laced into this work: "Being both travel and settlement stories, many [sagas] describe episodes of being lost at sea. They call it hafville, sea wilderness, sea wildering." "Hafville" is the name given to eight lyrics within section 2 ("Seafarer"), in which language falls to pieces most completely: "Hafville 5" consists of the letter "t" repeated over and over again over two pages. What should we make of this disassemblage? These repetitions of a glottal sound? It is almost as though the alphabet is a sea in which we drift (McMurtry 2018, p. 819). "Sailing starts to take place in the unfolding of the graphic work, in the textual shape, in the spatial markers" (Bergvall 2014, p. 153), she writes. Writing the poem is like being on a boat; drifting; left to die.

Her appropriation of the "Left to die boat" in *Drift* only narrowly avoids exploiting the spectacular violence that its casualties suffered. It does so because in the complexity of its formal experimentation one registers an integrity of purpose. For Bergvall this is to find a mode of representation appropriate to the conditions of migration that render people who move invisible to the extent that they are left to die. Focusing precisely on Forensic Archeology's report, she responds to the techniques that they develop in tracing the migrants' journeys through the remnants of their experience, retained in the various cameras and communication devices that observed the journey. These are like a palimpsest, which Bergvall reconstructs in the poem. Hence her interest in the graphic, expressed in her own drawings in sections 1 ("Lines") and 7 ("Block 16A6"); in the medieval ruling lines that fascinate her (Bergvall 2014, p. 146); in the lines on a map; and those that we see in the magnified photographs; the lines that connect the stars in the sky; lines that are writing, in different alphabets ("writing becomes tracks and traces and lines"); the lines that connect all languages. "Everything ripples in contact" (Bergvall 2014, p. 135), she writes. The forensic remains of the migrants are ripples; transitory, fugitive marks. But they express points of contact, and hold within them an implicit sociality, and assume an ethics of care that has been obliterated by the military security techniques. Bergvall's work develops this idea of rippling to repair the atrocity committed against the migrants when their plight was ignored on the ocean.

Within the various strands that make up *Drift*, the migrants in the "Left to die boat" constitute only a small component. In some ways we might see them as marginalized in the poem as they were in life—left to drift, and unattended to—as semi-invisible as the migrants in Haneke's film. In that light, the poem might be accused of being an act of appropriation and aestheticization. But in other ways, they are absolutely central to a work that deals precisely with drifting, and to a poetic practice that is concerned with many forms of social displacement. This multilayered epic is an attempt to find a language in which to account for the effects of drifting. As the ripples that the migrants' boat made on the water as they drifted to their deaths are transposed into its central image, *Drift* is, among other things, a fitting and respectful commemoration of their particular lost lives.

7
Aesthetic Poison

Edgar Garcia

Large, grainy cobalt salts dusted from the mining of nickel and copper ore. Cadmium impurities isolated in the production of zinc. Cerulean blue brought to life by heat applied to cobalt oxide. The pellucid appeal of manganese for artists in search of true cyan. Each of these minerals gives the pigment a different hue. In the color of blue, for instance, cobalt creates a quality of turquoise, as if the gem were melted into liquid form on the canvas—recalling the Aztec name for turquoise, *chalchihuitl*, which was said to be found where the grass grows high and flows, as if nourished from below by the "cool and moist exhalation" of the stones beneath (Sahagun qtd. in Nuttall 1901: 228). Cadmium blue has a more haunted feel, receding into its muted shade much like the silent howler of Edvard Munch's cadmium-rich *The Scream*. Cerulean takes its name from its sky-like appearance, but really it has the quality of a dusty sky, more like the hazy horizon of coastlines in Southern France before the tramuntane or mistral wind comes roaring through to clear the particle-hanging air. Manganese makes blue that is bright and vivid—full of light like the sky but, unlike the sky and more like the sea, infused with greenish luster and the mysterious exultation of the creatures living below that pearly sheen.

When I run a paintbrush through a glob of paint, I feel that I am stirring those creatures beneath the waves of pigment and vehicle, pulling them into the light reflecting in combinatorial and transformative ways on the other paints already on the canvas. In the instant of a brushstroke, earth's minerals, vast mining operations, chemical processes, and even animal bodies (some black paint is still made from burnt animal bone) shake into new life on the watching jelly of my eye. I see the paint come to life then, teaching me about itself as if it were what French philosopher Pierre Hadot called a goddess pulling the veil from the scene of life. But, as Hadot notes in his famous study of the idea of nature as a withholding entity, *The Veil of Isis* (2006), the goddess of nature does not only hide her secrets of life, she also reveals that secret of life's emergence as it unfolds from death, decay, ruin, and disappearance—corresponding "to the representation both of the earth that hides the body and of the veil with which the heads of the dead are covered" (9). In my paint there is plentiful death. Not only are there the charred bones of animals and the occluded mining operations in Zambia and the Democratic Republic of Congo (where most of global cobalt production takes place, alongside the violent Ituri conflict over this precious resource in addition to gold, diamonds, and oil), there is also the present toxicity of the minerals. Through inhalation or skin absorption, my body is exposed to highly corrosive and in some cases carcinogenic substances. When I run a paintbrush through a glob of cobalt, I am sending deathly particulates into the air all around me.

And, while I don't paint in anything like the famous hoarded chaos of Francis Bacon (open paints piled on paints amidst endless wet paintbrushes in a tiny crowded room) or with the derelict intimacy that Vincent van Gogh held for his paints (horrifying fellow students at the Cormon Studio in Paris by painting with thick globs of lead paint that ran down the paintbrush onto his hands, or by holding those paintbrushes between his teeth as he did something or other with his hands, or by smoking his pipe as he painted with his paint-soaked hands, ingesting in so many ways the lead that likely led to his lead poisoning or saturnism (González Luque and Montejo González 2004: 10)), I do nonetheless paint with toxic substances whose settling onto my skin, over my mouth, or into my lungs is unknown to me. As I pull the veil of Isis from the revealing canvas, she reminds me of my inevitable mortality. It is all vaguely nefarious.

This vague feeling reminds me of John Berger's analysis of the largesse inherent in the oil painting of the so-called Renaissance Masters—the way that the expense of an oil painting served to reflect the expenditure of its patron, and how this economic symbolization in turn sought to capture its primary representations: landscapes and women. It also brings me to consider the more recent controversy around paint companies' designation of "flesh tones" that have historically meant pale and peachy skin—as if flesh were primarily white and only aberrantly brown or black. Art supply company, Jackson's Art, has subsequently renamed its peachy "flesh tint" as "pale terracotta" and expanded its skin tone sets to include "burnt sienna" and "burnt sienna extra dark," reddish brown and blackish brown pigments (Solomon 2020). In terms of its symbolic entanglement with wealth, gender, and race, then, oil painting comes with heavy historical baggage, vaguely nefarious if you sit down for any length of time to think about where the pigment comes from and how it has acquired its meanings over the years. Even today, it is interesting to note that the pigmentary decentering of whiteness and the elevation of brown and black colors involve semantic relations to dirt: flesh made into terracotta (i.e., baked earth) in one instance, and in the other burnt sienna (named after Siena, Italy, where the reddish mixture of iron oxide and manganese oxide was found in abundance in the Renaissance) made into flesh. Paint is no innocuous thing; in so many ways it corrodes, contaminates, confuses, and occludes—even while it inspires, makes worlds, investigates its own conditions for creativity, and simply combines in light and gesture to stand out in striking composition.

It is at this intersection of creativity and crisis, of critique and ideological entanglement, that the form of painting takes its historical shape. It is here—at this intersection, which is also a kind of pinwheel—that artists engage with the world historical conditions of their art, while also indeed making art. It is here that the art object is caught in what German philosopher Walter Benjamin called apocatastasis—returning time and again to both its positive and negative aspects (its world creation and historical contamination) until as that sometimes mystical philosopher put it, the "initially excluded, negative component" of an art object finds that "by a displacement of the angle of vision (but not of the criteria!), a positive element emerges anew in it too—something different from that previously signified. And so on, ad infinitum, until the entire past is brought into the present in a historical apocatastasis" (1990: 459). This passage, which appears in Benjamin's intellectual collage-work, *The Arcades Project*, has been a source of constant inspiration and confusion for me. I've stayed with it because it seems to get at something that is profoundly important (i.e., the interfusion of creativity, critique, and ideology; the positive element emerging from cognition of that which was previously excluded, and hence from a consciousness of contradiction), yet I've also stayed with it because it is so evasive. Like the astrological concept with which Benjamin explains his idea—apocatastasis, which denotes the recurrent return of a star to the same place in the sky—I've returned again and again to this passage because I feel it is pointing me in the direction of something key to my own thinking about aesthetics, history, and politics.

In an earlier essay, I've analyzed this key in terms of risk analysis, especially with how Benjamin reconfigures risk into something like restoration and justice (Garcia, 2020: 272–5). Apocatastasis represents a form of risk analysis (astrology) in which reckoning with one's exposure in the world must return to its originating sources of violence until all those sources are remembered, restituted, and the whole of time redeemed. It is a classic version of Benjamin's fusion of materialist Marxist and messianic Talmudic analysis. But just as importantly, I feel now, is that strange moment of correction that he offers his readers—when he says that the art object achieves its recurrent historicity by shifting the angle of vision *but not the criteria*. What does he mean to specify by insisting that the criteria not change in the aesthetic work of historical recursiveness? The German here is "*Maßstäbe*," which is perhaps more ambiguous than criteria—*Maßstäbe* denotes also standards, measures, scales, rules, yardsticks, and models. Criteria are standards for judging, and the word carries a connotation of judgment and distinction. Still, *Maßstäbe* has to do with not only distinction but also discernment; another translation in this context might be "framework" or indeed "form." In considering that Benjamin wishes to hold fast to framework or form (the yardstick), his reckoning with the historicity of art objects takes on a special meaning: it is not so much the materials of the art object that hold their historical recursiveness, or that bear that power to shift a viewer's angle of vision from ideology into critique and world-creativity, but rather the conceptual architecture carried by those materials also shifts the angle of vision. The materials of an art object are not so much units of historical information as they are made historical by their particular assemblage of signification, symbolization, coordination, and composition. In keeping with Benjamin's astrological metaphor, we might say that the material histories of pigment only become such (i.e., historical) when they are seen as the signifying constellations that they in fact are.

This renewed analysis of Benjamin's comments on historical recurrence, prompted now by the idea of aesthetic poison, brings me to the poisonous quality of aesthetic form not just in its material dynamics—that is, not just with respect to corrosive minerals and problematic mineral extraction industries. Rather, in addition to those dynamics, the network of meanings carried by the paint also corrodes. And what fascinates me most about this corrosion is its complex involvement in the creation of a work of art. In the artistic endeavor to make worlds and resist harmful ideological systems, there is nonetheless the fact that the art object itself is made from harmful symbolizing systems. It compels me to think about aesthetic poison not just in terms of poisonous units of art, but indeed in the whole vial of poison that arrives in the making of an art object—the terrible admixture—and which the art object also consumes. Benjamin's emphasis on holding fast to the *Maßstäbe* bears a faith in the combinatorial ways that that art object ingests the poison of its symbolic system, metabolizes it, and makes it into something potently self-possessed.

1. Forms of Colonial Gold

This historical pharmacology is perhaps no better expressed in any pigment than in metallic gold. The material basis of gold paint isn't typically toxic. Sometimes it contains mica, which gives it a reflective shine that in earlier times was achieved by the use of actual gold (as in gold leaf) or tin sulfide (as in mosaic gold); but mica is only dangerous in its process of production into a pigment, when the inhalation of the fine particles of dry mica powder by paint makers can lead to pneumoconiosis or lung fibrosis. In the use of contemporary gold pigments (many of which do not even contain mica), there is no such danger. Still, that only accounts for a portion of the *Maßstäbe* of gold. Gold is of course synonymous with worth, wealth, money, and markets. Gold extraction has a dark history in colonial endeavors reaching back to the Romans in the British Isles and, later at a much more devastating scale, the Spaniards in the Americas.

It is here that the mythology of gold takes its primary historical inflection. It is here that gold becomes something dramatically other than its mineral composition. It is here that it is transformed into what French scholar and literary titan J.M.G. Le Clézio calls the dream of the Americas. Describing that dream, Le Clézio writes, there was the Spanish dream of gold, a devouring, pitiless dream, which sometimes reached the heights of cruelty; it was an absolute dream, as if there were something at stake entirely different from the acquisition of wealth and power; a regeneration in violence and blood to live the myth of Eldorado, when everything would be eternally new. (1993: 2–3)

In its entanglement with colonial expropriation in the Americas, gold is not only synonymous with wealth and power; it is also synecdochical of civilizational consumption. Feeling themselves consumed (in late medieval European geopolitics; in religious wars in Palestine and on the Iberian Peninsula), the Spaniards set out to consume the Americas as a source of rejuvenation—new blood for the new life that was the new world. They arrived with a rapacity for the gold that betrayed a deeper zeal for world transformation. Gold was a spiritual vehicle. It was the key ingredient for the colonial alchemy whose absolute aim was the violent, unprecedented entanglement of four continents into a unified effort of wealth extraction (Lowe 2020).

Strangely, in thus construing gold as a synecdochical key of world historical transformation, the Spaniards were mirrored in their fellow civilizations in the Americas. Among the Aztec, Maya, and Inca, gold was also a spiritual vehicle, a means of reckoning with the gods and the world historical destiny they held in their hands. But rather than raise this metal toward the heavens to propitiate world change, as did the Spaniards, the cultures of Mesoamerica used it to envision the earthliness of the gods and the godliness of the earth. Or, better put, gold helped them to consider what and how the gods digested with their bowels: the Nahuatl-language (i.e., the language of the so-called Aztecs) word for gold is *teocuitlatl*, meaning literally "god-excrement" (Restall 2003: 183); and the Yucatec Mayan-language word for gold is *takin*, meaning similarly "sun-excrement" (Le Clézio 1993: 13; Knowlton 2016: 327). In ancient Mesoamerica, gold was associated with regeneration, especially with regard to the filth, sickness, pollution, and putrescence that are necessary aspects of life cycles. The use of gold (literally and figuratively) in healing ceremonies served to emphasize the permeability between patient and environment, underscoring the act of healing as a symbolic parallel to the earth's phenomenal ability to churn new life out of waste, disease, and pollution (Knowlton 2016: 328–9). Goldwork was therefore deeply connoted with techniques, styles, and ideas of transformation, especially therapeutic change.

Of course, this could not be more different from how gold was conceptualized by the Spaniards. When they expropriated the gold of the Americas, they did not consider its therapeutic relation to earth and bodies. They did not even bother to transport the *Maßstäbe* of Mesoamerican gold, whatever those criteria were, back to Spain. What I mean is that the Spaniards did not take back to Europe the Mesoamerican gold headdresses, bracelets, earrings, nose rings, necklaces, talismans, regalia, embroidery, chalices, musical instruments, and other ceremonial

164   AESTHETIC POISON

objects. They melted all these things down to coins, *escudos*, cobs, and ingots. Such objects were not only easier to pack into the galleons, they could also be stamped with symbols of a Spanish maritime dominion that bordered on messianic self-affirmation: the Christian cross, the Spanish King's coat of arms, and the pillars of Hercules at the Strait of Gibraltar intersected by the bold acronym P.U.A. (which revised the famous warning on those pillars—*non plus ultra*, "beyond this nothing"—into *plus ultra America*, "further beyond, America"; hence revising a world historical orientation reaching back to classical antiquity) all feature on the coins, *escudos*, cobs, and ingots. Charles V, King of Spain from 1516 to 1556 and Holy Roman Emperor from 1519 to 1556, made the *plus ultra* his personal motto, and it came to denote a colonialist Spanish self-understanding: always reaching *beyond*, always acquiring *more*. When the Spanish stole the gold from the Americas it was a double theft: they took the material gold, obviously, but they also eliminated the form in which such gold held its symbolic, intellectual, aesthetic, and therapeutic values.

2. Infinite Regress

These considerations came into a new light for me in a collaboration with Peruvian American visual artist Eamon Ore-Giron. Ore-Giron's best-known work is a series of large format paintings titled *Infinite Regress*. The paintings of this series are highly geometric, drawing on the visual styles of abstraction and spatial mathematics found in Andean weaving and architecture. On first glance, the paintings appear to represent time's movement in a visual field of orbs and intersecting planes—much as one might track the movement of time by watching the sun or moon move into and out of alignment with pyramidal steps, corbelled arches, bisecting pillars, ceremonial platforms, and astronomically orientated passageways and vaults. Apocatastasis indeed. But, again, apocatastasis in reference to more than celestial recurrence or return. One of the core components of Ore-Giron's work is the use of gold paint—a tremendous amount of gold in the finely delineated architectonic work through which the orbs pass and, less often, in the orbs themselves. In their interlocking geometry, these gold paintings also look like elaborate ceremonial jewelry, talismans, and tunics hanging from the untreated linen canvases. The canvases are thick with gold and their gold is thick with the abstraction of Andean aesthetic form and the history of that form in its colonial expropriation. Ore-Giron's goldwork serves to remind its viewers of what was stolen *and* indeed that so much was stolen—not just the gold stuff itself, but its formal dynamics in a culture complex spanning the Americas.

My collaboration with Ore-Giron has primarily consisted of his artist book *Infinite Regress* (2020), for which I provided the writing. In doing so, I came to appreciate the living interaction between materiality and abstraction in his work. I wrote such things as:

> It is not just embroidery. It is the embroidery idea. It is not just magic. It is the magic idea. Is immanence of the abstract in the creature who is the mirror, who mirrors. Concave, like history in its natures, made into "figurative spatial simultaneity."

And:

> The concept is the "little leap into its opposite." It is contradiction at the level of the idea, the rhythm. In its less compulsive instances, it is contradiction at the level of syntax or, still more disparately, at the level of a logical construct. But, like a disc of paint cudgeled from crushed stones, those instances could be incorporated in the fabric, that "rhythmic tick-tock... closer to the ears of the gods."

And:

> My god must be getting sheared again, his skeleton
> scraped for what's left, because today—this morning—
> I remembered my dreams like an empty tube,
> a clear glass that had passed between us but pale, now,
> like a sun in mist, an unattainable ~~gray~~ shadow;
> he must be shiny as linoleum, sleek as backsplash.

And, perhaps most directly: "And it, conversely, passes through a scene like a volute whose return makes the stitch of vertices that are all edge. The myth is in the nodes." In each of these passages I tried to convey what I felt to be a constant animating contradiction at the heart of Ore-Giron's work, which draws so enthusiastically from the goldwork traditions of the Americas but which, at the same time, places this goldwork in a visual field of abstraction and spatial mathematics. Like a tapestry, the composition of his work weaves Andean ideas about space and form into the materiality and material history of gold paint. In doing so, it gets to that therapeutic function that gold form has in the Americas—but, crucially, it does not do so by way of nostalgia.

In one of our public conversations (hosted by the Anderson Collection at Stanford University), I asked Ore-Giron about the uses of gold in his work, considering its many complicated connotations for an artist engaged with the histories of the Americas. The two things that stood out to me from his answer were mentions of *ritual* and *glue*. He said that the byzantine intricacy of the goldwork in his paintings staged a kind of ritual for him—that he certainly did not give it any initial cultural connotations. Rather, he found himself caring for the gold paint in a way that he had not cared for other paints previously—so that after spending "twenty hours on a painting" there was a particular mindset that was created, "like putting yourself in the mind state of a ritual, but in yourself." This brought me to consider the therapy-work associated with gold in its indigenous contexts, where its conceptualization as god-shit allowed for human patients to disidentify with their personal bodies and, via the very putrescence and disease afflicting them, become absorbed in environmental and divine sensibilities that either heal them or dignify their transition to some other state of life and death.

This profoundly liminal understanding of gold was further materialized in Ore-Giron's description of the adhesive component for the paint—that which not only adheres the paint to the canvas but that with which the paint absorbs the canvas into itself. He says he uses the now rather outdated adhesive of rabbit skin glue (in use since at least the 1400s and possibly earlier) because he

> likes cooking the glue up and the effect that it gives the linen—and what it does to the linen, which is act almost like a starch. It's a protein essentially, it takes up the linen and it really kind of makes it almost a living thing. So when you paint these paintings with rabbit skin glue they really bow. They almost look like they're going to break and then overnight they relax and get flat again.

It strikes me that his description of the adhesive offers metaphorical resonance for the gold paint: it not only sticks to the canvas, it grabs it, transforms it, and brings it to life in its hygroscopic process, that is, in its variable absorption of moisture from the atmosphere. Such life-giving component in the paintings makes the composition itself appear to participate in ritual: it makes the canvas bow, bringing it to a point where it might break, until it is allowed to relax and lay flat again. It becomes a patient indeed. And this is not to mention also the presence of animal flesh in the admixture—further making the gold-painted canvas into something like a substance permeated by animal beings and environmental considerations.

If a painted canvas is something like a scene of a crime, involving centuries of violent wealth expropriation and status display, involving also present conditions of resource extraction and mineral toxicity, if these are its *Maßstäbe*, then it is truly a patient in need of ritual transformation. And if its *Maßstäbe* involve gold, then it is all the more so in need of the therapy of gold-shit. This is not a retrospective position because expropriation of the wealth of the Americas is ongoing, and indeed because the phenomenological effects of the stolen forms continue to be felt in every artist or writer of the Americas who must encounter their histories and cultural inheritance as a gap, loss, erasure, forceful elimination, or continued prohibition. Ore-Giron has pointed out to me that the earliest gold metallurgy in the Americas (c.2000 BCE) is found near Lake Titicaca in present-day Peru and Bolivia. There is no returning to that moment of creation without the thick film of five hundred years of colonial depredation and the contemporary extraction industries (a lot from China these days) still operating heavily in those lands. This is not to mention the internecine wars and conflicts in the Americas that preceded Columbus's arrival, or the various meanings that diverse cultural interpretations in the pre-Columbian Americas give to gold and, hence, to gold paint in the perpetual apocatastasis of the contemporary canvas.

Recently, this thick film has been theorized as a kind of "saturation" by scholars C. Riley Snorton and Hentyle Yapp, who see such saturation as a point of material convergence between colonial histories and aesthetics, contemporary art markets, racist legacies and racial legibility, and the dynamics of paint and color. Ore-Giron's painting is thick with all that. But the special framework of gold gives such saturation a particular meaning in a Mesoamerican context: it is not just saturation, it is saturated filth compressed—by skill, technique, and pedagogies of perception—into the substance of ritual healing. It is the poison or toxic element that is ingested and metabolized to make historical sickness into a symbolic parallel of life cycles and necessary transformation (like a painterly version of the classic ghost dance tradition, in these works colonial theft of gold and much else is the ill that necessitates the therapeutic conception of gold and paint; the gold-shit is both the pollution and purifying element). It is, as Ore-Giron calls it, an infinite regress or, as I have called it, an apocatastasis that will keep coming back to its negative and eliminated elements until those elements are transvalued in real justice, equity, and social transformation. Perhaps the regress is infinite, or perhaps its alchemical moment is coming. Or maybe it has never gone away. There has always been shit in the world, there continue to be artists who swallow the poisons and sweat orichalcum, and the gods must know where and how all their gold churns unsettled even today.

In Hadot's study of our magnified wish to find out the secrets of such gods, he discusses gold sparingly, and then really only through the first century CE writings of Ovid, Seneca, and Pliny the Elder. Hadot notes that these Roman writers had a lot of anxiety about gold extraction. For instance, the philosopher and encyclopedist Pliny (perhaps considering Rome's own colonial mining industries in the British Isles and elsewhere) felt that gold mining was motivated only by cupidity, so could inspire only the same; just as iron mining was motivated only by hatred and war-mongering, so could inspire only war. It is all still more offensive to Pliny because the earth's surface provides everything needed for healthy, happy lives: "How innocent and happy our life would be, nay, how refined it would be, if we only lusted for what is on the earth's surface; that is, what is right at our feet" (qtd. in Hadot 2006: 142). In Ovid's description of the same offensiveness of mining operations, he seems to echo a Mesoamerican conception of gold as godly excrement: "Mankind was no longer content to ask the fruitful earth for harvests and the food she owed, but he penetrated as far as her entrails, and tore from her what she had hidden,...the treasures that aggravate our evils" (qtd. in Hadot 2006: 141). The difference between Ovid's conception of earth's gold-filled bowels and the Mesoamerican one is that Ovid has no access to a therapeutic possibility for the divine excrement. For Ovid, the gold would be better left untouched, whereas for Mesoamerican ritual practice in its form and ideation it is a necessary point of contact. Moreover, in its Mesoamerican conception, the gold in the bowels of the earth makes available a type of contact that—as anthropologist Claude Lévi-Strauss wrote in discussing a similar healing ritual in the Kuna culture of Central America—creates a vector or opening point "from the physical universe to the physiological universe, from the external world to the internal body." Citing this passage, anthropologist and scholar of Maya religions Timothy Knowlton notes that the particular rhetorical relation between gold-shit and the bowels of an earth goddess in the Mesoamerican patient–healer relation not only creates an opening between physical and physiological worlds, but also transforms that opening into a filter for purifying pollution:

> The very permeability of the body that makes it susceptible to pollution is addressed through identification of the diseased parts with the deity herself. Moving roughly from lower body to upper body, ultimately the corporeal polarity between goddess and patient is reversed, as the lower orifices of the underworld goddess become the upper orifices of the patient. Bit by bit it is revealed what golden accoutrements of Ix Hun Ahau [Maya Goddess of Earth, sexuality, pollution, and purification] entered the patient's body, until the now purified excrement of the one exits the mouth of the other, and the vital breath of the goddess becomes the patient's vital breath as well. (2016: 329)

The Maya corporeal relation to the toxicity of gold could not be more dramatically transformational (at least, in this instance, in which Knowlton is working with the *Ritual of the Bacabs*, a colonial Yucatec Maya medical text that, he argues, bears traces of a Mesoamerican medical tradition dateable as early as 1200–1500 CE and extant in various forms to this day). In this therapeutic framework by which the pollution gives way to purification, the toxicity of the social history of gold can *not* only *not* be avoided; it must be integrated into the patient's self-perception as a harmful element that, by way of synonymy with the filth of gods, brings a sense of contact with the gods themselves—making their lower orifices into our upper orifices and vice versa, so that any person's inescapable putrescence is seen and smelled in the vital breath that keeps all life going.

Considering the contemporary significations of gold that come with gold paint, the *Maßstäbe* or even *saturation* of gold painting, the above passage suggests that that too is inescapable. The artist of the Americas must ingest the poison of colonial historicity and, compositionally blurring the distinction between historical worlds and physiological worlds, transform that poison into a kind of self-possession that is historical redemption. They must eat lead and sweat orichalcum; they must breathe pollution and speak poetry. They must reckon with these hard histories and make of such crisis tremendous efforts of creativity and world creation. There is simply no other way. Or, put another way, if there is an attempt to get around it, the artist fails to be grounded in the lands in which they make their art, and the art is subsequently groundless, watery, even airy in its formation. Either it is underworlds all the way through or it is without its world thoroughly. Our allotted paints are inescapably thick with aesthetic poison.

8
Aesthetic Criticism and the Postcolonial

Ankhi Mukherjee

"A classic is a work that comes before other classics; but those who have read other classics first immediately recognise its place in the genealogy of classics," writes Italo Calvino in *Why Read the Classics?* (1999: 7). A classic is first among equals in the cabinet, on the curriculum, in the collective literary unconscious: to read a classic is to know its place and know our place, belated and second-rate in relation to it. Calvino's musings on reading classics—the examples he mentions are Lucretius, Lucian, Montaigne, Erasmus, Quevedo, and Marlowe—depict the contemporary world, "banal and stultifying," in the throes of an epochal definitional crisis, upon which only a classic can bestow form and purpose. Without its guardianship, the present would lose itself in a "timeless haze" (1999: 8). The dominant mode of literary criticism seems unable to discuss the classic without activating the temporal logic of the civilizational lag, and this explains why posterity's engagement with classics—Graeco-Roman as well as the Western literary canon—is doomed to be a one-sided, non-mutual relationship. While postcolonial studies painstakingly parses textual references to Shakespeare in Jean Rhys's *Good Morning, Midnight*, a Creole Ophelia drowning in addiction in Paris is unlikely to add interpretive dimensions to *Hamlet* scholarship. Similarly, while the specter of European Romantic "Satanism" is routinely invoked to read nineteenth-century Bengali poet Michael Madhusudan Dutt's revisionist epic, *Meghnadbadhkabya*, the Milton or Blake industry remains untroubled by the exertions of the Calcutta-born member of what Blake, with reference to Milton, dubbed the "Devil's Party."[1]

As a US-trained Victorianist scholar who teaches English literary history (from 1760 to the present) at the University of Oxford and researches on three seemingly disconnected fields—nineteenth-century literature and culture, psychoanalysis and the history of medicine, and postcolonial studies—it frustrates me that literary and critical work done by authors deemed "postcolonial," on topics deemed "postcolonial," is widely perceived by mainstream literary critics as political. Political here stands for literature that is not beautiful, that is anti-style; it is

---

[1] The logic of the supplement that inspires much of postcolonial (or decolonizing) curriculum revision would recommend the reading of Dutt's blank verse epic not instead of but with Milton's *Paradise Lost*, expanding and troubling traditional Western understandings of the "Devil's Party."

taken to be didacticism unmitigated by contrarian wit, self-reflexiveness, and willed purposelessness. It may be argued that if postcolonial writing and theory, their provenance tied to the nefarious politics of Empire, colonization, and the tricontinental slave trade, are not seen as aesthetic it is because the aesthetic itself, as Jonah Siegel observes, was seen for most of the twentieth century "to be either divorced from politics and ethics or in an unhappy partnership with the worst versions of both" (2016: 562). The intellectual tradition of the aesthetic, the modern concept traceable to the philosopher Alexander Gottlieb Baumgarten's definition in 1750, distances it from history and life. Our aesthetic theorists have, in singular ways, estranged the relationship between the object of aesthetic inquiry and the material object itself: Adorno likened the aesthetic to "the conceptual without the concept" (1997: 96); Kant separated aesthetic judgment from social and political concerns; Benjamin described the work of art as a funeral pyre, the enigma of the fire promising simultaneous blindness and illumination.

"What aesthetics refers to is not the sensible. Rather, it is a certain modality, a distribution of the sensible," Jacques Rancière states (2009: 1). This distribution, Rancière explains, has three implications: a certain configuration or re-configuration of the given; a calibration of the relation between sense (understanding) and sense (sensibility); a conjunction or disjunction in the relationship between the faculties which dictates which sense is higher and which the lower. The aesthetic dimension, Rancière argues, is a "dissensus": not conflict but a perturbation and distribution of the ethos which posits one sense over another (3). This intervention in the distribution of the sensible is the politics of the aesthetics. Rancière comments also on the aesthetics of politics: politics, he points out, is not simply "laws and constitutions" (8) but invested in a mode of "dissensus," a supplement to the consensual game of domination and rebellion. The example he uses is democracy, with its "disjunctive junction of power and the demos" (10). Political "dissensus" puts two heterogeneous logics—that of the difference *within* the demos and the oligarchic functioning of power which seeks to neutralize such difference—in the same world. The political understanding of this democratic supplement, Rancière argues, is aesthetic, in that the supplement is "a conflict of sensory worlds" (11). The aesthetics of knowledge he proposes is a form of supplementation that redistributes the configuration of the topoi, whether aesthetic or political, thereby changing the "topography of the thinkable" (19).

As Raji Vallury argues, in Rancière's interpretation, aesthetics is more than a theory of art: "It is a mode of intelligibility for conceptualising ways of doing, seeing, and understanding art forms" (2014: 245). Rancière does envision forms of critical art which will bridge the gap between the aesthetic and the political, feeling and understanding, the autonomy of art and the heteronomy of life. Gayatri Chakravorty Spivak's rereading of the canon also pivots on the idea of an "epistemic transformation" (2012: 45) through introducing a dissensus of reason (Spivak's term is "fracturing"). Spivak's redefinition of aesthetic critique and

Rancière's aesthetics of knowledge have in common the idea (or promise) of equality (Rancière) and of upward social mobility (Spivak). The framework is international, though not universalizable, and the readings of literature, in Spivak's case, are locally situated within global, international, or planetary frameworks. The version of the aesthetic Spivak adapts for postcolonial lifeworlds comes not from Kant's third *Critique* (although she acknowledges the force of the Kantian counterintuitive) nor does it have affinities with Schiller (who lends the "aesthetic education" of her title). Schiller, according to Spivak, undoes binaries and double binds, forming new totalities and turning "the desire inscribed in philosophy into its fulfilment" (2012: 19). The aesthetic, in her redefinition, is a training ground of the imagination for epistemological performance and (epistemological) transformation. In an interview with Cathy Caruth, Spivak mentions the UN Committee on the Status of Women, where the discussions had centered on the provision of basic needs such as food, shelter, and clothing, and on education as a vocational need. She was reminded of Du Bois saying that the "Negro" needs food, shelter and clothing as well as communication with the stars. Aesthetic education, a completed education, supplements the human-rights discourse of global literacy with "communicating with the stars" (Caruth and Spivak 2010: 1023).

1. Postcolonial Critique: Is Critique Inherently Postcolonial?

"The idea of the post-colonial has taken such a battering from post-colonial theorists that to use the word unreservedly of oneself would be rather like calling oneself Fatso," Terry Eagleton (1999) wrote with characteristic irreverence in an LRB review essay on Spivak's *A Critique of Postcolonial Reason*. The review was perhaps neither to the point nor fair, but Eagleton was right to see auto-critique as a persistent mode of contemporary postcolonial discourse. This is hardly unexpected: postcoloniality works best as a futurity or a vision of the future, the utopian promise of a receding horizon, for history shows that erstwhile colonies have not got rid of colonialism altogether. Postcolonial theory is increasingly confronted with challenges, both to its intelligibility and to its conceptual range in the face of the asymmetries of power in the global world, the inseparability of neocolonialism from "unlimited capitalism" and neoliberalism, and the escalation of violence—global, internecine, ethnic, communal, or gendered—in erstwhile colonies. The very size and expandability of the postcolonial world have gone against a coherent and systematic formulation of it. As David Chioni Moore observes:

> The colonial encounters of the past two hundred years – from Dakar to Calcutta, Samarkand to Jamaica, Skopje to Tallinn, or Vladivostok to Seattle by the long

route – were so global and widespread, in unstandardizable diversity, that every human being and every literature on the planet today stands in relation to them: as neo-, endo- and ex-, as post- and non-. (2001: 124)

Moore's own scholarship supplements the geopolitical scope of Ella Shohat's "Notes on the postcolonial," adding the Soviet portion of the Second World War to Shohat's map of the First and the Third. The trouble is that even if one were to add China ("for China has been buffeted by the Mongols, Manchus, Japanese, and British, and today it imperially-colonially controls Tibet and the giant Turkic Muslim Xinjiang Uighur region," Moore 2001: 123) to this, even if all these regions were cross-hatched on a map, certain smaller zones would remain unmarked. The problem is quantitative as well as qualitative—no one mode of postcolonial critique can do justice to all the numerous determinants and interpellations of the multiply located subject positions it represents. It is like the Great North Road of E.M. Forster's *Howards End*, "suggestive of infinity," as it resonates back on the banal highway, lending it *noumen* and nobility at the same time, as Fredric Jameson puts it.[2] Does postcolonial critique, inhabiting the spatial gap between the banal and the noumenal, the concrete and the metaphysical, dare speak its name? If, as in the Kantian mode, postcolonial reflection is inseparable from the critique of postcolonial reflection, and it is doomed to realizing itself in the form of antinomy, what has aesthetics to do with it?

In the introduction to *The Postcolonial Unconscious*, Neil Lazarus states that he wishes to move from the "'negative' moment of critique to the more 'positive' moment of reconstruction":

> While I still believe that it is important to write in the mode of critique, I will be concerned here also to propose alternative readings and conceptualisations, to be set alongside and compared with those currently countervailing. (2011: 1)

Elsewhere, while discussing Ania Loomba's treatment of anti-colonialism, he conflates critique with deconstruction (67). As his riff on Fredric Jameson's 1981 title (*The Political Unconscious: Narrative as a Socially Symbolic Act*) reminds us, the urgent critical task at hand in that book is to heed the political occlusions and denials that are still in place. This is because not only is the range of literary works typically addressed by postcolonial scholars remarkably attenuated, and I am quoting Lazarus's reading here, but "the same questions tend to be asked,

---

[2] Fredric Jameson cites this section of *Howards End* in his essay "Modernism" to discuss the "spatial perception" of industrial modernity, particularly as it intersects with empire. It is Jameson's argument that the Great North Road is a "noble idea" that resonates back on the "banal highway, lending it noumen and thereby transforming it into the merest promise of expressivity without having to affirm it as some official 'symbol'" (1988: 54–5).

the same methods used, the same concepts mobilised, and the same conclusions drawn" (19).

A very interesting case of reconstruction of what Lazarus calls the "new history of the present" can be seen in the book's pivotal second chapter. There, Lazarus offers a defense and justification of Jameson's controversial and widely pilloried argument about "Third World" literature in the 1986 *Social Text* article, "Third-World Literature in the Era of Multinational Capitalism." Lazarus is referring to Jameson's seemingly sweeping hypothesis that "All third-world texts are necessarily... allegorical, and in a very specific way: they are to be read as what I will call national allegories" (cited in Lazarus 2011: 92). The assertion has played a significant role in stereotyping and undermining the vast, eclectic, and diverse body of postcolonial literary and cultural production and has frequently been refuted in postcolonial studies, largely along the lines laid down in Aijaz Ahmad's influential rebuttal: "For the further I read," Ahmad wrote in his rejoinder to Jameson, "the more I realized... that the man whom I had for so long, so affectionately, albeit from a physical distance, taken as a comrade, was, in his own opinion, my civilizational Other" (1995: 84). Lazarus, however, sees Ahmad's reading as inadequate, showing that it is quite possible to defend Jameson from the charge of "Third-Worldism."

Does Fredric Jameson need saving? Does Lazarus's riposte to Ahmad's riposte give us the critical resources to reconstruct the aesthetics of the postcolonial for the twenty-first century? If we can sweep these inconvenient questions aside, Lazarus is at his acerbic and entertaining best on the two Marxists, Jameson and Ahmad. His point is devastatingly simple: what Jameson *actually said* was not that third-world texts valorize nationalism as the overarching political value, but that they tend to be apprehended by first-world readers (here represented by the American intellectual) in this unsatisfactory way. "Jameson explicitly disavows this 'first-world wisdom,'" Lazarus states. Jameson wrote the "Third-World Literature" essay for a memorial lecture to a largely US audience, with its "schooled inability to grapple with cultural difference" (Lazarus 2011: 103) and there is no doubt in Lazarus's mind that Jameson is critical of the first-worldist perspective that would have it that nationalism has been put to bed on this side of the imperial divide. He goes so far as to say that "third world" in the Jameson essay "functions more as the name of a political desire (as in 'Cuba very much identifies itself with the third-world') than as the descriptor of an actual place" (106) and that literature which rises to the challenge of "third-worldness" thus defined will, of necessity, allegorize the nation.

Lazarus's argument is that Jameson did not mean that third-world literature is hung up on national allegory, but that these writings seem to require such an hypothesis: if Jameson had not made his "national allegory" hypothesis, we would have had to invent it. Jameson and his political unconscious prove to be winners, while Ahmad has not only blatantly misread Jameson's intentions but, in invoking a "rhetoric of otherness" in Jameson is complicit with a climate in which, Lazarus thunders on, "the strategic production of the race card was becoming a formidable weapon in the competition of symbolic capital, within the academy as well as in the wider circuits of culture and society" (103). The real losers in this debate are, of course, postcolonialists, bloody-minded readers lost in the muddy morass of received meanings. Lazarus, at least five of whose critical works have the word "postcolonial" in their title, takes this parting shot: "Scholars in postcolonial studies should therefore seize the opportunity today to reread [Jameson's 'Third-World Literature' essay], as though for the first time" (107).

In Lazarus's "sociological" counterargument, postcolonial theory is anti-historicist and anti-Marxist, a critical practice opportunistically consolidated on the decline of liberationist ideologies. It is accused of using tropes and terms which are not only *not* attuned to the social reality of non-Western literature but are actively alienated from them. In the book's bluster against the "pomo-postcolonialists" (25) it overlooks the substantial work of Marxist and Subaltern Studies postcolonial critics, but that is irrelevant to this discussion. *The Postcolonial Unconscious*, in its polemic against postcolonial theory, differentiates the primary and secondary texts of postcolonial criticism, privileging the emancipatory charge of the literary over the theoretical. This falsifies a field whose foundational texts use philosophy, history, literature, and culture interchangeably. Spivak's *Critique of Postcolonial Reason*, for example, offers several counterarguments to Lazarus's description of postcolonial critique as destruction, particularly in the way she traces the figure of the native informant through fictional representations.

Ethnography denies the native informant autobiography, even as this figure is generative of a text of cultural identity. The literary or philosophical texts that Spivak reads here are not ethnographic: the human norm is European, but here too the Native Informant is *both* needed and foreclosed. After 1989, Spivak states, a certain self-marginalizing and self-consolidating postcolonial subject has been appropriating the Native Informant's position. Whether a metropolitan migrant or the citizen of a decolonized nation state, he or she serves as a facilitator for exchange between metropole and nation and or transnational corporation and country of origin. It is for this usurper figure, the class of "functionary intelligentsia" (Spivak 2012: 61) participating in international civil society, that the meaning of critique—which tests its relation to truth and measures its degree of interestedness—must remain not only relevant but urgent.

Spivak's critique, Mark Sanders says, is "broadly Kantian": "there are limits to what human beings can know...and therefore any claim to know, to have information, is to be subjected to a kind of examination called critique" (2006: 9). If we choose to read critique as negative criticism, Spivak's strongest criticism of postcolonial as a figure is that "it masquerades as and overrides the foreclosed position" she calls "the native informant." Spivak proposes that a different standard of literary evaluation, necessarily provisional, can emerge "if we work at the (im)possible perspective of the native informant as a remainder of alterity, rather than remain caught in some identity forever" (352). Spivak finds such a remainder of alterity in Christophine, Antoinette's Martinican nurse in *Wide Sargasso Sea*, Jean Rhys's rewriting of Charlotte Bronte's *Jane Eyre*. Despite her commodification—she is a wedding present—Christophine is briefly entertained as an affective and enunciative subject in the text. She is an adept mediator between cultures and also someone who understands the limits of cultural translation (it is she who judges that culture-specific black ritual practices cannot be used by whites as cheap remedies). A post-emancipation consciousness—"No chain gang, no tread machine, no dark jail either. This is a free country and I am a free woman" (*Wide Sargasso Sea*, cited in Spivak 1999: 130)—Christophine is given the license to talk back to Rochester about his gross exploitation of Antoinette. Soon after the exchange, however, she is "quietly placed outside the story," Spivak observes, "with neither narrative nor characterological justification" (131). Spivak reads in her parting words in *Wide Sargasso Sea*, "Read and write I don't know. Other things I know," "a singular strength, not a weakness" (131).

If Spivak has trained herself to read the voice consciousness of the native informant here, it is difficult to replicate this reading or brand it as postcolonial criticism: herein lies its aesthetic charge and efficacy. The site of the native informant can only be read, "by definition, for the production of definitive descriptions"—she cannot be reclaimed, Spivak cautions, as a reading position. "I am calling for a critic or teacher," she says of the foreclosed native informant in Kant's *Critique of Judgement*, "who has taken the trouble to do enough homework in language and history," and who can analyse the address structure of the text, with its own openings and foreclosures, in the interest of "active interception and reconstellation" (1999: 50). The stakes of postcolonial aesthetics in "the singular and the unverifiable" are not easily grasped by institutional and instrumental knowledge (2012: 2). The corrective is not advocacy on behalf of the silenced but going out of one's self—in the act of reading—to figure a lost perspective. The other cannot be self-ed. The aesthetics of postcolonial literature and criticism lies in the impasse of the political in a reading such as Spivak's reclaiming of Christophine. The challenge it throws out is how to find a way to proceed from raising the question to moving to activism, unavoidable because vulnerable subjects in the postcolonial context come with vulnerable, endangered environments. The native informer is that curious guardian at the margin and of the margin who will not inform: however, she will be enabled by the hard-earned knowledge and skill of the postcolonial critic to innovate, create, and bring about change.

"[T]he intellectual or political payoff of interrogating, demystifying, and defamiliarizing is no longer quite so evident." So claim Elizabeth Anker and Rita Felski, unambiguously positing "critique" as the mode of intellectual argumentation guilty of the joyless actions described above. In this reading, the critique-minded critic is the psychoanalyst "treating the text as a patient" (2017: 4); the psycholinguist unravelling its "contradictions, slippages, elisions" (5); the Foucauldian forensic detective of knowledge/power entanglements; the Marxist curator of "fragments of social totalities" which are corrupted by these very totalities (5). Oversimplifying a heterogeneous body of complex (and painstakingly developed) acts of reading that involve self-vigilance and "unlearning one's privilege," as Spivak memorably put it (2013: 4), the editors posit critique as made paranoid and enervated by its own reactive, hypervigilant, codic critical stances. The affective register of these practitioners of critique includes skepticism, negativity, antagonism, depression. As with Lazarus's Ahmad in particular and postcolonial critics of Fredric Jameson in general, these "impoverished"[3] reading practices neutralize what Rancière calls art's dissensus by seeking a correspondence between "aesthetic virtue and political virtue" when, according to Rancière, no criterion for establishing such a correspondence exists (Rancière, cited in Anker and Felski 2017: 17). Critique—and the mode of aesthetic reception that is postcolonial criticism seems particularly vulnerable to this term of opprobrium—fails, with all its "negativity and opposition" to justify the "aesthetic or social importance of literature or our practice as critics" (20).

There is no space here to elaborate further on the fallacies and willed misrepresentations inherent in Anker and Felski's takedown of the "ethos of critique" (20)—or dwell on the alternatives this publication proposes—but the second half of my chapter will demonstrate by example the interpretive richness mobilized by postcolonial literary criticism from postcolonial literature.[4] I have chosen two novels and a collection of essays which assume revisionist stances in relation to canonical figures, texts, and forms of English literature. My textual analyses of the aesthetics of these canonical extrapolations touch on the political imaginary of literature without arresting its motion and development. The transactions between canon and latecomer, author and critic, writer and reader are individual and unrepeatable, but they are, if not always happy, hopeful of the promise of textual encounters and engagements.

2. Postcolonial Literary Aesthetics

"Can Rancière's concepts allow us to view the politics of postcolonial literature as something other than a derivative (or determined) epiphenomenon of a truer and

---

[3] This term is borrowed by Anker and Felski from Saba Mahmood in this instance (14).
[4] See Bruce Robbins's "Not So Well Attached" (2017) for a powerful rejoinder to Rita Felski's argument in *The Limits of Critique* (2015) that critique is out of date and a spent force. Robbins's insights on critique and its relation to the critique of power, and the relation of the critique of power to a critique of social injustice, are relevant to the connection between critique and postcolonial criticism I am making in this chapter.

deeper historical reality?" Vallury asks (2014: 251). When it emerged in the eighties (some scholars date it to a lecture given by Edward Said at the University of Kent in August 1989, others to the mid-eighties), the term "postcolonial" came to represent not only anti-colonial and decolonizing ideals but acts of resistance to neo-colonial regimes and home-grown despots. Simon Gikandi calls postcolonialism "a code for the state of undecidability in which the culture of colonialism continues to resonate in what was supposed to be its negation" (1996: 14). Its remit was inhabitants of erstwhile colonies as well as the postcolonial metropolis and the diaspora. The Anglophone postcolonial tends to be seen as self-marginalizing and anti-assimilationist—an anarchy perversely sustained by the (English and Comparative Literature) departments whose traditional curricula and methodologies it criticizes—and derivative and mimetic at the same time. How can postcolonial literature and method be subversive *and* aesthetic? How can they be subversive enough when they are written in English and caught up in the publishing protocols, pedagogic demands, or value criteria of the Western academy?

The works of postcolonial literature discussed here examine the vicissitudes of the performativity that Spivak associates with the aesthetic. Junot Diaz's *The Brief Wondrous Life of Oscar Wao* (2007) and Helen Oyeyemi's *Icarus Girl* (2005) are interlocutions between the USA and Dominican Republic, or Europe and Africa. Combining history and fantasy, the language of these novels interrupts and intervenes in discourses of the dominant. As the concluding reading of Teju Cole's *Known and Strange Things* (2016) brings home, the classic extrapolations of postcolonial writing are not merely a writing back or a striking back. Haunted by its own influence, relation, and comparatism, postcolonial literature strives instead to "uncompare the comparative situation to which it has been assigned," Robert Young observes (2013: 688). In the first part of this chapter, I have argued against the spurious separation of the postcolonial and the aesthetic—and the tendency of criticism to see the aesthetic as separated from the subject, which automatically denies postcolonial literature and theory, its subjects, "handcuffed to history," aesthetic status and claims. Here, reading postcolonial novels through the lens of postcolonial criticism, I show what is aesthetic about both.

Discussing *Brief Wondrous Life*, his Pulitzer-winning novel, in an online journal, Junot Diaz traces the book idea to Mexico City, where he had spent the year of his Guggenheim fellowship:

> Anyway, one time after a night of partying I picked up a copy of *The Importance of Being Earnest*, and I said Oscar Wilde's name in Dominican and it came out 'Oscar Wao.' A quick joke, but the name stayed with me, and the next thing you know, I had this vision of a poor, doomed ghetto nerd, the kind of ghetto nerd I would have been had I not been discovered by girls the first year out of high school.[5]

---

[5] See https://www.bookbrowse.com/author_interviews/full/index.cfm/author_number/1496/junot-diaz.

The Brief Wondrous Life of Oscar Wao combines historiography, magic realism, and the so-called "nerd genres"—sci-fi, comics—to tell the story of the DeLeon family during the reign of the Dominican dictator Rafael Trujillo, whose formation of the modern Dominican state was predicated on the genocide of Haitians and Haitian-Dominicans. The teller of the story is Yunior, a homodiegetic narrator who is also a quasi-omniscient author and annotator. The anti-hero or accidental hero of the novel, Oscar DeLeon Cabral, gets his nickname at a Halloween party when his prize Doctor Who costume makes him look, Yunior thinks, "like that fat homo Oscar Wilde." Melvin mishears Wilde as "Wao" and asks "Oscar Wao, quién es Oscar Wao." "And the tragedy? After a couple of weeks dude started *answering* to it," adds Yunior, the narrator (180).

This random act of naming, and the botched relay of meaning it signifies, proves to be a legitimating appellation for Wao, a cosmic misfit, a creature of fatal misrecognitions and missteps. A game fanatic who can't dance and can't get women, he is a failed Dominican stereotype (please note, however, that just because he is not a stereotype doesn't mean he is a genuine article by default). Diaz's point, of course, is that "[N]ot all Dominican men are macho peacocks, and not all sci-fi, anime, and Dungeons and Dragons fanatics are white boys," as the *New York Times* review puts it.[6] Haunted by history yet utterly powerless to change it, Oscar lives in the world of fantasy and science fiction, the "more speculative genres," as he airily calls them, as he plots his own masterpiece. Book-obsessed, thesaurus-dependent, his heart sick with desire for a string of unattainable women, Oscar is eventually destroyed by the random corruption and everyday violence of the post-Trujillo Dominican Republic (despite his not assuming a proactive political stance either for or against it).

The canon, in this novel, is both J.R.R. Tolkien (Oscar calls himself the Dominican Tolkien) and Gabriel García Márquez, in particular the Márquez of *One Hundred Years of Solitude*; Oscar Wilde; Derek Walcott; the *Fantastic Four* comic classics; the philosophical works of Édouard Glissant. In its self-reflexive moments, *The Brief Wondrous Life of Oscar Wao* thinks of itself less as a novel, more as genre fiction. Genre, Yunior seems to say, is more flexible than novel or history, yet more embodied and embedded than fantasy. We get this definition of "genre" from one of Yunior's footnotes on Oscar:

> Where this outsized love of genre jumped off from no one quite seems to know. It might have been a consequence of being Antillean (who more sci-fi than us?) or of living in the DR for the first couple years of his life and then abruptly, wrenchingly relocated to New Jersey – a single green card shifting not only worlds (from Third to First) but centuries (from almost no TV or electricity to plenty of both). (21)

---

[6] See https://www.nytimes.com/2007/09/30/books/review/Scott-t.html.

Genre here is larger than life, alt history and secret history. There are frequent references to lost or stolen books—the secret history that Oscar's grandfather Abelard writes about the Dark Powers of the President, a history that is now lost. Genre is sci-fi in that it is a telepathic scoping and writing of the center from the margins. Genre is high literary science fiction and space melodrama. Genre is a commingling of kitsch and literary, cultural memory, and personal intimacy. In a letter that reaches his family Oscar writes about his private happiness, short-lived as it is: "So this is what everybody's always talking about. Diablo! If only I'd known," writes Oscar. This is followed by the book's closing counterpoint to Mister Kurtz's "The horror! The horror" in *The Heart of Darkness*: "The beauty! the beauty!" (335).

It might be clear by now that the eponymous novel is not really about Oscar: it is a coming-to-America story that makes much of the enunciative non-correspondence of "Wilde" and "Wao," an uncanny place in which the nameless life can be entertained. Its entrenched literariness draws attention to the ways in which canonical and emergent literature risks apprehending and depicting social reality through form, and about the new ways in which their fictive powers may be allowed to gloriously fail. The novel, which has masses of untranslated, glossed, and semi-glossed Spanish, Spanglish, "Negropolitan" and street slang as well as thirty-three lengthy footnotes ("For those of you who missed your mandatory two seconds of Dominican history" (2)), is not simply highlighting pre-existing cultural hierarchies and marginalization (white North America's limited knowledge of Dominican history, for one): by multiplying unknown words and phrases that do not presuppose a consensual readership or even lend themselves to a contextual understanding, *The Brief Wondrous Life of Oscar Wao* is blatantly mimicking the idiom of metropolitan arrival to baffle the Western(ized) reader's investment in the translators and translated characters who make this genre of the mixed (global and local) novel viable for the world literary marketplace. In *Monolingualism of the Other*, Derrida anticipates heterological openings in monological and tautological languages. What Diaz's postcolonial rewriting seems to say is that English literature can hardly reach itself, or self-actualize as metalanguage, if it no longer knows where it is coming from.

The Nigerian-born British author Oyeyemi wrote *Icarus Girl* when she was 18 years old. In this novel, the protagonist's pathology, her propensity to fits and screams, is attributed to her hybrid or "half-and-half" identity; another child mocks, "Maybe Jessamy has all of these 'attacks' because she can't make up her mind whether she's black or white!" (86). The novel's epigraph is an Emily Dickinson quotation—"Alone I cannot be – / For hosts do visit me – / Recordless company" and ends with a Yoruba poem translated into English. The text's twins, mirrors, shadows, and echoes do not function as neat doubles, copies, or halves: they show, instead, how heteroaffection supervenes on the self. Oyeyemi recalls Fanon's melancholic reading of the failure of the (Lacanian) mirror stage in the identity formation of the black subject; she is referencing also the preponderance of twins in Yoruba visual culture, displacing the spirit children from what Christopher Ouma calls their "natal geography" to a continental context. The *Icarus* twins "mirror" each other, but this mirroring is "out of proportion." To use auditory similes, this doubling is like "singing out of sync with the radio...like an echo," as Jess's Aunty Anike does, or the unnerving split-second delay Jess registers in the phone calls from Nigeria (36).

"Two of me," Jess thinks, "No, *us*. TillyTilly, JessJess, FernFern, but that's three" (251). Jess creates a double in her grandfather's Ibadan compound to reconcile herself to her Yoruba heritage. Mimesis in *Icarus Girl* is difference, deferral, a dissociative identity disorder, textual interruptions *bringing into being* radical alterations in perceived reality. However, Jess and Tilly defy white/black, English/Nigerian binaries and also provide a new classic-modern relationality that subverts the "West vs. the rest" model of canon revision. Their twinned corpus is exscripted, written out, taken away from the breath and the tongue and transformed into corpuscular texts and philosophies. Tilly and Jess, their inmixed identities both conjured up and made unstable by the vagaries of text, display a strong interest in "amending books" (59), to quote Oyeyemi, with Jess not only heavily annotating but correcting her mother's copy of *Little Women*. All books, of course, African and English, are vulnerable to ruin and alteration:

> Bose, with her hands coated with spicy *adun*, had nearly destroyed the wine-coloured leather bindings of his specially commissioned copies of *Things Fall Apart* and *A Dance of the Forest*. (49)

Despite the novel's lusty tearing up of Ibeji (spirit double) paintings and shattering of mirror reflections, doubles, twins, and likenesses organize our aesthetic response to it. Critics have noted how *Icarus Girl* is also a veritable echo chamber of the African epistemologies mined by Nigerian classics: John Pepper Clark and Wole Soyinka's "abiku" poems; Achebe's representation of Okonkyo's daughter Azinma as a spirit child; the figure of Azaro in Ben Okri's *The Famished Road* trilogy. In Jess's grandfather's study in Nigeria, the two girls delve into Coleridge's poetry, Arthurian legends, even the Bible. Literature or literariness here is not an enclosed circle of confirmed meanings but an ongoing sharing of words, senses, voices, the sharing of a corpus or the corporeal.

> Tilly smiled. 'Let's look around,' she said.
> She took Jess's hand and guided her slowly past each shelf. She passed the candle over rows of leather-bound and hardback books, bringing the flame so close to some that Jess's breath caught in her throat with amazement at her daring.

'You might set them on fire,' she warned, and Tilly looked at her seriously, the ends of the string in her hair bobbing as she nodded.

'I know!' (53)

As Natalya Din-Kariuki (2017) points out, the metrical form of the poem Jess and Tilly collaboratively write—*'I asked if I could go to her / To find my thoughts, to think one day'*—echoes the iambs of spoken English, as well as the specific use of iambic tetrameter in English and Scottish ballads. The eight-line poem's rhymes (head/dead, her/prefer, day/stay) suggest a symmetry, the possibility of being neatly cut in half, which is semantically disrupted by both its content and Oyeyemi's narrative of interrupted and discontinuous heteroaffection. The ending does not promise a happy reconciliation of clashing worlds and imperatives, but it does promise an awakening. Oyeyemi writes that Jess, following a coma-inducing road accident, undertakes a journey into the wilderness at the end of which she both enters TillyTilly's body and goes "back into herself" (322). And then, Jessamy Harrison wakes "up and up and up and up" (322).

I will end this discussion on the aesthetics and beauty of postcolonial literature with an examination of Teju Cole's canonical extrapolations in his book of essays, *Known and Strange Things*, published in 2016. The preponderance of canonical works and authors as the "imperishable" things Cole ponders in this collection of essays is unsurprising, beginning, as it does, with an epigraph from Seamus Heaney's *Beowulf*. The title of the book itself refers to Heaney's evocation of the fleeting sensation of full receptivity, the heart "a hurry," a condition of urgency, "through which known and strange things pass." Many gems in this book illuminate the topic in hand, but I will focus on a curious homage piece to the Caribbean Nobel laureate V.S. Naipaul, titled "Natives on the Boat."

In a later essay, titled "Housing Mr Biswas," Cole writes that it is a book that "shelters the one who reads it," but the precursor-latecomer relationship is in choppier waters in "Natives on the Boat." The immediate occasion is a glittering private party on the Upper East Side to mark the publication of Naipaul's 2010 *The Masque of Africa*; in lieu of a book launch the Nobel-winning author had requested a quiet dinner with a group of young African writers. "This is how I came to be invited," Cole says, though they end up discussing La Rochefoucauld, Twain, O'Connor, and Hemingway, not the African masters. Cole seems to surprise himself with the warmth he feels for a man [and I quote him here] "so fond of the word 'n*****,' so aggressive in his lack of sympathy toward Africa, so brutal in his treatment of women" (23). "Natives on the Boat" is haunted also by Joseph Conrad, the progenitor of Naipaul's novelistic craft (pun intended) in the Congolese travel diaries and documentary writing on Africa that Cole discusses in the essay. We learn that Cole is writing the Conrad retrospective in an architectural folly, the enclosed upper deck of a boat named *Roi des Belges*.

In 1890 Joseph Conrad piloted a steamship down the Congo on a boat with the same name. That journey became his inspiration for *Heart of Darkness*, a puzzling novella with nested narrators who unfold a shadowed, strangled, brutal tale.... So, this perch on which I sit above the Thames – the sky is blue now, the 180-degree view of it full of long stratus clouds – this perch in which the city is exposed to me but I am not to it, is an homage to Conrad's bitter vision. What might it mean when the native pilots the ship? What happens when the ones on the shore, numerous, unindividuated, are white? (20)

A cynical reading would be that Cole is cannily positioning V.S. Naipaul's documentary writing between Conrad's travelogues and the multimedia experimentation of his own traveling theory and flaneurist iconology. But if Cole is breaking into the classic heart-of-darkness tradition, interrupting and correcting, he himself is not immune from classic interruptions.

In *Self and Emotional Life*, Adrian Johnston and Catherine Marabou's study of subjectivity at the intersection of philosophy, psychoanalysis, and neuroscience, they use the medical term "syncope" to describe an interrupted touch between the self and the other. Syncope is a temporary loss of consciousness experienced, Marabou and Johnston explain, by a blockage of blood to the brain or a drastic plummeting of blood pressure. Cole's interaction with the literary precursors he must survive, outwit, and overwrite is a touch that doesn't know about itself. "An affect touches me but I don't know what 'me' means" (2013: 24). What struck me as uncanny about this passage about Cole on a boat was that the existential crisis on the roof (Cole's and also Sir Vidia's, who, we are told, is afraid of heights), the unsure native piloting the ship, the nested narrators of the "shadowed, strangled, brutal tale" with whom Cole ambivalently associates, had already been prefigured by Naipaul in his now-forgotten 1984 *New Yorker* essay "The Crocodiles of Yamoussoukro," republished in *Finding the Center: Two Narratives* (1984). As critics such as Rob Nixon have pointed out, the crocodiles kept by President Houphouet-Boigny in an artificial lake do "a great deal of figurative work" in this essay in that they come to signify "the ineluctable ills of the Ivory Coast" (76). Naipaul self-consciously creates a tissue of quotations by social outsiders— European, American, and Caribbean travelers—to foreground his own misgivings, from the boat, about the African modernity on shore. "Crocodiles" is valuable also for the Conradian rhetoric of chance and accident—"to allow oneself to be carried along, up to a point, by accidents"—which Naipaul co-opts to describe the "creative and imaginative" drift of his documentary writing (1984: x). What is aesthetic in this representation inheres in the semi-conscious and half-acknowledged intergenerational relay between literary antecedents and successors. While postcolonial criticism might contextualize this relay in the epistemological disquietude and confabulations of Anglophone writers in the postcolony, it is also itself organically linked to these mnemonic processes and will desist treating the phenomenon as a strategic or opportunistic political alignment on the part of either Naipaul or Cole. The passage with which I will close, eerily similar to Cole's speculations on the *Roi des Belges*, occurs in Chapter 11 of Naipaul's "Crocodiles," after an expatriate in Africa has offered a very gruesome portrait of child-sacrifice:

> I dreamed I was on a roof or bridge. The material, of glass or transparent plastic, had begun to perish: seemingly melted at the edges. I asked whether the bridge would be mended. The answer was no. What had been built had been built; the roof or bridge I was on would crumble away. Was it safe, though? Could I cross?
> (1984: 155)

PART 4
READING CLOSELY
Form and Meaning

9
On the Last Paragraph of the 1859 Edition of Darwin's *Origin of Species*

Myra Jehlen

My text for this very brief reflection on the *Origin of Species* is the last paragraph of the first edition (1859) which differs from the closing paragraph of the five subsequent editions by three words.[1]

The words are "by the Creator." I will suggest that Darwin should have stuck with this first version, which is both coherent and complete, and that conversely the Creator's presence in the five later editions makes the paragraph read not only awkwardly but even incoherently.

Actually, "the Creator" appears very little in the *Origin* as a whole, only eight times in the first edition, nine in the five more editions published in his lifetime. On each occasion Darwin concludes a brief speculation about His position on whatever the issue is by saying that since His ways are transcendent, he, Darwin can't know what He thinks. But in the *Origin*'s closing paragraph, which is my text, Darwin invokes the Creator without any explanation. Maybe it's the excitement; for the closing paragraph outright exults and Darwin's writing grows visionary. This transformation is the more striking because the last sentence of the penultimate paragraph also projects a vision but its writing stays soberly declarative: "And as natural selection works solely by and for the good of each being, all corporeal and mental endowments will tend to progress toward perfection."

Here in contrast is the closing paragraph:

It is interesting to contemplate an entangled bank, clothed with many plants of many kinds, with birds singing on the bushes, with various insects flitting about, and with worms crawling through the damp earth, and to reflect that these elaborately constructed forms, so different from each other, and dependent on each other in so complex a manner, have all been produced by laws acting

---

[1] The full title being, *The Origin of Species By Means of Natural Selection; Or, The Preservation Of Favoured Races In The Struggle For Life*. I have consulted in particular two histories, Robert J. Richards's *The Romantic Conception of Life* (University of Chicago Press, 2002), especially its concluding chapter, "Darwin's Romantic Biology," and Jessica Riskin's *The Restless Clock* (University of Chicago Press, 2016), especially Chapter 7, "Darwin Between the Machines."

around us. These laws, taken in the largest sense, being Growth with reproduction; Inheritance which is almost implied by reproduction; Variability from the indirect and direct action of the external conditions of life, and from use and disuse; a Ratio of Increase so high as to lead to a Struggle for Life, and as a consequence to Natural Selection, entailing Divergence of Character and the Extinction of less-improved forms. Thus, from the war of nature, from famine and death, the most exalted object which we are capable of conceiving, namely, the production of the higher animals directly follows. There is grandeur in this view of life with its several powers, having been originally breathed into a few forms or into one; and that, whilst this planet has gone cycling on according to the fixed law of gravity, from so simple a beginning, endless forms most beautiful and most wonderful have been, and are being evolved.

It would have been hard not to take a breath after the last words of the preceding paragraph's last sentence, "...progress toward perfection" and it needs a new breath to start off again: "It is interesting to contemplate an entangled bank..." For the rest of this last paragraph, Darwin is not only describing but celebrating, lyrically counting the ways.

One way is the abundance of plants he imagines to be clothing the bank; there are birds singing, insects flitting, worms crawling. It's a lovely serene scene. Plants, birds, insects, and worms seem not to prey on one another, the birds are not pulling up worms, the insects not chewing on plants. This bank is more pacific than a Henri Rousseau Peaceable Jungle, where on occasion a hungry lion does bring down an antelope.

Then, halfway through the first sentence, Darwin moves from contemplation ("It is interesting to contemplate") to reflection ("...and to reflect"). The relations of the bank's denizens change commensurately, from equivalence and equality to difference and interdependence. Plants, birds, insects, and worms are no longer just cohabiting but interacting ("these forms so different from each other, and dependent on each other in so complex a manner"). Interaction brings in laws. The first sentence rejoices in many distinct survivors. On second thought, in a new clause, it emerges that the distinct kinds (pushing up through the dirt, buzzing, flying, slithering), though different, are also interdependent, according to ways established by those laws setting the terms of each kind's survival and as well the community's.

There follows a list of the conditions of survival, to which list capitals lend a categorical authority. Growth, Inheritance, Variability, Ratio of Increase, Struggle for Life, Natural Selection which results in Divergence of Character and for some species, Extinction. With Extinction we've come a distance from the benevolent and plentiful coexistence of the first half of the paragraph's first sentence. Besides thriving growth, the bank also features "famine and death."

But all is not lost; in fact nothing is lost. Extinction turns out to be life giving as "famine and death" clear the way "for the production of the higher animals." This is the moment in creation myths for the advent of the Creator, whose stock in trade is Death and Redemption.

Darwin imagines the opposite: an advancement that's not special to humankind but common to the whole category of "the higher animals." A progress whose principle is a process: an immanent, inherent, organic process. There is no interstice between Nature's lower and higher species: "the production of the higher animals directly follows." That gap across which the Creator on the ceiling of the Sistine Chapel sends man the spark of life is closed in Darwin's *Origin* story by the higher animals' joining the parade of "endless forms most beautiful and most wonderful," while the earth, following the same laws, goes on cycling "according to the fixed laws of gravity."

I have been reading the *Origin*'s last paragraph as if it were a literary text, as I take it to be. The passage from the last sentence of the penultimate paragraph to the last paragraph (from "...progress toward perfection" to "It is interesting to contemplate...") crosses from one kind of writing to another: from expository writing to literary writing. "Progress toward perfection" has an idealistic thrust and its alliteration is consciously elegant. But the change in rhythm in the first sentence of the final paragraph calls for a different kind of attention, an attention to the linguistic look and feel of the writing itself. This new demand is especially compelling in the paragraph's last sentence.

I'll repeat that last sentence here in order to read it up close. Having finished his survey of the progress of life from the lower denizens of the entangled bank to the higher animals, Darwin concludes:

> There is grandeur in this view of life with its several powers, having been originally breathed into a few forms or into one; and that, whilst this planet has gone cycling on according to the fixed law of gravity, from so simple a beginning, endless forms most beautiful and most wonderful have been, and are being evolved.

The grandeur is in the view of life with its several powers having been breathed: it's not in the breathing nor in the breather. The interpolation of "by the Creator" in the later editions comes here (see italics): "...breathed *by the Creator* into a few forms or one," and it is clearly contrary to Darwin's argument. In the religious plot, the crucial event is a divine act ("In the beginning, God...") but here that event, established but not attributed, is the extant fact of the bank's abounding nature, for life already exists: in Darwin's world, Creation is lower-case and literally a pre-text.

Having stipulated both the emergence of life and the law of gravity, almost at the end of his last sentence, Darwin gets to his argument, though he represents it as a mere exposition. He says that from so simple a beginning—referring to both the coming about of the earth and the emergence of life—has come about a world to marvel at, a world in which endless forms most beautiful and most wonderful have been (he's now invoking all of history past, present, and future) and are, once, still and forever evolving.

That last sentence of the *Origin* ("There is grandeur in this view of life with its several powers...") while proposing an idea of life that makes life its own highest authority is also rhetorically incontestable: "There is...," it says and that being so, everything follows. For Darwin doesn't own up to proposing a theory in this sentence: he's only observing, just saying. There is; and there being, "from so simple a beginning," it just keeps on going.

As he began the paragraph in the impersonal—"It is interesting to contemplate"—he now ends it at an even further remove, the impersonal passive tense: "...from so simple a beginning, endless forms most beautiful and most wonderful have been, and are being evolved." The first and only time the word "evolved" appears in the original *Origin* it's not an argument but an evidence. Like Nature.

10
Wild Aesthetics
D.H. Lawrence's "Art for *My* Sake"

Philip Davis

The first paragraph of Lawrence's "Study of Thomas Hardy" (1914) concerns the human drive for self-preservation: a creature between sky and land, at home in neither, always fighting for more food, more clothing, more shelter, on and on and on, unable ever to feel utterly satisfied or completely safe.

But the second paragraph, marking as so often in Lawrence a changed axis, speaks of "something more" again, only at a different level—a level where Lawrence's language is no longer that of survival or gain or conservation of energy, but of wildness and waste and all that is exuberantly in excess of the prudential. Think of the poppy, says Lawrence, and the reckless fleeting red of the wild flower. Its excess is not really a surplus extra, an aesthetic add-on of pretty redness, but "the thing itself at its maximum of being" (*Phoenix*, pp. 399–400, 402). And that is the purpose of anything living: to come into "its own fullless," "as a tree comes into full blossom, or a bird into spring beauty, or a tiger into lustre" ("Democracy," *Phoenix*, p. 714). It is what, in humans, mind first exists to register: "the pure joy of consciousness" (*Fantasia of the Unconscious*, p. 190). It is only when we talk of species and nations that we speak merely in terms of *existence*, says Lawrence: when it comes to individuals we speak rather of what is better expressed as *being*, with an extra qualitative dimension for the sake of which the whole species is a preparation ("Reflections on the Death of a Porcupine," *Phoenix II*, p. 468). Every infant is an entirely new birth.

This wilder second-order principle, almost cutting free of the first principle of self-preservation, is Lawrence's alternative evolutionary idea. Its shorthand name—though it's a pity it's "such an ugly little word," he says—is "*sex*" (*Phoenix II*, p. 527). An existence made free and calm and peaceful, a loving sense of a beautiful fittingness within the world: these may be for Lawrence the final word when "look! we have come through!";[1] but he will barely ever speak it, for fear of trespassing upon the sacred by naming it too easily and too early. Eros is for Lawrence untamed in the midst of life, beyond ideas of origin or end, and defiant

---

[1] The title of his collection of poems (Chatto and Windus, 1917) on the achievement of his marriage to Frieda.

of being only a means of attraction and reproduction. "They say a peacock puts on all his fine feathers to dazzle the peahen into letting him satisfy his desire for propagation," he writes in "Sex Versus Loveliness," but he adds with his chirpy carelessness, "Oh highly aesthetic peahen!" But really: why should not *she* "put on fine feathers...to satisfy *her* desire" for eggs? And is "her sex-urge so weak that she needs all that blue splendor"? (*Phoenix II*, p. 527).

What Lawrence sees is the trumping of survival by life itself—the needs of an individual vitality that exists insubordinate, desirous, and unpurified. "They are wrong – they are all wrong," says an incensed Louisa, looking around her family in "The Daughters of the Vicar" (1911); "They have ground out their souls for what isn't worth anything, and there isn't a grain of love in them anywhere. And I *will* have love" (*The Prussian Officer and Other Stories*, p. 92).

And not what Lawrence calls lovey-doveyness: what right has such as *that*, says Louisa, to be called goodness! (p. 83). What is the norm for men nowadays? demands Lou Witt in the novella "St Mawr." It is to be either clever or nice. But "it seems to me," she says, "there's something else besides mind and cleverness, or niceness or cleanness," or else "the last bit of wild animal" has died in such men (*St Mawr together with The Princess*, p. 58).

1. I Will Have It

The imperative in that tone suits Lawrence because, like Louisa, he is always of the second generation, himself a son rather than a first-generation parent, trying to become a new man. His signature note is also like that of young Will Brangwen in *The Rainbow* proposing to marry his cousin Anna even while her parents, the older Brangwens, Tom and Lydia, tell him the couple shouldn't yet be thinking of marrying, so imprudently. "You have no experience," says Lydia.

> "What experience do I want, Aunt?" asked the boy.
> And if [Tom] Brangwen's heart had not been hard and intact with anger, like a precious stone, he would have agreed.   (*The Rainbow*, ch. 4)

The father would have agreed, were his life not now going backwards. Forwards without knowledge in advance is what vitality means to Lawrence: "In his fullest living he does not know what he does..." he writes in the "Study of Thomas Hardy," "heaving into uncreated space" (*Phoenix*, p. 431). In his heart Tom Brangwen knows, from his own youthful love of Lydia, that you can't *have* experience, in advance, in order to qualify *for* experience.

"What experience do I *want*, Aunt?" There is in Will's naïve shrug a defiant flourishing, a flowering of young brio, in celebration of which Lawrence is like Ruskin in *The Queen of the Air*:

The spirit in the plant—that is to say, its power of gathering dead matter out of the wreck round it, and shaping it into its own chosen shape—is of course strongest at the moment of its flowering, for it then not only gathers, but forms, with the greatest energy.

And where this life is in at full power, its form becomes invested with aspects that are chiefly delightful to our own human passions; namely, at first, with the loveliest outlines of shape; and, secondly, with the most brilliant phases of the primary colours, blue, yellow, and red or white, the unison of all; and, to make it all more strange, this time of peculiar and perfect glory is associated with relations of the plants or blossoms to each other, correspondent to the joy of love in human creatures, and having the same object in the continuance of the race. (*The Queen of the Air*, 1869, para. 60)

This joy of love in the continuance of the race was Ruskin's language for sexual reproduction: he would deny it was only a euphemism for a more technical and unfeeling name. But where Darwin had said that "the final end of the flower, with all its parts, is the production of seed," to Ruskin as to Lawrence it had to be the other way round or else the ongoing process made no sense and had no purpose:

we are wrong in speaking as if the object of this strong life were only the bequeathing of itself. The flower is the end or proper object of the seed, not the seed of the flower. The reason for seeds is that flowers may be; not the reason of flowers that seeds may be. (*The Queen of the Air*, para. 60)

Lawrence simply does not care if the flowering is transitory. As he puts it in his little poem (against) "Self Pity," "I never saw a wild thing / sorry for itself." For him, despite his darker side, there is always above all the heliotropic principle: like plants following the sun, humans are naturally in search of life and warmth and energy even in difficult emotional climates, even through the struggles in the roots of darkness (Elliot 1999). Shadow, says Lawrence, comes only temporarily and transiently when something intervenes between us and the sun: as soon as the intervening object is removed, shadow ceases to exist. "We can think of death, if we like, as of something permanently intervening between us and the sun," he writes in "Flowery Tuscany" (1927)—where "if we like" sounds the defiant warning note. But "as far as experience goes, in the human race, the one thing that is always there is the shining sun, and dark shadow is an accident of intervention" (*Phoenix*, pp. 57–8). Creatures are here to use and even to use *up* their lives, such that health becomes something more than just surviving without disease. In that setting, death is more like an accident, a nothing.

It is in this mood that Lawrence is unsatisfied by the idea of sexual selection, as a counter-force to natural selection—*unless* it also lets nature dangerously back in again at another level. Only then, by risk of venture, "sex and beauty are one thing, like flame and fire" (*Phoenix II*, pp. 527–8). "Beauty is an *experience*, nothing else. It is not a fixed pattern... the plainest person can look beautiful, can *be* beautiful. It only needs the fire of sex to rise delicately to change an ugly face to a lovely one. That is really sex appeal" (*Phoenix II*, p. 529).

In his own version of courtship, Birkin keeps telling Ursula, I *can't* get right, I *can't* get straight, with all the twisted and messed up stuff inside him. But at least I *know* it, he says, the last and only rightness left in him (ch. 11, "An Island"). Birkin is what Lawrence in *Apocalypse* was to call a whirlpool, an almost chaotic maelstrom, revolving around its own contradictory forces until out of its deepening fullness a center is formed and some resolve breaks through (*Apocalypse*, p. 81; see also Deleuze 1998: ch. 6). And so Birkin insistently holds that swirling mess of tense ugliness together, tighter and tighter, resisting false escapes, in order to try to force out of it its bursting resolution. Until then and done the right way, no safe distance, no idealized satisfaction, no pure beauty can be tolerated instead.[2] Birkin has told Ursula that there is a lovely golden light in her, and that even if she thinks she doesn't know of it, he wants her to give it to him. She storms off in furious argument, throwing aside the rings he gave her. "He wanted her to come back," it says in one paragraph. "She was coming back," it says in the next, quite independently of the anxiety of that wish. "See what a flower I found you," she says, not going back over the past but as out of nothing. "Pretty" is all he says, taking the flower. "Everything had become simple again, the complexity gone in to nowhere." Then Birkin badly wanted to cry—"except that he was weary and bored by emotion" and did not want to go backwards or spoil the new achievement (ch. 23, "Excurse"). "Beauty is an *experience*." It has austerely to come through all that is not beautiful.

2. In the Wild

"Pretty," the exhausted Birkin said gently, because only a child's short, basic word could steady him. But the emergent beauty of his reconciliation with Ursula is not the same as "prettiness," which is a tame and domesticated aesthetic, a bourgeois emotion, only serving to quench the natural fire (*Phoenix II*, p. 265).

> And the ideal lovey-dovey "explanation" of sex as something wonderful and extra lovey-dovey, a bill-and-coo process of obtaining a sweet little baby—well, it just makes one sick. It is disastrous to the deep sexual life. But perhaps that is what we want. (*Fantasia*, p. 161)

---

[2] See Ngai (2005) on socially inconvenient emotions, including Nietzsche's assault on "something beatific about being poor, weak or disenfranchised" (p. 34), and, conversely, Kant's opposition to those feelings that "destroy not only 'aesthetic satisfaction' but the disinterestedness on which it depends" (p. 335).

Like his Birkin, Lawrence does not want these emotional substitutes and sly placebos: better the ugly and painful, and far better working-class Nottingham dialect than polite bill-and-coo. He hated the false consciousness created by "sublimation," human beings' evolutionary trick instead of substituting the bloodlessly mental, conceptual, and ideal for the reality of the physical, transient, and dynamic. We think we need to turn the wild into the socially acceptable:

> We have made the idea supplant both impulse and tradition.... there is substitute for everything—life-substitute—just as we have butter-substitute, and meat-substitute, and sugar-substitute, and leather-substitute, and silk-substitute, so we have life-substitute. We have beastly benevolence, and foul good-will, and stinking charity, and poisonous ideals. (*Fantasia*, p. 207)

Better to leave a gap painfully empty and feel it as such—a thing unknown, or missing and irreplaceable, or barely quite nameable—than polyfilla it with the easy tone and language of cosily betraying euphemisms. And better to use the word sex instead of the lovey-dovey. Speaking in "The Novel and the Feelings":

> I say feelings, not emotions. Emotions are things we more or less recognize. We see love, like a woolly lamb...hate like a dog chained to a kennel...Our emotions are our domesticated animals...
>
> Convenience! Convenience! There are convenient emotions and inconvenient ones. The inconvenient ones we chain up, or put a ring through their nose. The convenient ones are our pets. Love is our pet favourite. (*Phoenix*, pp. 756–7)

He is not interested in tamed and socialized pets, in pet aesthetics. Sex is an *in*convenient and *un*tamed force, a happening more sudden than calm; and if calm and renewing, only after climax and fulfilment. Lawrence has "feelings," closer to the body than mental emotions, which, he says, are variously like roaring lions and twisting snakes and bleating lambs, like warbling linnets and dumbly darting fishes and just occasionally opening oysters. "A pure animal man," adds Lou Witt in "St Mawr," "would be all the animals in turn, instead of one fixed automatic thing" (p. 61).

Lawrence was all the animals in turn. It was always said of him that, like Tolstoy, he could throw himself into anything alive, as if he were an instrument finely tuned to sense what it was like to be a plant or a tree, an animal or a child, in the sun or in the dark, but always in the live moment.

So, I call to my black cow, Susan, he says in "Love Was Once a Little Boy," and sometimes she comes but sometimes she doesn't, till I seek her out and "she rises with a sighing heave": "My calling was a mere nothing against the black stillness of her cowy passivity" (*Phoenix II*, p. 446).

Or I notice a small infant: "how often it seems to be gazing across a strange distance at the mother; what a curious look is on its face, as if the mother were an object set across a vast gulf." The mother, says Lawrence, will want to chase away that look with kisses (*Psychoanalysis*, p. 102).

Or, here I am writing now, outside, with my back to a tree, says Lawrence. "It's no good looking at a tree to know it": it has no face. But if you "sit among the roots and nestle against its strong trunk," then you feel it can grow unlike us in its two directions, down into the dense and damp middle earth, and up and about in the high-reaching air (*Fantasia*, p. 45).

Or there's the child, again, when it asserts its distinction from the mother in giving a little "kick" of roguish glee, or a "crow"' of tiny exultance—"this sheer joy of a young thing in its own single existence" (*Fantasia*, pp. 32–3).

All of these are non-verbal or pre-verbal experiences, because Lawrence never believed that in the Beginning was the Word. It is the sense of the flesh that comes first to Lawrence through what in *Fantasia of the Unconscious* and *Psychoanalysis and the Unconscious* he calls the sympathetic centers of his nervous system. But at the same time he feels in each of my extracts that "strange distance" across which there is something or someone not at that moment at all sympathetic but resistant or oblivious, individual and separate of will. Lawrence doesn't mind that, rather relishes it, even if it is to his own particular disadvantage or inconvenience: there are times when self-interest is not very important in life, even to the so-called self. In the child, the cow or the flower is an assertive principle felt in the very set of the shoulders, or the wall of the back, or the toss of stalk or head. That is why suddenly "you touched me" (the title of a short story) can make such a quick and vital difference, like a turn-around. It is in washing a young coal miner's back, when his dying mother cannot do it, that Louisa's love is clinched in "Daughters of the Vicar," and what she first feels is not "convenient"—but rather that it hurt her. It is never simply two sympathies cosying up to one another; a circuit is created only by tension between the poles and across the levels, and that connection is not automatic but comes and goes. But the worst is not the risk of the clash; the worst is when "a force flashes and has no response": from the earliest days, if a baby finds no vital connection coming back from its mother, its force dies away for want of any reception, and there is only devastation (*Psychoanalysis*, p. 65).

But then, even when the family bond is established as the basis of the social, there must come what Lawrence called "the hour of the stranger," that rupture when family love is no longer sufficient and a person's life has almost to begin again at a different level (*Fantasia*, p. 146). Then all the more, the great generative work in the world is carried out through the primal dialectic of sameness and difference—and all the more intimately in the sexual driving force that goes beyond the initial power of attraction, into the attempted union of two in one.³ The old gods, as Lawrence put it in *Apocalypse*, held "things asunder to make a space": into that space there came time, for the working out of human experience; and there came sex, for "sex is a holding together of two things asunder, that birth may come through between them" (*Apocalypse*, p. 129). For Lawrence sex can then create the birth of what he calls "the third thing" between the to-and-fro friction and surge of the pair: the relationship itself, which at best is beyond the unbalancing control of either party, and is where marriage comes from (*Twilight in Italy*, p. 153). And that is the maximal meaning of consummation, of coition and mutual orgasm in Lawrence. It means the simultaneous and inseparable sense of my affecting you even as you are affecting me, of each being both subject and object in the "organic grammar of life."⁴ It means the unappeasably impossible desire of you being me and I being you, bursting into temporary release of what is too much to be contained within a single person any more. "For bodies cannot pierce, nor be in bodies lost: / As sure they strive to be, when both engage / In that tumultuous momentary rage"; "Agen they in each other wou'd be lost / But still by adamantine bars are crossed."⁵

So it is in the sexual rhythms of *The Rainbow*, union and separation coming and going between Tom and Lydia: "For him to feel her there, absorbing the warmth from him, giving him back her weight... So close on him she lay, and yet she answered him from so far away..." (ch. 1). "What was it then that she was, to which he must also deliver himself up, and which at the same time he must embrace, contain?" (ch. 2). "*At the same time*" is the key dynamic for sameness and difference together.

3. Sex—That Ugly Little Word

Like a man short of a protective skin, Lawrence never quite got over being to varying degrees shocked by anything that was suddenly revealed as quite other than himself and different from dulled convention. There was a deep early part of him, the mother's boy, that was vulnerably sensitive to thresholds, to unfamiliar movements towards other people and to impressions from the world outside, and suffered from new contact. And yet it was precisely this fear, lived down, that gave to any new encounter something genuinely and startlingly new. It made sex the

---

³ Cf. Wordsworth in "Preface to Lyrical Ballads" (1800), on the perception of similitude in dissimilitude: "This principle is the great spring of the activity of our minds and their chief feeder. From this principle the direction of the sexual appetite, and all the passions connected with it take their origin" (Wordsworth 1974: vol. 1, p. 148).
⁴ Trigant Burrow's phrase, (1927: 184), in book reviewed by Lawrence in *Phoenix*, pp. 377–82.
⁵ Scruton (2006: 94–5), Dryden's translation of Lucretius. There is relation here to Coleridge's idea of double touch (see Marshall 2018: 7).

most searing of these encounters because, as Bertrand Russell put it with a nasty twist, "in sex alone he was compelled to admit that he was not the only human being in the universe," and that made him conceive of sexual relations as almost painful (Russell 1973: 359).

Jessie Chambers, Lawrence's first love and the model for Miriam in *Sons and Lovers*, had hated it when all Lawrence's early sympathetic delight in the familiar life around increasingly turned, she felt, into hardness and anger and frustrated hate. Something happy and innocent and beautiful turned ugly in him, she thought, because of sex and the conflicts caused by its demand and strain.[6] For such as Paul Morel, there was Freud's diagnosis: "Where they love, they have no desire, and where they desire, they cannot love" (Freud 2001: vol. 11, p. 183). Yet equally for Paul Morel, as for Lawrence in relation to Jessie, what Miriam wanted was itself too spiritual in denial of the sexual and what the sexual stood for. "'I think it is terrible to be young.... Because we all make a very, very bad start today, with our idea of love in our head, and our sex in our head as well" (*Fantasia*, p. 198).

But what *did* the sexual more truly stand for? One of the reasons for writing the "Study of Thomas Hardy" was the challenge posed by Hardy's terrible fear, especially in *Jude the Obscure*, that modern human love was no more than an unstable sublimation of animal sex; a transient and not even permanent falsification determined essentially by biological drives from below. It horrified Jude that deep within himself, for all his well-meaning consciousness, he might still be no more than a self-deceptive seducer, forcing Sue into sex, when all she wanted was what Lawrence says the male in Jude cannot give: "passionate love without physical desire" (*Phoenix*, p. 509). This was Hardy's own torment, including the terrible pull of sexual desire that such as Boldwood feels before Bathsheba: "His equilibrium disturbed, he was in extremity at once. If an emotion possessed him, it ruled him" (*Far From the Madding Crowd*, 1874, ch. 18). This terrible tension in Hardy Lawrence understood as resulting from the "over-development of one principle of human life at the expense of the other" (*Phoenix*, p. 509) when civilization pretended it could tame the sexual. But the sexual kept coming back. Human beings, Hardy believed, had accidentally *over*-evolved, developing civilized mental and spiritual ideals that transcended their origin in physical nature, but without ever being able actually to work free of it. The machinery of Darwinism in its unthinking and runaway selections had produced in the human creature something beyond a machine, but still a botched and self-divided hybrid: mind opposed to body, sex against love, theory at odds with practice, nature revolting against the civilization it had helped create. "A woeful fact—that the human race is

---

[6] See Chambers (1935: 106, 128, 173) on (respectively) the loss of easy young delight, the tenderness checked by iron will, and the loss of the wonderful man he could be through (as she saw it) the separation of sex from love (70).

too extremely developed for its corporeal conditions, the nerves being evolved to an activity abnormal in such an environment" (Hardy 1984: 227). It was nerves that jarred emotions and memories in Hardy, and it was nerves that made Lawrence so sensitive, so obliged at times to put on a hard carapace in protection or attack. That is why his readers so often feel his work getting under their skin and getting on their nerves.

But instead of the division between the sexual and the spiritual that Paul Morel was instinctively fighting, this is what Paul says to Miriam about his own mother and father. "My mother, I believe, got *real* joy and satisfaction out of my father at first":

> "That's what one *must have*, I think," he continued—"the real, real flame of feeling through another person—once, only once, if it only lasts three months. See, my mother looks as if she'd *had* everything that was necessary for her living and developing. There's not a tiny bit of feeling of sterility about her."
>
> (*Sons and Lovers*, ch. 12)

It was clear again as she began to wash the back of Walter, the old miner:

> "You should have seen him as a young man," she cried suddenly to Paul, drawing herself up to imitate her husband's once handsome bearing.
>
> Morel watched her shyly. He saw again the passion she had had for him. It blazed upon her for a moment. He was shy, rather scared, and humble. Yet again he felt his old glow. And then immediately he felt the ruin he had made during these years. He wanted to bustle about, to run away from it. (*Sons and Lovers*, ch. 8)

These feelings, not emotions, belong to what I am calling a wilder natural aesthetic. It registers "what one *must* have" through that passionate heliotropic shift in a feeling-language from "flame" and "blaze" and "glow," and then to the vulnerably diminished "shy," as in shying away, and "ruin" and then "bustle... away." It knows how Walter Morel "had denied the God in him" (*Sons and Lovers*, ch. 4).

Lawrence knew that Hardy had felt his own life turn against him, his own strong feelings and powerful memories reverse their current back upon him. "Physician heal thyself" said Lawrence to Hardy, do not go on making art only out of what is sick and wrong. "A man is as big as his real desires," and not just ironically hurt and diminished by them (*Phoenix*, pp. 405, 489). "We have a right to what we want" is what Lydia replies to little Ursula when she asked if anyone would love her when she was grown up and living outside the family (*The Rainbow*, ch. 9). But Ursula knows even then how strange it is that humans have to find their own way alone. There were terrible moments always for Lawrence when he still felt the old Hardy within him, and suddenly found himself "feeling again the old, old lack in himself," losing his hard-earned core of right, and going backwards (Luhan 1932: 38). It was as if there was some first nature in him that could never be wholly overcome—or had to be overcome again and again by a core need that would not be cowed, as Lawrence believed Hardy's was. Aldous Huxley said that along with such blows and setbacks, both physical and psychological, existence was for Lawrence "one continuous convalescence; it was as though he were newly re-born from a mortal illness every day of his life." "Vitality," Huxley added, "has the attractiveness of beauty and in Lawrence there was a continuous springing fountain of vitality" (*Lawrence Letters*, pp. 1265–6). Vitality is beauty. Lawrence loved the idea of a beautiful renewal of the atmosphere, after both physical and mental thunderstorm, after sex; fresh air, fresh blood after times of conflict or dormancy (*Fantasia*, pp. 277–8). And, in keeping the rhythms of the world, he thought it would be good to think when one's night-time self was ready for sleep: Here dies the man I know; and next morning, not that lowering sense of here we go again but of rising fresh from the source (*Fantasia*, p. 271).

Art for *my* sake, says Lawrence in a letter to Ernest Collings, December 24, 1912—where the art has to be what registers an instinctive feel of *more or less* life and health, of *more or less* shadow or failure. This affective calibration is going on somewhere almost all of the time deep in his characters. There are in Lawrence's work secret messages of judgment, instinctive measurings of greater life or increased death at any moment of a continuing human existence. After his marriage Will Brangwen is ashamed at times to realize that he needs Anna more than it seems she needs him. Knowing that he has failed to become articulate or to give expression to himself, he will still have to live on in that way.

Life and death have become psychological terms here: such is the process of evolution once physical survival is secured. For then, so far from resting safely content, the evolutionary force goes on again at another level. Its further challenge is to take on, to contend with, the defences of mental survival, and to go even where we do not want to. It is "psychoanalysis alone," says Lawrence, that "has the courage necessary to conduct us through these last stages" (*Psychoanalysis*, p. 32).

4. The Use of Lawrence's Wild Aesthetic

What I am finally about is *using* Lawrence to make an argument for a psychological aesthetic that can be applied as an untamed way of thinking outside art as well as within it. *Psychological*, because it is probing within the novel's feelings at a level beneath conventional consciousness, unsure of what may come out. *Aesthetic*, because it is a version of what "agnostic" now means within religion: the almost over-full place in which all the not-knowing has to go. This is the use of the mind, not as director or controller but as a "great indicator and instrument"

(*Psychoanalysis*, p. 127). In the novels, consciousness *happens*, it does not control but it comes into being, answering some message it hears.

It works within an agnostic language that is not to do with substitutive names and prescribed values, but with indicators and instruments. There are words such as "love" and "soul" that Lawrence wanted not to be used again for a hundred years, and one might add to that his own buzz-word "life," plus a hundred others in contemporary discourse that have turned into idols of the mind. But really, Lawrence perhaps best loved the word "*It*":

> We are only the actors, we are never wholly the authors of our own deeds or works. IT is the author, the unknown inside us or outside us.
> (*Studies in Classic American Literature*, p. 26)[7]

"The term *unconscious* is only another word for life" (*Psychoanalysis*, p. 108). That is not the Freudian unconscious which Lawrence identified as no more than an inverted product of the consciousness, of all that it does not want to think, but "IT," the more primary and unknown thing. At his finest Lawrence is good at closing the eyes of the mind, and going across the threshold back to IT, to a physical sense of thinking in the immediately registered present. So it is with Walter Morel and his wife waiting for their eldest son to return home for Christmas, "it was getting so late: it was getting unbearable":

> "He's here!" cried Morel, jumping up.

And then, the next sentence, new paragraph:

> Then he stood back. The mother ran a few steps towards the door...
> (*Sons and Lovers*, ch. 4)

In the silent space between those sentences, the jumping up and the standing back, the reader feels with a physical sinking what was to be spelt out only later: "And then immediately he felt the ruin he had made..." *Immediately*.

It is vital language, and Lawrence was right to want to transfer it back, via writings such as *Fantasia of the Unconscious*, to the doing of thinking outside art. Psychoanalysis in some form may have this courage. In *Forms of Vitality* the psychologist Daniel Stern argues that there is no use directly and over-explicitly asking a man uncertain of his marriage whether he wants to stay in the relationship or leave it. That is a dead, not an alive language. Instead the therapist asks the man when he met his wife at the airport after an absence of several weeks and first

---

[7] I prefer the capital IT as it appears in later editions.

saw her emerge, "Did something jump up or fall down inside you?" (2010: 129). It is like those neo-physical thoughts of immediate "feeling," when Lawrence felt his heart drop at the return of some old, old lack, or rise at a connection unexpectedly resumed or a core re-found. And it begins, like the work in *Fantasia* and *Psychoanalysis and the Unconscious*, by minutely observing the founding of pre-verbal inter-relations between babies and mothers so that the two were in emotional attunement. It is the earliest aesthetic in dynamic form and the basis of all future social relations. Stern describes a child of ten months: she gets a piece of her puzzle in the right place after several failed efforts, then looks up to her mother, opening up her face and raising her arms in synch. The mother intuitively responds by saying "Yeah!" in an elongated up-and-down intonation that matches the contours of her daughter's facial-kinetic movements. The woman had "switched to a different modality (from seen action to heard sound) but she kept the dynamic features faithfully," matching the vitality not through the *what* of content so much as the *how* of style. It would not have been the same if the mother had merely imitated the girl's actions: there would have been no genuine exchange-circuit of sameness across difference (Stern 2010: 41).

In aesthetics, as in psychotherapy, this realization of the pre-verbal form of vital communication can go even further, within verbalization itself. W.R. Bion, Samuel Beckett's psychoanalyst in 1934–5, wanted to do what he called his wild thinking,[8] by conducting his sessions without their being tamed and prematurely humanized by ready-made concepts and pre-determining diagnoses. All he instinctively sensed was whether with his client he was getting closer to or further from what he decided to call "O," where O was a regulative sign for the really real, however approximate and fallible our recognition of it. O marks what cannot ever be known but only felt and experienced—like a moment of breakthrough, of intense joy or utter trauma in sudden realization. Bion wanted no more initially than a non-verbal indicator to point out: *It* is more or less *here*.

Lawrence looks at a poem and is not sure it means anything, not at any rate anything that can be turned into a message: "And yet it has something to say." It even carries a dim sense, he says, "of that which refuses to be said." The poem is, he concludes, "a glimpse of chaos not reduced to order" (*Phoenix*, p. 258).

And it is that agnostically or aesthetically interesting place of instability between extreme chaos and complete order, across difference and sameness, in which Lawrence insists on trying to get his art to remain. It is a dense zone of immanence, a saturated solution, out of which wilder thoughts come, leap into being, become stable for their time, and make for re-positioning. And the role of the novelist is to make the aesthetic zone as dense and as full of human matter as possible, beyond easy control, creating a secondary counterpart to biological

---

[8] See Bion *Taming Wild Thoughts* (1997) and his examples of wild aesthetic thinking in the poetry of Shakespeare and Milton in *The Tavistock Seminars* (2005), especially seminar 2.

evolution, such that the larger the quantity of rich material the better the selection of mutations and variations.

Lawrence's sense of the nervous system may be idiosyncratic but physical thinking is not mumbo-jumbo. There are synapses, electrically transmitting messages, in the gut as well as in the brain. Recent brain-imaging research confirms, moreover, that the quality of conscious states depends on the whole neural system's state of entropy—the degree of unpredictability in its activity (Carhart-Harris et al. 2014: 140–61). Higher-end entropy is reflected in conditions ranging from mental flexibility all the way to mental chaos, from divergent and creative thinking to the wildest psychosis. By contrast, normal waking consciousness, typically more structured and economic, is associated with lower entropy, characterized by rigid, bounded thinking, and shown in its lowest form in depression or obsessive compulsive disorder.[9] By providing opportunities to work between active/passive, unorganized/organized states of mind, literature has evolved to take individuals away from everyday routines into more primary forms of emergent consciousness. In this way, in his fiction's remaining realism, Lawrence has his own version of ontogeny replicating phylogeny: there are in his individuals continual returns to origins, retreats to the center, deep physical experiences that recreate again and again a consciousness that is never wholly transcendent or permanent. For him this is art-thought, the only form of thinking Lawrence finally believes in to register what is really happening in human beings.

The point is that, in this realm of the immanent aesthetic, readers can use the idea of O ahead of any other form of notation, to go into art-thought without betraying it. This pointing is particularly apt for the journeying of prose, lineally continuous and unmarked by clear signs of formal artifice, and especially prose as fluent as Lawrence's, balancing as he goes.

> Is there really any huge difference between my hand and my brain? Or my mind? My hand is alive, it flickers with a life of its own.... My hand, as it writes these words, slips gaily along, jumps like a grasshopper to dot an *i*, feels the table rather cold, gets a little bored if I write too long, has its own rudiments of thought, and is just as much *me* as is my brain, my mind, or my soul. (*Phoenix*, p. 533)

As it goes along, *this* is where *It* is: *this* is where something happens or emerges; *this* is where something shifts and changes in the midst of things; *this* is where a paragraph opening makes a difference, going closer to or further from the reality O; *this* is where even along the *lines* there is a sudden otherwise unmarked modification of *level*:

---

[9] Priesemann et al. (2013); Martindale and Dailey (1996); Schwartz (2014).

the emotional consciousness of man has a life and movement quite different from the mental consciousness. The mind knows in part, in part and parcel, with a full-stop after every sentence. But the emotional soul knows in full, like a river or a flood. (*Apocalypse*, p. 184)

It looks like a full stop, but Lawrence loves to begin another sentence at once with "And" or "But" and "So," mainly omitting the explanatory words for mental connectives like "Therefore." It is not a 1:1 correlation between the sentence and its meaning; thought is not coterminous with the sentence's literal beginning or material end; and there is no smooth progress or certain conclusion. Instead, as the hand goes forward, there is invisible matter left behind to resonate between the sentences, while at the sentence-end there is often some excess still looking for a place or a future for itself. The punctuation Lawrence loved best was the vital dash which his printers would replace with more conventional punctuation, the full-stop, the semi-colon. But the hand alive relished the rhythmic flow of the sentences, the informal freedom of abrupt leaps and changes in the continuing beat of the present.[10] "My hand, as it writes these words..." All this calls for aesthetic or agnostic markers of what even in passing is important to emotional consciousness: the instinctive sensing of more or less life, of jolts and turns, and lifts and falls and sudden, strange connective circuits. The art in this is an emotionally transmuted form of natural selection, seeking more than what most easily fits, and by that excess raising the level of existence:

He *felt* the ruin he had *made*
So *close* on him she lay, and yet she answered him from so far *away*

Or as the Christmas dialogue between Morel and his eldest son went on:

"*Well* **Dad**!" "*Well* my **lad**!" The two **men** shook hands.... Morel's eyes were **wet** ... Then the son **turned round** to his **mother**.

—where the two italicized "Wells" are Lawrence's own indicators of the initial circuit or field, while the words in bold mark his wild blood beats and surges within it. So in the example of Lydia lying upon Tom, somewhere unlocatable between her closeness and her awayness is O, silently asking, "What was it then that she was?" The most important first act in aesthetics lies in the ability to point to the nerve-like messages of an art that gets under the skin; to feel the synaptic messages inside the words, through and between or across them, like code: **what**

---

[10] I am indebted to John Worthen (private correspondence) where, for example, he points out that the manuscript version of the hand-alive passage has it: "Is there really any difference between my hand and my brain?—or my mind? [Not: Or my mind?] My hand is alive..."

was it then that **she** *was*?[11] This is the way in which a psychology of style, blindly following the "how" of any "what, feels its way in exploration.

This half-blind notation through the nerves and instincts is particularly vital for a reading of Lawrence, when for many readers he gets so much under their skin. "He hurts and shakes me," said one middle-aged man from the community of readers involved in shared reading groups.[12] "I have led a pretty conventional life. And it embarrasses me when I'm reading Lawrence and find myself reacting, stupidly: 'What *ought* I to think about this, what am I *meant* to be thinking here?' I cannot get out of the ideas I have had for such a long time. All I can do is point to what bursts them and where."

That wilder way with art is hard, hard won. It feels, in the words of William James whom Lawrence read with interest in his mid-twenties, like a real fight with life:

—as if there were something really wild in the universe which we, with all our idealities and faithfulnesses, are needed to redeem; and first of all to redeem our own hearts from atheisms and fears. For such a half-wild, half-saved universe our nature is adapted.
("Is Life Worth Living?" in *The Will to Believe* (1896), James 2000)

If just one person, one couple can get it right and make a breakthrough, it feels as if, says James, something "is eternally gained for the universe by success." A first nature is redeemed and remade by those human beings, within their own mixture of wild and tame, fighting for peace.

It is terrible to be young.—But one fights one's way through it, till one Is cleaned: the self-consciousness and sex-idea burned out of one, cauterized out bit by bit, and the self whole again, and at last free.... But I must say, I know a great deal more about the craving and raving and sore ribs than about the accomplishment.
(*Fantasia*, p. 198)

There, even in the very dash between sentences, "It is terrible—But one fights one's way through it," is the moment, the O, of exuberance well done.

---

[11] *Poetry Explorer* is an application for tablets that we have designed for just this purpose of registering, through highlights like these and arrowed links between the words, the sudden magnetic and electric forces that are the poetry within such prose. See ****[PD I am hoping that the inclusion of two extra footnotes as indicated above will mean that this footnote does not run over] https://cgi.csc.liv.ac.uk/~phil/PEApp/. As Georges Bataille said of the relation of physical sexuality to eros, this app can show the brain within the mind of the poetry or prose—where "brain" is not something reductive, but alive and untamed by conceptual consciousness, electrically excited at the very origins of cognition (Bataille [1957] 2012: 94).

[12] See the shared reading groups provided by *The Reader* (http://www.thereader.org.uk), the research by CRILS (Centre for Research into Reading, Literature and Society) at the University of Liverpool (https://www.liverpool.ac.uk/humanities-social-sciences-health-medicine-technology/reading-literature-and-society/) and Davis (2020).

11
"Whose Eye Darted Contagious Fire"
Aesthetic Form, Performative Action, and *Paradise Lost*

Richard Eldridge

1. Egoism and the Problem of Justice in Modernity

For a variety of good reasons, our regnant paradigms of knowledge and its acquisition strongly emphasize impersonality and disinterestedness. Descartes, in describing and defending the new kind of knowledge of nature that is characteristic of modern physics, proposes to open "to each one the road by which he can find in himself, and without borrowing from any, the whole knowledge which is essential to him in the direction of his life, and then by his study succeed in acquiring the most curious forms of knowledge that the human reason is capable of possessing" (Descartes 2000: 305). This is to say that the experimental method, certified as reliable by a priori argument and applied in laboratory research, is both open to anyone, without regard to political or moral stances or to historical, cultural situation, and in the service of more fulfilling, better directed life. Nowadays, given the manifold, collaborative achievements of the diverse contemporary experimental sciences, no single individual can be in a position to check all the data in favor of any result whatsoever step by step. In addition, political and moral considerations, associated with lived ideals within historical situations, do sometimes enter into the choices of domains of study, often surreptitiously, even if they do not necessarily figure in the establishment of results within those domains.[1] Nonetheless, freeing the pursuit of knowledge of physical nature to a significant extent from the sways of prejudice, superstition, and ritual was a momentous historical achievement—modern technologies of medicine, transportation, and communication, as well as modern individualism and widespread breaks from authoritarianism, are inconceivable without it—and impersonality, detachment, and a consequent tendency to distinguish facts from values remain central parts of our cultural inheritance.

---

[1] For the fullest, most careful, and most accurate account of where and how political and moral values, distinct from cognitive values, do and do not figure in the practice of science, see Lacey (1999).

Despite its manifold benefits, however, this cultural inheritance has also had its costs. Absent shared, lived value stances certified by an authoritative common religion (if such a thing ever fully existed even locally), instrumentalism, egoism, and frenzies of self-conceit (as Hegel put it) threaten to dominate cultural life. In our contemporary situation, with massive, human-induced climate change, the breakdown under Covid-19 of food supply chains dominated by big agriculture and profit extraction (Pollan 2020: 4–6), and the exploitation and comparative immiseration of the working class and poor, driven by a cult of efficiency and profit maximization (Robinson 2020: 43–6), this threat seems realized, and industrial-technological capitalism, backed by and reinforcing egoism and instrumentalism, seems in crisis.

All this raises a set of interrelated, high-level, fantastically difficult questions. How, if at all, might we retain and build upon the virtues of technological modernity and avoid its vices? Here it will not do simply to criticize instrumentalism and egoism, as long as we are unable to identify and argue for alternative self-understandings, values, and forms of life.

Can we achieve a culture of justice, understood as a good enough, fair ordering of a society, in which no one has reasonable grounds for resentment? If so, what might it look like, and what considerations might support it? How, if at all, might we break with instrumentalism, egoism, and the cult of efficiency on a large scale and achieve knowledge of ourselves as capable of life within more sustainable and less exploitative commitments? What, if any, might the vehicles of such knowledge be, and how might they reasonably contest and modify the commitments to impersonality and detachment in the experimental sciences that support exploitative instrumentalism and egoism, yet without reversion to a new fundamentalism or authoritarianism?[2] If we cannot at least begin to articulate persuasive answers to these questions, answers to which many might resonate for good reasons, then we face the threat of collapse into an at best semi-civilized war of all against all within pervasive structures of competition and exploitation.

Here it is the great merit of literature, via its aesthetic-formal powers of imagery, diction, and emplotment, to solicit, sustain, and test powers of imaginative, reflective, and emotional engagement on the parts of attentive readers in such a way that their senses of themselves, their powers, and their human interests may be productively reshaped. Such reshaping will not happen for every reader on every occasion; literature cannot achieve and should not aspire

---

[2] In *A Theory of Justice*, John Rawls appeals to a sense of justice—that is, a settled willingness to live with others non-exploitatively, under conditions of fair competition—as one of two shared human fundamental moral or conduct-shaping powers. (The other is the ability to articulate and live according to a conception of the good for oneself.) (See Rawls 1999: xii–xiii). However valuable this suggestion is, one must nowadays wonder whether the existence of any such sense can be taken for granted, or whether it has largely been suppressed or exhausted under the practices of global neoliberalism and its pervasive instrumentalism.

to the impersonality and disinterestedness that are characteristic of some central regions of scientific practice. Its productive effects presuppose backgrounds of prior immersive reading[3] and contexts of critical discussion with others.

Among writers who solicit and sustain productive self-shaping imaginative engagement via aesthetic immersion, none is more pre-eminent than Milton. This is especially true in *Paradise Lost*, whose central subject is the roots of self-consciousness and the proper use of associated powers of imagination, reflection, and choice. *Paradise Lost* might, then, have some chance to teach us, or at least some readers who are able to draw on the appropriate imaginative resources and contexts of discussion, something about inherent human tendencies to egoism and instrumentalism and how, *en mésure*, to acknowledge and moderate them. It is worthwhile to consider, then, exactly how it might do this work through its formal organization, imagery, and diction.

2. Self-Consciousness, the Fact of Self-Assertion, Sin, and Shame

Human beings are complicated animals, and the complications have to do among other things with the fact of self-consciousness (as awareness of alternatives among which one as a continuing subject might choose) and with the will (as the power to choose). But why should these complications further entail, per se, as Milton argues in *Paradise Lost*, "guilty Shame" (1058),[4] "anger, hate, mistrust, suspicion, discord" (1123-4), "inward state[s] of mind now tossed and turbulent" (1124, 1126), "mutual accusation" (1187), and "vain contest" with "no end" (1189)? Why couldn't or can't we just choose better, in accordance with the requirements of morality and divine command, so as to live in harmony with ourselves, with one another, and with nature? In other words, why does Eve, and then Adam, eat the forbidden fruit? Why do they use their freedom *that* way? And what might this use of freedom—once we understand its motivation—show about us, or at least about Milton's understanding of us? How by way of a story might Milton teach us something fundamental about ourselves?

C.S. Lewis makes a start on answering this question by tying Eve's choice to our own exercises of will, in remarking that "the reader is involved in the same illusion as Eve herself" (Lewis [1942] 1961: 121-2). But what is the nature of this illusion?

---

[3] Without having learned, usually as young children, to immerse oneself in narratives (fictional or otherwise), it is difficult for adults to enjoy literary experience fully and to take it seriously. Happily, imaginative involvements can also be mobilized by direct experience of others and by other forms of art, with reciprocal effects for literary experience. Unhappily, epistemically speaking, there are never any neutral certainties about courses of imaginative involvement.

[4] All citations to *Paradise Lost* are given in the text by line number of Book IX, as here, unless preceded by the line number of another book.

Why does she, as Lewis puts it, seek "Godhead" (Lewis 121, citing 790) and to be Adam's "superior" (Lewis 121, citing 817–25)? What does it mean to seek Godhead, and what does her search for it have to do with us?

One stretch of argument that Eve rehearses, after Satan's flattery of her, runs as follows:

(1) If knowing and choosing bring death, then God-given inward freedom to choose is not good. ("what profits then / Our inward freedom?" [761–2])
(2) God-given inward freedom is good. (Tacit, but see 756–7, to be discussed presently)
(3) Therefore knowing and choosing do not bring death.

This argument is a sophism, since premise (2) is clearly false. God-given inward freedom and its exercise are not per se good, but are good only insofar as that freedom is exercised in accordance with God's command. But why then does Eve accept premise (2)? Why, that is, does she accept that it is her right and destiny to choose as she will?

Lewis helpfully adds that the way in which Eve chooses involves a common-enough use of tendentious act-redescriptions. That is to say, when we err in choosing, we are prone to tell ourselves a story about how we didn't really tell a lie (but only were less than forthcoming) or didn't really kill someone who was innocent (because the victim was really planning something awful). We think, as Lewis puts it,

> those others "don't understand." If they knew what it had really been like for [us], they would not use those crude "stock" names. With a wink or a titter, or in a cloud of muddy emotion, the thing has slipped into [one's] will as something not very extraordinary, something of which, rightly understood and in all [one's] highly peculiar circumstances, [one] may even feel proud.   (Lewis 122)

Just so with Eve. She tacitly accepts premise (2) in order to deny that what she is on the point of doing genuinely, in these circumstances, counts as a transgression; it counts rather as what she is to do, given her possession of the power to choose, mistakenly regarded by her as per se good. Still, Lewis's accurate description of the process does not yet explain *why* it is that Eve thus argues to herself and re-describes her incipient act in such a way as to make it appear good. What moves her to do this? How do what Lewis calls "folly, malice, and corruption" first *enter* Eve's mind and will, and Adam's, and ours, "unobtrusively and naturally" (Lewis 122), as Lewis puts it? What makes this turn of mind and will *natural* to us?— Lewis remarks in passing that Adam, unlike Eve, "fell by uxoriousness" and that "we are not shown the formation of his decision as we are shown the formation of Eve's" (Lewis, 122). While this is right as far as it goes, it fails to make clear exactly *why* Adam is unable to "forgo / [Eve's] sweet converse and love so dearly joined" (908–9). Something in that converse—as well as and beyond her being "flesh of flesh, and bone of my bone" (914–15)—must count for Adam, but what? And if, as Lewis puts it, again, "the reader is involved in the same illusion as Eve herself" (Lewis 121–2), what is the nature of that illusion, and might Adam, too, be involved in it, in virtue of the character of their sweet converse with one another? This possibility, too, then raises the question: How might a movement toward transgression enter naturally and unobtrusively into anyone's consciousness, as a result of the very nature of the power of choice, at least in relation to the presence of another? Does Eve really stand in for, or exemplify, what is entailed by possession of will as such? What reasons might there be to think *that*?

G.K. Hunter comes closer to providing an explanation of how self-consciousness and will might by their very natures motivate transgression in remarking that for Eve and Adam, "freedom becomes...a claim on enough space to exercise personal power, rather than a loving choice to contribute to the power of the pair." Rather than answering in innocence and "with a patient inclination of the will" (1982: 184) to "the activity of the Garden in calling for response," Eve and Adam abandon, according to Hunter, what "the pastoral tradition [calls] *otium*, or ease, [in favor of] *care* or *busyness*, seen as the defining characteristics of courtly or metropolitan life" (Hunter, 184, 180, 183). They give up what Hunter calls "the real meaning of work—real, that is, by the approval of God—[which] lies in its expression of mutual need, mutual support, [and] the direction of daily life towards a single God-pleasing end" (Hunter, 185) in favor of the exercise of merely personal power. Yes, exactly: but why do they do *that*? Why is patient inclination to do God's will supplanted by the exercise of personal power *as personal* rather than as guided by divine command? And are such supplantations—such substitutions of the personally willed for the divinely commanded—as Lewis suggested in any way natural to us? We will not really understand what Eve and Adam do as an action that is done *for a reason* unless and until we can make sense of it as something we, too, might also do for a like reason, but, also, simultaneously, naturally and unobtrusively.

My suggestion is now that we might make some advance in thinking about how Eve and Adam, and we along with them, might naturally and unobtrusively, and for a deep and unarticulated reason, choose the exercise of personal power as personal over patient abiding with the divinely ordained and pastoral by turning our attention to a famous passage from Plato's *Republic*: Socrates' description of the first ideal city. In addition, this passage will help us to see how Milton, echoing it, motivates his fundamental thoughts about will and ego through aesthetic form.

Socrates offers this description as he and his interlocutors begin their effort to imagine an ideal city in order to find justice in it, so as to become clearer about *its* nature. Socrates completes his description with the following flight of oratory:

First, then, let's see what sort of life our citizens will lead when they've been provided for in the way we have been describing. They'll produce bread, wine, clothes, and shoes, won't they? They'll build houses, work naked and barefoot in the summer, and wear adequate clothing and shoes in the winter. For food, they'll knead and cook the flour and meal they've made from wheat and barley. They'll put their honest cakes and loaves on reeds or clean leaves, and, reclining on beds strewn with yew and myrtle, they'll feast with their children, drink their wine, and, crowned with wreaths, hymn the gods. They'll enjoy sex with one another but bear no more children than their resources allow, lest they fall into poverty or war.   (Plato 1992: *Republic* 372a–b, p. 47)

This is an astonishing passage, dripping with irony about the pastoral, marked in the words "adequate," "honest," "recline," and "hymn" among others, and concluding with the suggestion that sex with one another will be enjoyed without resulting in excess children. Glaucon interrupts this ironic fantasia on the part of Socrates to say, "It seems that you make your people feast without any delicacies" (372c, p. 47), an interruption which prompts Socrates to continue the irony:

True enough, I said, I was forgetting that they'll obviously need salt, olives, cheese, boiled roots, and vegetables of the sort they cook in the country. We'll give them desserts, too, of course, consisting of figs, chickpeas, and beans, and they'll roast myrtle and acorns before the fire, drinking moderately. And so they'll live in peace and good health, and when they die at a ripe old age, they'll bequeath a similar life to their children.   (372c–d p. 47)

And this is too much for Glaucon, who abruptly interjects, "If you were founding a city for pigs, Socrates, wouldn't you fatten *them* on the same diet?" (372d, p. 47).

The point that Glaucon is making here—and that Socrates may be deliberately inviting him to make with the ironies of his excessive emphases on simplicities, ironies that Glaucon as an alert interlocutor may be presumed to have registered—is that he, and we, would not, do not, want to live this way. Something in us demands what Socrates will go on to call *luxuries* and *feverishness* (and what Hunter calls metropolitan life), all the while himself defending the first city as the genuinely healthy one, but conceding that it "won't satisfy some people" (373a, p. 48).

Why not? What in Glaucon, and in us, wants and demands luxuries, not only for the sake of more refined pleasures of consumption, but also for the sake of whatever the next additions to the city—prostitutes, artists, poets, actors, choral dancers, contractors, adorners of women, servants, tutors, wet nurses, nannies, beauticians, barbers, chefs, cooks, and swineherds (373a–c, p. 48)—will provide. The answer, I suggest, must be that what Glaucon wants, and what we want, is the opportunity to display his, and our, individual, particular intelligence, personality, and impress of will to and for others, in performance, for endorsement as exemplary. Above and beyond the simple consumption of material goods such as might be available in pastoral life, we seek distinctive self-display and its endorsement. Human action in general flows from the attraction of interest toward an object or anticipated outcome, where initially, in childhood, the primary attractions arise via eye, ear, touch, scent, and taste. But as we grow up out of infancy, we also become aware of multiple attractions among which we must choose, and we become aware, often under the direction of others, that various objects of attraction are, despite appearances, good or bad for us in various ways. We begin not only to feel attractions and to respond to them, but also to understand that there are often enough reasons in view for pursuing one attraction and dropping another, reasons backed by the rewards and punishments of authoritative others.

And then we wonder: in being attracted specifically to this—this object, this course of action—am I responding in a way that is both mine (felt by me, as part of my set of natural attractions) and also reasonable? Can both I over time and others find sense in my acting and living in this way rather than that? Can and do others, some of whose stances I have internalized as authoritative, find sense in what I do? As Glaucon then suggests, simple, automatic, natural persistence in doing what is natural is, even if God-ordained, not something that is either possible or satisfying for beings with our degrees of self-consciousness and our awareness of alternatives and of the presence of others.

One can hear Glaucon's thought registered in two passages from *Paradise Lost*. The first is the description in Book IV of what pastoral life in Eden is like, as it is first seen by Satan.

> Under a tuft of shade that on a green
> Stood whispering soft by a fresh fountain side
> They sat them down and after no more toil
> Of their sweet gard'ning labor than sufficed
> To recommend cool Zephyr and made ease
> More easy, wholesome thirst and appetite
> More grateful, to their supper fruits they fell:
> Nectarine fruits which the compliant boughs
> Yielded them sidelong as they sat recline
> On the soft downy bank, damasked with flowers.
>
> (IV, 325–36)

This outburst of pastoral should remind us immediately of Socrates' description of the first city, including talk of reclining, the enjoyment of natural agricultural products as wholesome food, and sweet labor unclothed. (Is Glaucon's outburst in your ear as you follow this passage imaginatively?)

Glaucon's rejoinder to Socrates is then echoed by Milton in his own voice at the beginning of Book IX, as he announces the turn in the plot:

> No more of talk where God or angel guest
> With Man as with his friend familiar used
> To sit indulgent and with him partake
> Rural repast, permitting him the while
> Venial discourse unblamed. I now must change
> Those notes to tragic: foul distrust and breach
> Disloyal on the part of Man, revolt
> And disobedience.
>
> (1–8)

These lines announce a turn in the plot. But equally important is the fact that there would not *be* a plot—that is, nothing we could recognize as a story of human actions—if the account remained in the register of pure pastoral, just as Glaucon is unable to recognize himself or human beings as he knows them in the Socratic pastoral. At least above a certain minimal age, human beings do not respond to the promptings and possibilities of their experiences smoothly and automatically, in the way that a bud opens into a flower, but instead in ways that are mediated by will and the demand for recognition of its exercises as reasonable.

In fact, that a turn away from pastoral must take place in anything that will count as a narrative of human life is already intimated in Book IV, where Adam describes to Eve a difference between themselves and other animals. As Adam explains to Eve:

> Other creatures all day long
> Rove idle unemployed and less need rest.
> Man hath his daily work of body or mind
> Appointed which declares his dignity
> And the regard of Heav'n on all his ways
> While other animals unactive range
> And of their doings God takes no account.
>
> (IV, 614–21)

Here Adam registers all at once a sense of a distinction between labor and rest, a sense of a difference from other animals who rove idle unemployed, without significant planning or regret, a sense of dignity in having their work appointed—named as something they must hold before them in consciousness and stick to—and a sense of being jointly under the scrutiny of another, hence also under one's own and each other's scrutiny as scrutinized. These senses of labor vs. rest, of a categorial difference from other animals, of having appointed work, and of being under scrutiny are parts of the very structure of human discursive consciousness and self-consciousness, and it is these senses that make simpler life in the pastoral an unfit home for the human.

The actual processes of choosing to eat the fruit are then for both Eve and Adam more consequences of their growing awareness of and insistence on this fact of the unfitness of the pastoral for humanity, of the persistent wish to act with exemplary self-command, than they are results of merely momentary confusion or contingent error. Eve and Adam both enact and discover to themselves their distinctly human identities through their courses of coming to choose, in relation to and in awareness of each other. This process of simultaneous enactment and discovery of the complexities of the human is shown first and most strongly in Eve's progress, but it is not fundamentally different in Adam's. In each case, a sense of being always already beyond the merely animal, in possessing both awareness of alternatives and the power to choose, exercised under the gaze of a human other, drives the progress of the plot.

The action begins, notoriously, with Eve's suggestion to Adam that they might work apart in order to avoid distraction by one another and thus get more done. To Adam's worry that left alone Eve might be insulted and distracted by Satan's mere tempting of her, albeit certain to fail, Eve replies that they would

> rather double honor gain
> From his surmise proved false, find peace within,
> Favor from Heav'n, our witness, from th' event.
>
> (332–4)

Eve here shows concern for winning, gaining, honor, and in being seen to do so, suggesting that until that happens she lacks peace within, suggesting further that "virtue unassayed" (335) counts for less than virtue put to the test and passing it.

To these suggestions, Adam aptly asks, "Wouldst thou approve thy constancy?" (36). Here the verb "approve," as in the French *éprouver*, carries the senses of *put to test* and *confirm*. The *OED* lists for "approve" "to make good a statement or position; to show to be true, prove, demonstrate," "to corroborate, confirm, or attest a thing with some authority," "to demonstrate practically or to the experience of others, display, exhibit, make proof of," and "to display or exhibit to advantage." Examples of usage in these senses reach back to Wycliffe's 1382 translation of the Bible (*OED*, s.v. "approve"). Adam similarly speaks later of Eve's having sought "needless cause t'approve / The faith they owe" (1140–1) and of her having sought "Matter of glorious trial" (1177). Making a show of something to oneself and others, for confirmation of its value, status, or worth, is central to this approving. And this—to make a show and to have the virtue thus shown confirmed and proved as shown—is exactly what Eve wants.

It is scarcely a surprise, then, that Satan's arguments—less than compelling in themselves if one takes God's authority seriously and does not seek self-display—work on Eve, thus motivated. Among these arguments are Satan's questions, "Who sees thee? (and what is one?), who shouldst be seen / A goddess among gods adored and served" (546-7), as if display and its confirmation mattered. The comparative, "a goddess among (plural) gods," appeals further to Eve's wish for distinctive, exemplary standing in the eyes of many others. All this should not matter to Eve, who ought to be committed to fulfilling God's ordinances. But it does matter, because it already matters to Eve, in her wish to have her constancy approved and her virtue thus displayed, even before Satan appeals to her vanity.

Satan's further arguments then appeal similarly to the sense that she might win a status that she already craves. It is, he says, "right thou shouldst be obeyed" (570); if you and Adam eat, you will know "both good and evil" and "be as gods" (709-10); if, by eating "I of brute human, you of human gods" (712). And then the following impossible dilemma. Either the gods (note, again, the plural) have not produced everything—"I question it," says Satan (720)—so that the things of the earth are simply there to be used as one wills, and there is no already fixed standard of good and evil—a stance of metaphysical naturalism that encourages individualist instrumentalism. Or the gods have produced everything, including this tree, so that it must be good, and if God is omnipotent, He can in any case not be injured by your eating, nor can He envy you your standing (722-30).

Again, these arguments are sophistic for anyone who possesses and is prepared to live according to a sense of God as a source of absolute normative authority. But Eve is not prepared to live according to that sense, precisely because she already wishes to exercise normative authority on her own, to display that exercise, and to have it endorsed. She wouldst approve her constancy in doing what she distinctively does. In her final reflections before eating, she reasons that "For good unknown sure is not had; or had, And yet unknown, is as not had at all" (756-7). She is in the grip of a will to possess and exercise normative authority on her own—to have it and to know herself to have it, as Eve, through her own authoritative judgment—and to be conspicuously exemplary in that possession and exercise. In the grip of such a will, prohibitions against knowing "bind not!" (760)—and so she eats: not simply out of unstructured vanity, or because of the force of Satan's arguments, but because a wish to be tested, to perform, and to win recognition has been always already part of the structure of her consciousness, in possessing awareness of alternatives and the power to choose.[5]

Adam's case, though less closely described, is fundamentally similar. He works out for himself a number of sophistic arguments. Since the serpent did not die,

---

[5] Here it is also worthwhile to compare both Milton and Plato with Hegel's parable of the development of self-consciousness as inherently involving the seeking of recognition from another in Chapter IV of *The Phenomenology of Spirit*.

perhaps his tasting of the fruit has made it safe for us (927)—a clear case of wishful thinking and failing to take God's normative authority to be absolute. Since the serpent became human as a result of eating, we might become gods (936)—the very "proportional ascent" (712) argument that Eve has already accepted from Satan, and an argument that is compelling only if one is committed already to seeking ascent. God will not destroy us and all his works and thus "labor lose" if we eat, as if the loss of labor might matter to God, and as if labor is already burdensome in itself, rather than a natural means of praising God. If God were to destroy us and His works, He would thus show himself "fickle" (948), and Satan could then point this out to the other angels and incite rebellion—again, clearly a matter of no concern to a God who is omnipotent and omniscient.

Behind Adam's articulation and acceptance of these sophistic arguments there lies, as in the case of Eve, an already existing wish for ascent, a wish for the acquisition, exercise, display, and endorsement of normative authority. This same wish for recognized personal normative authority motivates in turn the crucial thought on Adam's part, addressed to Eve in inward reflection, that he must eat too because he cannot "live without thee" (908), cannot "forgo / Thy sweet converse and love so dearly joined / To lie again in these wild woods forlorn" (908–10). The crucial questions to raise here are: Why does life without Eve count for Adam as forlorn? Why does her "sweet converse" matter so much to him? As he recognizes, God might create another Eve (911–12). Why does he not abide in God's will in faithfulness to this possibility? In short, why does Eve matter more to him than God?

The answer to these questions must be that Eve is that particular like but different being to and for whom mutual display and endorsement of attraction and interest through converse have been possible thus far, and *that*—mutual display and endorsement (the sense that a like but different present other of equal standing approves one's powers or virtues in actual converse) must matter more to Adam than having God alone as his distant creator, witness, and judge, just as it mattered more to Eve to display and test her character and judgment to herself and to Adam than to obey God. And this wish for display to and endorsement by a particular human other must, too, be part of the very structure of Adam's human discursive consciousness. Otherwise he would not work out sophistic arguments for himself and would not count only life with Eve as a life worth having. "To lose thee were to lose myself" (959) *because* self-consciousness and will crave display to and endorsement from *her*.

Once transgression has taken place, the quality of experience is itself altered, as if to heighten the difference between human beings and other animals, the difference between experience on the part of creatures with awareness of alternatives and the power to choose and creatures without these features. Eve observes to Adam that the apple to her has "Taste so divine that what of sweet before / Hath touched my sense flat seems to this and harsh" (986–7), significantly in virtue of the fact that she now not only enjoys the fruit, but enjoys her enjoying the fruit and Adam's enjoying of her enjoyment. She tastes with "opened eyes, new hopes, new joys" (985), not as other animals more simply feed. More explicitly, Eve and Adam now enjoy sexual relations self-consciously, as something involving performance, mutual recognition, and mutual enjoyment of each other's enjoyment of each other. Adam is moved "to dalliance" with Eve (1015), that is, to tarrying in self-conscious enjoyment as opposed to simpler immediate action. He forebears "not glance or toy / Of amorous intent, well understood / Of Eve whose eye darted contagious fire" (1034–6).

In the case of Eve, at least, it is not clear that she wholly regrets or repents having been brought to allow self-consciousness and the power of choice to express themselves by claiming normative authority and seeking endorsement of performance. "Was I," she asks Adam after the fact, "t'have never parted from thy side? / As good have grown there still a lifeless rib!" (1153–4). Here, for her, parting from Adam (and from God's will) is required by what it is first to have and then to seek to express *life as a self-conscious being*. Adam's understands Eve's fall as stemming from "that strange / Desire of wandering this unhappy morn [that] / (I know not whence) possessed thee!" (1135–7). That he takes Eve to be possessed by desire he knows not whence already intimates that this possession is due to the very structures of self-consciousness and will rather than to any independently identifiable occurrence that simply happened to her. Eve's non-regretful question, "Was I t'have never parted from thy side?" (1153), comes, moreover as an answer to Adam's thought that she has been somehow possessed, as if to suggest that the possession has been deeper and more justified, more ineradicable and inevitably acted upon, than any talk of happenstantial occurrences might explain.

3. How the Text Moves Us into Self-Assertion and Reflection on It

Milton's view—echoing Plato, expressed in ironic overstatements of the charms of the pastoral, and made explicit in Eve's and Adam's accounts of what they seek—is, then, that nothing that happens to us externally causes our transgression. Instead, there is a kind of vanity that is built into the very structure of self-conscious, discursive awareness of alternatives and the power to choose: a deep wish to choose for oneself, out of one's own attractions and aversions, and thence to act performatively, not only for the sake of satisfaction, but also for the sake of the recognition and endorsement from another like-minded but different human other, of having thus exercised one's powers *in that way* as one's own.[6]

---

[6] Again, this bears comparison with Hegel's argument in Chapter IV of the *Phenomenology* that seeking recognition from another is inherent in the structure of self-consciousness.

But why, if at all, should the fact that Milton forwards these views in *Paradise Lost* by way of plot, diction, and imagery count for us? Surely that fact alone is not sufficient to compel agreement with those views. In the grip of a picture of objectivity that is associated with impersonality and detachment, for good reasons, some readers—many readers—if they read Milton at all will be tempted to dismiss the views in the text as nothing but his opinions. Yes, it may be conceded, Milton solicits us to recognize our temptations and transgressions *in* Eve's and Adam's, and yes, he proposes that we might do otherwise. As Tzachi Zamir eloquently puts it, Milton's aim in *Paradise Lost* is to "invite more complex routes for unification with God"—through gratitude, meaningful agency, or the sense of being alive— "that involve a responsive hosting of God's available presence" (Zamir 2018: 25), to which we might turn through having recognized ourselves in Eve and Adam. Hence Milton's methods are maieutic; they are to help us to see our lives and psyches more fully and to feel and respond to this vision of ourselves more aptly. But, again, why should any of this count for us, for anyone?

There are no easy answers to these questions, and it is an undeniable fact that Milton's vision is overwhelmingly likely not to count immediately for everyone or even for many, at least as our habits of life, reading, and judgment stand now. And yet the poem also has ways of enabling reshapings of those habits by way of imaginative engagement with its development. Like all great poetry, *Paradise Lost* solicits and sustains imaginative engagement and animated attention. As Kant puts it in the *Critique of Judgment*, poetic art at its highest reaches of achievement "animates the cognitive faculties and combines spirit with the mere letter of language" (Kant 2001: 35). Readers can be bound imaginatively, and suitably attentive readers are bound imaginatively, to the form of attention, involving both thought and feeling, to the phenomena that the text presents (see Eldridge 2009). This explains the self-sustaining flow of absorption that characterizes our most involved forms of reading.

Significantly, the phenomena that the text presents are not only the incidents of the plot that it represents. Absorbed reading is directed all at once to the textual surface (diction, acoustic contour), represented action (plot), the general possibilities and tendencies of human life that the represented incidents exemplify (theme), the presented authorial persona, and the emotions and attitudes that are expressed toward all of these in their courses of development. Absorbed attention is simultaneously both distributed across these phenomena and unified in being directed toward the text and the courses of thought and attitude that it both represents and makes available (see Cohen 2012: 75–6).

This fact entails important complexities with respect to the reading of *Paradise Lost*. In the represented plot, Eve and Adam (and Satan) each narcissistically assert and stand on their own powers of individual choice in the service of seeking recognition of themselves as distinctively valuable beings on their own. Milton's overt argument, as Zamir notes, is that this is not a necessary human action.

Human beings might instead, as Zamir puts it, host God, or become "part of a structure created by God (thereby an element housed by God) and also part of a structure that may wholly house God," hence part of an unfolding divine order (Zamir 2018: 79). That is, one might say, the official view of meaningful life that *Paradise Lost* forwards. At the same time, however, it is difficult not to notice a certain pride, even narcissism, that attaches to Milton's own authorial stance. Why does Milton undertake the project of justifying the ways of God to men? Couldn't God take care of that well enough himself, if he chose and if it's somehow necessary? Who demands this justification? And why does the poem begin "Sing Heavn'ly Muse"—a formulation that self-consciously echoes the opening of *The Iliad*—"Sing, goddess, the wrath of Achilles"? (p. 1) The pride of Milton in responding to God's lavish creation and seeking to assert his own distinctive place within it directly parallels Eve's and Adam's assertions of self-will. No surprise, then, that William Blake notes that Milton "was a true poet, and of the Devil's party without knowing it" (Blake 2005: 49).

And now the reader, too, or at least an alert reader, may notice that she too, like Eve in responding to Eden, and like Milton in responding to the whole of creation, is likewise housed within and absorbed by a lavish, overwhelming structure of manifold attractions—Milton's own text. The reader stands to the text of *Paradise Lost* as Milton stands to creation (and to Homer and Virgil) and Eve stands to God. Like Eve and like Milton, she will find herself being pulled toward this or that sensuous experience, being stunned by her attractions and their sublime proliferation, and then wishing as a result somehow to test and assert herself and her responses as a reader as apt (to approve her constancy). With its contagious fire of diction, imagery, plot, and expressed attitudes, the reader will find herself forced into Eve's and Milton's transgressive position in seeking to enact, express, and come to terms with who she is. If she is alert, then she will reflect on this and find herself bound up in the work of acknowledgment—the difficult, reflective, practical task of participating in and responding to self-assertion (see Russell 2020). And if all this happens, then she will find herself participating in and reflecting on human reality—that is, in courses of fallen, distinctively human life that express shifting ego-investments. Such participation coupled with reflection offers a chance to engage with stances that we may not be able to confront otherwise and that we may be moved to reshape by the experience of poetic art.

There will be no recipe for doing this. Given the participations of Eve, Adam, Milton, and the attentive reader in transgressive narcissism, we have very little if any idea either of what non-transgressive, pacified life on the part of recognizable human beings might look like or of how it might be achieved. But this fact makes the ongoing work of acknowledgment and imaginative practical response to human reality only more urgent. By inviting, sustaining, and shaping active imaginative and reflective engagement in an ongoing process of self-scrutiny, the contagious fire that is the fully absorbing poem (like other works of poetic art, including history, music, and painting, among others, at their highest reaches of achievement[7]) offers our best hope for coming to terms with who we are and what we have made of ourselves. In a poem entitled "Weather," commissioned by *The New York Times* to address "this historic moment in our country," the Black American poet Claudia Rankine writes:

> Whatever
> contracts keep us social compel us now
> to disorder the disorder...
> ...There's an umbrella
> by the door, not for yesterday but for the weather
> that's here.
>
> (Rankine 2020: 1)

Poetry does not solve problems of public policy. It does not disinterestedly record facts about the non-human material world. But it can challenge and reshape our self-conceptions and the commitments that express them. It can disorder the disorders in which we live, respond to the weather that's here, and offer possibilities of acknowledgment bound to glimpses of less death-dealing forms of human life.

---

[7] Both Aristotle and Hegel characterize all art as poetic, that is, as proceeding from powers of *poesis*, or the making of representations for other than theoretical or practical purposes, but instead for the sake of acknowledgment. For an explication of Aristotle on *poesis*, see Eldridge (2014, pp. 26–28). For an explication of Hegel on poetic truth and acknowledgment, see Eldridge (2016).

12
Tennyson's Tears, Brooks's Motivations

Susan J. Wolfson

1. "Tears, idle tears"

There are texts I don't teach because I know I'll tear up, to the confusion or embarrassment of my students. I've discussed this with them, the miracle of words as agents of visceral responses (not just tears), but I have not embodied it for them. I'm aware of this double bind of professional reading and personal reading, sometimes but not always, in productive interaction. My personal reading is intellectually active and emotionally engaged, but my tears are not for classroom display, even as I put both heart and mind into my teaching, which my students appreciate and remember. This ongoing, negotiated relay sharpened my attention to the most peculiar chapter in Cleanth Brooks's landmark of public pedagogy, *The Well Wrought Urn:* "The Motivation of Tennyson's Weeper"—the protagonist of *Tears, idle tears*.

Brooks's enduring fascination with this lyric throughout his brilliant career is palpable. He had it in the classroom-revolutionizing *Understanding Poetry* (1938), summoned it as a "test case" in *The American Scholar* to argue against the charge that "New Criticism" was hostile to feelings (1944), adapted this defense for the chapter in *Urn* (1947), and applied ever more forcible pedagogy in subsequent editions of *Understanding* (1950, 1960, 1976).[1] All this care, curation, and protection are inflected by Brooks's devotion to professional literary study, emerging in the 1930s with twin goals: to liberate it from the constrictions of philology and literary history (sources, allusion), and to claim parity for it with the sciences, in distinction from she-coded book clubs of soft-hearted, soft-headed appreciation.

The first edition of *Understanding Poetry* (1938) convenes a male-coded demographic: two he-editors, addressing him-students with a mostly male-authored syllabus. *Tears* was quietly tucked into a unit on *Tone and Attitude*, about a poet's relationship "toward his subject and toward his audience" (295), rendered by a "speaker" in a "dramatic organization" (23). It summoned no full lesson, just a brief EXERCISE: "its subject is vague... How does Tennyson achieve his success?" (365). By historical irony, Brooks's first critical work-up came in a dramatic

---

[1] In *American Scholar*, Brooks introduces the "case" of *Tears* as "taken from my own work" (1944: 285), apparently worked out and first published here.

conflict, launched by Darrel Abel in a wartime essay for *The American Scholar* (Autumn 1943), which charged "New Criticism" with impoverishing poetry into an "intellectual exercise," denying "value" to "its appeal to the feelings" (414); "readers lose the exciting consciousness of being in communication almost immediate with hearts of alien circumstances, hearts wonderfully the same as their own" (419). Abel diagnosed a "melancholy" professional pathology (428). Brooks retaliated in the summer 1944 *American Scholar* with a vigorous reading of *Tears* that he would later export to *Urn*.

Brooks introduced a gothic caricature of Abel's villain: a "bloodless creature who can enjoy a poem only by first mummifying it into a drily intellectual 'form,'" on which a New Critic "dotes" with an epicurean taste for "paradoxes and abstruse symbols" and anything "ironical," and a sneering "distaste for simplicity" (285). Brooks then subpoenaed *Tears* as a "test case" to demonstrate the emotive power of "irony, paradox, and complex symbol" (286), along with "ambiguity, and ironic contrast" (292), in dramas of struggle for expression. Able was Brooks, but Abel wasn't buying it: the flourish of "technical operations" were less about the poem's heartful communication, he replied in Autumn 1944, than a demonstration of critical "ingenuity in discovering irony, paradox, and dramatic evolution" (501).

Brooks called back his defense in 1947 for a chapter in *The Well Wrought Urn*, a smart and scrupulous work of attention that launched *Tears* into wide critical respectability for its shaping a "psychological problem" into complex aesthetic expression (157). Yet Abel haunts about the shape of the chapter in three new fortifications: its title, the two paragraphs of introduction, and a summoned foil, *Break, break, break* (160–1). These girders become their own spectacle on the centrifuge of Brooks's struggle to contain strains and contradictions, not of over-intellection but of unoriginated affection at odds with the site-plan of professional criticism. His *Urn*-title, "The Motivation of Tennyson's Weeper," advances *Motivation* to beg in advance the question of *idle*. Then, the curtain-raising new sentence: "Tennyson is perhaps the last English poet one would think of associating with the subtleties of paradox and ambiguity" (153)—quite a limit-case for the platform that "the language of paradox is the language of poetry" (3)! Brooks says this not in confession but as impresario. The subtitle of *The Well Wrought Urn* is *Studies in the Structure of Poetry*. By *structure*, Brooks means no static design, but a "dynamic drama" that "builds conflict" as "*an action*": "the structure of poetry is that of drama" (186–7). A "pang experienced in...immediately personal life" becomes poetry with a development of "dramatic elements"; *Tears* is a palpable poetry of pang: "complexity is no marked characteristic...it moves simply forward with a sweetly plangent flow"—this is F.R. Leavis in 1945 (53–4, 59), a year after Brooks's defense in *The American Scholar*, and the same year that he and Robert Heilman produced *Understanding Drama* (1945). While Brooks doesn't cite Leavis in *Urn*, his stressed "Motivation" and his definition of character, a totalized Weeper, are acutely tuned to drama-logic.

2. Brooks's Motivated Weeper

The Weeper is a dramatic character named for this expression; the critical character in the wings is named Paradox. If Tennyson is "not...successful in avoiding the ambiguous and paradoxical," this is the "saving grace" that gains his place in *The Well Wrought Urn* (153), bolstered by the paradox-acts of eight other chapter-lessons therein. All the exercises are braced by "The Language of Paradox" (chapter 1) and an antithetically rhymed "The Heresy of Paraphrase" (chapter 11). Brooks privileges *para*dox as the trope for incongruous situations and sensations ("contradictory" to habitual expectation) in refusal of any *para*phrase ("alongside"). Tears are a perfect occasion, because the form is not the "envelope" of a content (178) but simultaneous with it.

> Tears, idle tears, I know not what they mean,
> Tears from the depth of some divine despair
> Rise in the heart, and gather to the eyes,
> In looking on the happy Autumn-fields,
> And thinking of the days that are no more.
>
> Fresh as the first beam glittering on a sail,
> That brings our friends up from the underworld,
> Sad as the last which reddens over one
> That sinks with all we love below the verge;
> So sad, so fresh, the days that are no more.
>
> Ah, sad and strange as in dark summer dawns
> The earliest pipe of half-awakened birds
> To dying ears, when unto dying eyes
> The casement slowly grows a glimmering square;
> So sad, so strange, the days that are no more.
>
> Dear as remember'd kisses after death,
> And sweet as those by hopeless fancy feign'd
> On lips that are for others; deep as love,
> Deep as first love, and wild with all regret;
> O Death in Life, the days that are no more.

This is the text presented in all editions of *Understanding Poetry*, always with a subscript: "(*The Princess*)." The absence of this subscript in *American Scholar* and *The Well Wrought Urn* is a strange contradiction to the stress on "dramatic context."² I shall return to *The Princess*; for now I want to mark the gender transpositions that this suppression allows. In *The Princess*, a maiden sings the lyric to an audience at an all-female university, amid them a trio of secretly cross-dressed lads. In the lesson of *The Well Wrought Urn*, Brooks recasts the lyric as a man speaking to men. His new opening paragraph is not even coded: here is a poet who "struggles manfully" with "'big' questions.... Like his protagonist in 'In Memoriam,' Tennyson 'fought his doubts'" (153). Hard *fought* to well *wrought*: not for nothing does Gerhard Joseph, writing in the wake of Brooks, deem *Tears* one of Tennyson's "perfectly wrought works" (152)—this by force of "creative distance" from personal sorrow, and fully appreciated by knowing the struggle.

Brooks's chapter in *Urn* meets the spectacle of a man's "idle tears" head on, with italics-fortified rhetorical questions, against any gainsaid "not":

> Are they *idle* tears? Or are they not rather the most meaningful of tears? Does not the very fact that they are "idle" (that is, tears occasioned by no immediate grief) become in itself a guarantee of the fact that they spring from a deeper, more universal cause? (153)

On the stage of "Motivation," Brooks unfolds a dramatic struggle for expression (154–5). Like a dream-interpreter, he knows the weave of meaning on the warp of unmeaning. *Tears* opens "impulsively," in "dramatic boldness," and develops "a bold and violent reversal of the speaker's first characterization of his tears." Brooks deftly brings the two scenes of affective action—*in the heart* (not *from*) and *on happy Autumn-fields*—together in the tenor of *thinking on the days that are no more*, a "line of development" with "dramatic power" (157–60).

He then aligns the prepositions *in* and *on* with the emotionally invested imagery of surfaces and depths in the second stanza, fraught with sensations at once *fresh* and *no more*. The visual "field" is imagination's delicate analogy: *Fresh as the first beam glittering on a sail* (this line finely suspended on the page and by a comma) ahead of the figural event, the sail as metonym for a ship first coming *up* from geographical antipodes then sinking *below the verge*. Brooks plumbs *underworld* for its "Greek mythology, the realm of the shades, the abode of the dead" (155), involved with a pathos of Orphean poetic power, winning a reprieve then failing its license. Carefully building his grammar of paradox, Brooks notes the force of "the same basic symbol" (the sunlit sail on the verge) for both bringing and removing as a language for the affective "linkage," *So sad, so fresh*. This is symbol (literally "together thrown") dramatized, reprising *sad* for a new link to *strange* in the "figure developed" for stanza three.

---

² *American Scholar*, 288; *Urn*, 141, 151, 154. The *Urn*-text (263) also elides the first-line indentations of *Tears* and lower-cases "Autumn," corruptions not in *American Scholar* (286–7), nor any edition of *Understanding Poetry*.

Feeling lives in the analogical mode as well as the indicative. *Linkage* is Brooks's recurrent trope, a depth psychology that manifests as poetic metaphor. He shows us how to read the delicately pained image of a casement pane slowly growing to a *glimmering square* as a figural replication of the *glittering* sail, images with a "dramatic clarity and sharpness" for the "intensity" of desire in the ache of *no more*. The overlaid conjunction, *sad and strange*, is "explicitly linked" on the developing logic of ironic contrast, the emergence of day from a dark summer dawn in the sensorium of *dying eyes* and *dying ears*. The final stanza, the most passionate, floods four analogies, not by images but in fragments of sensation for the "intimate presence of what is irrevocably beyond reach" (156–7): *Dear as / sweet as / deep as / Deep as* are "tantalizingly vivid and near"—a tacit mythology (Brooks doesn't pause over it) from the eponym of eternal desire and torment. The adverb is tuned to the effect, "precious because of the very hopelessness": here, remembered kisses after death, kisses futilely feigned in fancy, and depths of actual love, suddenly totalized into a radiant "wild with all regret" (158). Psychological density materializes in the density of words. "Something has happened to the grammar here" (Brooks muses out loud) in the drama of struggling for adequate explanation.

This "something" condenses in the dramatically charged "culminating paradox":

O Death in Life, the days that are no more.

So Brooks insets this cry on page 157, as if an epigraph speaking to a "deeper, more universal cause" (154). Yet for all this general power, Brooks worries the grammatical indeterminacy of *O Death in Life* so meticulously that William Empson seems to have slipped in a page from *Seven Types of Ambiguity* (1930):

What is the status of the exclamation, "O Death in Life"? Is it merely a tortured cry...? Or is it a loose appositive: "the days that are no more are a kind of death in life"?

Brooks recognizes the multiple vectors: a transitory thematic apostrophe, a vocative prosopopoeia, a cry of identificatory naming.[3] He means to sort it out, "to accord it justification... on closer examination" (158) into "paradox, the assertion of the union of opposites" (reiterated in "The Heresy of Paraphrase," *Urn* 194). Empson likes dramatically interesting indeterminacy. Brooks summons italics to lecture on dramatic coherence (160).

---

[3] Although Hillis Miller reiterates the grammatical multiplicity of this *O* (387), his resistance to New Criticism suppresses Brooks's precedence.

I have no wish to intellectualize the poem—to make conscious and artful what was actually spontaneous and simple. Nevertheless, the qualities of ironic contrast and paradox *do* exist in the poem and they *do* have a relation to the poem's dramatic power.

In *American Scholar*, he wrapped, and wrapped up, his defense on these stresses, tied up into the vital involvement of "*what* is said" with "the *way* that a thing is said," how words from the lexicon of "common sense" gain "uncommon sense" in poetic structuring. He offered this analysis as a service to understanding, neither a substitute clinical account nor an "expression of the critic's own emotional response" (293–5).

3. The "stuff" of Brooks's Motivations

I have no wish to satirize Brooks's delineation of poetic structure, which is often the target of reductive critique. Nevertheless, I want to read some tenacious effects of his pedagogical master-plot that he is recurrently at pains to deflect. These press the unified field of "The Motivation of Tennyson's Weeper" into a genre I shall call "Critical Dramatic Monologue" and, in this case, "The Motivation of Tennyson's New Critic." One tenacity for Tennyson (Brooks knows this, but rules it out as extra-literary motivation) is the sudden death of his beloved friend and champion Arthur Henry Hallam in 1833. Hallam is the tacit referent of an untitled lyric that Tennyson (his "widow" and "widower") wrote soon after, then added to *Poems* 1842, finding a late placement on some spare unnumbered pages at the end of volume two. Brooks summons it into the chapter in *Urn* as a foil to *Tears*, because it aptly draws on the same "emotional habit" (as Spitzer puts it, 55), and distills the same lexical climate, with a sibling pathos of exclamation and a refrain of profound temporal melancholy.

> *Break, break, break,*
>   *On thy cold gray stones, O sea!*
> *And I would that my tongue could utter*
>   *The thoughts that arise in me.*
>
> *O, well for the fisherman's boy,*
>   *That he shouts with his sister at play!*
> *O well for the sailor lad,*
>   *That he sings in his boat on the bay!*
>
> *And the stately ships go on*
>   *To their haven under the hill;*

> *But O for the touch of a vanish'd hand,*
> *And the sound of a voice that is still!*
>
> *Break, break, break,*
> *At the foot of thy crags, O sea!*
> *But the tender grace of a day that is dead*
> *Will never come back to me.*

Brooks brings this lyric on board to judge it a "much thinner" poem, "coarser" and "more confused," its imagery asserted and "conventional," without a "psychological exploration" of "dramatic force" (160–2). Fixed on the template of *Tears*, Brooks can't hear a different key: no self-accounting climaxing in existential paradox, just choked speech, so alienated from the living world that even metaphor is impossible. But this, too, is a plausible lyric mode, divergent, not necessarily inferior. The first staccato thumps, comma-choked, evoke the monotony of the waves, a sound still more expressive than the utterly arrested tongue.[4] What Brooks calls the "dramatic boldness" with which *Tears* opens registers here, too: three phantom iambs nearly homologous to the three stresses of "Tears, idle tears." Verbal repetition possesses both poems.

Here, though, no analogies accrue for Tennyson. The waves evoke only to resist pathetic fallacy (that the world should mirror our emotions), even seem to mock it with indifferent mechanical motion. *Break, break, break* opens in alienated arrest, in implicit pained obverse to what Hallam had praised in Tennyson's *Poems, Chiefly Lyrical* (1830): a "distinctive" skill with "the exquisite modulation of harmonious words and cadences to the sweep and fall of feelings expressed" (621). No hope for *feelings expressed*, this song is an auditorium of estrangements, blank sounds and hollow sighs. The vivid information of the external world is edged in antitheses: the singing and shouting voices of the young, ships that impersonally *go on*, their very *haven under the hill* evoking, to refuse, any graveyard. Tennyson's contemporary R.H. Hutton praised his power to render "the dumb spirit of human loss," and he found *Break, break, break* "closely analogous" to *Tears* in exactly this way: "No poet has ever had a greater mastery over the power of real things ... to express evanescent emotions that almost defy expression" (373–4). Much drama in *almost*.

So, too, we might say, of those *happy Autumn-fields* upon which the speaker of *Tears* looks with sad estrangement. Focused on the semantic "linkage" of *autumn* and *days that are no more*, Brooks elides *happy* when he cites the line, missing how

---

[4] Derek Attridge reads the subtle tensions of meter versus rhythm in affective reading, especially how the commas induce metrical pauses in place of the unaccented syllables (41), and Isobel Armstrong brings fine attention to the dramatic force of ungoverned "polymetrics" ("Meter and Meaning" 35–41).

Tennyson uses this utterly conventional word for the pathos of the "ironic contrast" that Brooks reserves for the final stanza (158). Whether its sense is fortunate unconsciousness or positive delight, *happy* is further pained for usurping the tradition of "Autumn" with vanishings and dying. Were Brooks to think through rather than around *happy*, he might have recognized the kinship of the two poems he sets in contrast, allowed *Tears* a "drama" of paralysis, *happy* a benign treachery, more kin to than different from the living world of *Break, break, break*. It is telling that Brooks (unaccountably) lower-cases both *Autumn* and the *Sea* of *Break, break, break* with the effect of depleting the affective force of a futile gesture to responsive personification.[5]

The drama of *Tears* climaxes in a single *O*, erupting from the vibrations of *know not, no more, below, so (sad, fresh, sweet)* and subsiding into a last *no more*. *Break, break, break* gives *O* a primary role on its rolling sound-stage. First, a vocative to the sea; next, two inward sighs; last, a volta break: *But O*, pained with a tactile ache for *a vanish'd hand*, panged against the indifferent returns of *Break, break, break*. All this summons *The voice that is still* onto an Empsonian double-grammar with a vengeance: *dead-still* in the world and *yet-still* in memory, stasis become temporality. The refrain, *Break, break, break* is also a syntax that continues, *At the foot of thy crags, O sea! / But*, with a chiasmus of *But O*, teetering from the craggy meta-metrics of *at the foot* into the most ironic *grace* that ever was, a death-in-life, not in so many words, let alone a culminating paradox, just a starkly monosyllabic *Will never come back to me*. Less a degraded contrast to *the days that are no more*, this is Tennyson's historical prequel and Brooks's pedagogical sequel. The connective tissue in and between both poems is a repetitive *and* that refuses to be progressive, and performs, instead, a fractured "linkage" of psychological associations.[6]

It's not just that Brooks problematically divorces the poem he hates from the one he loves, but that he feels compelled to bring this warp into his critical dramatic monologue:

> Of course, the poet need not be concerned with... the nature of memory as "Tears, Idle Tears" explores it. At moments, men are unaccountably saddened by scenes which are in themselves placid and even happy. (*Urn* 162)

Men again, here absent of "Motivation": *unaccountably*. Then he returns to the lesson-core of *Scholar*, with this closing statement: the achievement of *Tears* is its "imaginative grasp of diverse materials... so sure that it may show itself to the

---

[5] He also puts a comma after *O* in line 5 of *Break, break, break*.
[6] For a fine reading of the "puzzling obliqueness of logic or argument," strung on the "elusive thread" from injunction to conjunctions, see Christopher Ricks's note, with a generous enlistment of Hutton (*Tennyson*, 133–4).

reader as unstudied and unpredictable without for a moment relaxing its hold on the intricate and complex stuff which it carries" (162). Yet nothing could be more unaccountable than *stuff*. It feels anti-climactic, but Brooks had the word ready from *Understanding Poetry* (1938), explaining how "the special characteristics of formal poetry" are different from the "'stuff of poetry' appearing in ordinary life... rooted very deep in human experience" (9; cf. 27).

Should criticism be made of sterner stuff? The *stuff* that Brooks wants to name but doesn't unpack presses with an affective force that he recognizes enough to leave there for deflection. If the figure of stately ships in *Break, break, break* is "idle and irrelevant," if the language of "thinking" feels "frozen" at the level of "conventional prose," these are arguably dramatically meaningful effects, hung (and sung) on ironic juxtapositions of broken linkages. Brooks (in a parenthesis) entertains this, but only to call it a "forced" interpretation, of small yield (161). Yet when convention is a motivated language, when a dramatic scene is frozen, when the poetics are of fragments and breaks, this too is a structure of poetry. Brooks's partisan comparison remains oversold and underexamined. He surely would know Robert Frost (a poet with presence in *Understanding Poetry*) on this score: "I like to drag and break the intonation across the meter as waves first comb and then break stumbling on the shingle."[7] On the beach with Tennyson.

4. "I know not what they mean"

Brooks's disdain of the images of *Break, break, break* as "idle" and "irrelevant" haunts his chapter as specters of corruption to his investment in *Tears, Idle Tears*. This is the uncanny flux of Brooks's retrojection of a Tennyson who prefigures the critic: "when the poet is able... to analyze his experience, and in the full light of the disparity and even apparent contradiction of the various elements, bring them into a new unity, he secures not only richness and depth but dramatic power as well" (*Urn* 162). The "reader would do well to look deeper into the poem," Brooks coaxes in the fourth (1976) edition of *Understanding Poetry* (243), replicating his "depth" reading of *Tears*. The discursive relay commands a noticeable phalanx of *must* in the final pages of "The Heresy of Paraphrase" (*Urn*, 194–6), summoned sixteen times for the mandate of unity, to "dramatize the oneness of the experience" on the field of "paradox and ambiguity."

It is a dramatic vocabulary for sure, but it is not dramatically structured. It is a critical motive circuited though Brooks's motivated protagonist. Brooks knows that *I know not what they mean* is a patent challenge for pedagogy no less than for understanding drama. If you consult *Understanding Drama* on "Motivation" you

---

[7] To John Cournos, July 8, 1914: *Selected Letters* 128.

will encounter a circular, self-referential semantics. "Motivation" must be "logical" (29) and legible in outward "effects" (80). A substantial Glossary entry (36-9) winds up glossing itself. A "motivated" action must have "an adequate 'motive'"; "successful characterization" will supply "*concrete* evidence (actions, thoughts) that accounts specifically" for a character and "adequate provision for all actions which spring from character...made apparent in concreteness of presentation." Evidence spells a logic for motive; motive spells the logic for action; character is the lodge of action, and action expresses character. The antonym *unmotivated*—when "events and occurrences appear to lack a proper cause, reason, or justification"—is on the same level as *idle and irrelevant*.

No idle word, *idle*. Graham Hough put it succinctly: the "sense of dereliction... formed a tangled and aching knot somewhere deep in Tennyson's being" (35). For the protagonist of *Tears*, "idle" is a self-judgment conscious of self as spectacle. Empson, who liked the "bite" of Brooks's reading, still wanted to tease him about his privileging a metaphysics of depths when "idle" seemed a matter of "good manners more than anything else," as a concession to social self-consciousness ("Thy Darling", 691). You can sense this in the opening lines of Tennyson's *Ulysses* (1833, also in 1842): *It little profits that an idle king*, an existential self-accounting in a social network. Brooks's focus on the drama of finding that "idle" is otherwise elides the idling of Tennyson's repetitions and arrests. Not the least is the after-echo of "I" from *idle*, then its phonic dissipation into the words of tearful passion: *Rise, eyes, dying, dying, wild*, and evacuated *Life. I know not what they mean* is the only instance of the first-person pronoun (twin to *I would that my tongue could utter*), and the only independent sentence in twenty lines. Everything following is a pendant syntax of apposition, repetition, and loops of analogy. The "anamorphic adverb 'as'"—Isobel Armstrong's nicely flexed term for this (117)—is a strain for approximations: *fresh as / Sad as / Ah, sad and strange as / Dear as / deep as / Deep as*. Each flux of syntax is a strain of temper anything but idle.

Brooks's focus is on the temporality of *as* on a "line of development" that joins poet to critic: "as the tears unexpectedly start," the critic doubles the Weeper, "as he searches for an explanation" (*Urn* 154-5). It is peculiar that a formal structure that might have interested Brooks does not come into play. This is a stanza form of finely crafted quintains and refrains, in a score of iambic pentameter, caesura-paused by marked or rhythmic punctuations. "Few know that it is a blank verse lyric," Tennyson remarked, half in marvel and half in congratulation about the effect (*Memoir*, 1:253). Miltonic blank-verse is "sense variously drawn out from one Verse into another: not in the jingling sound of like endings" (said the poet in his headnote to *Paradise Lost*, "The Verse"). *Tears* is not this cadence, nor even, for all its readiness for "dramatic framing," the thinking-out-loud or audience-confiding of Shakespearean soliloquy. The rhyme blanks are overcome by the rhyme-effect of phonic modulations, rhythm, and repetition. One chord is that adverbial/conjunctive *as*. Stronger vibrations draw across the words *Tears, tears,*

Tears, despair, Dear, tears, dear, deep, depth, Death, days, dying, eyes, and the repetitions of *Fresh, sad, sad, fresh, sad, strange, sad, strange, dear, death, sweet, deep, love Deep, love*. There is even a rhyme in *Rise / eyes*. Most conspicuous, formally and phonically, is the refrain: *the days that are no more—are* ever *more* in accumulation, as recognition, inspiration, and poetic formulation. Hough calls it a "formal stress" (330), and Herbert Tucker discerns a "formal stanzaic contract" of increasingly recognized doom (365). To say "no more" is not to confirm an absence, but to make the absence affectively present.

It is as if Tennyson had already feared the loss to come, in eight-line preview, "No More," published in 1831 in the literary annual, *The Gem* (p. 87), and never collected thereafter:

>Oh sad *No more!* Oh sweet *No More!*
>Oh strange *No more!*
>By a mossed brookbank on a stone
>I smelt a wildweed-flower alone;
>There was a ringing in my ears,
>And both my eyes gushed out with tears.
>Surely all pleasant things had gone before,
>Lowburied fathomdeep beneath with thee, NO MORE!

To cry out four times, "No More!"—with a climax in capitals—is to set meaning and expression into contradiction. Tennyson distilled the usually hyphenated compounds into totalized *Lowburied* and *fathomdeep* for this occasion, deepening *deep* with the syllable *beneath... thee*.

The phonic texture is just as critical in the sequel *Tears, idle tears*, because it spills into and spells a psychic arrest that strains the differential of *Break, break, break*. Walt Whitman, who would hold a place for *Break, break, break* in his esteem of Tennyson (403), also confessed to some warning in Tennyson's "finest verbalism... such a latent charm in mere words, cunning collocutions, and the voice ringing them" (1). I love the verbal incarnation, *cunning collocutions*. The refrain is the epitome of this art, a meta-poetic resounding, "rooted in a rhetorical self-consciousness," as John Hollander arrays the double-sensed "burden" of musical form and cognitive pressure (133). His introduction of the term "burden" could have been written for Tennyson: "a returning burden whose name, *refrain*, is etymologically *refractus*, broken back or rebroken" (133). When its word is *break* in psychic synonymy with *never* and *no more*, the poetics of refrain stage a contradiction beyond paradox, an oxymoron of *no more* in duration. On this temporality, the close of *Tears* is a formal stop that affectively is no closure.

The Poet Laureate of Refrain, Poe, spins the genesis of that most manic of refrain-poems, written just ahead of *Tears*, *The Raven* (1845), throbbing the lexeme *more* into a refrain *evermore, nothing more, nevermore*. Refrain is the *black plume* of a demonically penned, unified "poetic principle" (1846: 165). Tennyson's iteration of *no more* is what Hollander calls a "timing device" (130) in two treacherous senses, a formal destination and a temporal vision. The overwhelming of the "I" of *Tears* by these burdened repetitions has drawn two fine readers, Herbert Tucker and J. Hillis Miller (innocent of Tucker's precedence), into stories of disintegrated subjectivity, over and against Brooks's production of "a living man" (157) discovering a "universal cause" (154). Tucker describes a scene of "impersonality," its "persona poetics" dissolving into a "place of extreme and decontextualized lyricism" (363). Miller traces a "figurative strategy" that entails "failed prosopopoeia, the ruin of the trope of personification" into a language that "has nothing to do with persons" but is "merely" a register of "human temporality" (287). While Brooks is no such clinician, he knows the symptoms.

These plague his swerves around two high-stakes theological moments: the colloquially vague *depth of some divine despair* and the grammatically overproduced, depth-driven, despair *O Death in Life*. In the first, quieter formulation, a vague *some* attenuates a potential double scandal to Christian theology: not only a radical cancellation of faith in *despair* but also an ambiguously modifying *divine*. A divine despair is a god with a difference; and if *divine* means only an aesthetic effect, then that's dicey, too. The second crux is the prized paradox, *O Death in Life*, an existential epiphany reversing the Christian metaphysics of *Life* released *in Death*. Coleridge, a literary theorist of multiple appearances in *The Well Wrought Urn*, is strangely absent on this page, where we would most expect to find him. He is the author of the curse of Night-mare *Life-in-Death* on the Ancient Mariner (*Poems*, 2:9), and of the auto-epitaph: he who "Found death in life, may here find life in death!" (2:152). While Brooks despises words "frozen at the conventional prose level," he is ready to issue a pass to the formulaic *Death in Life* as the poetic heroism of a "culminating paradox" (159).

This accolade swerves strangely around the wording of despair in un-Latinate English: *hopeless fancy feign'd* (despair: without hope, hopeless). Tennyson and Brooks know Keats's imagined "all the gardener Fancy e'er could feign," a phrase near the end of *Ode to Psyche*, for a delicately negotiated infinitive of success, "To let the warm Love in!" And all poets know how to ring the cunning collocations of *feign*, from *fain* into fictive and factitious. Tennyson's compressed, alliterated *fancy feign'd* is at once *hopeless* and *wild with all regret*. No less than Empson, Brooks loves this last phrase for the amorphously explosive *wild*, possessing the present speaker in the vivid breaking forth of memories "buried but not dead." Does speaking release *wild* regrets from depths into poetic forming; or, by stanza four, is poetry's formative power the agent of these regrets? Brooks writes out (or himself into) another circuit of motivation and effects:

does the man charge the memories with his own passion, or is it the memories that give the emotion to him?... we come to a point where the distinction lapses. Perhaps I should say, more accurately, adopting the metaphor of the poem itself, we *descend* to a depth where the distinction lapses. (159)[8]

For the critic who argues that form is content, this *or* is a false distinction. Brooks's deep grammar is unembarrassed not only about persona-poetics, but also its reach into the living persons of present critic and present reader, in existential in-the-moment dramatic monology. "Can there be anything more moving than the description of man's unhappy condition performed with all the intellectual craftsmanship of which man is capable, than a thing of beauty made out of human despair, than the mournful triumph of art?" asks Spitzer (75), doubling the question for Tennyson and for Brooks.

5. Brooks's Motivations in the "cultural matrix"

Spitzer means *craftmanship* in general, but a gender-coding is critical for the mid-century professional man struggling with the "cultural matrix" of philology and source-study. This is the quietly feminized regime from which New Critics executed their prison-break—as the Preface to *The Well Wrought Urn* spells it out (x)—into vigorous male aesthetics: "The men whose poems are considered in this book evidently thought that they were able to transcend the limitations of their own generation" and the discipline that would limit literary study to this (xi). Yet men are more than the sum of their craft, and Brooks's attachment to *Tears, idle tears* betrays a devotion in excess of its professional consideration. Reading *The Well Wrought Urn*, a brace of American allies in mid-century criticism, W. K. Wimsatt and M.C. Beardsley, were prompted to call this out in "The Affective Fallacy," an essay in *Sewanee Review* 1949.

> "The last stanza," says Brooks... "evokes an intense emotional response from the reader." But this statement is not really a part of Brooks's criticism of the poem—rather a witness of his fondness for it... the ground of some ultimate emotional state which may be termed the aesthetic... It may well be. The belief is attractive; it may exalt our view of poetry. But it is no concern of criticism, no part of criteria. (47–8)

This critique got installed in *The Verbal Icon*. In their lights, *the reader* is Brooks's affective front for a personal *fondness* at odds with the professional aesthetic

---

[8] Empson proposes that what Brooks describes as a lack of distinction is a "regular function" of "the trope" of "transferred epithet" ("Thy Darling," 691–2).

criteria. The distinction is "theoretically of the greatest import," they insist, because the "polar opposites in criticism" are "classical objectivity" and "romantic reader psychology" (48).

While Brooks's chapter provokes this teasing, he is also admirable for his willingness to entertain what Wimsatt and Beardsley would cordon off to "cognitively untranslatable" psychology (47). Between Brooks's iterations in *The American Scholar* and *Urn*, Leavis cited *Tears* as a "habitual indulgence" for Tennyson, "emotion for its own sake without a justifying situation" (59). Brooks keeps fending this off, seeking justification for his habitual fondness. Leavis's bottom line (literally, his closing one) is that "the critical discipline that is capable of justifying formal literary study is a discipline of intelligence, and one that no one who is committed to using language for disciplined thought can afford to forgo" (71). This is an economy of professional self-preservation, with a sense of *discipline* as both practice and enforcement.

This is Brooks's pedagogical drama in the three post-*Urn* spins of *Understanding Poetry*. In the second edition (1950, three years after *Urn*), he exports *Tears* to *Imagery*, urging students to "be on the alert for the implications that imagery may have... for the full meaning of the poem" (366). The third (1960) is less coy: "imagery affects meaning," he advises; it is "a means to insight" by "implicit rather than explicit" suggestion (269-70, 273). Its "Exercise" is more detailed, more coercive. "Are the tears idle (that is, meaningless) or are they the most meaningful of tears? What occasion prompts them? Does the speaker himself know?" "What do the tears mean? is this a weepy, sentimental poem or is it something quite different?" (318). No questions really, it is the chapter titled "Motivation" in Socratic recast. In the final (fourth) edition (1976) Brooks issues a two-page lecture against the felt pressure of *unmotivated*: "Tennyson's attempt to define what overcame him as a fit of unmotivated melancholy may in fact exhibit a real thinking through images": "he has actually succeeded in telling the reader what the tears *do*, in fact, mean"; *Tears* is not "weepy and sentimental" but "in reality something quite different" (243). The flexing of *has actually/in reality* and the oxymoron *may in fact* are the "stuff" of opaque personal investment straining pedagogical patience, on the rails of a vaguely worded, intensely motivated, *something quite different*—those wayward effects that cling to the overwrought urns of interpretation.

It is characteristic of Brooks that his assertion of *something quite different* betrays something not so quite. Two chapters before "Motivation" in *The Well Wrought Urn*, Brooks is contending with the "Paradox of Imagination" in Wordsworth's "Immortality" Ode, as he makes poetic capital out of sensations of loss in "Thoughts that do often lie too deep for tears." In this Critical Dramatic Monologue, Brooks admits, "I must confess that I feel the solution is asserted rather than dramatized"; it is caught up in "distracting confusions" that should have been "enriching ambiguities." Brooks admits his "desperate effort" to construct a paradox, implicitly mindful of being "overingenious" (137). A "vagueness" in Wordsworth's argument sends its "rich multiplicity" splaying out into "some loose ends." Critic Brooks feels mirrored in this splay, with "suspicion" about "this kind of poetic strategy" (138). I find this thinking-out-loud quite moving. It's not pedagogy disingenuously packaged, but a sensation of the shadow that uncertain Wordsworth may cast forward to *Tears, idle tears*.

One loose end in Tennyson's paradox—*the* loose end—is the *no more* of Hallam, borne back dead to England on a ship from below the verge of the horizon, up from the underworld to no Orphean Tennyson. It is threaded with Wordsworth. Hallam was buried near Tintern Abbey, a charged Wordsworthian site for a calculus of loss and poetic gains. Tennyson said he was "moved" to write *Tears, idle tears* there (*Memoir*, 2:73).[9] "The passion of the past, the abiding in the transient," he said, "was expressed in 'Tears, Idle Tears,' which was written in yellowing autumn-tide at Tintern Abbey, full for me of its bygone memories" (1:253). This sentence is a prose-poetry in the prepositional mode: three iterations of *in* align the existential sensation, the expressive song, and the impressive scene, and the quiet contradiction of *bygone* and *full for me*, an intuitive repetition of Wordsworth's ache of memory, "Felt in the blood, and felt along the heart" in remembering the environs of Tintern Abbey. Tennyson insists on aesthetic woe, in distinction from "real woe," and on a generic "passion" that all "young people," including himself "when he was a youth," may experience "for that which seems to have passed away from them for ever" (*Memoir*, 2:73). This sounds like a special pleading that anticipates Brooks, performing disinterested analysis but exposing an overdetermined motivation.

> That time is past,
> And all its aching joys are now no more,
> And all its dizzy raptures...

So Wordsworth sighs, feeling the totality of *aching joys* and *dizzy raptures* in alternation with the flat assignments *is past* and *now no more*. The ache of poetry contests the "Abundant recompense" from "a sense sublime / Of something far more deeply interfused" (*Poems* 2:77).

What abides for Tennyson is not the sense sublime, however, but a sublimation of memory into lyric arrest, not expelled by Wordsworth's account-book, nor by Tennyson's generalizing *we* and *our*, nor by the categorical *the* for the registrations of *Tears*. It's not that Brooks, writing up "The Motivation of Tennyson's Weeper,"

---

[9] Miller, in passing, dubs *Tears* "Tennyson's 'Tintern Abbey'" (280). Armstrong revives this wording to title an argument that, in a Brooksian practice, sets Wordsworth's security in "purer thought" as a foil to Tennyson's existential collapse (116–17). This is a familiar "Victorianist's 'Wordsworth'"; but *Tintern Abbey*, I have argued elsewhere (2014), bears a collapsing pressure in just about every subordinate clause that brings it quite intimately into Tennyson's ache of *no more*.

is "unaware of this discrepancy" (Paul de Man's charge of the critical blindness in the practical insights of American New Criticism, ix), but that he is too aware. The honesty of Brooks's chapter is the way its argument negotiates a force field of recognitions in quarrel with it.

Of the most famous of motive-hunters, Iago, Empson remarks: "he is quite open to his own motives or preferences and interested to find out what they are" (*Structure* 223). If Brooks is not "open" to this degree, he is never closed. Empson's tacit interlocutor is Coleridge, describing the paradox of "motive-hunting of motiveless Malignity":

> It is a matter of infinite difficulty, but fortunately of comparative indifference, to determine what a man's motive may have been for this or that particular action. Rather seek to learn what his objects in general are!—What does he habitually wish? Habitually pursue?—and thence deduce his impulses, which are commonly the true efficient causes of men's conduct; and without which the motive itself would not have become a motive.... Iago ... is represented as now assigning one, and then another, and again a third, motive for his conduct, all alike the mere fictions of his own restless nature. (*Shorter Works*, 1:310)

Eliot's famous term for this determination is "objective correlative": a "set of objects, a situation, a chain of events which shall be the formula of [a] *particular emotion*" (his italics), as if this were a clinical procedure (92). While Eliot arraigns its absence—"unexplained" (89); "inexpressible" (92)—as a problem for drama, this is as debatable as Brooks's contempt of *Break, break, break*. Character as action; plot-logic over psychology: Eliot's criterion is legibly motivated action. Substitute Brooks for Eliot's Hamlet or Coleridge's Iago; substitute critical fixation for the fictions of a *restless nature*; write "pedagogically pursue" in place of *habitually pursue*, and you are pretty close to "The Motivation of Tennyson's Weeper."

In *American Scholar*, Brooks concludes his essay by insisting that his critical analysis "does not pretend to constitute an expression of the critic's own emotional response of the poem," then adds, "I have deeply enjoyed the poem," then clarifies that this is irrelevant to professional analysis, though not distinct from the pleasures of "intellectual criticism" (293–5). While these human oscillations are ethically different from bloodless Iago's, they share the grammar of restless motive-hunting that fissures the essay framed for *The Well Wrought Urn*. The "unity...achieved by a dramatic process" does not fully contain the psychic energies that made this poem interesting to Brooks in the first place, or Brooks interesting to us.

6. "So sweet a voice and vague, fatal to men"

In *The Well Wrought Urn*, Brooks emphasizes "dramatic context" (154). So what of the original dramatic context, Tennyson's *The Princess: A Medley*? Here, it is sung by a nameless maiden to an audience in a female academy, including that cross-dressed trio, at once legally evading and socially materializing the mandate on the gate: LET NO MAN ENTER IN ON PAIN OF DEATH (33).[10] Brooks's restructuring of this school into a school of male-coded criticism is imprinted by the re-gendering, not least, of *Tears*-disdaining Princess Ida into Alpha Professor of the master-class on *Tears*.[11] The pedagogical imaginary of *The Well Wrought Urn* (and its genesis from the "he" student-demographic of *Understanding Poetry*) yields chapters on men's poetry that, Brooks contends, "touch on the heart" of "the Humanities" in "normative" and "universal" ways (xi). Tennyson's Princess Ida has founded a "University for maidens" devoted to another, gender-specific, urgent task in the humanities, the struggle for the rights of women.

Among those in drag is a nameless Prince betrothed (by paternal arrangements) to Ida in their infancy. Already sporting his hair "like a girl" (I.2), he provokes the question of disclosure in disguise. It feels like sheer redundancy to say that Tennyson is distributed all over the scene of the song: he is the author; his avatar is the she-singer; he is relay-figured by the she-men; and he is the scripter of Ida's reproof of the song in a twenty-two-line counter-lyric (44–65). Such mournful songs, she scolds in this sequel, "haunt / About the mouldered lodges of the Past" with "So sweet a voice and vague, fatal to men." Were songs of "moans about the retrospect" merely "fancies hatched / In silken-folded idleness," she would insist that they follow Ulysses' command to his crew as the sirens sing: "cram our ears with wool / And so pace by... trim our sails, and let old bygones be" (44–51). But no ears are closed to *Tears*. If *idle* (summoned only three times in *The Princess*) sounds in implied antithesis to *Ida*, Tennyson plays it loud in the first three letters of self-declaring Ida's cry, "*I* dare / All these male thunderbolts" (478–9).

The reviewer for *Athaeæum* certainly saw the gender trouble. The Princess is "a modern blue, to be quizzed and bantered," at best "a stately Amazon." And "Tears, idle tears"—"full of plaintive beauty"—is a gender-lesson: it "delicately indicates that bias of Woman's heart toward the affections which neither the example nor the discipline of the Princess had been effectively to counteract" as a "biting satirist and subtle metaphysician" (7). Yet if "Amazon" is the *Athaeæum*'s name for

---

[10] Tennyson kept the song in context in all his collected works, though (according to Christopher Ricks, in a personal correspondence, April 8, 2021) he countenanced its excerpt, along with several other songs, out of context for the volume in Moxon's Miniature Poets, *A Selection from the Works of Alfred Tennyson, D. C. L, Poet Laureate* (London: Edward Moxon, 1865), 203–4.

[11] Edward Vandiver lodged one of the first responses to Brooks's chapter on this score, proposing a maiden weeping in song about what she's lost from enlisting in this all-female academy.

unnatural woman, Tennyson's *medley*, for all its plotting of this course correction, does not dispel the sensation of Ida's conversion to love and marriage as a deformation, against an admirable motivation. So concluded one review of Gilbert and Sullivan's Tennyson-based operetta, *Princes Ida, or Castle Adamant* (1884), no doubt catching the tuning of *Adamant* to satirize her very name.

> The Laureate's heroine is essentially a tragic character. She is possessed by an *idée fixe*, perhaps we should say an ideal—the liberation of her sex from the thraldom of man... One may hold all idea of "woman's rights" in condign detestation, and yet see that such a heroine, when at last she yields to the common sway of love, surrenders her ideal significance and *raison d'être*, and that therefore Tennyson's poem is... a tragedy in spite of its "happy ending."

It is Princess Ida who might well sing "Tears, idle tears" about what is no more.

Brooks's chapter is a peculiar escape from this source, at once suppressing it and provoking knowledgeable readers with this suppression—provoke, too, the reception history of *Break, break, break* which ably assigned a female lodge of anguish, as a somber plate in *The Illustrated London News* (1897) shows (fig. 12.1). It is a mournful woman in black on a stormy shore. The professor who in 1944 lectured readers of *American Scholar* (channeling A.E. Housman) that "the skin may bristle so as to defeat the razor when a man is confronted with true poetry... but skin-bristling is not criticism" (294) calls up a metaphor exclusively for a man speaking to men. If we take Brooks at his word, "that the *way* a thing is said determined *what* is said," then what is said by critic Brooks is that men can understand the poetry of manly tears, in the domain of "'intellectual' criticism after all" (295). But when tears are unaccountable and intention ungovernable, "studies in the structures of poetry" are provoked. Brooks's relay of analytical "rigor" (286) and visceral affect is also the dynamic of the song that compels his enduring critical discipline.

Yet men will weep and know why, in the affective currents of aesthetic experience, in private, in a communal imagination, or in social collocution. "The usefulness of the aesthetic" is not "directly 'practical,'" argues our humane convener, George Levine; "its value lies in its peculiarly humanizing force, in its capacity to expand boundaries of thought and feeling beyond the practical norms of every day and the linear thinking of non-fiction." Brooks's "test case" is at once humanly motivated and theory-tagged for the wartime young men in his pedagogical imaginary. When he paraphrases the motivation of Tennyson's weeper as this crisis, "The past *should* be tamed, fettered, brought to heel; it is not. It is capable of breaking forth and coming to the surface" (159), the imperatively italicized *should* is contested by dramatic sympathy—and not just for Tennyson. *Breaking forth*—or put it another way for Tennyson, *Break, break, break*—is poetry's verbalist aesthetics, suspended between sound and sense, between

Figure 12.1 Engraving first published in The Illustrated London News, 28 August 1897

description and exhortation, between similitude for wordless heartbreak, and the indifference of material nature. I endorse Levine's view of aesthetic experience as "one medium through which all of us experience emotion, uncover emotion, share emotion." "I have found it humbling and enlightening to work with people who have fought in Iraq and Afghanistan, and witnessed war at its most devastating," reports Duncan Wu of his evening class for veterans just returning to the workforce. He was deeply moved to hear from them that this is "the sole forum in which they are able to share their experiences." It made this "one of the most fulfilling experiences of my teaching career" (11). Sometimes aesthetic mediation provides an enabling "cover." Sometimes it uncovers what oft was felt and suddenly arrested in being so well expressed.

PART 5
OVERVIEW

13
Do Birds Disagree?
The Place of Aesthetic Value in Advocacy for the Humanities

Helen Small

Late in the narrative of Kazuo Ishiguro's most recent novel, *Klara and the Sun* (2021), his android narrator takes a walk into the countryside and describes for us a scene replete with significance for her:

> The Sun's rays coming from the back of the barn were too intense to face directly, so though it might seem rude, I turned my gaze once more to the drifting shapes to my right, perhaps hoping to glimpse Rosa... But now the Sun's pattern had fallen across the front alcove, momentarily illuminating it, and I saw there not an AF, but a large oval-shaped photograph fixed to the wall. It showed a green field on a sunny day, dotted with sheep, and in the foreground, I recognized the four special sheep I'd glimpsed from the Mother's car returning from Morgan's Falls. They seemed even more gentle than I'd remembered, lined up as they were in a neat row, their heads lowered to partake of the grass. These creatures had filled me with happiness that day,... and I was pleased to see them again, if only in this oval photograph. But something was wrong: although the four sheep were positioned in a line in just the same formation I'd seen from the car, here they'd become oddly suspended, so they no longer appeared to stand on the surface of the ground. As a result, when they stretched down to eat, their mouths couldn't reach the grass, giving these creatures, so happy on the day, a mood of sadness.[1]

Klara has been designed for two key competencies: accurate analysis of her physical environment, so that she can navigate it and manipulate objects successfully; and correct assessment of human emotions, enabling her to perform optimally as an Artificial Friend or "AF." An advanced product of robotic engineering, Klara conducts her ordinary tasks efficiently and labors at her higher purpose, alleviating the loneliness of the teenager she is purchased to serve. "Robot," as

---

[1] London: Faber and Faber Ltd, p. 274.

cultural critics like to remind us, derives from the Czech *robota: serf* or *enforced laborer* designating "high-powered laborers" (as the first English translators of Karel Čapek's *R.U.R. expressed* it): "automats...good for nothing but work."[2] Klara, on the contrary, is good for a great deal. In the dystopian near-future America Ishiguro asks us to imagine, the human need of friendship has generated a specialist market in artificial intelligence (AI) for privileged families raising their children in isolation, maximizing their competitive advantages through biogenetic modification that puts their lives at risk and all but erases the conditions for normal social development. Solar-powered, Klara devises a form of magical thinking, as it seems to others, based on the animating power of the sun, offering a rationale for hope in a world that has moved beyond religion. To the extent that she wins over the AI skeptics in her vicinity, she does so by the emotional intelligence with which she works to normalize teenage life and prevent death. A remarkable achievement of Affective Computing, she can interpret the physiological signs of loneliness (complex eye movements, unstable tonalities of voice...), detecting sadness even in sheep.

Like many other science fiction writers before him, Ishiguro has largely forfeited a once prized idea that what distinguishes human life from its robotic simulacra is the capacity for emotion. When Klara tells us that she is "filled... with happiness," we have no grounds for challenging her semantics though we may want to dispute the quality of experience she lays claim to. If her "happiness" remains under suspicion—just the word generated when a situation meets formal criteria (close, in this case, to those a literary critic would associate with pastoral)—the next thought must be: on what grounds does her linguistic performance disqualify her from authentic experience? Would "genuine" happiness sound qualitatively different? "Filled with happiness" has the thin timbre of automatic diction, but if we are going to require originality of expression as evidence of humanity we are on bad terrain. (What sort of person judges the authenticity of a person's testimony by their capacity to give it eloquent expression?) Besides, Klara is far from bland. Her speech patterns, verbalizing alternative pathways of reasoning, are quaintly askew from ordinary language, generating odd animisms (to turn one's back on daylight "might seem rude," from the Sun's point of view) and retrospectively supplied motives for actions (not least her own: "perhaps" she was "hoping to see Rosa"—an AF in the store where she was purchased, unlikely to be in this remote barn). By affording his narrator a persistently defamiliarizing and to that extent "literary" voice, Ishiguro protects the novel from lapsing into speech the reader would find "robotic," below the aesthetic standard for a work of literature. Klara, on the other hand, has no appreciation of why her patterns of

---

[2] *R.U.R.: (Rossumovi Univerzální Roboti)* (1921); *R.U.R.: (Rossum's Universal Robots): A Fantastic Melodrama in Three Acts and an Epilogue*, trans. Paul Selver (Garden City, NY: Doubleday, Page & Co., 1923), p. 3.

speech might interest others. Even so sophisticated an artificial intelligence has, to borrow terms from Isobel Armstrong (this volume, Chapter 5, p. 125), no way of apprehending the "excitement of words" as it can arise from "the interaction of cognitive and aesthetic experience."

Having a functional vocabulary for pleasure and displeasure but none for beauty makes Klara an appropriate avatar, as much as technological fix, for a society well on the way to forgetting why a qualitatively rich idiom ever mattered. The word *beauty* is used in her presence, and she can process the grammar of its articulation, but she experiences neither aesthetic pleasure nor disgust, and makes no aesthetic judgments beyond observing degrees of mimetic accuracy in art. She decodes visual scenes much as a digital lens arranges what comes within its frame, adjusting the resolution in ways that generate brief fantastic interludes for the reader, but not for her. A delay in focus-stacking, for example, causes a momentary image-processing error: a "large creature with numerous limbs and eyes" develops "a crack...down its centre" then settles into "two separate people—a runner and a dog walk woman...who for an instant happened to be passing one another" (217). The visual processing challenges of the barn interior are less cleanly resolved. We can't be sure whether Klara is correct in identifying "a large oval-shaped photograph fixed to the wall." Possibly this is a window; more likely (given the location) a cheap poster, picture, advertisement, or calendar, and a drawing not a photograph (which would explain the free-floating appearance of the sheep). For attuned readers, the reference to Philip K. Dick's *Do Androids Dream of Electric Sheep?* (1968) will carry more significance. Worrying over the appropriate registration of mood if sheep may no longer safely graze—an updated Rick Dekkard no longer demoralized by electronic sheep—Klara is the object, not the author, of an intertextual joke. She falls short of presumptive criteria for being human not because she is cognitively imperfect but because she has been designed (by Ishiguro, and within a long literary tradition) as the vehicle for a cultural conversation, ongoing, about what it means to be human.[3]

In offering a feeling and language for the aesthetic, rather than a capacity for empathy, as the final ground of our human difference from machines, *Klara and the Sun* offers an apt provocation from which to begin responding to these essays on *The Question of the Aesthetic*. In his introduction, George Levine identifies two larger ends for this volume beyond the opportunity to grapple, again, with the appeal and the limitations of Kant's "purposeless purpose." Those ends are:

---

[3] Klara has been programmed to detect jokes—for example, suspecting humorous intent when a higher-grade robot initiates an aggressive line of conversation—but she is signally without the capacity for humor. It is of course the case that Ishiguro might have made Klara more "human" still, but the distinction between her position within the artwork of fiction and ours as its aesthetic interpreters would remain. I discuss below the potential role of comedy in adjudicating claims to human-like agency.

- "resistance" to the idea that "concern for the aesthetic" in literary criticism is somehow in contention with the purpose of serious moral, political and social engagement;
- insistence on the importance of "attention to the aesthetic" in our efforts to explain why critical study of the arts and humanities deserves economic and political support.

A third claim, important to the volume's framing but (tellingly and, as I see it, quite properly) attracting different levels of agreement and engagement from the contributors, is that

- we have much to learn from "Darwin's 'aesthetic' view of life, the view that across the animal kingdom the work of the aesthetic is fundamental and consequential."

In adopting the first two purposes, and contemplating, locally, the purchase of the third, Levine and his fellow contributors offer to refine our terms of critical debate for something we are not, it seems, as adept at doing as we might be. With the practically and emotionally hyper-competent and yet aesthetically incompetent Klara in view, it is worth asking "why not?": why, with at least three centuries of argument over the importance of aesthetic judgments behind us, are we not better—or more confident—at incorporating into the work of the Humanities the feeling for beauty and, to borrow a term from the philosopher Mary Mothersill, the work of "commending" it? ("Commending" in its widest sense: not only promoting beauty, "present[ing it] as worthy of favourable acceptance," but "direct[ing] attention" to it, showing it to be "worthy of notice or regard."[4]) Specifically, why in a professional context where most Humanities scholars are unembarrassed about expressing "serious moral, political and social engagement[s]," should the claims of Beauty—and the basis of those claims—seem so difficult to commend?

In sponsoring to the degree that it does a claim for the natural basis of our concern with beauty, *The Question of the Aesthetic* is pushing against a direction of travel that has, with some prominent exceptions,[5] come to seem very hard to reverse (better pursued as a specialist form of criticism within our disciplines than

---

[4] Mary Mothersill, *Beauty Restored* (Oxford: Clarendon Press, 1984), p. 217. *OED online*, v. 2.
[5] Among them, see esp. Elaine Scarry, *On Beauty and Being Just* (Princeton, NJ: Princeton University Press, 1999); Susan Stewart, *Poetry and the Fate of the Senses* (Chicago, IL: University of Chicago Press, 2002); Michael Wood, *Literature and the Taste of Knowledge* (Cambridge: Cambridge University Press, 2005); and Angela Leighton, *On Form: Poetry, Aestheticism, and the Legacy of a Word* (Oxford: Oxford University Press, 2007). For a more extended critical reflection of the return to aesthetic value in the early 2000s, see Helen Small, "Caprice: Individual Subjectivity in Literary Criticism," in Rónán McDonald, ed., *The Values of Literary Studies: Critical Institutions, Scholarly Agendas* (Cambridge: Cambridge University Press, 2015), pp. 27–43.

as a public rationale for their support). In under two hundred years, Jonah Siegel argues trenchantly in this volume, we have gone "from a situation in which Tennyson might fear our humanity is at risk if we allow ourselves to be dominated by a love of beauty" over goodness and knowledge, "to one in which it is *only* a claim of either knowledge or goodness that justifies the presence of beauty at all" (this volume, Chapter 3, p. 73). It is an analysis confirmed and extended into very recent criticism—and reaccented—by Isobel Armstrong's critical account of surface reading and other forms of "depthless immersion" now often recommended in place of critique.

As Siegel and the other contributors to this volume present the problem, the relegation of Beauty from the front line (as it were) of literary and cultural criticism has multiple sources, chief among them modernity's loss of confidence in the aesthetic as a mode of critique. An earlier, in its time widely influential, edited collection of essays, Hal Foster's *The Anti-Aesthetic* (1983)[6] serves as a key text in Siegel's explanation of how, allegorically speaking, we got from a time and place when Beauty seemed powerfully autonomous, sufficient unto herself and intensely desirable, to casting Beauty as the driving force of oppositional critique (Adorno her last-ditch defender in that role), to permitting her to be so thoroughly eclipsed that critics, publicly committed to her sisters, Knowledge and Goodness, have struggled to give a public account of their ongoing relationship to "the most attractive sister, the one who puts the other affections at risk" (p. 72). Pivoting the occasion of this volume against the "anti-aesthetic" moment of Foster's collection, Siegel asks pointedly "How is that working out for us? Has the anti-aesthetic in fact fostered a practice of resistance" that is having any good political effect on the culture around us? The implied answer is, plainly, no: rejecting the power of the aesthetic (both its attractive power and its potential role in critique) has left us politically enfeebled. When power is seen to be at home in Mar-a-Lago or Gelendzhik, a *political* anti-aestheticism, in Siegel's view, no longer looks coherent. Once Beauty no longer associates with Power, what sense is left for a politically motivated critique of Beauty?

Accounting historically for Beauty's reduced presence in the arena of critical debate provides some of the answers for why aesthetic value finds an uncertain reception within advocacy for the Humanities. There are also, no doubt, valid and interesting things a psychologist might have to say on the subject—particularly around the difficulties of critically adjudicating what may or may not be beautiful to any one individual or group. (It is not easy to forget, once read, Bruce Robbins's response to Elaine Scarry's *On Beauty and Being Just*: "Kant's Third Critique defines beauty as a perception that demands to be universalized. Yet when Scarry assumed the universality of her perception of the beauty of a palm tree, I wanted to

---

[6] *Essays on Postmodern Culture* (Port Townsend, WA: Bay Press).

scream. 'It is everything I have always loved...lustrously in love with air and light.' I have nothing against palm trees, but I found myself viscerally opposed to being told that Scarry's loves would henceforth be mine."[7]) The felt coercion of other people's strongly-affirmed tastes (and aversions) and the potential *exclusivity* of aesthetic experience that this felt coercion alerts us to is a topic to come back to. Before getting to that point, there seem to me some objective difficulties, necessary to consider, in the way of pressing aesthetic value in public debate given the kinds of evaluative claim that find argumentative traction today.

The boldest challenge this volume poses to business-as-usual in advocacy for the Arts and Humanities is George Levine and Richard O. Prum's third claim and what it implies: that aesthetic activity is of value to society because the making of artful things, the experience of desiring them, of being in the aesthetic "event" (as Derek Attridge encourages us to frame our thinking here), and laboring to apprehend, appreciate, and assay the relation of aesthetic experience to other things we value—*all these are activities in our nature and may viably be defended on that ground*. It is bold, because "naturalistic arguments" for the value of the Humanities have not fared well of late. The word does not make discussion easier, given that the adjective "naturalistic" may be used both loosely to dismiss arguments for public goods that appeal to "the natural order of things"[8] (also those that are naturalized, i.e., habituated) and in the more technical sense whereby economists reject would-be normative, empirical claims of the kind usually deemed inadmissible in arguments over rivalrous public goods. When the former UK Minister for Universities and Science David Willetts observes that universities are now "big businesses" set within modern economic and governance cultures where they can "no longer rely upon naturalistic arguments" but must be able to evidence the benefits they return for public investment,[9] he is, I take it, employing the word with a technical leaning.[10] The prohibition almost certainly resonates more loudly in the ears of Humanities advocates than in the ears of scientists or social scientists—though there will be variation by discipline.

---

[7] "Is Literature a Secular Concept? Three Earthquakes," *Modern Language Quarterly* 72.3 (2011), 293–317 (299).

[8] *OED online*, adj. 4.

[9] Lecture given to the *State of the Arts* debate series hosted by the Ax:son Johnson Foundation at the British Academy, London, March 19, 2014.

[10] For a helpfully succinct economist's account of where art and culture sit in the range of public goods between those few that count as "pure," "non-rivalrous...non-excludable" (such as public defense) and the great majority that are at least partly rivalrous and excludable, see Jason Potts, "The Price of Everything," *The Conversation*, August 6, 2014, https://theconversation.com/are-the-arts-and-culture-a-public-good-29939 [last accessed April 29, 2021]. And for a critically pointed assessment of how economic and literary-philosophical conceptions of public goods became gradually "eviscerated" of normative thinking over the course of the late nineteenth and twentieth centuries—moving (in "close parallel[l]) toward formalist criteria of operation"—see Regenia Gagnier, "On the Insatiability of Human Wants: Economic and Aesthetic Man," *Victorian Studies* 36.2 (1993), 125–53, and the subsequent book-length articulation of the argument, *The Insatiability of Human Wants: Economics and Aesthetics in Market Society* (Chicago, IL: University of Chicago Press, 2000), esp. ch. 4.

In this political context it is not hard to see why a naturalistic claim for aesthetic value meets with different levels of enthusiasm (which it is not to say that it may not be right). Banning normative assumptions about the importance of our human investment in the arts, and thus the value of studying, curating, criticizing them, the economistic language of public debates over funding reminds us of a lesson Humanities scholars have already conned well: *Be wary of appeals to nature*. The readiness of many, but by no means all, advocates for the Humanities to accept such a constraint on how we justify the value of our work to public life is not just a sign of hard-acquired economic realism; it owes much to discipline-specific forms of training in distinguishing between culture and nature, and understanding how profoundly our access to the latter goes by way of the former.[11] Nietzsche, an attentive reader of Darwin, remains a figure to be reckoned with, scorning appeals to nature wherever they take on an ethical dimension: "'according to Nature'?... what a fraud is this phrase!... boundlessly extravagant, boundlessly indifferent, without purpose or consideration, without pity or justice, at once fruitful and barren and uncertain: imagine to yourselves INDIFFERENCE as a power."[12]

Such widespread inhibitions notwithstanding (not least on the part of those unpersuaded by recent work in the field of "literary Darwinism"[13]), if Prum and Levine are right the biological sciences have something important to offer Humanities scholars at this juncture by way of sharpening our understanding of what a naturalistic claim for the value of the aesthetic correctly entails in the early twenty-first century. A *coevolutionary* account of beauty, in the detail and depth with which Prum elaborates it here, asks us to understand our aesthetic cultures within a comprehensive picture of life on earth where we differ from other animals in our formal, technological, and reflective sophistication but not in our fundamental drive to create and curate art objects, and (though there is more dispute here) to evaluate them. The view of the aesthetic that results is lateral, comparative, and very wide indeed. It is set out by Prum in terms of a detailed vocabulary for taking account of the variety of co-existent "artworlds" or "aesthetic communities"—

---

[11] See especially the clarificatory debate that arose, on the limits of arguments for culture over nature, in response to "the Sokal Affair": John Guillory, "The Sokal Affair and the History of Criticism," *Critical Inquiry* 28.2 (2002), 470–508. Also his subsequent exchange of views with Christopher Newfield: "Critical Response I: The Value of Nonscience," *Critical Inquiry* 29.3 (2003), 508–25; Guillory, "Critical Response II: The Name of Science, the Name of Politics," *Critical Inquiry* 29.3 (2003), 526–41. For discussion of how those arguments impact upon advocacy for the Humanities, see Helen Small, *The Value of the Humanities* (Oxford: Oxford University Press, 2013), ch. 1.

[12] *Beyond Good and Evil: Prelude to a Philosophy of the Future*, ed. Rolf-Peter Horstmann and Judith Norman, trans. Judith Norman (Cambridge: Cambridge University Press, 2002), ch. 1, §9, p. 10.

[13] Armstrong's essay touches on some of the marked lines of dissent and disagreement around the work of E.O. Wilson (esp. *On Human Nature*, 1979) and, especially, Joseph Carroll (see this volume, Chapter 5, pp. 121–2 Prum takes an emphatic distance on this line of thinking ("faux profundities" that attempt to "explain away human agency scientifically as the product of a natural process"; "an intellectual dead end" (p. 42)).

sometimes entirely independent, sometimes overlapping, and, when overlapping, sometimes co-operative, sometimes conflicting.

Deeply indebted to Darwin but more keenly alert even than he was to how ubiquitously variation puts pressure on normative descriptions of any species' behavior,[14] this is a perspective that sets human aesthetic impulses and capacities in the richest of comparative contexts. To adopt it is to recognize the profusion of artistic activities and tastes generated from "a currently incalculable number of independent origins in the history of life" and "continu[ing] to diversify into aesthetic radiations among species." Darwinian in its delightful contemplation of variety, it is equally Darwinian in the rebuke it tenders to "the universal narcissism of men" (we are asked to look "*horizontally* at, not down upon, the [...] aesthetic agencies [and achievements] of other species" (p. 61)).

There are innumerable cultural contexts today in which the critical challenge of a Darwinian perspective remains potent. Humanity is not free (probably never can be entirely free) of social factors that made evolutionary theory so confronting to nineteenth-century world views: widespread religious faith; desires to ground morality—and life itself—in "precedent Idea," as Gillian Beer puts it[15] (theological or otherwise); the sheer force of conventionality (moral, social, also aesthetic); and (even in the midst of ecological crisis and pandemic) a common *operative* presumption that nature is ours to shape, or break, or mend. On the other hand (such is the variety of human culture and society), Darwinian lessons have been keenly absorbed in many quarters: the calibration of human agency against other agencies, and the predication of all life on principles of variation, transformation, supplementation, amid (ineluctably) loss, (ultimately) extinction, are well understood. Confronting that knowledge, and incorporating it into our philosophy has been part of the business of much art and literature, as well as ethics, for over a century and a half.

Cultural non-alignment of ideas over the ultimate source of the great plurality in aesthetic tastes is, probably, here to stay, and will matter to some, though (in the context of public advocacy) it seems to me among our lesser concerns. What *has* changed is the environmental context and thus the political point of engagement with Darwin in the philosophical framing of what Humanities scholars do— change helpfully highlighted by Myra Jehlen's brief critical meditation on the close of the 1859 *Origin* (this volume, Chapter 9). By broad if not complete agreement, we are heading not, as the penultimate paragraph of the first edition

---

[14] Not that Darwin wasn't keenly alert, but it is easier for us now to see the blind-spots and inhibitions of a mid-Victorian, privileged Englishman. For, by way of example, a concise summary and response to feminist readings of Darwin, see Elizabeth Grosz, "Darwin and Feminism: Preliminary Investigations for a Possible Alliance," *Australian Feminist Studies* 14.29 (1999), 31–45. Penelope Deutscher gives a fascinating account of Victorian feminist appropriations of Darwinism, in "The Descent of Man and the Evolution of Woman," *Hypatia* 19.2 (2004), 35–55.

[15] Gillian Beer, *Darwin's Plots: Evolutionary Narrative in Darwin, George Eliot and Nineteenth-Century Fiction* (London: Routledge & Kegan Paul, 1983), pp. 12, 79.

has it, "toward perfection," as Darwin (moving up a rhetorical gear) was prepared to venture, but toward a world which confirms and deepens Victorian reasons for skepticism[16]—a world in which reparative action is urgently required if we are not to face global environmental disaster; also (keeping Ishiguro in sight) one in which artificial intelligences will increasingly co-operate with our human intelligence, for better and/or worse. The professional habitus of Prum's writing makes a difference: in asking us to preserve our "humanistic focus on human agency" amid a richer set of agencies, he is providing a "post-humanist" perspective, emanating from a Department of Ecology and Environmental Biology, that is quite unlike the dominant theoretical conceptualization of post-humanism in the Humanities in that it explicitly excludes futuristic visions of overcoming our nature. (Post-humanism is, from this perspective, the last redoubt of Humanism: an "overcoming" rather than a "relinquishment" of priority [Prum, this volume, Chapter 2, p. 43]). Not that Prum cannot credit the possibility of radically altered forms of existence, but utopian and dystopian scenarios alike—projected futures in which Human minds and bodies are for better or worse free of "natural" constraints on our capacities (even our basic life expectancy)—"leave [him] cold" (p. 43).

This is (confessedly) a personal political and aesthetic preference on Prum's part. Drawing attention to it nevertheless helps to flush out some key differences between his position and those of other contributors to a volume in which political terms of agreement are easily stated, philosophical terms less easily so. As I see it, the crucial question is what we critics can agree to mean by "agency."

Consider the bowerbird—as Prum, like Darwin before him, asks us to do (p. 64).[17] And then consider why we are considering him. An "aesthetically extreme" case, the males of the species construct and painstakingly curate their bowers of seduction over several years. Darwin devoted several paragraphs of *The Descent of Man and Selection in Relation to Sex* (1871) to them as evidence of a highly evolved avian sense of taste, with marked differences in aesthetic preference between genera. The Satin bowerbirds observed in John Gould's *Handbook to the Birds of Australia*, 1865 (a key source for Darwin) relished "gaily-coloured articles such as the blue tail-feathers of parrakeets"; the Spotted bowerbirds preferred "very profuse" arrangements of tall grasses; the Regent bowerbird "described by Mr. Ramsay, ornament[ed] its short bower with bleached land-shells... [and]

---

[16] See esp. Andrew H. Miller, *The Burdens of Perfection: On Ethics and Reading in Nineteenth-Century British Literature* (Ithaca, NY: Cornell University Press, 2008).

[17] With birds so much to the fore in this volume, it seems important to note that we could vary our examples: octopuses, whales, chimpanzees have all attracted the attention of aestheticians. Equally, it seems important to note how contested these claims are within contemporary evolutionary biology. See esp. Stephen Davies, *The Artful Species: Aesthetics, Art, and Evolution* (Oxford: Oxford University Press, 2012), chs. 1 and 2. Davies takes a strong line against considering bowerbird performances as "art." He also considers, critically, the aesthetic or quasi-aesthetic activities of chimpanzees, elephants, bees, nightingales, whales.

'berries of various colours, blue, red, and black, which give it when fresh a very pretty appearance.'"[18] A quick internet search of nature documentary footage shows that while some bowerbird tastes have remained the same, there has also been change. The New Guinea Vogelkop Bowerbird community has incorporated plastic bottle tops, straws, and the clear nozzles of squeezable bottles into its repertoires, for example. Nature documentaries strengthen the picture of individual differences in taste within genera: one Vogelkop male has "a very appreciative eye for colour...favour[ing] red and orange flowers" and pale orange fungus; another prefers a more minimalist palate—"darker colours...deer dung and charcoal."[19] The appearance of white sprouting fungus on his dung arrangement is a source of agitation and additional labor for him. He pecks as much as he can away, with evident annoyance. Unsurprisingly, the female bowerbird opts for the more relaxed mate with brighter decor.

Both Darwin and Prum want us to recognize human-like aesthetic agency here (the Satin Bowerbird puts Prum in mind of "a human using an egret plume to decorate a hat," just as the seductive efforts of birds, generally, put Darwin in mind of "women everywhere" decking themselves with "plumes"), but the driver behind analogy has subtly shifted. For Darwin, what mattered was evidence from nature that the "Sense of Beauty" is not confined to man. For Prum, the role of Beauty in driving sexual selection was a lesson conned a long time ago; what counts for more at this point in our cross-disciplinary conversations is the *descriptive consequence* of holding that human beings operate aesthetically in tandem with many other species/sub-species, all making "multiple, ontologically distinct kinds of judgements." When we take pleasure in footage of bowerbird bowers, or inhale the famously rank scent of a *Amorphophallus* corpse flower (Araceae), or admire a domesticated hybrid rose, we are "human evaluators" of "biotic artworks" that run a gamut from independently evolved objects with their own "ecological communities" to objects that reflect a high degree of human engineering. In providing a technical vocabulary for the complex intermeshing agencies that result, Prum is not just inviting us to rethink the arrogation of "aesthetic agency" to the Human; he is providing a way of conceptualizing what other aesthetic agencies amount to. In his own terms, he is "recontexualiz[ing]" the idea of agency through recognizing "the qualities, properties, and consequences of non-human biological and material agencies" (p. 43).

The birds are delightful. Prum's image (p. 65) has sat on my desktop for some days, reminding me that curation of one's domestic environment might count as an art of courtship not drudgery. But they tempt me, as they tempt Prum and

---

[18] *The Descent of Man, and Selection in Relation to Sex*, 2 vols. (London: John Murray, 1871), II, pp. 112–13.
[19] *Life—The Vogelkop Bowerbird: Nature's Great Seducer—BBC One*, https://www.youtube.com/watch?v=E1zmfTr2d4c, at 00:30–52, and 02:20–28.

tempted Darwin, to a perilous kind of identification that can feel at once heartfelt and, inevitably, comic. In part this is the comedy that sits in near proximity to all analogy: "in analogy the pleasure and power of the form is felt in part because it is *precarious*," Beer rightly notes: "We experience a sense of trepidation as we follow the analogy through its various stages lest we are arriving at the point where the parallels dispart."[20] Siegel gives this form of comedy rich play as he pursues Beauty, Truth, and Goodness through their nineteenth- and twentieth-century fortunes and up to the present day. We are, moreover, prey, at this point in the conversation to a "meta" comedy (which may well be in Beer's sights, too) attaching to our *flirtation with* analogy, our decision to *play* within the very evident limitations of comparisons that set us in a kind of familial company with creatures who for the most part have (presumptively) rather less interest in their similarity to us than we have in ours to them.

Edward Lear (who illustrated both Darwin and Gould) seems to me the presiding genius of this terrain: in love with birds, keenly alert to the hapless identifications we human observers make when asserting their kinship to us while having to concede their profoundly alien existence, and thereby opening the door to comedy and to nonsense. "Should any transmigration take place at my decease [...] I am sure my soul would be uncomfortable in anything but one of the Psittacidae," quips Lear,[21] his recourse to Latin archly conceding the gap between man and parrot. Nonsense is what happens, Matthew Bevis suggests, when human imagination meets and concedes its limits (lines of poetic flight, hankerings after free flight that, with our heavier bodies, more complex minds, and our capacity for questioning ourselves, elude us). Bevis homes in on the psychological import of the avian identification: "the parrot is uncanny not simply because it is the talking animal, but because, in mimicking me, it reminds me that I am a mimic." In some contexts, more than others, that reminder may have a monitory force well beyond any intent attributable to birds: Tennyson's parrot, Bevis notes, used to murmur "Oh God" when the family knelt down to pray...[22]

Comedy seems to me the good conscience of an argument that cannot *but* bear witness to the profound difference in agency that comes with the ability to wield language beyond mimicry. My mother's parrot (since these are partly questions of family and its limits, as well as aesthetics, I feel bound to introduce my mother), had a ropier background than Tennyson's. Brought into her shared 1950s London flat, having once been in the possession of an opera singer and recently acquainted with sailors, it began its vocal exercises with implacable regularity at 5 a.m. "La – la – la ..." up and down the melodic scale, starting from middle C, working upwards

---

[20] *Darwin's Plots*, p. 80.
[21] Quoted by Matthew Bevis, "Some Birds," *Poetry Magazine*, March 2, 2020, https://www.poetryfoundation.org/poetrymagazine/articles/152456/some-birds [last accessed May 24, 2021].
[22] Ibid.

till it reached a high B: "la...la...la...SHIT!" I am perfectly happy to say that Polly Oliver had something we can call a sense of aesthetic pleasure. I am much less convinced that it was exercising aesthetic judgment (though, on this question generally, the jury remains out among ornithologists[23]). I am quite sure that it was not entering the terrain of the "discussable," where, Isobel Armstrong suggests, aesthetics starts to meet politics (p. 127).[24] Our aesthetic co-existence with these creatures, in other words, may matter as much or (I would hazard) *more* in this context for what it tells us about our peculiar nature than about our shared nature; our identification with them may be, on the same basis, more revealing in what it says about *identification* than about identity.

If shared "aesthetic agencies" with other species cannot sufficiently ground a naturalistic claim for the value of a Humanistic concern with Beauty, the deeper scrutiny that the pluralization of agency invites to the concept can certainly be of help. "It is," Steven Connor proposes, an "effect of the wide acceptance of the value of what is called 'agency,'" that "everything that does not allow for or might require the restraining of agency" seems "puzzling or provoking." Birds, as it happens, intrude metaphorically when he proposes that what we are really talking about when we invoke "agency" (or, now, "agencies") is not "action," but a "potential for action" apprehensible only through contemplating the language that expresses it:

> Despite my rising irritation over the last few years with the unreflective parroting of the need and value of "agency", agency is a complicated notion.... Agency

---

[23] My thanks to Alex Kacelnik and Irene Pepperberg for assistance in isolating the vocal range of a gray parrot (since Polly Oliver was sadly unrecorded, I am estimating a top B). Pepperberg's celebrated thirty-year study of the gray parrot Alex, demonstrating some capacity to reason at a basic level and use words creatively, makes the parrot, more than the bowerbird, the ideal test case here. Aesthetic *judgment* and, especially, the capacity for aesthetic *discussion* still seem to me to go further than any evidence yet permits. I realize that I am making a point closely akin to one Simon Blackburn makes, in reviewing Martha Nussbaum's *Upheavals of Thought: The Intelligence of Emotions* (2001):

Talking of two dogs, she says:

They showed a dejection when the men were temporarily absent, and a boisterous joy when they returned home, that showed that they had put these two men into their lives in a much more than instrumental way—still eudaimonistic, in the sense that the men were central to their scheme of goals and projects, but not simply survival-linked in the way of many of the eudaimonistic emotions of animals.

I have no difficulty with the boisterous joy that dogs can show, but I do have a lot of trouble with the dewy-eyed belief in "their scheme of goals and projects," and I certainly do not know how that scheme could be described as eudaimonistic unless the animals were thinking in terms of their own flourishing, a feat that is surely beyond them. ("To Feel and Feel Not," The New Republic, December 24, 2001, https://newrepublic.com/article/66029/feel-and-feel-not [last accessed May 10, 2021]

I take it, on the basis of his claims about evaluation, that Prum might go so far as to identify "evaluator disagreements" beyond our species, glimpsed, for example, in the neighboring bowerbirds' unlike tastes (though I wonder how strong a reading of "disagreement" he would endorse).

[24] It is beyond my scope here to go into the subject of whether non-human animals' capacity for art should be judged in terms of their capacity to generate "subtle forms of conceptual art." On that subject, see Davies, *Artful Species*, pp. 29–31.

names a theory about the possibility of the kind of action I am able to perform. Wherever there can be agency which sees and knows itself as such, it is something more or other than simple action. In knowing itself for what it is, and in being experienced as future possibility, agency must no longer be the elementary and unreflective doing of a thing that it is supposed to be.... Agency... signifies the power to perform actions that themselves signify my power to perform them.[25]

This is precisely the ground of Milton's radicalism, as Richard Eldridge accounts for it: re-imagining "man's first disobedience" as the recognition of his own capacity to "choose the exercise of personal power... over patient abiding"—a capacity realized by means of poetry's ability to "animat[e] the cognitive faculties and combin[e] spirit with the mere letter of language" (this volume, Chapter 11, pp. 210, 218, quoting Kant's Third Critique).

Connor's interest is in how attention to agential power in language may help us to think and talk better about the ways in which the power we could look to assert is, instead, moderated, its positive force "subtracted" or "retracted." Why, he asks, have we become collectively so keen on asserting, attributing, defending agency as a good, so inattentive to the ways in which social and political life are tolerable only because agency is restricted? Eldridge's concern may seem quite the opposite: namely, with how, under the inspiration of the aesthetic, we "become aware of multiple attractions among which we must choose" and thereby understand our own power to act; aware also of the moral implications of that power (we see "that various objects of attraction are, despite appearances, good or bad for us in various ways" [p. 212]). Connor and Eldridge are, in fact, training our attention on two ends, two *consequences* if you will, of our ability to grasp our potential to act through contemplating the language that gives that potential conceptual form. To know our own agency through language, both suggest, is at once a kind of liberation into and a constraint on action (it is, in the moment of reading or hearing, potential not realized action). Milton's genius, as Eldridge describes it, was to rewrite the biblical account of the origin of morality and free will as a genealogy of politics, locating its genesis in the seductive power of aesthetic form. There is—and here Eldridge channels Milton's thought in the direction of Darwin—"vanity... built into the very structure of self-conscious, discursive awareness of alternatives and the power to choose" (p. 217).

Understanding and negotiating the linguistic delimitation of our human agency not just as an individual experience but as social experience is, indeed, a large part of what we do in the Humanities. It is what all the contributors to this volume are in practice about as their essays address the repercussions of unevenly shared or

---

[25] Steven Connor, *Giving Way: Thoughts on Unappreciated Dispositions* (Stanford, CA: Stanford University Press, 2019), p. 10.

distributed aesthetic agency in the production and reception of art and literature, looking to test our "own experience [...] against the experiences of others" (Attridge, Chapter 1, p. 30), then setting about necessary or desirable adjustments of critical perspective with reference to different, new, or excluded experiences. I read Attridge's account here of the political activation of art and literature in the moment of its experience as an extension of his earlier, important work defining the "singularity" of the reading event and its ethical implications. Here he gives wider ambit to that ethical effect, arguing that, at its most potent, the artistic event calls upon "the full engagement of mind and body," plus any knowledge we possess of its creation and the accrued history of its engagements, plus the connections set running by "the environment" in which it is experienced anew. Ben Jonson's elegy to his first born son, channeling private grief into public utterance, has struck many chords over the centuries; re-read by Attridge in the context of millions of Covid-19-related deaths worldwide, including (at the point of writing) 231 children under the age of 15, "On My First Son" allows us to weigh the reality of an individual death amid daily announcements so repetitive, and overall numbers so large, they can no longer elicit deep grieving.

The four chapters grouped in Part III provide the volume's strongest concentration of attention on how politics is currently entering into experience of the aesthetic. "It comes down to language," Armstrong argues (I take it she, like McDonagh, would include images). Let me summarize the political point of address in these essays succinctly, with a view to isolating what they have in common, despite differences in political focus and methodological articulation:

- Armstrong's essay (Chapter 5) is written in urgent pursuit of the kind of political and aesthetic accountability for criticism that much recent critical theorizing misses, and, by missing, fails (a) to connect with why non-academic audiences value aesthetic experience; (b) to say anything by way of meaningful resistance to the rise of New Fascisms.
- Josephine McDonagh's (Chapter 6) account of migrant representations in the contemporary arts and literature alerts us to the strengths and weaknesses, political and aesthetic, of a field of artistic endeavor substantially driven by desire for social justice and by indignation at a collective international failure as yet to deliver anything like justice.
- Ankhi Mukherjee's essay (Chapter 8), closely allied in its concerns, makes a bid for stronger, less opportunistic connections between the political and aesthetic work of criticism and "postcolonial" critical theory—the gain from which would be genuine openness to new "enunciating subjects," the *price* of which would be that some politically motivated texts must be "allowed to fail" aesthetically.
- Edgar Garcia's essay (Chapter 7) gives fresh aesthetic and political point to a kind of material criticism more often practiced in the way of historical

literary critique: he tracks the art of painting back to source in the extraction and manufacture of its materials (beautiful pigments, dyes, minerals), revealing how intimately they have borne and still bear with them the poison, literal and figurative, of colonialism and its legacies.

Reading across these essays, I am struck not only by their confirmation of the two more-readily agreed aims of the volume, but by the combined case they make for the social and political value of the aesthetic as (in Connor's terms) it mediates and moderates—rather than asserts—human aesthetic agencies. All four critics are wedded (it would be surprising if they were not) to the power of art to redistribute our attention, with a striking recurrence of Rancière's definition of aesthetic experience as the *distribution of the sensible*, a disturbance of the relation between sense as understanding and sense as sensory perception (elegantly redescribed by Mukherjee as "a perturbation and distribution of the ethos which posits one sense over another") (p. 171; see also Siegel, Chapter 3, pp. 82–4). To put the point more simply (if less compactly), these essays deepen and give political content to the idea that aesthetic experience empowers us with a proper sense of what agency amounts to, reorienting our perception and our understanding of the potential for action in the world around us. That potentiality is, as they show, both individually felt and complexly shared in the way of experience tested, argued over, often disputed *and accruing public value as much via disputation as via agreement*. The strongest implication to be taken from such an account of the aesthetic is that it is possible to talk meaningfully of such a thing as aesthetic justice and aesthetic injustice. Once we recognize aesthetic value as accruing through the interpretative acts of agents interacting with one another socially, comprehending and adjudicating aesthetic value in a language that figures vividly the potentiality of agency, we are on the way to articulating a political philosophy of aesthetics grounded in language.[26]

Arguments about which aesthetic experiences we hold in high value and which we esteem less—or, indeed, disvalue altogether—are ubiquitous, their political implications often latent rather than explicit. Several of the contributors here worry about the specific refinements in judgment, and the accompanying

---

[26] Elaborating the terms of such a philosophy is plainly beyond the scope of this chapter, and I take to heart George Levine's clarification in stating that the current volume is not intended primarily as a contribution to philosophy. The term "aesthetic injustice" is credited, by analogy, to Miranda Fricker, *Epistemic Injustice: Power and the Ethics of Knowing* (Oxford: Oxford University Press, 2007). See esp. chs. 4 on "The Virtue of Testimonial Justice" and 7 on "Hermeneutical Injustice." More recent contributions to this rapidly growing area of interest include Gustavo H. Dalaqua, "Aesthetic Injustice," *Journal of Aesthetics & Culture* 12.1 (2020), 1–12, defining the term as "denoting any harm done to someone specifically in their capacity as an aesthetic being." See also the work of Dominic McIver Lopes: *Being for Beauty: Aesthetic Agency and Value* (Oxford: Oxford University Press, 2018), esp. chs. 6 and 12; and work in progress toward *Aesthetic Injustice* (the subject of his Mark Sainsbury Lecture, March 16, 2021). To the best of my knowledge, this work has not yet directed attention to literature as the aesthetic mobilization of language in ways that channel recognition of justice and injustice.

separation between popular and academic aesthetic experience, that follow from a Humanities higher education in literature, history, art, music, philosophy (an education that—almost by definition—alters what we are inclined to commend, though Mothersill is surely right that we may not command[27]). Armstrong, especially, voices concern about the separation between academic aesthetic tastes and those that galvanize non-academic publics: the lyrics of Pink Floyd, for example, not often taught, even, to the best of my knowledge, in cultural studies departments though we are decades past the point where it might seem contentious.[28]

Philip Davis's vivid attestation to D.H. Lawrence's "wild aesthetics" (his search for a "feeling-language" apt to the "heliotropic shift" we undergo in sensing beauty) takes an alternative route to the same concerns around specialist training and, more especially, the effect of specialist languages—typically abstract, technical, too often exclusionary (this volume, Chapter 10). Assaying Lawrence's style, he reminds us that the feeling for "'beauty," the *desire* for beauty, are not abstract things ("an experience of the aesthetic"): they touch us powerfully, physiologically. Too much writing on the subject failed, for Lawrence, at the first hurdle: its language dry, categorizing, euphemistic, "cosy," "easy," riskless, sexless. He sought words, rhythms, repetitions, paragraph constructions, grammar, punctuation that put literature, and us with it, vitally at risk from instinct. Humanities scholarship now, at least as much as in Lawrence's lifetime, may struggle to exonerate itself from his fierce repudiation of academic thought: the "thin, spurious mental conceit... all that is left of the mental consciousness once it has made itself exclusive."[29] On the other hand, Davis suggests, few writers better reward revisiting, equipped with the insights of recent work in embodied cognition. *Un*persuaded by Darwinian sexual selection, Lawrence nevertheless crafts an "immanent aesthetic" (as Davis terms it, p. 203)—a hard-fought-for/fought-with art that stimulates not just brain but "gut," skin, nerves, whole body.

The Ruskinian and, indeed, Hardyan strands of inspiration accounted for in Davis's reading of Lawrence chime with Herbert Tucker's encouragement to look before and after Darwin for assistance in grasping the wide political stakes of literary-aesthetic value (this volume, Chapter 4). Here, too, but with a wider comparative remit, we are helped to recognize a form of political urgency that is quite distinct from, ultimately far more ambitious in its scope, than the ends-driven agendas generated by the "rush to relevance in contemporary humanities study" (p. 98). The "unruliness" of the Romantic and Victorian poetic language and forms on which Tucker trains our attention disclose pre-Lawrentian forms of "wild" creativity emanating not just from the energy of individual (or, indeed,

---

[27] Mothersill, *Beauty Restored*, p. 217.
[28] For *Jacqueline Fowler v. The Board of Education of Lincoln County* (1987), see https://law.justia.com/cases/federal/appellate-courts/F2/819/657/245113/ [last accessed May 24, 2021].
[29] D.H. Lawrence, *Phoenix II: Uncollected, Unpublished and Other Prose Works*, ed. Warren Roberts and Harry T. Moore (London: Heinemann, 1968), p. 596.

collaborative) aesthetic endeavors but from the ongoing participatory, "processive" energies of aesthetic reception. The "reciprocation of beauty with truth" as the poem is read is not subject to decision or closure, Tucker urges: (risking an application of Darwinian metaphor) it is, rather, a "collective and ongoing... aesthetic *evolution*." Shelley, Keats, Browning, Tennyson, Arnold, Swinburne, Ruskin, Pater—these are canonical figures, but Tucker's readings draw out their capacity still to radicalize the terms of entry into aesthetic debate by "disavow[ing] principles" for prose and poetry, eschewing didacticism, laboring rather under a "mandate whose outcomes and applications were radically unknown to the present, and for that very reason [remain] speculatively precious to the future" (p. 98).

The particular appeal of Victorian aestheticism, like the particular appeal of Lawrence, may split readers. It would be, in a sense, a failure for writers so willing to risk disapprobation and give offense to the arbiters of taste in their day if they had lost that power. Disagreements, uncertainties, ambivalences are in the nature of our aesthetic experience, understood not "just" as an evolved variety of aesthetic responses, nor by reference to agreed standards (Kantian or otherwise), but as a form of responsiveness to aesthetic stimuli that is in our nature but constantly under pressure from cultural change and subject to adjustment all our lives. Educable, certainly, but individually characteristic of us up to a point, taste is also, often, vagrant. Much of the best critical writing about aesthetics, in recent years, has been about the ordinary, everyday density of our reactions to aesthetic experience, the ambivalences it can induce in us, and the social and political implications they bear even without taking a long view.[30] And it is to the point here that even the most generously pluralizing approach to our descriptive categories for criticism of art and literature can be thought open to a charge that taxonomic subtlety may miss the point (too many fresh conceits, Merve Emre suggests, can start to "curdle": "one is left suspicious of the category—of all aesthetic categories"[31]). In refining our language, in other words, cultural theory may fine-sieve what we care to argue over; or it may harden our resolve to keep something of the power of our aesthetic experience out of the classroom, where, if we are not careful, it stands to lose as well as gain from our professional acuity.

Any Humanities reader will identify with the resulting "double bind of professional reading and personal reading" described by Susan Wolfson (this volume, Chapter 12): the embarrassment of emotion in response to beauty that generates

---

[30] See, esp. Sianne Ngai, *Ugly Feelings* (Cambridge, MA: Harvard University Press, 2007); *Our Aesthetic Categories: Zany, Cute, Interesting* (Cambridge, MA: Harvard University Press, 2012); and *Theory of the Gimmick: Aesthetic Judgement and Capitalist Form* (Cambridge, MA: Harvard University Press, 2020). Ngai's description of *Ugly Feelings* as "a bestiary of affects... filled with rats and possums rather than lions" seems apropos here.

[31] "Our Love-Hate Relationship with Gimmicks," *The New Yorker*, November 16, 2020, https://www.newyorker.com/magazine/2020/11/16/our-love-hate-relationship-with-gimmicks [last accessed May 24, 2021].

this sense of wanting to keep something of our response to beauty in reserve. Tearing up over beauty, no less than gushing over it, tends to "the confusion or embarrassment of...students," Wolfson remarks. Pregnancy exacerbated the hazards, in my own case. Welling up, reading Keats's "This living hand..." to three second-year undergraduates, I flapped a hand in the air in an effort to dispel emotion, and met with eye-rolling despair from a less susceptible 19-year-old Anthony: "It's good, but I'm not gonna *cry*!" Tracing the signs of Cleanth Brooks's struggle, over more than thirty years, to acknowledge, and at the same time account intellectually for, his deep attachment to Tennyson's *Tears, Idle Tears*, Wolfson draws attention back, with a difference, to the way in which acknowledgment of the emotional power of aesthetic experience seems to prompt questions of agency and *motive*. What is it that acts upon us when we feel poetry, or any other art, deeply? (It seems salient that we are, again, considering a poem about grief, written in the knowledge of many earlier poems that have captured its various intense shadings—despair, regret, remorse, longing. Grief, no doubt, adds gravitas to what we might say, with no less truth, on behalf of pleasure.) "Does [the act of] speaking *release* wild regrets from depths into poetic forming," Wolfson asks, or "is poetry's formative power the agent of these regrets?" "For the critic [Brooks] who argues that form is content," the "or" is "a false distinction."[32] Overdetermination of motive then generates, at the level of the critical phrase, a "grammar of restless motive-hunting," drawn to the surface by Wolfson's acute close reading. She directs us to a quality of Brooks's writing that is the more interesting for being unresolved: expression (up to a point "admission") of uncontained psychic energies that repeatedly escape the critic's attempts at professionalizing and controlling them within the professional practice of accounting for art's workings.

Collectively, these essays seem to me to be worrying—and worrying well[33]—around what is, ultimately, not a weakness in our ability to advocate for the Humanities but an aspect of their value for us, individually and collectively, that resists easy condensation. Let me nevertheless (and at whatever risk of dry academicism) attempt, with their assistance, a "6th claim" for the public benefit of the Humanities to be added to the five identified in *The Value of the Humanities* (2013). By contrast with some familiar, readily sloganized claims ("democracy needs us," "intrinsic value") the claim is comparatively complex and delicate, which is not to say tentative:

---

[32] I am quoting Wolfson out of turn, here, but not, I hope, misplacing her meaning.

[33] Adam Phillips helpful invites us to think about worrying as 'a form of thinking. At one end of some imaginary spectrum, there is something akin to creative rumination. At the other end, there is the stalled thought of obsession. If worrying can persecute us, it can also work for us, as self-preparation...' 'What, Me Not Worry?', *The New York Times*, 13 December 1996, https://www.nytimes.com/1996/12/13/opinion/what-me-not-worry.html [last accessed 24 May 2021].

- The Humanities have a special interest in experiences of beauty (more broadly, experiences of the aesthetic) as they alter the quality of our perception and our understanding of the world—recognizing that what moves us is at once private and shared, conventionally determined and constantly subject to change. Among the most important work Humanities subjects undertake is the calibration of these experiences in language, recognizing that it is in the process of acknowledging, discussing, debating, disputing aesthetic experience and commending it to others that much of our social and political thinking takes place. Critical to that thinking is the power aesthetic experience affords us to apprehend the idea of agency through language, and thus be in a position to respond better to the reality of injustice.

Works Cited

Abel, Darrel. "Intellectual Criticism." *American Scholar* 12.4 (Autumn 1943): 414–28.
Abel, Darrel. "On 'The New Criticism.'" *American Scholar* 13.4 (Autumn 1944): 500–2.
Achebe, Chinua. *Things Fall Apart* [1958]. London, Penguin Books, 2010.
Adichie, Chimamanda Ngozi, *Half of a Yellow Sun* [2006]. London: 4th Estate, 2017.
Adorno, Theodor W. *Aesthetic Theory*, ed. Gretel Adorno and Rolf Tiedemann, trans. Robert Hullot-Kentor. London: Athlone Press, 1997.
Agamben, Giorgio. "The End of the Poem." In *The End of the Poem: Studies in Poetics*, trans. Daniel Heller-Roazen. Stanford, CA: Stanford University Press, 1999, pp. 109–15.
Agamben, Giorgio, *Taste*, trans. Cooper Francis. London: Seagull, 2017.
Ahmad, Aijaz. "Jameson's Rhetoric of Otherness and 'National Allegory'." *The Post-Colonial Studies Reader*, ed. Bill Ashcroft, Gareth Griffiths, and Helen Tiffin. London: Routledge, 1995, pp. 84–7.
"Amazing! Bird Sounds From The Lyre Bird – David Attenborough – BBC Wildlife." BBC Studios, February 12, 2007. Video, 2:54. https://www.youtube.com/watch?v=VjE0Kdfos4Y
Anker, Elizabeth S. and Rita Felski, eds. *Critique and Postcritique*. Durham, NC: Duke University Press, 2017.
Archambeau, Robert. *Poetry and Uselessness: From Coleridge to Ashbery*. New York: Routledge, 2020.
Armstrong, Isobel. *The Radical Aesthetic*. Oxford: Blackwell, 2000.
Armstrong, Isobel. "Meter and Meaning." *Meter Matters*, ed. Jason Hall. Athens: Ohio University Press, 2011, pp. 26–52.
Armstrong, John. *The Secret Power of Beauty*. London: Penguin Books, 2005.
Arnold, Matthew. *Poetry and Criticism of Matthew Arnold*, ed. A. Dwight Culler. Boston, MA: Houghton Mifflin, 1961.
Athenaeum 21.1053, January 1, 1848: 6–8. Review of Tennyson, *The Princess*.
Attridge, Derek. *The Work of Literature*. Oxford: Oxford University Press, 2015.
Attridge, Derek. *The Singularity of Literature* [2004], 2nd edn. Abingdon: Routledge, 2017.
Attridge, Derek, Mir Ali Hosseini, Anirudh Stridhar, eds. *The Work of Reading. Literary Criticism in the 21st Century*. Cham: Springer Nature, 2021.
Bakhtin, M.M. *The Dialogic Imagination. Four Essays*, ed. Michael Holquist, trans. Carl Emerson and Michael Holquist. Austin: University of Texas Press, 1981.
Barrett Browning, Elizabeth. *Aurora Leigh: Authoritative Text, Backgrounds and Contexts, Criticism* [1856], ed. Margaret Reynolds. New York: Norton, 1996.
Bataille, Georges. *Eroticism* [1957], trans. M. Dalwood. London: Penguin, 2012.
Baucom, Ian. *Spectres of the Atlantic: Finance Capitalism, Slavery and the Philosophy of History*. Durham, NC: Duke University Press 2005.
Beer, Gillian. *Darwin's Plots: Evolutionary Narrative in Darwin, George Eliot and Nineteenth-Century Fiction*. London: Routledge & Kegan Paul, 1983.
Bell, Clive. *Art* [1914]. Oxford: Oxford University Press, 1987.
Belting, Hans. *The Invisible Masterpiece*. London: Reaktion, 2001.
Benjamin, Walter. *The Arcades Project*, trans. Howard Eiland and Kevin McLaughlin. Cambridge, MA: Harvard University Press, 1990.

Bennett, Jane. *Vibrant Matter: A Political Ecology of Things*. Durham, NC: Duke University Press, 2010.
Berger, John. *Ways of Seeing* [BBC TV series 1972]. London: Penguin, 2008.
Bergvall, Caroline. *Drift: Performance for Spoken Voice, Electronic Text, and Percussion*, 2014, https://carolinebergvall.com/work/drift-performance/.
Berubé, Michael. *The Employment of English: Theory, Jobs, and the Future of Literary Studies*. New York: New York University Press, 1998.
Best, Stephen and Sharon Marcus. "Surface Reading: An Introduction." *Representations* 108 (Fall 2009): 1–21.
Bevis, Matthew, ed. *The Oxford Handbook of Victorian Poetry*. Oxford: Oxford University Press, 2013.
Bevis, Matthew. "Some Birds." *Poetry Magazine*, March 2, 2020, https://www.poetryfoundation.org/poetrymagazine/articles/152456/some-birds.
Bion, Wilfred R. *Taming Wild Thoughts*. London: Karnac Books, 1997.
Bion, Wilfred R. *The Tavistock Seminars*. London: Karnac Books, 2005.
Björgvinsson, Erling, Nicholas De Genova, Mahmoud Keshavarz, and Tintin Wuli. "Art and Migration: Editorial Introduction," in *Migration*, ed. E. Björgvinsson et al., *Parse* 10, 2020, https://parsejournal.com/journal/#migration.
Blackburn, Simon. "To Feel and Feel Not." *The New Republic*, December 24, 2001.
Blake, William. *The Marriage of Heaven and Hell*, in Blake, *Selected Poems of William Blake*, ed. G. E. Bently, Jr. London: Penguin, 2005.
Blanchot, Maurice. *The Space of Literature*, trans. Ann Smock. Lincoln: University of Nebraska Press, 1982.
Bloom, Harold. *The Anxiety of Influence: A Theory of Poetry*. Oxford: Oxford University Press, 1973.
Blumenberg, Hans. *Shipwreck with Spectator: Paradigm for a Metaphor for Existence*, trans. Steven Rendall, Cambridge MA: MIT Press, 1979.
Bollas, Christopher. "The Fascist State of Mind," in *Being a Character: Psychoanalysis and Self-Experience*, London: Routledge, 1993, pp. 193–217.
Born, Georgina. "The Social and the Aesthetic: For a Post-Bourdieuian Theory of Cultural Production." *Cultural Sociology* 4 (July 2010): 171–208.
Bourdieu, Pierre. *La distinction: Critique sociale du jugement*. Paris: Editions de Minuit, 1979.
Bourdieu, Pierre. *Distinction: A Social Critique of the Judgement of Taste* [1979], trans. Richard Nice. Cambridge, MA: Harvard University Press, 1984.
Bourdieu, Pierre. *The Rules of Art: Genesis and Structure of the Literary Field* [1992], trans. Susan Emanuel. Cambridge: Polity Press, 1996.
Bourdieu, Pierre. *Practical Reason: On the Theory of Action*, trans. Randal Johnson and others. Palo Alto, CA: Stanford University Press, 1998.
Boyd, Brian. *On the Origin of Stories: Evolution, Cognition, and Fiction*. Cambridge, MA: Harvard University Press, 2009.
Brilmayer, Pearl S. and Filippo Trentin. "Toward an Inessential Theory of Form: Ruskin, Warburg, Focillon." *Criticism* 61 (Fall 2019): 481–508.
Brooks, Cleanth. "The New Criticism: A Brief for the Defense." *American Scholar* 13.3 (1944): 285–95.
Brooks, Cleanth. *The Well Wrought Urn: Studies in the Structure of Poetry*. New York: Reynal & Hitchcock, 1947.
Brooks, Cleanth. "Thy Darling in an Urn." *Sewanee Review* 55.4 (1947): 691–7.

Brooks, Cleanth and Robert Penn Warren. *Understanding Poetry*. Henry Holt, 1938; 2nd edn., 1950; 3rd edn., Holt, Rhinehart & Winston, 1960; 4th edn., 1976.
Brooks, Cleanth and Robert B. Heilman. *Understanding Drama*. Henry Holt, 1945.
Brown, Marshall and Susan Wolfson, eds. "Reading for Form." Special issue, *Modern Language Quarterly* 61.1 (2000).
Browning, Robert. *The Poems*, 2 vols., ed. John Pettigrew and Thomas J. Collins. New Haven, CT and London: Yale University Press, 1981.
Bürger, Peter. *Theory of the Avant-Garde* [1974], trans. Michael Shaw. Minneapolis: University of Minnesota Press, 1984.
Burrow, Trigant. *Social Basis of Consciousness*. London: Kegan Paul, Trench, Trubner and Co., 1927.
Calais Migrant Solidarity. December 4, 2015, https://calaismigrantsolidarity.wordpress.com/2015/12/04/the-border-takes-another-life/.
Calvino, Italo. *Why Read the Classics?* Trans. Martin McLaughlin. Boston, MA: Houghton, Mifflin, Harcourt, 1999.
Čapek, Karel. *R.U.R. (Rossum's Universal Robots): A Melodrama in Three Acts*, trans. Paul Selver. Garden City, NY: Doubleday, 1923.
Carhart-Harris, R.L., R. Leech, P.J. Hellyer, M. Shanahan, A. Feilding, E. Tagliazucchi, ... and D. Nutt. "The Entropic Brain: A Theory of Conscious States Informed by Neuroimaging Research with Psychedelic Drugs." *Frontiers in Human Neuroscience* 8 (2014): 140–61.
Caruth, Cathy and Gayatri Chakravorty Spivak. "Interview with Gayatri Chakravorty Spivak." *PMLA* 129.4 (October 2010): 1020–5.
Cavell, Stanley. *Must We Mean What We Say? A Book of Essays* [1969]. Cambridge: Cambridge University Press, 1976.
Chambers, Jessie. *D.H. Lawrence: A Personal Record*. London: Jonathan Cape, 1935.
Chatterjee, Ronjaunee, Alicia Mireles Christoff, and Amy R. Wong. "Undisciplining Victorian Studies." *Victorian Studies* 62 (Spring 2020): 369–91.
Chow, Andrew R. "A Play About Refugee Camps Is Coming. With Refugees in the Cast." *New York Times*, June 20, 2018, https://www.nytimes.com/2018/06/20/theater/the-jungle-a-play-about-refugee-camps-is-coming-.html.
Chubb, Emma. "Differential Treatment: Migration in the Work of Yto Barrada and Bouchra Khalili." *Journal of Arabic Literature* 46 (2015): 268–95.
Clune, Michael W. "Judgment and Equality." *Critical Inquiry* 45 (2019): 910–34.
Cohen, Ted, *Thinking of Others: On the Talent for Metaphor*. Princeton, NJ: Princeton University Press, 2012.
Cole, Teju. *Known and Strange Things*. London: Faber & Faber, 2016.
Coleridge, Samuel Taylor. *Poetical Works*, 2 vols. London: Pickering, 1834.
Coleridge, Samuel Taylor. *Shorter Works and Fragments*, eds. H.J. Jackson and J.R. de J. Jackson. Princeton, NJ: Princeton University Press, 1995.
Collingwood, R.G. *Speculum Mentis: Or, The Map of Knowledge*. Oxford: Clarendon Press, 1924.
Collingwood, R.G. *The Principles of Art*. London: Oxford University Press, 1938.
Connor, Steven. *Beyond Words: Sobs, Hums, Stutters and other Vocalizations*. London: Reaktion Books, 2014.
Connor, Steven. *Giving Way: Thoughts on Unappreciated Dispositions*. Stanford, CA: Stanford University Press, 2019.
Coombs, David Sweeney. *Reading with the Senses in Victorian Literature and Science*. Charlottesville: University of Virginia Press, 2019.

Curry, Patrick. 2019. *Enchantment: Wonder in Modern Life*. Edinburgh: Floris.
Daily, Patricia. "Questions of Dwelling in Anglo-Saxon Poetry and Medieval Mysticism: Inhabiting Landscape, Body and Mind." *New Medieval Literatures* 8 (2006): 175–204.
Dalaqua, Gustavo H. "Aesthetic Injustice." *Journal of Aesthetics & Culture* 12.1 (2020): 1–12.
Dangarembga, Tsitsi. *This Mournable Body*. London: Faber and Faber, 2020.
Danto, A.C. "The Artworld." *Journal of Philosophy* 61 (1964): 571–84.
Danto, A.C. *The Transfiguration of the Commonplace*. Cambridge, MA: Harvard University Press, 1981.
Danto, A.C. "The End of Art," in B. Lang, ed., *The Death of Art*. New York: Haven Publishers, 1984.
Danto, A.C. *After the End of Art*. Princeton, NJ: Princeton University Press, 1997.
Darwin, Charles. *On the Origin of Species by Means of Natural Selection, or The Preservation of Favoured Races in the Struggle for Life*. London: John Murray, 1859.
Darwin, Charles. "Letter to Asa Gray," April 3, 1860, Darwin Correspondence Project, no. 2743, http://www.darwinproject.ac.uk/entry-2743.
Darwin, Charles. *The Descent of Man, and Selection in Relation to Sex*. London: John Murray, 1871.
Davis, Philip. *Reading for Life*. Oxford: Oxford University Press, 2020.
Davies, Josh. *Visions and Ruins: Cultural Memory and the Untimely Medieval*. Manchester: Manchester University Press, 2018.
Davies, Stephen. *The Artful Species: Aesthetics, Art and Evolution*. Oxford: Oxford University Press, 2012.
De Genova, Nicholas, et al. "Migrant Crisis"/"Refugee Crisis," in *Europe/Crisis: New Keywords of the Crisis in and of Europe*, coordinated and ed. Nicholas De Genova and Martina Tazzioli. Near Futures OnLine, 2016, https://f7687beb-3eb9-469c-8cfb-f5a0fe324552.filesusr.com/ugd/4fd32d_cd94af72e46740868fa015ee1e6f00fe.pdf.
Deleuze, Gilles. *Essays Critical and Clinical*, trans. D.W. Smith and M.A. Greco. London: Verso, 1998.
Deleuze, Gilles and Félix Guattari. *One Thousand Plateaus: Capitalism and Schizophrenia* [1972], trans. Brian Massumi. Minneapolis: University of Minnesota Press, 2005.
De Man, Paul. "Foreword," in *Blindness and Insight*. Minneapolis: University of Minnesota Press, 1983, pp. vii–xii.
Demos, T.J. *The Migrant Image: The Art and Politics of Documentary During Global Crisis*, Durham, NC: Duke University Press, 2013.
Derrida, Jacques. *Of Grammatology*. Baltimore, MD: Johns Hopkins University Press, 1974.
Derrida, Jacques. "'This Strange Institution Called Literature': An Interview," in *Acts of Literature*, ed. Derek Attridge. New York: Routledge, 1992, pp. 33–75.
Descartes, René, "The Search After Truth by the Light of Nature," in Descartes, *Philosophical Essays and Correspondence*, ed. Roger Ariew. Indianapolis, IN: Hackett Publishing, 2000.
Desmond, Adrian and James Moore. *Darwin's Sacred Cause*. New York: Houghton Mifflin, 2009.
Deutscher, Penelope "The Descent of Man and the Evolution of Woman." *Hypatia* 19.2 (2004): 35–55.
Dewey, John. *Art as Experience* [1934]. New York: Penguin, 1980.
Díaz, Junot. "An Interview with Junot Díaz," 2007, https://www.bookbrowse.com/author_interviews/full/index.cfm/author_number/1496/junot-diaz.

Dickens, Charles. *Hard Times*, ed. George Ford and Sylvere Monod. New York: W. W. Norton, 1966.
Dillon, Elizabeth Maddock. *New World Drama: The Performative Commons in the Atlantic World, 1649–1849*. Durham, NC: Duke University Press, 2014.
Din-Kariuki, Natalya. "'Nobody Ever Warned Me About Mirrors': Doubling, Mimesis and Narrative Form in Helen Oyeyemi's Fiction," in Chloe Buckley and Sarah Holt, eds., *Telling It Slant: Critical Approaches to Helen Oyeyemi*. Brighton: Sussex Academic Press, 2017, pp. 59–73.
Dowling, J.L., D.A. Luther, and P.P. Marra. "Comparative Effects of Urban Development and Anthropogenic Noise on Bird Songs." *Behavioral Ecology* 23.1 (2011): 201–9.
Dowsett-Lemaire, Françoise. "The Imitative Range of the Song of the Marsh Warbler *Acrocephalus palustris*, with Special Reference to Imitations of African Birds." *Ibis* 121 (1979): 453–68.
Drndic, Dasa. *Trieste* [2007], trans. Ellen Elias Bursac. London: Maclehose Press, 2012.
Dufrenne, Mikel. *The Phenomenology of Literary Experience*, trans. Edward S. Casey et al. Evanston, IL: Northwestern University Press, 1987.
During, Simon. *Against Democracy: Literary Experience in the Era of Emancipations*. New York: Fordham University Press, 2012.
During, Simon. "The Postcolonial Aesthetic." *PMLA* 129.3 (May 2014): 498–503.
Dutton, Denis. "A Naturalist Definition of Art." *Journal of Aesthetics and Art Criticism* 64 (2006): 367–77.
Dutton, Denis. *The Art Instinct*. New York: Bloomsbury Press, 2009.
Eagleton, Terry. "In the Gaudy Supermarket." *The London Review of Books* 21.10 (May 13, 1999).
Eagleton, Terry. *The Ideology of the Aesthetic* [1990], ed. G.E. Bently, Jr. London: Penguin, 2005.
Elbiri, Bilge (2017) "Cannes's Beguilements," https://www.villagevoice.com/2017/05/25/canness-beguilements/.
Eldridge, Richard. *An Introduction to the Philosophy of Art*, 2nd edn. Cambridge: Cambridge University Press, 2000.
Eldridge, Richard, ed. *The Oxford Handbook of Philosophy and Literature*. Oxford: Oxford University Press, 2009.
Eldridge, Richard. "The Question of Truth in Literature: *Die Poetische Auffassung der Welt*," in Garry L. Hagberg, ed., *Fictional Characters, Real Problems: The Search for Ethical Content in Literature*. Oxford: Oxford University Press, 2016, pp. 119–38.
Eliot, T.S. "Hamlet and His Problems," in *The Sacred Wood: Essays on Poetry and Criticism*. London: Methuen, 1920, pp. 87–94.
Eliot, T.S. *Poems*, vol. 1, ed. Christopher Ricks and Jim McCue. London: Faber & Faber, 2015.
Elliot, Charles. *Locating the Energy for Change*, 1999, https://www.iisd.org/publications/locating-energy-change-introduction-appreciative-inquiry.
Emecheta, Buchi. *The Joys of Motherhood* [1979]), ed. Elleke Boehmer. London: Heinemann, 2008.
Empson, William. *Seven Types of Ambiguity*. London: Chatto and Windus, 1930.
Empson, William. *Some Versions of Pastoral; and Related Writings*. London: Chatto and Windus, 1935.
Empson, William. "Thy Darling in an Urn." *Sewanee Review* 55.4 (1947): 691–7.
Empson, William. *The Structure of Complex Words*. London: Chatto and Windus, 1951.

Emre, Merve. "Our Love-Hate Relationship with Gimmicks." *The New Yorker*, November 16, 2020, https://www.newyorker.com/magazine/2020/11/16/our-love-hate-relationship-with-gimmicks.

Etherington, Ben and Sean Pryor, eds. *Historical Poetics and the Problem of Exemplarity: Critical Quarterly* 61 (April 2019).

Evans, Richard J. *The Hitler Conspiracies: The Third Reich and the Paranoid Imagination*. London: Allen Lane, 2020.

Eyers, Tom. "Critical Response II: Theory over Method, or, In Defense of Polemic." *Critical Inquiry* 44 (Autumn 2017): 136–43.

Ezra, Elizabeth and Jane Sillars. "Hidden in Plain Sight: Bringing Terror Home." *Screen* 48.2 (2007): 215–21.

Falci, Eric. *The Value of Poetry*. Cambridge: Cambridge University Press, 2020.

Felski, Rita. *The Limits of Critique*. Chicago, IL: University of Chicago Press, 2015.

Field, Michael. "La Gioconda," in *Sight and Song*, 8. London: Elkin Matthews and John Lane, 1892.

Forensic Architecture. "The Left-to-Die-Boat," 2012, https://forensic-architecture.org/investigation/the-left-to-die-boat.

Forna, Aminatta. *The Memory of Love* [2010]. London: Bloomsbury, 2011.

Foster, Hal. "Postmodernism: A Preface," in Hal Foster, ed., *The Anti-Aesthetic: Essays on Postmodern Culture*. Port Townsend: Bay Press, 1983, pp. ix–xvi.

Freedgood, Elaine. "The Novelist and Her Poor." *NOVEL: A Forum on Fiction* 47.2 (2014): 210–23.

Freud, Sigmund. *Complete Psychological Works*, trans. and ed. James Strachey, 24 vols. London: Vintage Classics, 2001.

Fricker, Miranda. *Epistemic Injustice: Power and the Ethics of Knowing*. Oxford: Oxford University Press, 2007.

Frith, Clifford B., and Dawn W. Frith. *The Bowerbirds*. Oxford: Oxford University Press, 2004.

Fry, Roger. "An Essay in Æsthetics" [1909]. Reprinted in Fry, *Vision and Design*. New York: Brentano's, 1920, pp. 16–38.

Fulton, Dawn. "Known Unknowns: Michael Haneke's Caché and the Failure of Allegory." *Modern Language Review* 114.4 (2019): 682–99.

Gadamer, Hans-Georg. *Truth and Method*, 2nd rev. edn., trans. Joel Weinsheimer and Donald G. Marshall. New York: Crossroad, 1991.

Gagnier, Regenia. "On the Insatiability of Human Wants: Economic and Aesthetic Man." *Victorian Studies* 36.2 (1993): 125–53.

Gagnier, Regenia. *Literatures of Liberalization: Global Circulation and the Long Nineteenth Century*. Cham: Palgrave Macmillan, 2018.

Gallagher, Catherine. "Formalism and Time." *Modern Language Quarterly* 61.1 (2000): 229–51.

Garcia, Edgar. "A Migrant's *Lotería*: Risk, Fortune, Fate, and Probability in the Borderlands of Juan Felipe Herrera and Artemio Rodríguez's *Lotería Cards and Fortune Poems*." *Modern Philology* 118.3 (2020): 252–76.

Garcia, Edgar and Eamon Ore-Giron. *Infinite Regress*. Berlin: Bom Dia Books, 2020.

Garratt, Peter. *Victorian Empiricism: Self, Knowledge, and Reality in Ruskin, Bain, Lewes, and George Eliot*. Madison, NJ: Farleigh Dickinson University Press, 2010.

Gaskill, Nicholas. "The Close and the Concrete: Aesthetic Formalism in Context." *New Literary History* 47 (2016): 505–24.

Gelfand, Janelle. "Inside a Symphony Audition." *Cincinatti Enquirer*, November 24, 2015.

Gibson, James J. *The Ecological Approach to Visual Perception* [1979]. Hillsdale, NJ: Lawrence Erlbaum, 1986.
Gikandi, Simon. *Maps of Englishness: Writing Identity in the Culture of Colonialism*. New York: Columbia University Press, 1996.
Gikandi, Simon. *Slavery and the Culture of Taste*. Princeton, NJ: Princeton University Press, 2011.
Gilroy, Paul. "Shooting Crabs in a Barrel." *Screen* 48.2 (2007): 233–5.
Goldstone, Andrew. *Fictions of Autonomy: Modernism from Wilde to de Man*. Oxford: Oxford University Press, 2012.
González Luque, F. Javier and A. Luis Montejo González. "Vincent Van Gogh and the Toxic Colours of Saturn: Autobiographical Narrative of a Case of Lead Poisoning," trans. José M. Bueso. University of Salamanca, 2004, http://www.vggallery.com/visitors/summary.pdf.
Graves, Robert. *Collected Poems 1965*. London: Cassell, 1965.
Greenberg, Clement. 1986. *The Collected Essays and Criticism*. Chicago, IL: University of Chicago Press.
Grierson, Jamie, Kim Willsher, and Diane Taylor. "Teenager Found Dead Tried to Cross Channel in Dinghy with Shovel for Oars," 2020, https://www.theguardian.com/world/2020/aug/19/sudanese-teenager-found-dead-on-beach-near-calais-sangatte.
Grosz, Elizabeth. "Darwin and Feminism: Preliminary Investigations for a Possible Alliance." *Australian Feminist Studies* 14.29 (1999): 31–45.
Grosz, Elizabeth. "Art and the Animal." Talk given by Elizabeth Grosz at the Damien Minton Gallery, Redfern, Sydney, Australia, July 9, 2011.
Grosz, Elizabeth. *Becoming Undone: Darwinian Reflections on Life, Politics, and Art*. Durham: Duke University Press, 2011.
Guénoun, Solange. "Jacques Rancière's Ethical Turn and the Thinking of Discontents," in Gabriel Rockwell and Philip Watts, eds., *Jacques Rancière: History, Politics, Aesthetics*. Durham, NC: Duke University Press, 2009, pp. 176–94.
Guillory, John. *Cultural Capital: The Problem of Literary Canon Formation*. Chicago, IL: Chicago University Press, 1993.
Guillory, John. "Bourdieu's Refusal." *Modern Language Quarterly* 58.4 (1997): 367–98.
Guillory, John. "The Sokal Affair and the History of Criticism." *Critical Inquiry* 28.2 (2002): 470–508.
Guillory, John. "Critical Response II: The Name of Science, the Name of Politics." *Critical Inquiry* 29.3 (2003): 526–41.
Guillory, John and Christopher Newfield. "Critical Response I: The Value of Nonscience." *Critical Inquiry* 29.3 (2003): 508–25.
Guyer, Paul. "Editor's Introduction," in Immanuel Kant, *Critique of the Power of Judgment*, ed. Paul Guyer. Cambridge: Cambridge University Press, 2001, pp. xiii–lii.
Guyer, Paul. *A History of Modern Aesthetics*, 3 vols. Cambridge: Cambridge University Press, 2014.
Habermas, Jürgen. "Modernity—An Incomplete Project" [1980], in Hal Foster, ed., *The Anti-Aesthetic: Essays on Postmodern Culture*. Port Townsend: Bay Press, 1983, pp. 3–15.
Hack, Daniel. *Reaping Something New: African American Transformations of Victorian Literature*. Princeton, NJ: Princeton University Press, 2017.
Hadot, Pierre. *The Veil of Isis: An Essay on the History of the Idea of Nature*, trans. Michael Chase. Cambridge, MA: Harvard University Press, 2006.
Hall, Donald E. "Pied Studies." *Victorian Review* 33 (2007): 28.

Hall, George. "Sacconi Quartet/Padmore Review – a Terrible Tragedy Beautifully Expressed." *Guardian*, July 14, 2016, https://www.theguardian.com/music/2016/jul/14/sacconi-quartet-mark-padmore-review-jonathan-dove-kings-place.

[Hallam, A.H.] "On Some Characteristics of Modern Poetry, and on the *Lyrical Poems* of Alfred Tennyson." *Englishman's Magazine* 1 (August 1831): 616–28.

Haneke, Michael. *Happy End* (screen play), translator unknown, n.d., https://www.sonyclassics.com/awards-information/screenplays/happyend_screenplay.pdf.

Haraway, Donna. "Situated Knowledges: The Science Question in Feminism and the Privilege of Partial Perspective." *Feminist Studies* 14.3 (1988): 575–99.

Hardy, Florence Emily. *The Life and Works of Thomas Hardy*, ed. M. Millgate. London: Macmillan, 1984.

Hardy, John William, and Theodore A. Parker III. "The Nature and Probable Function of Vocal Copying in Lawrence's Thrush, *Turdus lawrencii*." *Ornithological Monographs* 48 (1997): 307–20.

Hardy, Thomas. *The Dynasts: An Epic-Drama of the War with Napoléon*. London: Macmillan, 1923.

Hartley, Lucy. "Beauty." *Victorian Literature and Culture* 46.3–4 (Fall/Winter 2018): 584–7.

Hegel, G.W.F. *Aesthetics* [1818–29], trans. T.M. Knox. Oxford: Clarendon Press, 1988.

Hewison, Robert. "Ruskin and Darwin." *The Ruskin Review* 14.2 (2020): 66–7.

Hollander, John. "Breaking into Song: Some Notes on Refrain," in *Melodious Guile*. New Haven, CT: Yale University Press, 1988, pp. 130–47.

Homer. *The Iliad of* Homer, trans. Andrew Lang, Walter Leaf, and Ernest Meyers. New York: Modern Library, 1946 [1891].

Hopkins, Gerard Manley. *The Journals and Papers of Gerard Manley Hopkins*, ed. Humphry House and Graham Storey. London: Oxford University Press, 1959.

Hopkins, Gerard Manley. "Pied Beauty" [1877], in *The Poetical Works of Gerard Manley Hopkins*, ed. Norman MacKenzie. Oxford: Clarendon Press, 1990, p. 144.

Hopkins, Gerard Manley. "The Wreck of the Deutschland" [1875–6], in *The Poetical Works of Gerard Manley Hopkins*, ed. Norman MacKenzie. Oxford: Clarendon Press, 1990, pp. 119–28.

Hopkins, Gerard Manley. *The Major Works*, ed. Catherine Phillips. Oxford: Oxford University Press, 2002.

Hough, Graham. "Tears, Idle Tears." *Hopkins Review* 4 (1951): 31–6.

Houston, Natalie M. "Towards a Computational Analysis of Victorian Poetics." *Victorian Poetry* 56 (Spring 2014): 498–510.

Hunter, G.K. *Paradise Lost*. London: George Allen & Unwin, 1982.

Hutton, Richard Holt. "Tennyson" [1876], in *Literary Essays*. London: Macmillan, 1892, pp. 361–436 [*Illustrated London News*, August 28, 1897, p. 299].

Ingarden, Roman. *The Literary Work of Art: An Investigation of the Borderlines of Ontology, Logic and the Theory of Language*. Evanston, IL: Northwestern University Press, 1974.

Iser, Wolfgang. *The Act of Reading: A Theory of Aesthetic Response*. Baltimore, MD: Johns Hopkins University Press, 1978.

Ishiguro, Kazuo. *Klara and the Sun*. London: Faber and Faber Ltd, 2021.

Jacqueline Fowler v. The Board of Education of Lincoln County (1987), https://law.justia.com/cases/federal/appellate-courts/F2/819/657/245113/.

James, William. *Pragmatism and Other Writings*, ed. G. Gunn. London: Penguin, 2000.

Jameson, Frederic. *The Political Unconscious: Narrative as a Socially Symbolic Act*. London: Methuen, 1981.

Jameson, Fredric. "Modernism and Imperialism," in Terry Eagleton et al., eds., *Nationalism, Colonialism and Literature*. Minneapolis: University of Minnesota Press, 1988, pp. 43–66.
Johnson, Brandon N., Erik A. Ehli, Gareth E. Davies, and Dorret I. Boomsma. "Chimerism in Health and Potential Implications on Behavior: A Systematic Review." *American Journal of Medical Genetics Part A* 182.6 (2020): 1513–29.
Johnston, Adrian and Catherine Marabou. *Self and Emotional Life: Philosophy, Psychoanalysis and Neuroscience*. New York: Columbia University Press, 2013.
Jones, David. *The Dying Gaul and Other Writings*, ed. Harman Grisewood. London and Boston, MA: Faber & Faber, 1978.
Jonson, Ben. *The Cambridge Edition of the Works of Ben Jonson Online*, ed. Martin Butler et al. Cambridge: Cambridge University Press, n.d., https://universitypublishingonline.org/cambridge/benjonson/.
Jonson, Ben. *Epigrams*, ed. Colin Burrow. In Martin Butler et al., eds, *The Cambridge Edition of the Works of Ben Jonson Online*, n.d., https://universitypublishingonline.org/cambridge/benjonson/.
Jonson, Ben. *Informations to William Drummond of Hawthornden*, ed. Ian Donaldson. In Martin Butler et al., eds, *The Cambridge Edition of the Works of Ben Jonson Online*, n.d., https://universitypublishingonline.org/cambridge/benjonson/.
Joseph, Gerhard. *Tennysonian Love: The Strange Diagonal*. Minneapolis: University of Minnesota Press, 1969.
Judd, Donald, "Specific Objects" [1965], in Thomas Kellein, *Donald Judd: Early Work, 1955–1968*. New York: D.A.P., 2002, pp. 86–97.
Junot, Diaz. The Brief Wondrous Life of Oscar Wao. London: Faber and Faber, 2007.
Kant, Immanuel. *Critique of the Power of Judgment*, trans. Paul Guyer and Eric Matthews. Cambridge: Cambridge University Press, 2001.
Kapil, Bhanu. *How to Wash a Heart*. Liverpool: Liverpool University Press, 2020.
Khalili, Bouchra. "Selected Works and Projects." 2019, http://www.bouchrakhalili.com/.
Keats, John. *Complete Poems*, ed. Jack Stillinger. Cambridge, MA and London: The Belknap Press of Harvard University Press, 1978.
Keats, John. "Ode on a Grecian Urn" [1819], in *The Poems of John Keats*, ed. Jack Stillinger. Cambridge, MA: Harvard University Press, 1978, p. 373.
Keats, John. *Selected Letters*, ed. Robert Gittings and Jon Mee. Oxford: Oxford University Press, 2002.
Keats, John. *John Keats: A Longman Cultural Edition*, ed. Susan J. Wolfson. London: Pearson, 2007.
Klonaris, Helen. "*Zong!* The Transformation of Language into Sacred Space." *sx salon* 3, 2011, http://smallaxe.net/sxsalon/reviews/zong-transformation-language-sacred-space.
Knowlton, Timothy. "Filth and Healing in Yucatan: Interpreting Ix Hun Ahau, A Maya Goddess." *Ancient Mesoamerica* 27 (2016): 319–32.
Koolhaas, Rem. *Delirious New York: A Retroactive Manifesto for Manhattan* [1978]. New York: Monacelli Press, 1994.
Kramnick, Jonathan. "The Making of the English Canon." *PMLA* 112 (1997): 1087–101.
Kramnick, Jonathan. "Against Literary Darwinism." *Critical Inquiry* 37.2 (Winter 2011): 315–47.
Kramnick, Jonathan. *Paper Minds: Literature and the Ecology of Consciousness*. Chicago, IL: University of Chicago Press, 2018.
Kramnick, Jonathan and Anahid Nersessian. "Form and Explanation." *Critical Inquiry* 43 (2017): 650–69.

Kramnick, Jonathan, and Anahid Nersessian. "Forms and Explanations: A Reply to Our Critics." *Critical Inquiry* 44 (2017): 164–74.
Kraus, Rosalind. *The Originality of the Avant-Garde and Other Modernist Myths.* Cambridge, MA: MIT Press, 1986.
Kurmanaev, Anatoly "A Battle of Singing Stars, With Wings and Feathers." *New York Times*, January 14, 2021, section A, p. 10.
Kurnick, David. "A Few Lies: Queer Theory and Our Method Melodramas." *ELH* 87.2 (2020): 349–74.
Lacey, Hugh, *Is Science Value Free? Values and Scientific Understanding.* London: Routledge, 1999.
Lawrence, D.H. *Sons and Lovers.* London: Duckworth, 1913.
Lawrence, D.H. *Prussian Officer and Other Stories.* London: Duckworth, 1914.
Lawrence, D.H. *The Rainbow.* London: Methuen, 1915.
Lawrence, D.H. *Twilight in Italy.* London: Duckworth, 1916.
Lawrence, D.H. *Fantasia of the Unconscious* London: Martin Secker, 1923.
Lawrence, D.H. *Psychoanalysis and the Unconscious.* London: Martin Secker, 1923.
Lawrence, D.H. *Studies in Classic American Literature.* London: Martin Secker, 1924.
Lawrence, D.H. *St Mawr* together with *The Princess.* London: Martin Secker, 1925.
Lawrence, D.H. *Apocalypse.* London: Martin Secker, 1932.
Lawrence, D.H. *Phoenix*, ed. E.D. Macdonald. London: Heinemann, 1936.
Lawrence, D.H. *Phoenix II*, ed. W. Roberts and H.T. Moore. London: Heinemann, 1968.
Lawrence, D.H. *The Letters*, ed. J.T.Boulton, Vol I, 1901–13. Cambridge: Cambridge University Press, 2002.
Lazarus, Neil. *The Postcolonial Unconscious.* Cambridge: Cambridge University Press, 2011.
Le Clézio, J.M.G. *The Mexican Dream: Or, the Interrupted Thought of Amerindian Civilizations*, trans. Teresa Lavender Fagan. Chicago, IL: University of Chicago Press, 1993.
Leavis, F.R. "Thought and Emotional Quality/Notes in the Analysis of Poetry." *Scrutiny* 13.1 (1945): 53–71.
Lee, Vernon and Clementina Anstruther-Thomson. *Beauty and Ugliness and Other Studies in Psychological Æsthetics.* New York: John Lane Company, 1912.
Lehman, Robert S. "Criticism and Judgment." *ELH* 87 (2020): 1105–32.
Leighton, Angela. *On Form: Poetry, Aestheticism, and the Legacy of a Word.* Oxford: Oxford University Press, 2007.
Levine, Caroline. *Forms: Whole, Rhythm, Hierarchy, Network.* Princeton, NJ and Oxford: Princeton University Press, 2015.
Levine, Caroline. Critical Response I, "*Still* Polemicizing After All These Years." *Critical Inquiry* 44 (Autumn 2017): 129–35.
Levine, Caroline. "The Long Lure of Anti-Instrumentality: Politics, Aesthetics, Sustainability." *Modern Fiction Studies* 67 (2021): 225–46.
Levine, George. *Dying to Know: Scientific Epistemology and Knowledge in Victorian England.* Chicago, IL: Chicago University Press, 2002.
Levine, George. *Realism, Ethics and Secularism: Essays on Victorian Literature and Science.* Cambridge: Cambridge University Press, 2008.
Levinson, Marjorie. "What is New Formalism." *PMLA* 122 (2007): 558–69.
Levinson, Marjorie. Critical Response III. "Response to Jonathan Kramnick and Anahid Neressian, 'Form and Explanation'." *Critical Inquiry* 44 (Autumn 2017): 144–55.
Lewis, C.S., *A Preface to* Paradise Lost. Oxford: Oxford University Press, 1961 [1942].

Liebling, Alison. "Appreciative Inquiry, Generative Theory, and the 'Failed State' Prison," in Jody Miller and Wilson R. Palacios, eds., *Qualitative Research in Criminology*. New York: Taylor & Francis, 2015, pp. 251-70.
Life – The Vokelkop Bowerbird: Nature's Great Seducer – BBC One." BBC, November 5, 2009. Video, 5:42. https://www.youtube.com/watch?v=E1zmfTr2d4c.
Loesberg, Jonathan. *A Return to Aesthetics: Autonomy, Indifference, and Postmodernism*. Palo Alto, CA: Stanford University Press, 2005.
Lootens, Tricia. *The Political Poetess: Victorian Femininity, Race, and the Legacy of Separate Spheres*. Princeton, NJ: Princeton University Press, 2017.
Lopes, Dominic McIver. *Being for Beauty: Aesthetic Agency and Value*. Oxford: Oxford University Press, 2018.
Love, Heather. Critical Response IV. "Strange Quarry." *Critical Inquiry* 44 (Autumn 2017): 156-63.
Lowe, Lisa. *The Intimacies of Four Continents*. Durham, NC: Duke University Press, 2015.
Luhan, Mabel Dodge. *Lorenzo in Taos*. New York: Alfred A. Knopf, 1932.
McDonagh, Josephine. *Literature in a Time of Migration: British Fiction and the Movement of People, 1815-1876*. Oxford: Oxford University Press, 2021.
McKeon, Michael. *The Secret History of Domesticity: Public, Private, and the Division of Knowledge*. Baltimore, MD: Johns Hopkins University Press, 2006.
McMurtry, Áine. "Sea Journeys to Fortress Europe: Lyric Deterritorializations in Texts by Caroline Bergvall and José F. A. Oliver." *The Modern Language Review* 113.4 (2018): 811-45.
Makumbi, Jennifer Nansubuga. *The First Woman*. London: Oneworld Publications, 2020.
Marchini Camia, Giovanni. "Cannes Review: *Happy End* is a Restrained Amalgamation of Michael Haneke's Oeuvre." 2017, https://thefilmstage.com/happy-end-review-michael-haneke-cannes/.
Maritain, Jacques. "An Essay on Art" [1930], in *Art and Scholasticism*, trans. J.F. Scanlan. London: Sheed and Ward, 1946.
Marshall, Tom. "Coleridge on Double Touch: A Phenomenological Analysis." *European Romantic Review* 29:2 (2018): 213-27.
Martindale, C. and A. Dailey. "Creativity, Primary Process Cognition and Personality." *Personality and Individual Differences* 20.4 (1996): 409-14.
Mathur, Saloni, ed. *The Migrant's Time: Rethinking Art History and Diaspora*. New Haven, CT: Yale University Press, 2011.
Miller, Andrew H. *The Burdens of Perfection: On Ethics and Reading in Nineteenth-Century British Literature*. Ithaca, NY: Cornell University Press, 2008.
Miller, J. Hillis. "Temporal Topographies: Tennyson's Tears." *Victorian Poetry* 30.3-4 (1992): 277-89.
Milton, John. "The Verse." *Paradise Lost*. London: S. Simmons, 1674.
Milton, John. *Paradise Lost: A Poem in Twelve Books*, ed. Merritt Y. Hughes. Indianapolis, IN: Bobbs-Merrill, 1962.
Milton, John, *Paradise Lost*, ed. Gordon Teskey. New York: W.W. Norton & Company, 2005.
Desmond, Adrian and James Moore. *Darwin's Sacred Cause*. Boston: Houghton Mifflin, 2009.
Moore, David Chioni. "Is the Post- in Postcolonial the Post- in Post-Soviet? Toward a Global Postcolonial Critique." *PMLA* 116.1 (January 2001): 111-28.
Moretti, Franco. *Graphs Maps Trees: Abstract Models for a Literary History*. London and New York: Verso, 2005.

Moretti, Franco. *Distant Reading*. London and New York: Verso, 2013.
Moretti, Franco. *The Bourgeois: Between History and Literature*. London: Verso, 2013.
Morgan, Benjamin. *The Outward Mind: Materialist Aesthetics in Victorian Science and Literature*. Chicago, IL and London: University of Chicago Press, 2017.
Morris, William. "The Defence of Guenevere." In *The Defence of Guenevere and Other Poems*. London: Bell and Daldy, 1858, pp. 1–17.
Mothersill, Mary. *Beauty Restored*. Oxford: Clarendon Press, 1984.
Naipaul, V.S. *Finding the Center: Two Narratives*. New York: Knopf, 1984.
National Museum of Mexican Art. Website, 2019, https://nationalmuseumofmexicanart.org/exhibits/woven-connections-and-meanings.
Nawi, Diana. "Other Maps: On Bouchra Khalili's Cartographies," 2015, https://www.ibraaz.org/usr/library/documents/main/other-maps.pdf.
Nealon, Christopher. "Reading on the Left." *Representations* 108 (Fall 2009): 22–50.
Ngai, Sianne. *Ugly Feelings*. Cambridge, MA: Harvard University Press, 2007.
Ngai, Sianne. *Our Aesthetic Categories: Zany, Cute, Interesting*. Cambridge, MA: Harvard University Press, 2012.
Ngai, Sianne. *Theory of the Gimmick: Aesthetic Judgement and Capitalist Form*. Cambridge, MA: Harvard University Press, 2020.
Nietzsche, Friedrich. *Beyond Good and Evil: Prelude to a Philosophy of the Future*, ed. Rolf-Peter Horstmann and Judith Norman, trans. Judith Norman. Cambridge: Cambridge University Press, 2002.
Nixon, Rob. *London Calling: V. S, Naipaul, Postcolonial Mandarin*. New York: Oxford University Press, 1997.
Nord, Deborah Epstein. *Gypsies and the British Imagination, 1807–1930*. New York: Columbia University Press, 2006.
North, Joseph. *Literary Criticism: A Concise Political History*. Cambridge, MA: Harvard University Press, 2017.
Nowell Smith, David. *On Voice in Poetry: The Work of Animation*. Basingstoke: Palgrave Macmillan, 2015.
Nuttal, Zelia. "Chalchihuitl in Ancient Mexico." *American Anthropologist* 3.2 (1901): 227–38.
Oyeyemi, Helen. *The Icarus Girl*. New York, Doubleday Random House, 2005.
Pangia, Davide. *Rancière's Sentiments*. Durham, NC: Duke University Press, 2018.
"Paris–Londres Music Migrations (1962–1989)," Le Musée National de l'Histoire de l'Immigration, https://www.histoire-immigration.fr/paris-londres.
Parker, Andrew. "Mimesis and the Division of Labor," in Jacques Rancière, *The Philosopher and His Poor*. Durham, NC: Duke University Press, 2003, pp. ix–xx.
Pater, Walter. *The Renaissance: Studies in Art and Poetry* [1873], ed. Donald L. Hill. Berkeley: University of California Press, 1980.
Pater, Walter. *The Renaissance: Studies in Art and Poetry*, ed. Adam Phillips. Oxford and New York: Oxford University Press, 1986.
Phillips, Adam. "What, Me Not Worry?" *The New York Times*, December 13, 1996, https://www.nytimes.com/1996/12/13/opinion/what-me-not-worry.html.
Phosphorous Theatre. [n.d.] Website, https://www.phosphorostheatre.com/.
Pinch, Alan and Michael Armstrong. *Tolstoy on Education: Tolstoy's Educational Writings 1861–62*. London: The Athlone Press, 1982, pp. 222–47.
Plato, *Republic*, trans. G.M.A. Grube, rev. C.D.C. Reeve. Indianapolis, IN: Hackett Publishing, 1992.

Poe, Edgar Allan. "The Philosophy of Composition." *Graham's American Monthly Magazine* 28.4 (1846): 163–7.
Pollan, Michael. "The Sickness in Our Food Supply." *The New York Review of Books* 67. 10, 2020, https://www.nybooks.com/articles/2020/06/11/covid-19-sickness-food-supply/.
Potts, Jason. "The Price of Everything." *The Conversation*, August 6, 2014, https://theconversation.com/are-the-arts-and-culture-a-public-good-29939.
Pound, Ezra. "A Few Don'ts" [1913], in *Literary Essays of Ezra Pound*, ed. T.S. Eliot. London: Faber, 1954.
Prettejohn, Elizabeth. *Beauty and Art: 1750–2000*. Oxford: Oxford University Press, 2005.
Priesemann, V., M. Valderrama, M. Wibral, and M. Le Van Quyen. "Neuronal Avalanches Differ from Wakefulness to Deep Sleep–Evidence from Intracranial Depth Recordings in Humans." *PLoS Computer Biology* 9.3 (2013): e1002985.
Prins, Yopie. "What is 'Historical Poetics?'" *Modern Language Quarterly* 77 (March 2016): 13–40.
Prum, R.O. "The Lande-Kirkpatrick Mechanism Is the Null Model of Evolution by Intersexual Selection: Implications for Meaning, Honesty, and Design in Intersexual Signals." *Evolution* 64 (2010): 3085–100.
Prum, R.O. "Aesthetic Evolution by Mate Choice: Darwin's Really Dangerous Idea." *Philosophical Transactions of the Royal Society of London B 367* (2012): 2253–65.
Prum, R.O. "Coevolutionary Aesthetics in Human and Biotic Artworlds." *Biology and Philosophy* 28 (2013): 811–32.
Prum, R.O. "The Role of Sexual Autonomy in Evolution by Mate Choice," in T. Hoquet, ed., *Current Perspectives in Sexual Selection*. New York: Springer, 2015, pp. 237–62.
Prum, R.O. *The Evolution of Beauty: How Darwin's Forgotten Idea of Mate Choice Shapes the Animal World – and Us*. New York: Doubleday, 2017.
Prum, R.O. "Ornament in Human and Biotic Artworlds," in G. He and K. Bloomer, eds., *Natures of Ornament*. New Haven, CT: Yale University Press, 2020, pp. 48–67.
Quammen, David. *The Song of the Dodo*. New York: Scribner, 1996.
Rancière, Jacques. *The Philosopher and His Poor*. Durham, NC: Duke University Press, 2003.
Rancière, Jacques. "The Ethical Turn of Aesthetics and Politics." *Critical Horizons* 7.1 (2006): 1–20.
Rancière, Jacques. "The Aesthetics Dimension: Aesthetics, Politics, Knowledge." *Critical Inquiry* 36 (Autumn 2009): 1–19.
Rancière, Jacques. *Aisthesis: Scenes from the Aesthetic Regime of Art* [2011], trans. Zakir Paul. London: Verso, 2013.
Rankine, Claudia, "Weather." *The New York Times Sunday Book Review*, June 21, 2020, p. 1.
Rawls, John. *A Theory of Justice*, rev. edn. Cambridge, MA: Harvard University Press, 1999.
Restall, Matthew. *Seven Myths of the Spanish Conquest*. Oxford: Oxford University Press, 2003.
Retallack, Joan. "The Ventriloquist's Dilemma," in *Bosch'd*. Brooklyn: Litmus Press, 2020, p. 13.
Retallack, Joan. *The Poethical Wager*. Berkeley: University of California Press, 2003, p. 45.
Rhys, Jean. *Wide Sargasso Sea*. New York: W. W. Norton, 1966,
Richards, I.A. *Practical Criticism: A Study of Literary Judgment*. London: Kegan Paul, 1929.
Richards, Robert J. *The Romantic Conception of Life: Science and Philosophy in the Age of Goethe*. Chicago and London: University of Chicago Press, 2002.
Ricks, Christopher. *Tennyson*, 2nd edn. Berkeley: University of California Press, 1989.

Riskin, Jessica. *The Restless Clock: A History of the Centuries-Long Argument over What Makes Living Things Tick*. Chicago and London: University of Chicago Press, 2016.
Robbins, Bruce. "Not So Well Attached." *PMLA* 132.2 (2017): 371–5.
Robbins, Bruce. "Is Literature a Secular Concept? Three Earthquakes." *Modern Language Quarterly* 72.3 (2011): 293–317.
Robinson, A. Mary F. "Art and Life," in *An Italian Garden*. London: T. F. Unwin, 1886, p. 96.
Robinson, Marilynne, "What Kind of Country Do We Want?" *The New York Review of Books* June 11, 2020, https://www.nybooks.com/articles/2020/06/11/what-kind-of-country-do-we-want/.
Rose, Jacqueline. "The Psychoanalytic Passion of Edward Said." *Raritan* 36.3 (2017): 1–23.
Rosen, Charles. *The Classical Style: Haydn, Mozart, Beethoven*. New York: W.W. Norton, 1997.
Ruskin, John. *The Works of John Ruskin*, 39 vols., ed. Edward Cook and Alexander Wedderburn. London and New York: Allen, Longmans, Green, 1903–12.
Russell, Bertrand. BBC talk in the Listener, July 24, 1952, reprinted in H. Coombes, ed., *D.H. Lawrence: A Critical Anthology*. London: Penguin, 1973, p. 359.
Russell, Francey. "'How shall we put ourselves in touch with reality?' James Baldwin, Film, and Acknowledgment." *Social Research, Special Issue on Apology* (Winter 2001).
Ryan, Michael J. *A Taste for the Beautiful: The Evolution of Attraction*. Princeton, NJ and Oxford: Princeton University Press, 2018.
Safina, Carl. *Becoming Wild: How Animal Cultures Raise Families, Create Beauty, and Achieve Peace*. New York: Holt, 2020.
Said, Edward. "Reflections on Exile." *Granta* 13 (1984): 157–74.
Sanders, Mark. *Gayatri Chakravorty Spivak: Live Theory*. London: Bloomsbury, 2006.
Sanders, Mike. *The Poetry of Chartism: Aesthetics, Politics, History*. Cambridge: Cambridge University Press, 2012.
Sanyal, Deborati, "Calais's 'Jungle': Refugees, Biopolitics and the Arts of Resistance," in Vanessa Agnew, Kader Konuk, and Jane O. Newman, eds., *Refugee Routes: Telling, Looking, Protesting, Redressing*. Bielefeld: Transcript-Verlag, 2020, pp. 159–92.
Saunders, George. *A Swim in the Pond in the Rain (In which Four Russians Give a Masterclass on Writing, Reading and Life)*. London: Bloomsbury, 2021.
Saville, Julia F. *A Queer Chivalry: The Homoerotic Asceticism of Gerard Manley Hopkins*. Charlottesville: University Press of Virginia, 2000.
Sayeau, Michael. *Against the Event: The Everyday and the Evolution of Modernist Narrative* Oxford: Oxford University Press, 2013.
Scarry, Elaine. *On Beauty and Being Just*. Princeton, NJ: Princeton University Press, 1999.
Scharres, Barbara. Review of *Happy End*, 2017, https://www.rogerebert.com/festivals/cannes-2017-happy-end-the-meyerowitz-stories-before-we-vanish
Schiller, Friedrich. *On the Aesthetic Education of Man* [1794], trans. Elizabeth M. Wilkinson and L.A. Willoughby. Oxford: Clarendon Press, 1985.
Schwartz, K. "On the Edge of Chaos: Where Creativity Flourishes," 2014, https://ww2.kqed.org/mindshift/2014/05/06/on-the-edge-of-chaos-where-creativity-flourishes/.
Scott, A.O. "Dreaming in Spanglish." *New York Times*, September 30, 2007, https://www.nytimes.com/2007/09/30/books/review/Scott-t.html.
Scruton, Roger. *Sexual Desire*. London: Continuum, 2006.
Scruton, Roger. *Beauty*. Oxford: Oxford University Press, 2009.
Shelley, Percy Bysshe. *The Major Works*, ed. Zachary Leader and Michael O'Neill. Oxford: Oxford University Press, 2003.

Shklovsky, Viktor. "Art as Technique" [1917], in *Russian Formalist Criticism: Four Essays*, trans. Lee T. Lemon and Marion J. Reis. Lincoln: University of Nebraska Press, 1965, pp. 3–24.
Siegel, Jonah. *Haunted Museum: Longing, Travel, and the Art-Romance Tradition*. Princeton, NJ: Princeton University Press, 2005.
Siegel, Jonah. "Victorian Aesthetics," in Juliet John, ed., *The Oxford Handbook of Victorian Literary Culture*. Oxford: Oxford University Press, 2016, pp. 561–79.
Siegel, Jonah. *Material Inspirations: The Interests of the Art Object in the Nineteenth Century and After*. Oxford: Oxford University Press, 2020.
Small, Helen. *The Value of the Humanities*. Oxford: Oxford University Press, 2013.
Small, Helen. "Caprice: Individual Subjectivity in Literary Criticism," in Rónán McDonald, ed., *The Values of Literary Studies: Critical Institutions, Scholarly Agendas*. Cambridge: Cambridge University Press, 2015.
Smith, Barbara Herrnstein. *Poetic Closure: A Study of How Poems End*. Chicago, IL: University of Chicago Press, 1968.
Smith, Caroline. *The Immigration Handbook*. Bridgend: Seren, 2016.
Snorton, C. Riley and Hentyle Yapp, eds. *Saturation: Race, Art, and the Circulation of Value*. Cambridge, MA: MIT Press, 2020.
Soliman, Francesca. "In the Name of Art? The Commercialization of Migrant Deaths," 2019, https://www.law.ox.ac.uk/research-subject-groups/centre-criminology/centreborder-criminologies/blog/2019/06/name-art.
Solomon, Tessa. "Art Supply Companies Contend with Racism as 'Flesh Tones' Come Under Scrutiny." *ARTnews*, August 27, 2020, https://www.artnews.com/art-news/news/artsup.
Spitzer, Leo. "'Tears, Idle Tears' Again." *Hopkins Review* 5 (Spring 1952): 71–80.
Spivak, Gayatri Chakravorty. *The Spivak Reader*. Eds Donna Landry and Gerald MacLean. Abingdon: Routledge 1996.
Spivak, Gayatri Chakravorty. *A Critique of Postcolonial Reason: Toward a History of the Vanishing Present*. Cambridge, MA: Harvard University Press, 1999.
Spivak, Gayatri Chakravorty. *An Aesthetic Education in the Era of Globalization*. Cambridge, MA: Harvard University Press, 2012.
Staten, Henry. *Techne Theory: A New Language for Art*. London: Bloomsbury Academic, 2019.
Stern, Daniel N. *Forms of Vitality*. Oxford: Oxford University Press, 2010.
Stevens, Wallace. "Sunday Morning" [1915], in *The Collected Poems of Wallace Stevens*, New York: Alfred A. Knopf, 1990, pp. 66–7.
Stewart, Heather and Rowena Mason. "Nigel Farage's Migrant Poster Reported to Police." 2016, https://www.theguardian.com/politics/2016/jun/16/nigel-farage-defends-ukip-breaking-point-poster-queue-of-migrants.
Stewart, Susan. *Poetry and the Fate of the Senses* Chicago, IL: University of Chicago Press, 2002.
Stonebridge, Lindsey. *Placeless People: Writing, Rights, and Refugees*. Oxford: Oxford University Press, 2018.
Stories in Transit (2021), http://www.storiesintransit.org/.
Swinburne, Algernon Charles. *Major Poems and Selected Prose*, ed. Jerome McGann and Charles L. Sligh. New Haven, CT and London: Yale University Press, 2004.
Tennyson, Alfred. [untitled] "Break, break, break." *Poems*, 2 vols. London, 1842, 2, p. 229.
Tennyson, Alfred. *The Princess: A Medley*. London: Edward Moxon, 1847.

Tennyson, Alfred. *Tennyson's Works*, 9 vols, ed. Hallam Tennyson. London: Macmillan, 1907–8.
Tennyson, Alfred. *The Poems of Tennyson*, ed. Christopher Ricks. London: Longman, 1969.
Tennyson, Alfred Lord. "The Lady of Shalott" [1833], in *The Poems of Tennyson*, ed. Christopher Ricks, 2nd edn. Berkeley: University of California Press, 1987, 1, pp. 387–95.
Tennyson, Alfred. "The Palace of Art" [1832], in *The Poems of Tennyson*, ed. Christopher Ricks, 2nd edn. Berkeley: University of California Press, 1987, 1, pp. 436–56.
Tennyson, Alfred. "To ___. With the Following Poem" ["The Palace of Art"] [1832], in *The Poems of Tennyson*, ed. Christopher Ricks, 2nd edn. Berkeley: University of California Press, 1987, 1, p. 436.
Tennyson, Hallam. *Alfred Lord Tennyson: A Memoir*, 2 vols. London: Macmillan, 1897.
Teukolsky, Rachel. *The Literate Eye: Victorian Art Writing and Modernist Aesthetics*. Oxford: Oxford University Press, 2009.
Thread Bearing Witness (2019), website https://threadbearingwitness.com/.
Ticktin, Miriam. "Calais Containment Politics in the 'Jungle'." *The Funambulist* 5 (2016): 28–33.
The Times, January 7, 1884: 7; review of Gilbert and Sullivan's *Princess Ida, or Castle Adamant*.
Trilling, Lionel. *Prefaces to 'The Experience of Literature.'* Oxford: Oxford University Press, 1981.
Tucker, Herbert. *Tennyson and the Doom of Romanticism*. Cambridge, MA: Harvard University Press, 1988.
Vallury, Raji. "An Incalculable Rupture? The Aesthetics and Politics of Postcolonial Fiction?" *NOVEL: A Forum on Fiction* 47.2 (Summer 2014): 242–60.
Vandiver, Edward P., Jr. "Tennyson's TEARS, IDLE TEARS." *Explicator* 21.7 (1963): 1–3.
Vargo, Greg. *An Underground History of Early Victorian Fiction: Chartism, Radical Print Culture, and the Social Problem Novel*. Cambridge: Cambridge University Press, 2017.
Volosinov, V.N. *Marxism and the Philosophy of Language*, trans. Ladislav Matejka and I. R. Titunk. Cambridge, MA and London: Harvard University Press, 1986.
V21 Collective. "Manifesto of the V21 Collective: Ten Theses." 2015. http://v21collective.org/manifesto-of-the-v21-collective-ten-theses/
Vygotsky, L.S. *Mind in Society: The Development of Higher Psychological Processes*, ed. Michael Cole, Vera John-Steiner, Sylvia Scribner, and Ellen Souberman. Cambridge, MA and London: Harvard University Press, 1978.
Wa Thiong'o, Ngũgĩ. *Decolonising the Mind*. London: Heinemann Educational, 1986.
Wa Thiong'o, Ngũgĩ. *Petals of Blood*. London: Penguin, 1977.
Weiner, E.S.C. and Simpson, J.A., eds., *The Oxford English Dictionary*, 20 vols., 2nd *edn*. Oxford: Oxford University Press, 1989.
Weitz, Morris. "The role of theory in aesthetics." *Journal of Aesthetics and Art Criticism* 15 (1956): 27–35.
Whitman, Walt. "A Word about Tennyson." *The Critic* 7.157 (January 1887): 1–2.
Wilde, Oscar. "The Decay of Lying" [1889], in *Complete Works of Oscar Wilde*, ed. Merlin Holland. Glasgow: HarperCollins, 1999, pp. 1071–92.
Wilde, Oscar. *The Picture of Dorian Gray* [1890], in *Complete Works of Oscar Wilde*, ed. Merlin Holland. Glasgow: HarperCollins, 1999, pp. 17–167.
Willett, David. *The State of the Arts – The Future of the Humanities in the UK*. Lecture delivered at the British Academy in London, March 19, 2014.
Wimsatt, W.K. and M.C. Beardsley. "The Affective Fallacy." *Sewanee Review* 57.1 (1949): 31–55.
Witchell, Charles A. *The Evolution of Bird-song, with Observations on the Influence of Heredity and Imitation*. London: Black, 1896s.

Wittgenstein, Ludwig. *Philosophical Investigations*. Oxford: Oxford University Press, 1953.
Wolfson, Susan J. *Formal Charges: The Shaping of Poetry in British Romanticism*. Palo Alto, CA: Stanford University Press, 1997.
Wolfson, Susan J. "Poem on the Wye," in Richard Gravil and Daniel Robinson, eds., *Oxford Companion to William Wordsworth*. Oxford: Oxford University Press, 2014, pp. 186–203.
Wood, Michael. *Literature and the Taste of Knowledge*. Cambridge: Cambridge University Press, 2005.
Woolf, Virginia. *Mrs. Dalloway*. London: Hogarth Press, 1925.
Leighton, Angela. *On Form: Poetry, Aestheticism, and the Legacy of a Word*. Oxford: Oxford University Press, 2007.
Wordsworth, William. "Lines Composed a Few Miles Above Tintern Abbey" [1798], in *Poems*, 2 vols. London: Longman, 1815, 2, pp. 73–80.
Wordsworth, William. *Works*, Vol. 1, ed. E.S. Haldane and G.R.T. Ross. Cambridge: Cambridge University Press, 1911.
Wordsworth, William. *Prose Works of William Wordsworth*, 3 vols., ed. W.J.B. Owen, and J.W. Smyser. Oxford, Clarendon Press, 1974.
Yeats, William Butler. *The Letters of W. B. Yeats*, ed. Allan Wade. London: Rupert Hart-Davis, 1954.
Yeats, William Butler. "Sailing to Byzantium" [1928], in *W.B. Yeats: Collected Poems, Revised Second Edition*, ed. Richard J. Finneran. New York: Scribner Paperback Poetry, 1996, pp. 204–5.
Young, Robert J.C. "The Postcolonial Comparative." *PMLA* 128.3 (May 2013): 683–9.
Zamir, Tzachi. *Ascent: Philosophy and Paradise Lost*. Oxford: Oxford University Press, 2018.
Zangwill, Nick. *The Metaphysics of Beauty*. Ithaca, NY: Cornell University Press, 2001.
Zon, Bennett. *Evolution and Victorian Musical Culture*. Cambridge: Cambridge University Press, 2017.

Index

Note: Figures are indicated by an italic '*f*', following the page number.
For the benefit of digital users, indexed terms that span two pages (e.g., 52–53) may, on occasion, appear on only one of those pages.

Abel, Darrel 221–2
Achebe, Chinua 133
Adiche, Chimamanda Negozi 133–4
Adorno, Theodor 80
Agamben, Giorgio 32n.9, 102n.3
Ahmad, Aijaz 174–5
Anker, Elizabeth 176–7
Anscombe, Elizabeth 121–2
Aristotle 28, 220n.7
Armstrong, Isobel 4–5, 10–11, 13–14, 20, 227n.4, 230, 235n.9
Arnold, Matthew 108–10, 149
Attridge, Derek 6–8, 18–20, 117–18, 227n.4
Auden, W.H. 12–13

Bacon, Francis 160
Bach, Johann Sebastian 19–20, 145–6
Badiou, Alain 31n.8
Bakhtin, Mikhail Mikhailovich 130–1
Barrett Browning, Elizabeth 75–6, 85–6, 123–4
Baudelaire, Charles 109n.9
Baumgarten, Alexander Gottlieb 1, 28
Beckett, Samuel 141, 202
Benigni, Roberto 117
Benjamin, Walter 8–9, 28n.3, 160–2
Bell, Clive 91–5
Bennet, Jane 43
Berger, John 160
Bergvall, Caroline 155–8
Best, Stephen 118–22
Biden, Joe 131–2
Bion, W.R. 202
Björgvinsson, Erling 143
Blake, William 218–19
Blanchot, Maurice 36–7
Block, Ned 121–2
Bloom, Harold 67
Blumenberg, Hans 152n.11
Bollas, Christopher 131–2
Born, Georgina 118
Bourdieu, Pierre 29, 76–80, 82–4, 86, 89–90
Brady, Andrea 126

Brilmyer, Pearl S. 126
Brooks, Cleanth 22–3, 221–6, 228–30, 232–3, 235–6
Browning, Robert 102–6, 108–10, 125–6
Büchel, Christoph 152
Bui, Thi 144–5
Burke, Edmund 28
Burrow, Colin 39n.17
Burrow, Trigant 196–7

Calvino, Italo 170
Chambers, Jessie 198
Charles V, Holy Roman Emperor 163–4
Chatterjee, Ronjaunee 120
Christoff, Alicia Mireles 129
Chubb, Emma 143, 147–8
Clune, Michael 2–3, 15
Cohen, Ted 218
Cole, Teju 178, 182–4
Coleridge, Samuel Taylor 197n.5, 232, 236
Collingwood, R.G. 31–2, 34n.12
Connor, Steven 130–1
Conrad, Joseph 150–1
Corral, Eduardo 146
Cotton, Robert 40–1
Curry, Patrick 106n.5

Dangaremba, Tsitsi 133
Danto, Arthur 44–5, 50, 66
Darwin, Charles 1, 6, 9, 12, 16–19, 21–2, 105, 107–10, 196, 198–9
Darwish, Mahmoud 146–7
Davis, Philip 5–6, 22–3
Deleuze, Gilles 31n.8
de Man, Paul 120, 122, 235–6
Derrida, Jacques 31n.8, 36n.13, 67
Descartes, René 206
Dewey, John 28–9, 32n.10, 45, 108–9, 109n.9
Diaz, Junot 178–80
Dickens, Charles 10–13, 153
Dillon, Elizabeth Maddock 63
Dilthey, Wilhelm 28n.3
Dove, Jonathan 145–6

Dowsett-Lemaire, Françoise 63
Dryden, John 196–7
Duchamp, Marcel 45
Dufrenne, Mikel 28–9
Dupré, John 121–2
During, Simon 28n.5
Dutton, Denis 46

Eco, Umberto 119
Eldridge, Richard 21–2, 218, 220n.7
Eliot, George 5
Eliot, T.S. 33n.11, 236
Emecheta, Buchi 133–4
Empson, William 28–9, 125–6, 225, 230, 232, 233n.8, 236
Epicurus 152n.11
Evans, Richard J 132
Eyers, Tom 122

Falci, Eric 100n.2
Farage, Nigel 143–4
Felski, Rita 122, 176–7
Field, Michael 75–6, 85–6
Forna, Aminetta 133–4
Foster, Hal 77–81
Foucault, Michel 31n.8
Freud, Sigmund 198, 201
Frost, Robert 229
Fry, Roger 92–3

Gadamer, Hans-Georg 28n.3
Gagnier, Regenia 128–9
Galileo 44
Garcia, Edgar 4–5, 21, 150–1
Gaskell, Elizabeth 90–1
Gauthier, Théophile 109n.9
Gibson, James J. 94
Gilbert and Sullivan 237–8
Gilroy, Paul 139n.2
Goethe, Johann Wolfgang von 99
Gove, Michael 131–2
Greenberg, Clement 52
Grosz, Elizabeth 2–3, 6, 12, 16–19, 21
Guillory, John 81–2
Guyer, Paul 28n.4

Habermas, Jürgen 77–9
Hadot, Pierre 159–60, 167–8
Hall, Donald E. 113–14
Hallam, A.H. 226–7, 235
Hamid, Mohsin 144–5
Haneke, Michael 137–9, 142, 152, 158
Haraway, Donna 43–4
Harduin, Fantine 139–40

Hardy, Thomas 105–6, 191, 198–200
Hegel, Georg Wilhelm Friedrich 86–8, 207, 215n.5, 217n.6, 220n.7
Heidegger, Martin 28n.3, 31n.8
Heilman, Robert B. 222, 229–30
Hempel, Carl 121–2
Hollander, John 231–2
Homer 219
Hopkins, Gerard Manley 75–6, 110–14
Hough, Graham 230–1
Houston, Natalie M. 128n.3
Humpherys, Anne 11n.2
Hunter, G.K. 210
Huppert, Isabelle 137
Huxley, Aldous 199–200

Ingarden, Roman 28–9
Iser, Wolfgang 28–9
Ix Hun Ahau 168

Jacobson, Roman 125
Jameson, Fredric 118–19, 122, 174–5
James, William 205
Jarvis, Simon 125–6
Jones, David 110n.10
Jonson, Ben 37–41
Joseph, Gerhard 223–4

Kant, Immanuel 18–19, 28, 76–7, 79, 82–3, 88–9, 91–3, 147, 218
Kapil, Bhanu 142–3
Kassovitz, Mathieu 139–40
Keats, John 85–7, 100–4, 108–10, 232
Kettle, Alice 145–6
Khalili, Bouchra 148–9
Klonaris, Helen 151n.10
Knapp, Steven 122
Knowlton, Timothy 167–8
Kramnick, Jonathan 8–9, 9n.1, 121–6
Kurdi, Alan 150

Lacey, Hugh 206n.1
Latour, Bruno 121–2
Lawrence, D.H. 22–3, 191–205
Leavis, F.R. 28–9, 222, 234
Le Clézio, J.M.G. 162–3
Lee, Vernon 96
Lehman, Robert S. 127
Levine, Caroline 5–6, 90–2, 96, 98n.1, 123–4, 126
Levine, George 109–10
Levinson, Marjorie 120, 122–3
Lévi-Strauss, Claude 167–8
Lewis, C.S. 208–10
Longinus 28

INDEX 283

Loughran, Trish 90–1
Love, Heather 123–5
Lucretius, Titus Lucretius Carus 196–7
Luiselli, Valeria 145n.5
Lyotard, Jean-François 31n.8, 149n.8

Macpherson, Sandra 123
Makumbi, Jennifer Nansubuga 133–4
Manet, Eduard 45
Marcus, Sharon 118–22
Maritain, Jacques 109n.9
Martial 40
Martialis, Julius 40
Martin, Meredith 126
Mathur, Saloni 143
McDonagh, Josephine 4–5, 21
McQueen, Steve 33
Mehta, Arjun 153
Michaels, Walter Benn 122
Miller, J. Hillis 225n.3, 231–2, 235n.9
Milton, John 101, 210, 212–20, 230–1
Mitford, Mary Russell 128–9
Moore, David Chioni 172–3
Moretti, Franco 86, 121–2, 128–31
Morris, William 12–13, 74–5, 88–9
Mukherjee, Ankhi 4–5, 21
Munch, Edvard 159

Naipaul, V.S. 182–4
Nealon, Christopher 119
Nersessian, Analid 121–5
Ngai, Sianne 84–5
Ngũgĩ wa Thiong'o 133–5
North, Joseph 4–9
Nowell-Smith, David 126

Ore-Giron, Eamon 164–7
Ovid 167–8
Oyeyemi, Helen 178, 180–2

Padmore, Mark 145–6
Pater, Walter 95–6, 109–10
Penn Warren, Robert 221–4, 228–9, 237
Philip, M. Nbourse 151–2
Pink Floyd 117, 126–7
Plato 210–12, 215n.5, 217
Poe, Edgar Allan 109n.9, 231–2
Pollan, Michael 207
Pound, Ezra 96, 104–5
Prins, Yopie 125–6
Prum, Richard 7–8, 15–21, 107n.6, 108–10
Pylyshyn, Zenon 121–2

Quammen, David 54

Rancière, Jacques 82–4, 86, 148, 149n.8, 171
Rankine, Claudia 211–12
Rawls, John 207
Richards, I.A. 6, 28–9, 96, 135
Robinson, A. Mary F. 85
Robinson, Marilynne 207
Rogowski, Franz 137
Rossetti, Christina 75–6
Ruskin, John 109–10, 126, 192–3
Russell, Bertrand 197–8
Russell, Francey 219
Ryan, Michael 18–19, 100, 112

Safar, Ali 145–6
Safina, Carl 109–10, 109n.8
Sahota, Sanjeev 144
Said, Edward 150–1
Saunders, George 28n.6, 36n.14
Saville, Julia 113–14
Scarry, Elaine 120
Schiller, Friedrich 1, 82–3
Scruton, Roger 50
Sedgwick, Eve Kosovsky 122
Shakespeare, William 12–13, 129–30, 134
Shelley, Percy Bysshe 99–100, 102–4, 108–9
Shklovsky, Viktor 96
Shohat, Ella 173
Siegel, Jonah 6–8
Siskin, Clifford 120
Small, Helen 14–16, 21–3
Smith, Barbara Herrnstein 32n.9
Smith, Caroline 153–5
Snorton, C. Riley 167
Soliman, Francesca 152
Spitzer, Leo 226, 233
Spivak, Gayatri Chakravorty 171–2, 175–7
Staten, Henry 34n.12
Stern, Daniel 201–2
Stevens, Wallace 85–6
Swinburne, A.C. 109–10

Tennyson, Alfred 22–3, 71–4, 88–9, 92–4, 97, 105–7, 222–4, 226–9, 231–8, 239f
Tolstoy, Leo 117, 195
Toto, Jackie 137
Trench, Richard 71
Trentin, Filippo 126
Trilling, Lionel 28n.6
Trintignant, Jean-Louis 137–8
Tuccio, Franco 152
Tucker, Herbert 3–5, 20, 222, 230–1
Turner, J.M.W. 151

Vandiver, Edward P. 237n.10
Van Frassen, Bas 121–2, 122n.1
Van Gogh, Vincent 160
Victor, Divya 146
Virgil 219
Voloshinov, Valentin 130–1
V21 Collective 118, 121
Vygotsky, L.N. 130–1

Warburg, Aby 126
Warhol, Andy 45
Weber, Max 77–8
Weitz, Morris 46
Whistler, J.A.M. 109n.9
Whitman, Walt 231
Williams, William Carlos 135–6

Wilde, Oscar 86–7, 90–1, 98
Wimsatt, W.K. and M.C. Beardsley 233–4
Witchell, Charles 106n.5
Wittgenstein, Ludwig 27n.1, 29, 46
Wolfson, Susan 5–6, 21–3, 123
Wong, Amy R. 120
Woolf, Virginia 129–30
Wordsworth, William 196–7, 234–6

Yapp, Hentyle 167
Yeats, William Butler 85–6, 102

Zamir, Tzachi 218–19
Zamora, Javier 146
Zangwill, Nick 84–5
Zon, Bennett 106n.5

The manufacturer's authorised representative in the EU for product safety is
Oxford University Press España S.A. of el Parque Empresarial San Fernando de
Henares, Avenida de Castilla, 2 – 28830 Madrid (www.oup.es/en or product.
safety@oup.com). OUP España S.A. also acts as importer into Spain of products
made by the manufacturer.

www.ingramcontent.com/pod-product-compliance
Lightning Source LLC
Chambersburg PA
CBHW071838290825
31867CB00003B/185